C000155633

Culture, Mind, and So

The Book Series of the Society for Psychological Anthropology

The Society for Psychological Anthropology—a section of the American Anthropology Association—and Palgrave Macmillan are dedicated to publishing innovative research in culture and psychology that illuminates the workings of the human mind within the social, cultural, and political contexts that shape thought, emotion, and experience. As anthropologists seek to bridge gaps between ideation and emotion or agency and structure and as psychologists, psychiatrists, and medical anthropologists search for ways to engage with cultural meaning and difference, this interdisciplinary terrain is more active than ever.

Series Editor

Rebecca J. Lester, Department of Anthropology, Washington University in St. Louis

Editorial Board

Linda Garro, Department of Anthropology, University of California, Los Angeles
Catherine Lutz, Department of Anthropology, University of North Carolina, Chapel Hill
Peggy Miller, Departments of Psychology and Speech Communication, University of Illinois, Urbana-Champaign
Robert Paul, Department of Anthropology, Emory University
Bradd Shore, Department of Anthropology, Emory University
Carol Worthman, Department of Anthropology, Emory University

Titles in the Series

Adrie Kusserow, *American Individualisms: Child Rearing and Social Class in Three Neighborhoods*
Naomi Quinn, editor, *Finding Culture in Talk: A Collection of Methods*
Anna Mansson McGinty, *Becoming Muslim: Western Women's Conversion to Islam*
Roy D'Andrade, *A Study of Personal and Cultural Values: American, Japanese, and Vietnamese*
Steven M. Parish, *Subjectivity and Suffering in American Culture: Possible Selves*
Elizabeth A. Throop, *Psychotherapy, American Culture, and Social Policy: Immoral Individualism*
Victoria Katherine Burbank, *An Ethnography of Stress: The Social Determinants of Health in Aboriginal Australia*
Karl G. Heider, *The Cultural Context of Emotion: Folk Psychology in West Sumatra*
Jeannette Marie Mageo, *Dreaming Culture: Meanings, Models, and Power in U.S. American Dreams*
Casey High, Ann Kelly, and Jonathan Mair, *The Anthropology of Ignorance: An Ethnographic Approach*
Kevin K. Birth, *Objects of Time: How Things Shape Temporality*

Andrew Kipnis, *Chinese Modernity and the Individual Psyche*

Katie Glaskin and Richard Chenhall, *Sleep Around the World: Anthropological Perspectives*

Naomi Quinn and Jeannette Marie Mageo, editors, *Attachment Reconsidered: Cultural Perspectives on a Western Theory*

Attachment Reconsidered

Cultural Perspectives on a Western Theory

Edited by

Naomi Quinn and Jeannette Marie Mageo

Divya -
Here's the skinny . . .
Also look at these 2 books:
1- Otto, Hiltrud & Heidi Keller (2014), eds.
"Different Faces of Attachment"
2- Vicedo, Marga (2013)
"The Nature & Nurture of Love"
Good reading! Naomi
5/21/16

palgrave
macmillan

ATTACHMENT RECONSIDERED

First published in 2013 by
PALGRAVE MACMILLAN®
in the United States—a division of St. Martin's Press LLC,
175 Fifth Avenue, New York, NY 10010.

Where this book is distributed in the UK, Europe and the rest of the world, this is by Palgrave Macmillan, a division of Macmillan Publishers Limited, registered in England, company number 785998, of Houndmills, Basingstoke, Hampshire RG21 6XS.

Palgrave Macmillan is the global academic imprint of the above companies and has companies and representatives throughout the world.

Palgrave® and Macmillan® are registered trademarks in the United States, the United Kingdom, Europe and other countries.

ISBN: 978–1–137–38671–7 (hc)
ISBN: 978–1–137–38674–8 (pbk)

Library of Congress Cataloging-in-Publication Data is available from the Library of Congress.

A catalogue record of the book is available from the British Library.

Design by Newgen Knowledge Works (P) Ltd., Chennai, India.

First edition: December 2013

10 9 8 7 6 5 4 3 2 1

This volume is dedicated to the Robert Lemelson Foundation. Psychological anthropology is a small if lively and productive field, and one underfunded by comparison with more sizeable and centrally positioned disciplines. Through the Lemelson/SPA Conference Fund, the Robert Lemelson Foundation has made possible a series of conferences on important topics in psychological anthropology, such as the one that culminated in the present volume. Through the Lemelson Student Fellowship Program, the foundation has also supported the initial dissertation field research of multiple cohorts of graduate students working in this area. This foundation has thus become by far the most dependable source of funding for psychological anthropology, playing a tremendous role in nourishing our subdiscipline. For this we are profoundly grateful. We hope that in a small way this dedication expresses our gratitude.

Contents

List of Illustrations ix

Part I A Framework

Attachment and Culture: An Introduction 3
Naomi Quinn and Jeannette Marie Mageo

Chapter 1 The Puzzle of Attachment: Unscrambling Maturational and Cultural Contributions to the Development of Early Emotional Bonds 33
Suzanne Gaskins

Part II Caregiving

Chapter 2 Cooperative Child Care among the Hadza: Situating Multiple Attachment in Evolutionary Context 67
Alyssa N. Crittenden and Frank W. Marlowe

Chapter 3 Cooperative Breeding and Attachment among the Aka Foragers 85
Courtney L. Meehan and Sean Hawks

Chapter 4 "It Takes a Village to Raise a Child": Attachment Theory and Multiple Child Care in Alor, Indonesia, and in North India 115
Susan C. Seymour

Part III Autonomy and Dependence

Chapter 5 Attachment in Rural Sri Lanka: The Shape of Caregiver Sensitivity, Communication, and Autonomy 143
Bambi L. Chapin

Chapter 6 Attachment and Culture in Murik Society: Learning Autonomy and Interdependence through Kinship, Food, and Gender 165
Kathleen Barlow

Part IV Childhood-Adulthood Continuities

Chapter 7 Toward a Cultural Psychodynamics of Attachment: Samoa and US Comparisons 191
Jeannette Marie Mageo

Chapter 8 Adult Attachment Cross-culturally: A Reanalysis of the Ifaluk Emotion *Fago* 215
Naomi Quinn

Afterword: Cross-cultural Challenges to Attachment Theory 241
Gilda A. Morelli and Paula Ivey Henry

Notes on Contributors 251

Index 255

Illustrations

Figures

3.1 Mean frequency of maternal holding, touching, and proximity 94
3.2 Mean frequency of maternal physical contact and access 94
3.3 Mean frequency of allomaternal holding, touching, and proximity 95
3.4 Mean frequency of allomaternal physical contact and access 95
3.5 Relationship between child distress and allomaternal sensitivity during mother-child separation 105

Tables

3.1 Sample description 92
3.2 Child attachment bouts, mean number of responders, and percentage of attachment bouts directed toward mothers, fathers, adult allomothers, and juvenile allomothers 97
3.3 Component loadings for responses to attachment behaviors 100
3.4 Mean component scores for mothers and allomothers 100
3.5 The percentage of child responses to their mother in the first minute and the first three minutes following a separation 103
3.6 The percentage of maternal responses to their child in the first minute and the first three minutes following a separation 104
5.1 Sinhala model of hierarchically ranked relationships 151

Part I

A Framework

Attachment and Culture: An Introduction

Naomi Quinn and Jeannette Marie Mageo

The fundamental argument that motivates this volume, namely that attachment theory's claims and constructs suffer from profound ethnocentrism, is not new. A handful of cross-cultural researchers have raised these worries since the early days of attachment theory, for more than a quarter century now. Most of these earlier critiques questioned the cross-cultural applicability of a category system that designated children's attachment to their caregivers as secure versus insecure, and measurement along this dimension by means of the Strange Situation (SS)—an experimental procedure for testing the child's relative security through absenting its mother from the laboratory. The current volume expands this critique beyond questions of classification and measurement, to question the cultural assumptions behind such a category system and such an experimental design, and extends this line of questioning to ethnocentric concepts beyond insecure attachment.

On the one hand, the influence of attachment theory in contemporary American psychology would be hard to overstate. On the other hand, the anthropological criticism of ethnocentrism has wider implications for the discipline of psychology, which so often unintentionally introduces psychologists' culturally biased assumptions into theory intended to be general, and is so devoted to culturally decontextualized experimental procedures that fail to challenge this ethnocentrism. Thus, we offer the current volume not only as a challenge to attachment theorists, but as an object lesson for psychologists of many other stripes.

Situating This Volume

Attachment theory, as is well known, originated with the work of John Bowlby. Bowlby was both a psychoanalyst and an evolutionary theorist. From the psychoanalytic study of human development, he took the foundational assumption that the infant's earliest experiences are the most consequential and form the basis of an internalized working model of human relationships. Inspired by evolutionary theory, Bowlby tried to identify adaptive behaviors such as proximity-seeking, one item in an hypothesized attachment system postulated to have evolved to ensure infant survival.

The Strange Situation Procedure and Its Cross-cultural Critique

Bowlby's colleague, Mary Ainsworth, took his ideas to Uganda in an admirable attempt to understand them in cross-cultural perspective. Ugandan infants, she discovered, were more or less constantly in contact with their caregivers, in sharp contrast to American infants. Upon her return to the United States, and to more conveniently analyze and classify infants' attachment to their mothers, Ainsworth devised the Strange Situation (often referred to in the literature simply as the SS or the SSP, the Strange Situation Procedure), a method for assessing attachment relationships between 12 and 72 months of age, which has become the standard by which the security of an infant's attachment is measured. As attachment theory became established, research within this paradigm came to be defined all too inflexibly by Bowlby's theory and Ainsworth's method.

The theoretical result was that an American cultural ideal of this period—the attentive, supportive stay-at-home middle-class mom—became a standard for promoting the psychological health of American children of all classes and subcultures, and indeed a standard for all the world against which the practices and norms of a vast variety of people were, we argue inappropriately, judged. The methodological result was no less inflexible. As Bretherton (1991:25) observed over two decades ago, and as is no less true today, with the proliferation of researchers trained in the tradition that Ainsworth had established, "Hundreds of studies using the Strange Situation appeared in print. Often it almost seemed as if attachment and the Strange Situation had become synonymous." This confounding of theory with instrument persists to this day.

Ainsworth originally devised the SSP for a sample of Baltimore infants (LeVine and Miller 1990:73–75). The laboratory-based procedure is made up of eight three-minute episodes. In some of these episodes, the mother leaves the infant alone in the room, and in other episodes she leaves the infant in the presence of a stranger. The episodes are meant to mildly stress the infant in order to activate the attachment system, and the procedure is designed in such a way as to escalate the level of stress experienced as the episodes progress.

Upon each of the mother's returns, a "securely attached" infant seeks proximity or contact with the mother and then resumes exploration of the environment, evidenced by play with the toys that are available in the room. An "insecurely attached" infant shows little or no tendency to approach mother on the mother's return (labeled *avoidant*) or, alternatively, makes efforts to contact mother but also resists her (labeled *resistant*). An additional category, *disorganized/disoriented*, was later added to accommodate a minority of infants whose attachment behavior fit neither category (see Solomon and George 2008:386–387; Weinfeld et al. 2008:80–81 for fuller descriptions of these categories).[1]

Anthropologists and others whose research has immersed them in other cultures cannot help but see contemporary attachment theory as resembling a folk theory. A folk theory abstracts elements of experience in a culture to formulate a view the human condition that is regarded as universal and is held, implicitly or explicitly, by most group members but is in fact reflective of experience within the group. In more complex economically tiered societies, folk theories tend to take the experience of a hegemonic class or classes as universally representative and normative. Attachment theory, like a folk theory, draws upon the way many middle-class Americans, and to a lesser extent members of this class in other Western and Western-influenced societies, think they should care for infants and small children, including ideas about how child-caregiver attachments are formed and fostered. Because this theory is so naturalized in American thinking, it can seem self-evident. Folk theoretical thinking often creeps into academic and other expert theories especially, as we have noted, when an academic psychology is based nearly exclusively on research in the United States and other Western countries and excludes the intercultural variation introduced by non-middle-class and minority populations in these countries. So it has been with the history of attachment theory and its methodological proxy, the SSP, which fail to assess very much about infant-caregiver relations cross-culturally.

In a 1990 commentary on the articles in a special topics issue of *Human Development*, Robert LeVine and Patrice Miller argue that culture-specific patterns of child care, in particular the frequency of maternal comings and goings, the length of these separations from mother, and the infants' familiarity with strangers, would influence responses to the SSP. Thus, Takahashi (1990:25) observes that the separation protest evinced by Japanese babies was so intense that the "infant-alone" condition had to be curtailed for fully 90 percent of subjects in her study. LeVine and Miller speculate that this effect, resulting in the classification of many Japanese infants as insecure-resistant, was due to the fact that these infants were so infrequently separated from their mothers in daily life. LeVine and Miller point out that Ainsworth herself had interpreted the difference between the Ugandans and her Baltimore sample similarly, with the American babies being accustomed to their mothers' frequent but brief absences, while the Ugandan babies had built up expectations that when their mothers left they would be gone, and inaccessible, for much longer periods.

Driven by field circumstances to an even more radical stance, Courtney Meehan and Sean Hawks (chapter 3) describe the impracticality of implementing the SSP altogether, in another, very different, cross-cultural setting. When Meehan arrived at her field site in 2000, she was planning to administer a culturally modified SSP. However, as Meehan and Hawks (chapter 3) report,

> While she could serve the role of stranger in the procedure, a variety of children's caregivers were always close by and often within the visual range of the focal child during the procedure. Isolating Aka children with her or a field assistant was not always an option. During the recordings there were often multiple individuals present and children crawled, scooted, or walked over to another caregiver; others stayed and signaled for someone to come to them.

Meehan could never be sure that interactions during these episodes were strictly dyadic, or whether children were reacting to the presence, sensitivity, and interactional history of, say, a grandmother just out of frame. Moreover, the focal child would often go to another caretaker or signal for another caretaker to come to them right in the middle of a recording. To solve these problems, Meehan abandoned the standardized SSP altogether and instead collected extensive natural observations by a method described in their chapter, and analyzed mother-child separations that occurred naturally during allotted intervals. Indeed, this is how these researchers discovered that, even though mothers were the most frequent caregivers, the variable sensitivity of allomaternal care, not that of mother's care, was what predicted the extent of children's distress during maternal absence.

LeVine and Miller (1990:76–77) go on to make the larger point that the conditions surrounding infant-caregiver separation and reunion in the SSP are at least partly defined by "the meaning of the mother to the baby," and that it is only possible to ignore this meaning "if one focuses exclusively on the reunion behaviors that are criteria for attachment classification and does not take into account the natural contexts that condition the child's responses to the Strange Situation." This point about the cultural meaning surrounding the child-caregiver relationship opens the way to further, more wide-ranging critiques of attachment theory, pursued in subsequent work by LeVine (LeVine and Norman 2001; LeVine 2009) and mounted in the ethnographic chapters to follow in this volume.

Positioning Ourselves

What unites the contributors to the volume is that every last one of us has conducted research in communities outside of Euro-America. In most cases, too, this research has taken us beyond the reach of industrialized society. These are important contrasts. One obvious example: the distinction between single and multiple mothering follows the fault line between postindustrial European and American communities and many other communities elsewhere in the world either that industrialization has not yet reached or in which, under industrialization, the extended family has not yet been rendered obsolete. In these societies unstudied by attachment theorists, there are routinely many child caregivers including, and often prominently, older children. Multiple caregiving patterns, described in chapters to follow, result in much wider variation in the forms of attachment than is captured in the contrast among Japan, the United States, and North Germany alone. More generally, and without exception, the communities in which we have worked and which we have grown to know present stark cultural contrasts to our own. All of us are attuned to the cultural meanings of attachment in these communities, which has given us a keen awareness of how profound the cross-cultural differences can be in the beliefs, values, practices, and institutions surrounding attachment.

Beyond these commonalities of cross-cultural experience and attention to cultural meaning, our contributors represent three different fields. The author of chapter 1 and the lead author of the afterword (about which no more will be said here, since it is, after all, an afterword) are cross-cultural developmental psychologists. Chapters 2 and 3 are the work of biocultural anthropologists (who also sometimes call themselves behavioral ecologists), and chapters 4 through 8 that of psychological anthropologists. Let us say briefly how these different disciplinary presences speak to one another and strengthen this volume.

What developmental psychologists add to this volume is their deep appreciation of attachment theory's history in their discipline. The theoretical breadth of psychologist Suzanne Gaskins's chapter derives from a background in and knowledge of contemporary work and past developments, positioning her to appreciate all that the field of psychology has to offer, and to recognize when psychological approaches require critique. Gaskins sets out a framework for the entire volume by asking how we can square the theoretical claim that attachment is a species-wide maturational process with the huge amount of cross-cultural variability in child care and the differing patterns of attachment that result. Her answer is that further investigation must sort out the two: the humanly universal from the experientially mutable and hence cross-culturally variable. Gaskins offers a preliminary sorting, and begins to illustrate her approach with analysis of her own Yucatec Maya research. Each of the volume's successive ethnographic chapters adds to this story, considering how such culturally variable practices as the differential availability of multiple caregivers, or different cultural styles of mothering, or different objectives for raising children, can and do change the cultural meaning accorded to attachment, starting in infancy and extending over the life course. As Gaskins emphasizes, this is only the beginning of such investigations, and studies of attachment expressly designed to sort out what is universal from what is cross-culturally variable are much needed.

The biocultural and psychological anthropological chapters that follow have disparate although also complementary concerns. The biocultural anthropologists are closely focused on allomothering and its implications for attachment. The psychological anthropologists take up a wider set of questions revolving around the divergent meanings that attachment can take cross-culturally. These questions emerge from observations made on the basis of research that has typically not yet been originally designed to test attachment theory assumptions.[2] In both cases, the aim is to refocus attachment observations to include phenomena beyond the behavior and values displayed by white Western middle-class mothers and infants and thus to provide a more adequate basis for future theory.

What the biocultural anthropologists in this volume (chapters 2 and 3) contribute to this nascent effort is to embark on the first half of Gaskins's agenda, specifically, research into a fundamental human adaptation: cooperative child care. The Cooperative Breeding Hypothesis, on which the research reported in these two chapters rests, calls attention to the long period of human children's dependency, due to their precocious birth and their extended maturation time. As a result, human mothers face the unusually high metabolic burden of having to care for as yet unweaned infants while simultaneously provisioning older but still immature children. This burden, coupled with the rest of a woman's normal workload, should make it adaptive for human mothers to share child care in order to lighten their burden of care. The assistance of allomothers has the ultimate advantage that it "can help mothers return to ovulation more quickly" (Crittenden and Marlowe, chapter 2) and thus be more reproductively successful. By this theory, modern middle-class nuclear families in which the mother is the primary attachment figure and also the main if not the sole child caregiver, such as those found in the United States and other industrialized societies, are outliers and not the normative human state of affairs. Thus, these two chapters jeopardize a central assumption of attachment theory. Studying multiple attachment among nomadic foragers brings evolutionary considerations into attachment theory, better situating attachment processes in the "environment that gave rise to them" (Chisholm 1996:22).

The chapters by biocultural anthropologists not only establish a starting point in the task of untangling the humanly universal from the cross-culturally variant but they also serve to remind psychological anthropologists of the fundamental importance of this evolutionary point of departure for the study of child rearing in all human societies. Indeed, the influence of the Cooperative Breeding Hypothesis on psychological anthropologists' thinking, especially as articulated in Sarah Blaffer Hrdy's (2009) recent argument for the evolutionary functions of allomothering, strongly influences several of the later volume chapters (see chapter 4 by Seymour and 6 by Barlow. At the same time, the reported range across human societies from multiple to nearly singular caregiving that the later chapters report is evidence that the practices surrounding attachment, and the cultural meaning of the child's attachment itself, can vary, and in this case do vary in correspondence to such constraints as local demands on mothers' workload and availability of alternative caregivers.

A note on terminology is in order at this juncture. Following in the tradition of primate studies from which their specialty emerged, biocultural anthropologists call this solution to human child care *allomothering*, or *allomaternal care*, or, more neutrally, *alloparenting* (just as they also borrow the term *breeding* from animal studies). Having independently observed this same practice and invented their own language to describe it, the psychological anthropologists in the volume tend to call it, instead, *multiple mothering* or *distributed caregiving*. We the editors have elected to leave contributors free to use their own terminology, which we also adopt in our discussion of each chapter.

For the obvious reason, their concern for evolutionary adaptation, biocultural anthropologists, including the authors of chapters 2 and 3, choose to study allomaternal care among foragers (also sometimes termed "hunter-gatherers" in the literature), peoples considered to most closely replicate the conditions under which humans are thought to have evolved, the so-called Environment of Evolutionary Adaptedness (or EEA).[3] These chapters explore the distribution of child care across caregivers in two different foraging societies, and pursue the implications of allomothering for the sustainability of a human mother's workload (chapter 2 by Crittenden and Marlowe) and for the child's pattern of attachment itself (chapter 3 by Meehan and Hawkes).

Parenthetically, it should not be assumed that the study of foraging societies is restricted to biocultural theorists, although those researchers have a principled reason for conducting their research in such societies. Indeed, one of the other chapters in this volume, chapter 6, by psychological anthropologist Kathleen Barlow, describes a marine foraging society in lowland New Guinea. Another psychological anthropologist justly famous for her ethnography of a hunting people, the Inuit, is Jean Briggs. Briggs's landmark account of Inuit child rearing (1998) has much to say about attachment and the cultural meanings surrounding it. Even though Briggs does not explicitly address attachment theory or the Cooperative Breeding Hypothesis, many of the emotionally powerful teasing episodes she so beautifully describes are intended "to cause thought" in small children about "the perils associated with attachment" (1998:110). It should be added that Jean was someone whom the co-organizers of the conference that led to this volume considered an essential conference attendee. She was, in the event, a vital and engaged discussant and is the silent interlocutor to this volume.

Following in Briggs's footsteps, what the psychological anthropologists contribute to this volume is a range of rich and diverse accounts of attachment, playing further variations in multiple caregiving on the findings of the biocultural anthropologists, documenting an array of other cultural meanings granted to attachment, and launching the second half of Gaskins's agenda: making sense of these cultural variations. Their preferred method, which may be largely unfamiliar to attachment theorists, but is the mainstay of cultural anthropology, is ethnography. Ethnography is the qualitative description of the life of a community that is gained from living in that community for a long time, making dense observations of life, and continually asking questions of inhabitants, whether they are proficient enough in the local language to do so themselves, or through interpreters. Psychological anthropologists, though they rely heavily on ethnography, may also depend on quantitative data. A fine example would be Susan Seymour's extensive quantitative record collected over her career-long longitudinal study in a North Indian town. Also, both biocultural anthropologists and cross-cultural developmental psychologists, while they may rely primarily on quantitative methods, typically combine these methods with ethnography. The difference is that what tends to be ethnographic background to the psychologists and the biocultural anthropologists who contribute to this volume is foregrounded by Seymour and the other psychological anthropologists.

Above all, ethnography has the advantage of capturing cultural meaning. And it is this, the culturally variable meanings that attachment can take, that is the chief concern of chapters 4 through 8 of this book. These contributors not only expand upon Gaskins's account of the Yucatec Maya, but also take up the call of a handful of earlier writers who have offered powerful critiques of previous cross-cultural studies by attachment theorists for their failure to consider the cultural meanings of attachment (see, e.g., LeVine and Miller 1990; LeVine and Norman 2001; Rothbaum et al. 2000, 2011). Their arguments go beyond the complaint, already noted, that the SSP decontextualizes cultural meaning. We next briefly summarize these earlier critiques as they pertain to the concerns of this book.

No anecdote better captures the gist of these critiques than psychological anthropologist Thomas Weisner's (2005:89) story of an American mother's reaction to her son's performance in the SSP: "I stood next to a mother who was watching (through a one-way window) her child being assessed in the Strange Situation Procedure (SSP)." According to his behavior profile, the boy had been labeled "avoidant."

> But the mother proudly commented that: 'This is what I have been working for by having him be with other kids and families while I am working. Look how independent he is! See how he can play by himself?' The mother was a single parent by choice. She had told us about her goals for independence for herself and her child, the importance of living a pro-feminist kind of family life, as she defined it, and her efforts to establish an ongoing convoy of friends and caretakers for her child to provide relational support and security. The meaning of the behaviors revealed in the SSP were positive to her, and her construction of the situation reflected a valorizing of her child's life path as well as the mother's. For her, the behaviors she saw meant that they both were on a positive, adaptive, virtuous path. Her child was not in fact 'at risk' for 'attachment disorder' nor relational insecurity in her frame of meaning, whatever the scoring of her child's behaviors might have been (and in fact, longitudinal follow-up through adolescence did not show any signs of risk either).

As this incident illustrates, the bias is in the labeling. While this mother labels her son's behavior as "independent," the theoretical category system labels him "avoidant." To label children raised according to a certain set of cultural practices as "insecurely attached" on the basis of their performance in an experimental situation, without understanding the meaning of the children's behavior both to their adult caregivers and to the children themselves, is bad scientific practice. This lesson applies not only to the middle-class American case, but also, and all the more, to research in other societies and among diverse subgroups in American society.

Psychologists' resistance to this caution against systems of classification overriding cultural meaning is captured in one well-known attachment theorist's comment on some early reactions by investigators themselves to Ainsworth's results from the SSP: "Frequently, the avoidant infants' behavior was interpreted as independence" (Bretherton 1991:24). This theorist goes on to argue that this (presumed to be erroneous) interpretation began to disappear once fuller findings, including home observations, from Ainsworth's Baltimore study and other studies "showing links between attachment categories and development in toddlerhood and early childhood became available." But could it not be that over time attachment theorists came to be so well-schooled in the classification system that what they learned to interpret as avoidant attachment might justly be regarded in some societies and cultural subgroups as valuable behavior to be actively cultivated in children? A well-known North German study that we will next have occasion to consider raises the same question.

Of those studies that have previously been critiqued from a cross-cultural perspective, we review two here, the aforementioned North German study and a set of Japanese studies of attachment, cases that are both especially pertinent to the objectives of this volume. We highlight the critical objections bearing on inattention to cultural meaning, and add our own two cents to these objections.

The North German Study and Its Critics

Robert LeVine (LeVine and Norman 2001:84) has usefully labeled the distinctive cultural meanings shared in every group, about how to raise a child into a desirable adult, the "cultural model of virtue" held by parents and enacted in their caregiving. LeVine and Norman (2001) apply this concept to a large and well-known study of infants in Beilefeld, North Germany, conducted by Karin and Klaus Grossman and their colleagues. Using the standard SSP, these researchers assigned fully 49 percent of the North German infants to the avoidant pattern, compared to 26 percent in the Baltimore study. Another 12 percent of the Bielefeld infants were categorized as ambivalent (compared to 17% in Baltimore), leaving only 33 percent of the North German infants assigned to the secure category, compared to 57 percent in the Baltimore sample. LeVine and Norman ask how it can be that the majority of a population can be insecurely attached? Instead, they (LeVine and Norman 2001:84) attribute this finding to the very different cultural model of virtue to which the North German parents ascribe, and according to which they raise their children. These authors (LeVine and Norman 2001:98–101) point out that, in the early part of the twentieth century, the American patterns of child rearing that preceded the emergence of attachment theory were "very similar to the patterns still observed in Germany more than twenty-five years later." They speculate that attachment theory was initially driven by the ideological battle of "child-centered freedom and equality against old-fashioned parentally imposed order and discipline" in the United States.

The nub of the issue seems to be the Grossmans' determination to conceptualize and label the difference they find between study infants in terms of security versus insecurity, which LeVine and Norman (2001:100) characterize as the "value laden conceptual terminology in attachment research." This despite the Grossmans' own observations of the strong demands for self-reliance made on the German infants, which included such attitudes and behaviors as discouraging infants from staying too close, being concerned not to spoil infants, evincing pride (as does the American mother in Weisner's story) that infants were able to play alone, and leaving infants alone at home in their beds for brief periods—the latter practice being considered an explicit part of self-reliance training. Indeed, the Grossmans themselves go on to interpret the much higher percentage of avoidant infants in the Bielefeld sample in terms of

> the cultural values that we believe to be dominant in North Germany, where people tend to keep a larger interpersonal distance. As soon as infants become mobile, most mothers feel that they should now be weaned from close bodily contact. To carry a baby who can move on its own or to respond to its every cry by picking it up would be considered as spoiling. The ideal is an independent, nonclinging infant who does not make demands on the parents but rather unquestioningly obeys their commands.

Thus the authors (1985:254–255) concede that what they call "a mother's lower sensitivity to infant signals" is due to "cultural norms" in the North German case, rather than a "rejecting attitude," as would be the interpretation of American findings. They conclude that the long-term consequences of such cultural patterns are "less grave" than insensitivity based on rejection.

Yet, in the face of their own cultural account of North German attachment, the Grossmans persist in labeling the North German babies as "insecurely attached" and "avoidant" and in glossing the mothering practices said to promote this insecure attachment as "insensitive," as "less than optimal mothering," or as demonstrating "lower sensitivity to infant signals" (Grossman et al. 1985:249, 253–254). These authors also note that the North German mothers, in comparison with American mothers, are "less tender, less careful and affectionate while holding the infant in their arms" (Grossman et al. 1985:245). They characterize these German mothers' demands for self-reliance as "premature" and offer such characterizations of these infants as being "under stress" and "ill at ease with their mothers at 12 months," and these mother-infant relationships as "less optimal" than those of American infants and mothers (Grossman et al. 1985:254–255). Compare LeVine and Norman's (2001:84) assertion that

> parents of a particular culture tend to promote infant behaviors they see as consistent with their culture's model of virtue, and further, that they are successful enough on average that their children manifest selected behaviors at a "precociously" early age by the standards of other cultures with different concepts of virtue.

The contrast between these two inclinations, to single out ways in which the behavior of infants in another culture is deemed "precocious," in line with a local standard of virtue, rather than being considered "premature," in line with the researchers' ideas about normal development, could not be more stark.

LeVine and Norman opt for a model of attachment that recognizes different "pathways of enculturation" (2001:86), replacing "the attempt to define a single norm of optimal development for all humans and its concomitant tendency to pathologize variation" (LeVine and Norman 2001:84). This notion of multiple, equally valid pathways, each meaningful in local cultural terms, from early attachment to adult relationships, is echoed by Gaskins in chapter 1, and by Weisner (2005:93), who speaks of "the plural pathways cultural communities provide for the socialization of trust in children," as against "the monocultural assumptions of good development that are . . . part of classical attachment paradigms."

Even the most devout of attachment theorists seem occasionally to entertain the possibility that, cross-culturally, any of the three attachment strategies may be "normative in the sense that it promotes inclusive fitness and general adaptation" (van IJzendoorn and Sagi-Schwartz 2008:881). One might imagine that when attachment theorists say such things they are embracing LeVine's and Weisner's idea of plural normative pathways, but they are not. Van Ijzendoorn and Sagi-Schwartz, for example, quickly back away from any implication that "normative" in another society necessarily means unequivocably good for children, continuing (2008:881):

> Nevertheless, one may wonder whether the secure attachment pattern is the primary strategy for adapting to a social environment that is basically supportive of the infant, and whether the insecure strategies should be considered as secondary in that they constitute deviating but adaptive patterns provoked by less supportive contexts.

Other attachment theorists make a parallel argument—that insecure strategies are less than ideal because they are adaptive to less supportive environments, or as Bretherton (1985:28) puts it, just "the best fit under the circumstances." Thus, in other societies as in the United States, attachment strategies that depart from the American middle-class "secure" pattern are painted as not just different, but lesser. When attachment theorists come to such conclusions, they seem to be thinking of societies such as those in the developing world in which economic and political environments might be regarded as "providing less supportive contexts." Of course the North German case does not fit this description. The volume chapters go further, showing that infants and children growing up in the developing world must be understood in their own cultural terms—as differently attached, not less securely so. This cross-cultural lesson, that different is not lesser, is a useful reminder not just to attachment theorists, but to all Western psychologists.

As Weisner argued in discussions opened at the conference leading to this volume, there are indeed conditions that produce unsuccessfully attached children—such as a chaotic environment, persistent violence and aggression around or toward a child as in cases of abuse, or severe neglect as in the cases of the post-institutionalized Romanian and other Eastern European children described by Margaret Talbot (1998). Such conditions, however, are exceptional and are never locally normative, and children do not prosper or, sometimes, even survive under them. Short of such extreme cases, stress surrounding attachment may be not only normative (see Quinn, chapter 8), but adaptive (as Jeannette Mageo argues in chapter 7).

Japanese Studies and Their Critics

In Japanese studies of attachment, the case to which we next turn, the pattern of "insecure" attachment is the reversal of that found in the Bielefeld study. Over several studies, the proportion of securely attached Japanese infants is tantamount to that found in American studies. However, there are few or no avoidant infants—unlike in the United States where the proportion of avoidant infants is around 20 percent—and the proportion of resistant infants is correspondingly larger than in American infant populations (16% in one Japanese study compared to the American average of around 10%). Indeed, upon reunification with the mother many Japanese infants are inconsolable.

One set of researchers raises the possibility of biologically based dispositional differences between Asian and European infants (Miyake et al. 1985:277–279).[4] Otherwise, researchers are inclined to explain the finding of few to no avoidant and a larger proportion of resistant infants in terms of cultural differences, this time distinctive features of Japanese child caregiving practices and corresponding cultural values. Implicated is "a more proximal mode of interaction (emphasizing physical contact, for instance)" (Miyake et al. 1985:280). Some of the practices exemplifying this mode of interaction are breast-feeding, co-bathing, sleeping together, communicating tactually, transporting the child on the mother's back, and toilet training the child by physically holding him or her above the toilet. Thus, Japanese infant-caregiver practices look quite different from North German ones with regard to proximity.[5]

The point not to be lost in this discussion of potential dimensions of difference in the forms attachment can take cross-culturally, is that child-caregiver relationships, child-rearing practices, and attachment outcomes in each society must be understood in their own culturally meaningful terms. Takahashi (1990:27) proposes that Japanese child-rearing practices avoid stressing infants by keeping them close. As for the absence or near absence of avoidant responses, this researcher points to the emphasis on harmony in Japanese interpersonal interactions, which "inhibits avoidant behaviors toward others, as impolite modes of interaction" (1990:28). She continues,

> Achieving this harmony is one of the main objectives of development. Children are carefully socialized not to direct avoidant behaviors toward others, because avoidance can mean the break of previous connections. Though 12-month-olds would be too young to have become fully socialized in this respect, they already would have had some experiences of being discouraged from showing avoidant behaviors.

Indeed, the "proximal" modes of interaction that Japanese mothers use with their infants make it practically impossible for these infants to avoid their mothers. The emphasis on harmony is a feature of the "cultural model of virtue" shaping Japanese child-caregiving practices. In contrast, in the American cultural model, "social independence or self-reliance is emphasized in the child's development," and even infants are encouraged to cope with being alone and to explore their environments on their own at a distance from the caregiver (Takahashi 1990:29). The divergent cultural meanings embedded in these practices are learned early.

Acknowledging that "There is no doubt that cultural factors constrain performance on social assessments like the Strange Situation," Miyake et al. (1985:294) conclude, "Thus we do not consider the classification of Japanese infants as C [resistant] to be 'insecurely attached.' " Takahashi (1990:28–29), however, is not so willing to concede the cultural relativism of attachment security and insecurity, insisting in the end that avoidant infants are to be found among Japanese populations, if only the diagnostic criteria be sensitive enough to identify them:

> In light of Japanese customs, avoidant behaviors, even when they are subtle, may be critical and thus should be given important diagnostic value, because avoidance goes against the grain of the culture. By modifying the criteria behaviors, we can identify at least some type A [avoidant] subjects among Japanese infants.

This insistence, that avoidant Japanese subjects are to be found if only sensitive enough criteria are used to identify them, seems to us to reflect a general tendency of psychologists to grant more credence to preexisting analytic categories than to field observations.

The major critique of these conclusions as to Japanese attachment comes from Fred Rothbaum and his colleagues (Rothbaum et al. 2000, 2011). As in LeVine and Norman's critique of the Bielefeld study, the issue is once again cultural context. Rothbaum and his colleagues make the insightful observation that the context of attachment has largely been ignored by theorists for the reason that "they, and the people they studied, were not themselves highly context dependent" (Rothbaum et al. 2011:154). These authors go on to propose that attachment and learning are related, and vary together across communities. For many American parents and children considered middle class, attachment and learning center on autonomous exploration. The qualities that promote this general orientation, such as individual accomplishments, self-confidence, and self-initiation, are encouraged and valued. Within many Japanese communities, by contrast, attachment and learning center on ways of harmonizing with others and adjusting to the social situation in which one finds oneself, as Takahashi has described. The qualities that promote this orientation, such as imitation, adherence to prescribed roles, and self-criticism, are encouraged and valued. These are two starkly different cultural models of virtue.

As Rothbaum et al. (2000:1100) note, "attachment theorists would be hard pressed to explain the many similarities between descriptions of insecure-ambivalent behaviors and behaviors widely regarded as adaptive in Japan"—including (all from an American perspective) exaggerated babyish behaviors, extreme expressions of neediness, extensive clinging and proximity seeking, helpless dependency, extreme passivity, blurring the boundaries between self and other, and failure to engage in exploration. "Many of these features," the authors conclude, "characterize the normal *amae* relationship in Japan."

Once again, cultural meaning is at issue. *Amae* is a central Japanese value that idealizes willing dependence and that typifies close relationships in Japan (Doi 1992). Rothbaum and colleagues cite other researchers who speculate that the close link between *amae* and attachment explains why both Japanese mothers and children experience more sadness and fewer feelings of fear than their American counterparts upon reunion in the SSP. In the Japanese case, researchers observe that attachment is activated "by loss more than by exploratory risk," and *amae* is an appropriate cultural means of deactivating this sense of loss (Rothbaum et al. 2000:1100).

Marinus van IJzendoorn and Abraham Sagi-Schwartz (2008) reject this interpretation. It is true that methodological issues bedevil these Japanese studies, making it difficult to evaluate their results—such as exceptionally small sample sizes, conflicting findings, longer-than-standard experimental episodes, and mothers' self-consciousness and deference toward experimenters during behavioral observations.[6] Acknowledging these problems, we wish to address the substantive argument that van IJzendoorn and Sagi-Schwartz level against Rothbaum et al.'s characterization of attachment in Japanese cultural terms. They argue (2008:892–896) that attachment security and *amae* are not the same kind of things, and that Rothbaum and his coauthors, by considering attachment and *amae* as "competing concepts," are "making a logical category error." As Rothbaum et al. (2011:174) respond, "[C]omparing security with *amae* is like comparing apples with fruit; the appropriate comparison is between security and *positive amae*." *Amae* is positive, they explain, when the child responds appropriately to interpersonal and situational contextual cues; it is negative when the child fails to attend to the contextual cues such as failing to attend to the needs of others.

We would go further: van IJzendoorn and Sagi-Schwartz are making an error of their own. Rothbaum and his colleagues are arguing that the behavioral expression of attachment is shaped by the uniquely Japanese cultural concept of *amae*. In this sense, *amae* is not competing with attachment, but is its Japanese version—its Japanese meaning.[7] The Japanese results do not threaten, and Rothbaum et al. do not attack, as van IJzendoorn and Sagi-Schwartz (2008:895) claim they do, what those authors (2008:881) call the "universality hypothesis"—the idea, fundamental to attachment theory, that all infants everywhere develop attachment relationships to their caregivers. Indeed, Rothbaum et al. (2000:1102) conclude only that, "Most of the basic tenets of attachment theory...are apt to be of greater value as they assume more culture-specific forms." As Gaskins (chapter 1) observes this argument, that attachment categories are simply inadequate to capture all cross-cultural variation in caretaker-infant bonding, is the most radical of all critiques of attachment theory.

Further Contributions of This Volume

The ethnographic chapters to follow take this most radical of positions. They are not critiques of the use of the Strange Situation Procedure or critiques of the way insecure attachment categories are assigned cross-culturally. Indeed, those issues (except when researchers wish to defend their nonuse of the SSP in the field, as do Meehan and Hawks in chapter 3, or fundamentally reformulate the concept of insecure attachment, as does Mageo in chapter 7) hardly receive commentary. Instead, these are deeper critiques of the cross-cultural applicability of a theoretical paradigm that decontextualizes, misunderstands, and so often pathologizes non-Western attachment (at the same time that it fails to recognize the psychological costs that can and typically do accompany Western-style attachment). The chapters that follow seek to expand the very way we think about attachment in the light of cross-cultural evidence. Depending upon and presuming another's love and indulgence as it does (Doi 1992), *amae* underpins healthy attachment relationships in Japan with their emphasis on accommodation and dependence. So in other places attachment styles are culturally distinctive in response to local conditions and according to local models of virtue.

By culturally distinctive attachment styles like *amae* we do not mean isolated and superficial practices of the sort that serves van IJzendoorn and Sagi-Schwartz (2008:882–883) as a stock illustration of cross-cultural variation in attachment, and that these authors seem to imagine when they think about such variation:[8]

> Gusii infants are used to being greeted with a handshake by their mothers and caretakers. During the reunions, the Gusii infants anticipated the handshake in the same way as North American or European infants anticipate a hug. The secure Gusii infants would reach out to an adult with one arm, to receive the handshake enthusiastically, whereas the insecure infants would avoid the adult or reach and then pull away after the adult approached.

The descriptions of cultural variation in attachment, beginning with Gaskins's (chapter 1) analysis of her ethnographic data on the Yucatec Maya, and continuing on through another seven ethnographic case studies, are much more far reaching. They are meant to show that the meanings of attachment in these other cultures are profoundly different from those in the United States and cannot be translated simply by substituting handshakes for hugs. Instead, they must be understood in their own cultural terms. Moreover, if we ever hope to derive culturally meaningful patterns of variation in attachment, we must deduce that variation from a large set of such cross-cultural studies, representative of the full range of human societies and human caregiving practices.

We caution that what we are not intending to do is to recast the existing categories of secure and insecure attachment in local terms, establishing a baseline "secure" attachment for each particular society, trying to capture how that society's system of attachment equips the majority of its children to become securely attached within their cultural, historical, and social circumstances. For such a project would be bound to fail. We would still be left with costs to the individuals in that society, costs in the form of inevitable anxieties and defenses against those anxieties, as we will address in a later section on the psychodynamics of attachment (and see chapter 7 by Mageo and chapter 8 by Quinn in particular). Neither have we set out to challenge the argument for the evolutionary basis of attachment or the universal biological adaptation that it is said to represent.[9] What we do insist upon is the cultural malleability of this universal adaptation, and the striking cross-cultural variability that results.[10] And we insist that adequate accounts of attachment must examine the relations among cultural practices, local psychodynamics, and models of virtue, rather than assuming that a narrow set of categories will be capable of defining ideal human development.

Until researchers have much more information than is currently available about the range and variability of attachment systems cross-culturally, it would be premature to propose an entirely new theory of attachment. That is where this volume comes in. The ethnographies that follow bring to the fore an array of differing cross-cultural circumstances from sub-Saharan Africa, South Asia, and the Pacific as well as Central America, and represent the full range of subsistence economies from foraging through horticulture to settled agriculture and postindustrial life. In being preindustrial (with the exception of Seymour's chapter, which compares India to the United States), all these case studies depart from earlier cross-cultural studies by attachment theorists in industrial societies. Thus, not only do they meet the urgent need for further cross-cultural evidence of attachment, but they also expand the range of possibilities with which to rethink it. Whenever appropriate, too, they suggest elements of a revised attachment theory beginning to emerge.

Each chapter focuses on one or more ethnocentric assumptions made in attachment theory, assumptions about the universality and normativity of beliefs and practices most of which are, in actuality, distinctively Western. In different ways the concepts challenged by the cross-cultural studies described in these chapters are absolutely central to attachment theory. These challenged concepts begin with (1) the assumed centrality of dyadic mother-child attachment, and include (2) the privileging of a Western style of sensitive mothering that is supposed to produce secure attachment; (3) the presumption that Western-style autonomy, and the independence that results from this kind of autonomy, are the only possible outcomes of secure attachment; (4) the dissociation of attachment from feeding and food; (5) the supposition that security is the singular effect of positive one-to-one attachments, to the neglect of negative experiences undercutting disfavored kinds of attachment; (6) the acceptance of adult pair bonding as the primary adult expression of attachment relationships; and, finally, (7) the picture of unproblematic continuity, uncomplicated by psychodynamics or developmental maturation, of a person's internal working model from earliest childhood to adulthood. Each contributor describes a case (or compares two cases) in which one or more of these seven assumptions do not hold, or must be radically modified.

Rethinking Dyadic Caregiving

The first of these ethnocentric assumptions, often implicit in the writings of attachment theorists, is that the only theoretically significant attachment is to mother (or in the case where there is no mother available, to a substitute mother). Indeed, some attachment theorists, including Bowlby himself, are careful to pay lip service to the idea that infants may attach to others—and, especially in the contemporary climate of shared parenting in Western countries, to fathers. Some researchers, such as Michael Lamb (see, e.g., Lamb 2010), have been arguing for the recognition of fathers' roles in child development for over 30 years. Nevertheless, the overwhelming majority of studies investigate attachment of children to their mothers. Even when multiple attachments are noted, they remain untheorized. So, for example, attachment theorists do not explore how children integrate multiple attachments into their internal working models of relationships. Guided by their knowledge of widespread multiple mothering in the anthropological record as well as observations of it at their own field sites, and spurred by Hrdy's (2009) recent work on allomothering, several of these studies contest the assumption that attachment is dyadic.

Despite the aforementioned terminological variants of allomothering and multiple mothering, all of these authors agree, and indeed their ethnographies collectively confirm, the universal fact that primary attachment is to mother or a singular mother substitute. This is so even in cases where the mother is not the infant's or child's routine caregiver. We are persuaded of this fact, we might add, not only by the evolutionary argument that is a paramount scientific contribution of attachment theory, and by our own and others' behavioral observations of infants and toddlers in many societies cross-culturally, but also by emerging neuroscientific findings, such as this tidbit (Purves et al. 2008:368):

> Infants recognize their mothers within hours after birth by smell, preferentially orienting toward their mothers' breasts and showing increased rates of suckling when fed by their mother compared to being fed by other lactating females, or when presented experimentally with their mothers' odor versus that of an unrelated female. This recognition ability in infants is matched by that in mothers, who can reliably discriminate their own infant's odor when challenged with a range of odor stimuli from other infants of similar age.

A caveat: Being Westerners, these writers do not consider whether an infant might develop a preferential orientation to multiple attachment figures where these exist—and especially where some of these may breast-feed the infant in the biological mother's absence, as is the case among the Aka (chapter 3), the

Alorese (chapter 4), and the Samoans (chapter 7). Our contributors explore new territory, asking how allomothering or distributed caregiving may be more or less prominent and widespread in a given community, may vary widely in the cultural style with which it is administered, can articulate with primary mothering in different ways, and can have strikingly different effects on children.

Chapter 2 on multiple caregiver attachments among the Hadza, by Alyssa Crittenden and Frank Marlowe, tests the Cooperative Breeding Hypothesis using infant holding as a measure of allomaternal support. They find that, indeed, shared child care as reflected in the number of others who hold the child reduces the amount of time that a mother herself spends holding her child, and thus "releases the recipient mother from some of the energetic burden of child care, which may function to reduce metabolic costs and help mothers return to ovulation more quickly," as the hypothesis predicts. Chapter 3, by Courtney Meehan and Sean Hawks on the Aka, fills in another part of this picture, demonstrating not only that infants and children are cared for extensively by allomothers—who account for around a quarter of the care of young Aka children—but that, in this world of dense social networks, children build attachments with some (on average six) of these other caregivers, as measured by attachment behaviors toward these allomothers. Furthermore, while Aka mothers are more sensitive to their infants and show more positive affect toward them, they are also more likely than allomothers to physically or verbally reject and ignore their child's attachment displays. Presumably, this is because mothers are reacting to the high demands these little charges put on their time, emotional energy, and attention to other work. By their rejection they may also be attempting to redirect their children's demands toward allomothers. Thus, while the Aka case does not dispute the theoretical premise that there is always one primary attachment figure, typically the mother, it does inflect that premise, calling attention to the nuanced and varied cultural meaning that this primary figure, and other attachment figures, may have for the attached child.

Susan Seymour's contribution to this volume, in chapter 4, sheds further light on the Cooperative Breeding Hypothesis, this time by comparison of two cases, one in which multiple mothering does assist the birth mother in child care in the way the hypothesis would predict, and another in which multiple mothering is more problematic. The ethnographic descriptions of both societies once again challenge attachment theory's focus on mother. Juxtaposed, they demonstrate that distributed caregiving can play out very differently in different societies. As this chapter and the previous two so convincingly demonstrate, attachment theorists cannot continue to operate as if the mother were the only caregiver of any theoretical importance.

Reexamining Sensitive Mothering

In attachment theory, the kind of mother said to cultivate secure attachment in her small child practices "sensitive mothering," defined as being accessible to the infant and responsive to its expressed needs. Bambi Chapin's case study in chapter 5 delves into the cross-cultural validity of this concept, using her research in a rural Sinhala-speaking Buddhist village on the island of Sri Lanka to do so. In this society hierarchy is especially valued, and with it, the deference and non-assertiveness that children learn as they grow older. In contrast, achieving the kind of independence and verbal communication that American middle-class child caregivers feel is so important, and that is so integral to attachment theorists' definition of "sensitive" mothering and its outcomes, is not valued in the Sinhala case. Rather, in the Sinhala cultural model of virtue, superiors are obliged to attend to juniors' needs, while juniors themselves wait patiently, whether as children waiting to be fed, or as young adults counting on their parents to arrange their marriages and guide them into professions. It is clear from this case that the cultural meanings of both maternal sensitivity and its desired outcome need to be broadened in order for such variations to be accommodated in attachment theory.

As Chapin and also Mageo in her chapter both observe, prominent features of mothering in American middle-class practice are gazing and face-to-face interaction, which establish something that psychologists call "attunement" between mother and infant. Indeed the mutual gaze, face-to-face interaction routine depicted in the cover photo of this book is so iconic in American cultural understanding that infants like the one in the photo begin learning it from their mothers as newborns. Once again, as Chapin notes, attachment theorists consider these cultural behaviors to be integral to sensitive mothering as well as a universal and necessary precursor to the development of a strong and secure attachment. Yet, these kinds of behavior are absent from many of the caregiving regimes described in this book (see Seymour, chapter 4, p. 127 for an explicit example; see also Greenfield 2009). These versions of mothering are no less sensitive, no less responsive to infantile needs, for their omission of mutual gazing.

Considering Autonomy and Independence

Chapin makes the further point that these Sinhala children do not lack autonomy; it is just that they practice a different kind of autonomy, requiring them to exercise self-control and discernment.[11] Chapter 6, by Kathleen Barlow, offers a case even more challenging to the place attachment theory accords to autonomy. Barlow describes patterns of attachment in a marine foraging society in which a child, in the exclusive care of its biological mother for the first few months, is later cared for by multiple community members. This sequence reflects, and perhaps goes some way toward explaining, a duality in the Murik cultural model of virtue. According to attachment theorists, secure attachment is the desired outcome of sensitive mothering and is evinced by the child's eventual independence, so central to adulthood in American society. Murik caregivers, however, foster both independence and dependence in their children, and both are subsequently important markers of Murik adulthood. The case thus offers an important corrective to the biased assumption in attachment theory that the universal goal of child rearing is to raise a child who is unequivocally independent.

Parenthetically, this dual emphasis on both independence and dependence also calls into question the distinction that has long been the subject of such lively debate in cultural psychology, sometimes posed as a dichotomy and other times as a continuum, between so-called collectivist and individualist societies, with their respective emphases on interdependent or independent self-construal. A reader might have already begun to wonder why this introduction has had nothing to say so far about that debate, since so many of the societies represented in these ethnographies would seem to fall into the collectivist category. As important as this debate is to some psychologists and cultural anthropologists, our contributors refuse to unduly dichotomize cultures or legitimize an assumed distinction between collectivist and individualist societies that has characterized much of the literature on this topic. Instead, our ethnographies suggest that collectivist and individualist tendencies are always present in societies. Researchers might better determine the specific relation between them in a given society rather than essentializing cultural orientations and thereby obscuring the complexities of cultural psychodynamics as well as intercultural variations. Barlow's ethnography of the Murik stands out for offering an extreme challenge to the collectivist-individualist contrast, demonstrating as it does that both interdependence and independence can be culturally valued in the very same society, both being components of the cultural model of virtue according to which children are raised. This pattern is possibly typical of foraging societies like the Murik, who live in an environment demanding at once extreme individual initiative for successful daily fishing and gathering, and readiness to fall back on the group during predictable times of economic crisis.

Incorporating Feeding and Food

Not only are Murik mothers initially their infants' exclusive caregivers and thereafter continue to be their children's primary caregivers, but they are cultural exemplars of the goodness and generosity that caregiving requires—reflected in their typical reliance on others to punish their children while they stand by to comfort them, and frequently also expressed through their role as suppliers of food, beginning with nursing. Here is a prime example of the way that feeding can become part and parcel of the cultural meaning of attachment. Bowlby, although he did not foreclose the possibility that feeding among other behaviors might become associated with attachment, argued that the attachment system evolved independently of feeding (for protection from predators). He was compelled by psychologist Harry Harlow's well-known demonstration that rhesus monkeys preferred terrycloth-covered surrogate mothers to bare wire-mesh ones even though the latter, but not the former, were equipped with food dispensers.[12] Without disputing the evolutionary independence of attachment from feeding, Barlow's and other contributions to this volume, particularly Seymour's analysis of both Alorese and North Indian caregiving (chapter 4) and Quinn's analysis of attachment on Ifaluk (chapter 8), show how central feeding and, by symbolic extension, food can become to the cultural meaning of attachment. This is especially so, perhaps, in societies that experience severe seasonal or periodic food shortages as the Murik and Ifaluk do. As Barlow observes, here is another dimension of the cultural meaning of attachment that has been neglected by attachment theorists.

Questioning Secure Attachment

Barlow's discussion of Murik disciplinary techniques is preface to the next chapter by Jeannette Mageo. In chapter 7, Mageo uses her field research in Samoa and in the United States to expand the notion of normative child socialization even more broadly, dismantling attachment theorists' notion of it even more radically. She makes the case that these theorists, by focusing so exclusively on secure attachment and the kind of mothering that is supposed to achieve it, have written out of their story a whole other side of attachment systems. This other side is the "distancing" practices, both physical and psychological, that work to undercut disfavored forms of attachment. As she explains, in Samoa distancing practices create separation anxiety and ultimately compel children to attach to, and rely on, the larger group for a support that is lifelong. Yet lack of intense maternal supervision also permits a surprising degree of personal independence. In the Northwestern middle-class US culture that Mageo studied, in contrast, distancing practices create dependency feelings that undermine personal boundaries and compel developing young people to intense interpersonal bonding coupled with defensive assertions of independence. Thus, Mageo's analysis adds yet another dimension of cultural meaning missing from attachment theory.

Reconceptualizing Adult Attachment

Several of these ethnographic case studies speculate about attachment over the life course and the consequences of early caregiving for the kind of adults produced by these cultural practices. Chapin, for instance, makes a strong case for continuity between the Sinhala style of early caregiving and later acceptance of one's junior place in a social hierarchy. Mageo considers how an emphasis on distancing practices in childhood translates into an adult Samoan world in which it makes emotional sense to depend upon the larger group for support. Adult attachment is, rather, the starting point of chapter 8, based on Naomi Quinn's reanalysis of Catherine Lutz's ethnography of the Ifaluk emotion term *fago*, and comparison of that case to the American understanding of adult *love*. Quinn is led to question the attachment theorists' notion of pair bonding as the universal adult outcome of early attachment (see also Seymour's discussion of this matter with respect to the case of India, in chapter 4). She adds a further, psychodynamic, layer of analysis to the understanding of individual-to-individual versus group bonding that contributors Barlow and Mageo discuss in relation to patterns of attachment.

Introducing Psychodynamic Defenses

Despite attachment theory's roots in psychoanalysis, and some current attempts to synthesize the two (see Fonagy et al. 2008), there has never been a critique of attachment theory from a psychoanalytic perspective. Although founders Bowlby and Ainsworth were psychoanalytic in their orientation, subsequent attachment theorists, in their determination to perpetuate what they considered ideal parenting, settled on a denuded version of psychoanalysis lacking the dimensionality of much preceding and subsequent psychoanalytic thought. Attachment theory gives us a rosy picture of normal human development and a benign vision of the securely attached person who results from this development (with perhaps a little help from attachment theorists and therapists).

In psychoanalytic theory, by contrast, the cultural crafting of self is always (and not only in instances of insecure attachment) in tension, and at least potentially at odds, with sensory and emotive elements of being and memory. As an intellectual tradition, one might say that psychoanalysis suspects that "civilization(s)" creates discontents and cannot be trusted to aim at greater human fulfillment—any more than chief executive officers can be trusted to better their workers' quality of life. Cultural conditioning is likely to promote compulsions like that toward money, success, or consumption (for an American example) that may help to reproduce society but that also may impede opportunities to live truly human lives. Freud saw the course of development he outlined not as ideal, but rather as productive of the psychopathologies of everyday life, pathologies to which society offered rehabilitating, but never entirely final, resolutions.

Chief among these partial resolutions, we believe, are what Melford Spiro (1961, 1965) called "culturally constituted defense mechanisms." Spiro argued that culturally constituted defensive formations are universal across societies. In subsequent decades, although psychological anthropologists remained interested in putatively universal psychodynamic "complexes" such as the Oedipal complex, culturally constituted defense mechanisms did not earn their attention. Perhaps, in reaction to earlier evolutionary ideas about the inferiority of so-called primitive societies and their cultures, these anthropologists were reluctant to examine defenses specific to other societies because any such focus might be interpreted as pathologizing those societies. Meanwhile in critical theory—for example in the work of Herbert Marcuse (1955) and Louis Althusser (1971)—the idea that cultures might be psychologically repressive flourished.

Chapters 7 and 8 by Mageo and Quinn, respectively, begin to correct psychological anthropologists' neglect of the defenses and attachment theory's neglect of psychodynamic processes more generally. They do so by considering the ways attachment plays out over life courses. As Mageo explores, it is not only attachments that are culturally patterned, but also insecurities and anxieties about those attachments, offering yet another dimension of caregiving variation. Mageo describes what she calls "culturally constituted reaction formations," through which Samoans and Americans differently manage infantile rage and dependency. Quinn addresses the cultural mechanisms that defend against inevitable and troublesome dependency feelings that follow attachment into adulthood. Through their comparative studies of attachment, these two chapters make it clear that culturally constituted defenses and the unresolved anxieties that engender them are found worldwide, while at the same time these defenses and their articulations with styles of attachment are culturally variable.

To Attachment Theorists

It would be a shame if attachment theorists did not take this volume seriously. A primary reason they might not be disposed to do so is because of the ethnographic methodology herein. While in many quarters "mixed methods" research is becoming acceptable and even desirable, attachment theory is still largely wedded to narrowly quantitative methods represented by the SSP (and its spin-off, the Q-sort; see discussion by Gaskins, chapter 1. Our suggestions are that attachment needs to be studied in the context of local meanings and child-rearing practices, along with cultural models of virtue and psychodynamics, all of which are best discovered through ethnography.

Ethnography, as represented in this volume, is decidedly qualitative. Chapters 2 and 3 in this volume on Hadza and Aka foragers, respectively, follow accepted practice in biocultural anthropology in presenting quantitative findings, and thus may seem more familiar to quantitatively oriented psychologists like attachment theorists. Even here, as we have already seen in the case reported by Meehan and Hawkes in chapter 3, the methods that attachment theorists rely upon are unsuitable in the naturalistic circumstances of the anthropological field. While the method Meehan designed still yields quantitative results, it is far from the SSP that attachment theorists know and trust.

The other five case studies in this volume are more thoroughly "ethnographic" in style, eschewing summary statistics for discursive reports. This is a deliberate methodological strategy. These authors are intent on building a rich ethnographic picture of attachment in given societies. Indeed, all the contributors to this volume, including the biocultural anthropologists, accomplish the work of ethnography by staying for long periods in and returning repeatedly to the field site, becoming more or less fluent in the local language, interviewing local actors extensively, observing ordinary everyday interactions with an eye to extracting the patterns in these little "dramas," and, as Chapin describes so well in chapter 5, trying to make sense of seemingly incomprehensible patterns with more questioning and more observing.

To have used, instead, an instrument measuring secure or insecure attachment, which could be administered reasonably quickly but which removed a behavior from its cultural context and failed to capture its cultural meaning, would have been to fall prey to the very error that we critique attachment theorists of committing.

One way to reconcile these different methodological traditions, in the spirit of the newer turn to mixed methods, is to recognize that both methodological approaches have their appropriate uses. It might be thought of as a choice between reliability and validity. Quantitative approaches reduce data so that they can be economically presented and reliably compared, but in doing so they squeeze out meaning; whereas so-called qualitative approaches preserve meaning, insuring that descriptions are valid, while making comparison more difficult. In general, meaning-preservation methods are usually best for developing theory, while data-reduction methods are often best for testing hypotheses. A way to restate the argument of this volume is that attachment theory has been testing cross-cultural hypotheses prematurely and needs to first develop a more universally adequate theory. To this purpose, ethnography is well-suited. Earlier in the introduction, we commented that the cross-cultural case studies in the following chapters would expand the range of possibilities with which to reassess attachment theory. They also provide the rich, contextualized, meaning-laden, and often unexpected material that promotes such rethinking. This is what anthropologists use and recommend ethnography for—to think and rethink theory.

For other reasons, previous critiques of attachment theory have not been heard. As LeVine (2009:2–3) has written so eloquently, attachment theory was and is infused with Bowlby's ideological fervor for more humane child care. Bowlby's crusade in the mid-twentieth century was directed against the then-regnant American school of thought that medicalized child care and advocated strict scheduling and discipline of young children. His zeal was further fueled by his encounter with orphaned and abandoned children in post–World War II Britain, and the near-criminal neglect of babies in American orphanages in the 1950s. In assembly-line style, rows of cribs lined some orphanages, the little ones picked up only as necessary to feed them. In its assertion that humans could develop only in the context of a tender, sensitive one-to-one bond, attachment theory militated against the dehumanizing tendencies of institutional care in industrial society. However, Bowlby then "made questionable recommendations about normal child care and tended to conflate extreme cases of severe separation and stress with moderate and even routine ones, as if they were part of a single continuum" (LeVine 2009:3). In the wake of Bowlby's writings, as a result, attachment theory became a blend of academic school and political movement. And, as Janet Spence (1985:1285, quoted in Rothbaum et al. 2000:1093) commented in her 1985 presidential address to the American Psychological Association, "When most investigators [have]...a common cultural or ideological position, the effect may be to retard or to corrupt the search for scientific knowledge by collectively blinding them to alternative conceptions." We believe that this has been the case with attachment theory's blindness to alternative "pathways to enculturation."

In addition to an assured career in academia, there are certain further "professional advantages," in LeVine's (2009; also see Rothbaum et al. 2000:1093) term, which come to some members of an established academic field. In the case of attachment theory, and springing from its aforementioned second life as a political movement with a vision of humane child care, these are the advantages of making a living in clinical practice or therapeutic intervention programs, or writing popular how-to books on early childhood attachment (see Talbot 1998). Such practitioners have an obvious vested interest in the paradigm they espouse.

Critiques of attachment theory have also been ignored simply because these critiques have not been written by attachment theorists themselves (or even, in many instances, by other psychologists), nor have they typically been published in venues read by attachment theorists. And those reevaluations that have arisen from inside the school itself have typically been tentative, presented as inconsequential to the theory or requiring only slight modifications of it rather than the radical challenges to it that they in fact pose. In addition, all the critiques taken together have been relatively few compared to the massive numbers of attachment theorists' published works. These commentaries have been swallowed up by the magnitude of the field they are critiquing, as well as being overshadowed by the academic success of that enterprise.

Psychology, of which attachment theory is a well-established and successful branch, is a vast academic discipline.[13] Attachment theory is massive in its own right. The Preface to the latest edition of the *Handbook of Attachment* (Cassidy and Shaver 2008:xi) reports,

> Anyone who today conducts a literature search on the topic of "attachment" will turn up more than 10,000 entries since 1975, and the entries will be spread across scores of physiological clinical, developmental, and social psychology journals; will include numerous anthologies; and will deal with every stage of life from infancy to old age.

Furthermore, the majority of these studies conform to a mold, as Bretherton's comment about the seeming equation of attachment with the SSP, quoted earlier, reminds us.

Sheer size makes intellectual endogamy easier, reinforcing an already natural disinclination of the members of any academic enterprise to venture across disciplinary boundaries. But there is another reason for this disinclination to attend to critiques from outside the field. Attachment theory itself has become an academic "industry." New PhDs tend to be conversant with a single approach and loyal to a single paradigm, rather than ever having been pushed to find their own way through a thicket of alternative approaches and theories—as those of us in smaller fields, who are exposed to multiple paradigms (and moreover, in cultural anthropology, then go off to conduct fieldwork in relative isolation), are willy–nilly forced to do.

In several other respects, what we are calling academic industries are especially resistant to outside critiques. To begin with, concepts and methods become highly standardized. Increasingly, their validity goes unquestioned; as is the SSP, they are simply applied and reapplied. To make one's academic career in attachment theory it is enough to tinker with one isolated concept or introduce one methodological modification. Fundamental rethinking of the theory is not encouraged, nor is it likely be taken seriously. Thus, Rothbaum et al. (2000:1094) talk about how attachment theorists "have examined the periphery of their theory more than its core." By this latter complaint they mean that analyses focus on the definition of specific behaviors such as proximity-seeking, or the incidences of different types of insecure attachment, rather than jeopardizing "core tenets of the theory involving the antecedents, consequences, and nature of attachment security." Significantly for the present enterprise, Rothbaum and his coauthors note that one important reflection of this theoretical timidity is how few cross-cultural studies of attachment have been conducted, an observation that still holds true today. Along with this allegiance to industry standards, narrow conception of research questions, and avoidance of obvious cross-cultural challenges comes a certain amount of readiness to dismiss or defend against other approaches.

For all these reasons, influencing attachment theorists is a formidable task. Entering professional life as our generation did in the wake of Thomas Kuhn's *Scientific Revolutions*, we certainly do not expect to reorient, with a single book, the entire attachment theory paradigm. We do hope to win some converts, especially younger ones, to our view that attachment theory is in need of profound rethinking. The time is long past due that psychological theory sheds its imperial perspective: that Americans and particularly the American middle class can legitimately serve as a generic unmarked case. The alternative we believe is to think in terms of culture.

Acknowledgments

This introduction benefited from wise suggestions and hard thinking from several volume contributors, not to mention the actual rewriting they did. Indeed, writing it began to feel very much like a collective effort.

Notes

1. To anticipate Suzanne Gaskins's (chapter 1) point this fourth category may have been an early sign of this category system's failure to fully encompass attachment responses and their variations.
2. All but the studies in chapters 2 and 3 are reanalyses of ethnographic material after the fact of its collection, in almost all cases drawn from the authors' own field research, but not originally gathered to study attachment. This is simply a result of

the fact that psychological anthropology has only lately begun to pay attention to attachment theory, and not necessarily either an asset or a drawback at this stage in the theory's rethinking. We look forward to future anthropological research explicitly designed for the purposes of studying cross-cultural patterns of attachment. Such future research, we anticipate, will go beyond observations of such behavioral indices as caregivers holding infants or distressed infants seeking attachment figures (as fundamental as these behaviors are to attachment), to directly investigate the implications for attachment of the cultural meanings accorded to, for example, style of maternal care, feeding and food, or adult expressions of dependency, all features of attachment touched upon in these chapters. Meanwhile, the findings of the reanalyses presented here can be surprising and suggestive.

3. And, presumably for the same reason, some cross-cultural psychologists as well study foragers. See, for one example, Tronick, Morelli, and Ivey (1992), an earlier critique of the Western bias in attachment theory's mother-centered account, based on the finding of what the authors call "multiple caretaking" among the Efe, a foraging people.
4. This is not such a far-fetched idea. It is supported by recent findings from the new field of cultural neuroscience that, for example, East Asian (including Japanese) populations have a much higher frequency of an allele associated with anxiety than is found in Euro-American populations (Chiao and Blizinsky 2010). It is unknown whether this genetic difference might have implications for patterns of infant and child care—although these authors make a leap that most psychological anthropologists would consider altogether unwarranted, positing an association of the two different distributions of alleles with collectivism versus individualism, broadly conceived. More conservatively, we might ask: Has the Japanese pattern of proximal care, to be described shortly, evolved to reassure especially anxious infants?
5. van IJzendoorn and Kroonenberg (1988, quoted in Sagi 1990:18), characterize this difference as a continuum running from "distal" forms of attachment at one end to "proximal" at the other.
6. See Rothbaum et al. 2001:172–173 for a critique of some of the methodological problems with the Japanese studies.
7. Thus, it is unsurprising that the Japanese experts and mothers asked would say, as van IJzendoorn and Sagi-Schwartz report that they do, that the Japanese idea of *amae* and the American idea of secure attachment (however rendered in the Japanese language) were different.
8. Quite independently, Rothbaum et al. (2011:175) had the same reaction to this example.
9. Of course there is no way to verify Bowlby's original speculation that this evolutionary development around proximity-seeking and maintenance was an adaptation to the danger of predators, but that story is not what we are contesting either (though see Gubernick 1981 for a broader view of the adaptive value of infant attachment); it makes reasonable sense as long as it is not overly narrowly construed with regard to present-day societies.
10. See Rothbaum et al. (2011) for a similar argument.
11. See also Miller (2002:105) on the emphasis on self-control in Hindu India, in contrast with either voluntarism in the American morality of caring or empathy-based responsiveness in close Japanese relationships.
12. For brief descriptions of these experiments and their influence on Bowlby's thinking, see Cassidy (2008:2) and Suomi (2008:183).

13. The American Psychological Association tops 154,000 members and boasts 54 topical divisions.

References

Althusser, Louis. 1971. "Ideology and Ideological State Apparatuses." In *Lenin and Philosophy, and Other Essays* (Ben Brewster, trans.). New York: Monthly Review Press.

Bretherton, Inge. 1985. "Attachment Theory: Retrospect and Prospect." In *Growing Points of Attachment Theory and Research*, Inge Bretherton and Everett Waters, eds. Monographs of the Society for Research in Child Development, Serial No. 209, 50:1/2:3–35.

Bretherton, Inge. 1991. "The Roots and Growing Points of Attachment Theory." In *Attachment across the Life Cycle*, Colin M. Parkes, Joan Stevenson-Hinde, and Peter Marris, eds., pp. 9–32. New York: Routledge.

Briggs, Jean. 1998. *Inuit Morality Play: The Emotional Education of a Three-Year-Old*. New Haven, CT: Yale University Press.

Cassidy, Jude. 2008. "The Nature of the Child's Ties." In *Handbook of Attachment: Theory, Research, and Clinical Applications*, 2nd edition, Jude Cassidy and Phillip R. Shaver, eds., pp. 3–22. New York: Guilford Press.

Cassidy, Jude, and Phillip R. Shaver. 2008. Preface to *Handbook of Attachment: Theory, Research, and Clinical Applications*, 2nd edition, Jude Cassidy and Phillip R. Shaver, eds., pp. xi–xvi. New York: Guilford Press.

Chiao, Joan Y., and Katherine D. Blizinsky. 2009. *Culture-Gene Coevolution of Individualism-Collectivism and the Serotonin Transporter Gene*. Proceedings of the Royal Society B: Biological Sciences 277:529–537.

Chisholm, James. 1996. "The Evolutionary Ecology of Attachment Organization." *Human Nature* 7(1):1–37.

Doi, Takeo. 1992. "On the concept of *amae*." *Infant Mental Health Journal* 13(1):7–11.

Fonagy, Peter, George Gergely, and Mary Target. 2008. "Psychoanalytic Constructs and Attachment Theory and Research." In *Handbook of Attachment: Theory, Research, and Clinical Applications*, 2nd edition, Jude Cassidy and Phillip R. Shaver, eds., pp. 783–810. New York: Guilford Press.

Greenfield, P. A. 2009. "Linking Social Change and Developmental Change." *Developmental Psychology* 45(2):401–418.

Grossman, Karin, Klaus E. Grossman, Gottfried Spangler, Gerhard Suess, and Lothar Unzner. 1985. "Maternal Sensitivity and Newborns' Orientation Responses as Related to Quality of Attachment in Northern Germany." In *Growing Points of Attachment Theory and Research*, Inge Bretherton and Everett Waters, eds. Monographs of the Society for Research in Child Development, Serial No. 209, 50:1/2:233–256.

Gubernick, David. 1981. "Parent and Infant Attachment in Mammals." In *Parental Care in Mammals*, David Gubernick and Peter Klopfer, eds., pp. 243–305. New York: Plenum.

Hrdy, Sarah Blaffer. 2009. *Mothers and Others: The Evolutionary Origins of Mutual Understanding*. Cambridge, MA: Harvard University Press (Belknap).

Keller, Heidi. 2007. *Cultures of Infancy*. Mahwah, NJ: Erlbaum.

Lamb, Michael E., ed. 2010. *The Role of Fathers in Child Development*, 5th edition. Hoboken, NJ: Wiley.
LeVine, Robert A. in press. "Attachment Theory as Cultural Ideology." In *Different Faces of Attachment: Cultural Variations of a Universal Human Need*, Heidi Keller and Hiltrud Otto, eds. Cambridge: Cambridge University Press.
LeVine, Robert A., and Patrice M. Miller. 1990. "Commentary." *Human Development* (Special Topic: Cross-Cultural Validity of Attachment Theory) 33(1):73–80.
LeVine, Robert A., and Karin Norman. 2001. "The Infant's Acquisition of Culture: Early Attachment Reexamined in Anthropological Perspective." In *The Psychology of Cultural Experience*, Carmella C. Moore and Holly F. Mathews, eds., pp. 83–104. Cambridge: Cambridge University Press.
Marcuse, Herbert. 1955. *Eros and Civilization*. Boston, MA: Beacon.
Miller, Joan G. 2002. "Bringing Culture to Basic Psychological Theory—Beyond Individualism and Collectivism: Comment on Oyserman et al. (2002)." *Psychological Bulletin* 128(1):97–109.
Miyake, Kazuo, Shing-jen Chen, and Joseph J. Campos. 1985. "Infant Temperament, Mother's Mode of Interaction, and Attachment in Japan: An Interim Report." In *Growing Points of Attachment Theory and Research*, Inge Bretherton and Everett Waters, eds. Monographs of the Society for Research in Child Development, Serial No. 209, 50:1/2:276–297.
Purves, Dale, George J. Augustine, David Fitzpatrick, William C. Hall, Anthony-Samuel LaMantia, James O. McNamara, and Leonard E. White, eds. 2008. *Neuroscience*, 4th edition. Sunderland, MA: Sinauer Associates.
Rothbaum, Fred, Gilda Morelli, and Natalie Rusk. 2011. "Attachment, Learning, and Coping: The Interplay of Cultural Similarities and Differences. In *Advances in Culture and Psychology*, vol. 1, Michelle Gelfand, Chi-yue Chiu, and Ying-yi Hong, eds., pp. 153–215. New York, NY: Oxford University Press.
Rothbaum, Fred, John Weisz, Martha Pott, Kazuo Miyake, and Gilda Morelli. 2000. "Attachment and Culture: Security in the United States and Japan." *American Psychologist* 55(10):1093–1104.
Sagi, Abraham. 1990. "Attachment Theory and Research from a Cross-Cultural Perspective." *Human Development* 33(1):10–22.
Solomon, Judith, and Carol George. 2008. "The Measurement of Attachment Security and Related Concepts in Infancy and Early Childhood." In *Handbook of Attachment: Theory, Research, and Clinical Applications*, 2nd edition, Jude Cassidy and Phillip R. Shaver, eds., pp. 383–416. New York: Guilford Press.
Spence, Janet T. 1985. "Achievement American-style: The Rewards and Costs of Individualism." (The 1985 American Psychological Association Presidential Address.) *American Psychologist* 40:1285–1295.
Spiro, Melford E. 1961. "An Overview and a Suggested Reorientation." In *Psychological Anthropology*, Francis L. K. Hsu, ed., pp. 472–497. Homewood, IL: Dorsey Press.
Spiro, Melford E. 1965. "Religious Systems as Culturally Constituted Defense Mechanisms." In *Context and Meaning in Cultural Anthropology*, Melford E. Spiro, ed., pp. 100–113. New York: Free Press.
Suomi, Stephen J. 2008. "Attachment in Rhesus Monkeys." In *Handbook of Attachment: Theory, Research, and Clinical Applications*, 2nd edition, Jude Cassidy and Phillip R. Shaver, eds., pp. 173–191. New York: Guilford Press.
Takahashi, Keiko. 1990. "Are the Key Assumptions of the 'Strange Situation' Procedure Universal? A View from Japanese Research." *Human Development* 33(1):23–30.

Talbot, Margaret. 1998. "Attachment Theory: The Ultimate Experiment." *New York Times Magazine*, May 24:24–30, 38, 46, 50, 54.
Tronick, Edward Z., Gilda A. Morelli, and Paula K. Ivey. 1992. "The Efe Forager Infant and Toddler's Pattern of Social Relationshiops: Multiple and Simultaneous." *Develomental Psychology* 28(4):568–577.
van IJzendoorn, Marinus H., and Pieter M. Kroonenberg. 1988. "Cross-Cultural Patterns of Attachment: A Meta-analysis of the Strange Situation." *Child Development* 59(1):147–156.
van IJzendoorn, Marinus H., and Abraham Sagi-Schwartz. 2008. "Cross-Cultural Patterns of Attachment: Universals and Contextual Dimensions." In *Handbook of Attachment: Theory, Research, and Clinical Applications*, 2nd edition, Jude Cassidy and Phillip R. Shaver, eds., pp. 880–905. New York: Guilford Press.
Weinfeld, Nancy S., L. Alan Sroufe, Byron Egeland, and Elizabeth Carlson. 2008. "Individual Differences in Infant-Caregiver Attachment: Conceptual and Empirical Aspects of Security." In *Handbook of Attachment: Theory, Research, and Clinical Applications*, 2nd edition, Jude Cassidy and Phillip R. Shaver, eds., pp. 78–101. New York: Guilford Press.
Weisner, Thomas S. 2005. "Commentary: Attachment as a Cultural and Ecological Problem with Pluralistic Solutions." *Human Development* 48(1/2):89–94.

Chapter 1

The Puzzle of Attachment: Unscrambling Maturational and Cultural Contributions to the Development of Early Emotional Bonds

Suzanne Gaskins

There is a tension that exists over the maturational and cultural contributions to the development of attachment bonds in infants. This chapter first lays out the general puzzle of how to resolve that tension and describes how it has been characterized in the formative work on attachment. Next, that discussion will be extended by reviewing the issues raised by the existing research on attachment in other cultures and discussing what these issues mean for defining the level of cultural analysis needed. Then, attachment is put into developmental (maturational) perspective by placing it in the context of a broader set of infant capacities that develop around the time that attachment also first presents itself. It will be argued that this set of new capacities sets the stage for infants to enter and to begin to make sense of their culturally organized social worlds. The fourth section of the chapter illustrates how complex that entry and sense making is, by providing concrete examples of cultural understandings and practices that influence specific attachment behaviors as they are negotiated by infants and caregivers. The chapter ends with a proposal of how to solve the puzzle of attachment, by working iteratively, and open-mindedly, between a universal theoretical concept and the complex facts on the ground.

The Puzzle of Attachment

Bowlby (1969) made the theoretical argument that attachment behaviors observed in infancy are evidence of the development of an internal working model of social relations. He developed an interest in the role of attachment in development when he observed how orphans and others without their mothers failed to thrive. Infants who were separated from their mothers at first appeared angry and then appeared depressed, and in the long run, failed to develop normal motor, cognitive, and social skills. He took an ethological perspective on attachment, which presumes that we have evolved in ways that maximize our chances of survival. He argued that, since human young stay dependent for a comparatively long time, we have developed a complex, reciprocal system of caregiver and infant bonding that promotes maximal proximity over the first few years of life, and thus, survival.

Attachment behaviors identified, both through theory and observation, typically include contact and proximity seeking; use of others as a secure base for exploration of objects, people, and environment; and use of others for consolation (Bowlby 1988). In addition, two forms of distress can occur that are seen as additional evidence of such a working model: separation anxiety and stranger anxiety. Even when willing to go quite a distance away from the caregiver, the infant likes to know that the caregiver is available; thus it is stressful for the infant if the caregiver leaves—this is called "separation anxiety" (Bowlby 1960). Likewise, unknown people and objects come to be recognized as potential threats to the infant, and they become hesitant to approach them (especially without the secure base of the attachment figure available)—this cautious stance toward unknown people is called "stranger anxiety." (See Rheingold and Eckerman [1973] for a review of the concept as it was understood at the time Bowlby was developing his theory.)

In the cultures that have been studied the most—that is, mainstream cultures in Europe and North America—these behaviors tend to emerge in the final quarter of the first year of life. The most basic characteristic of the working model is an understanding by infants that their needs will be met by other members of their immediate, everyday social world. Bowlby (1958, 1969) assumed that the model would be centered on one member of that world—the infant's mother. Furthermore, Ainsworth and her colleagues (Ainsworth 1979; Ainsworth, Bell, and Stayton 1991; Bell and Ainsworth 1972) demonstrated in their empirical work that *sensitivity* of the caregiver to an infant's needs in the preceding months predicts a high level of trust in the infant that those needs will be met through contact and supervision by the caregiver, along with a reduction in the amount of crying and an increase in obedience. Thus, we have a candidate for a human universal—if infants experience an environment where their needs are consistently attended to and responded to effectively, they come to develop an emotional bond to their caregivers based on trust; that is, they develop a working model of social relations based on their interactions with those who take care of them. This model leads them to assume that their needs will be met by their caregivers. In short, seeking and maintaining contact with caregiver (or with infant by caregiver) is an effective way to insure that the infant remains safe and comfortable.

Those who have since studied the concept of attachment (including Ainsworth herself) have taken this basic original theoretical claim of Bowlby's and Ainsworth's and simultaneously expanded their claims about the significance of attachment in structuring future social relationships while narrowing the scope of topics and methods used in their investigations. They have expanded the theoretical claim to suggest that the working model of social relationships constructed in infancy is a direct and significant influence on characteristics of older children's and adults' relationships (e.g., Berlin, Cassidy, and Applebard 2008; Main and Cassidy 1988; Main, Kaplan, and Cassidy 1985; Thompson 1999; see also Karen 1998 for a review). In addition, from a statistical analysis of the clustering of behavioral responses (i.e., factors), they have argued that there are only three or four basic ways of being attached, and of these, one is dominant and clearly seen as more desirable, as is evidenced by its positive label "secure attachment" (Ainsworth et al. 1978). Furthermore, attachment has come to be studied almost exclusively through being measured by a handful of assessment tools that have been developed in investigators' labs in Europe and North America, primarily the "Strange Situation" developed by Ainsworth (Ainsworth, Salter, and Bell 1970) and the "Q-sort" (Waters and Deane 1985).

Thus, despite Ainsworth's first attempts to study the concept of attachment in naturalistic settings and across cultures (Ainsworth 1967, 1977), the practice of studying attachment has become narrowed and has moved away from an exploration of the range of variation in the expression of an *evolutionarily valuable*, shared commitment of caregivers and infants in their everyday lives and moved toward a *clinically defined* set of specific behaviors that can be elicited in an artificial setting to assess individual differences (e.g., Carlson and Sroufe 1995). Ainsworth (1967) first studied Bowlby's theoretical concept of attachment ethnographically in Uganda (where infants' experiences, even during their first year or two, are significantly different from those of infants in the United Kingdom or the United States). Her second attempt to study the concept of attachment in the United States was through naturalistic observation in children's homes (Ainsworth 1977). The burdensomeness of both of these studies led her and her colleagues to seek a simpler assessment measure, which came to be called "the Strange Situation," that could be administered in a lab (Ainsworth and Bell 1970). During this process, the intellectual task moved away from describing the social organization of attachment as social practice between infant and caregiver and toward viewing attachment as a stable characteristic of individual infants, one that constrained variation across individuals to a limited number of clusters of behavior, endured over time (even into adulthood), with reliable social precursors and consequences. This conceptual shift allowed for a shift in methodology as well, and a commitment was made to assessing this stable, individual characteristic in a lab, using a standard assessment procedure, gaining control and comparability while losing any understanding of contextual factors. (A second method of studying attachment, the Q-sort [Water and Dean 1985], uses a predetermined set of codes—based heavily on understandings developed from the Strange Situation—to apply to observations of infant-caregiver behaviors.)

Perhaps the most surprising thing about these changes made by Ainsworth and her colleagues is that few researchers have objected to the narrowing and morphing of the theoretical concept or the methodology used to study it. Those who have objected most consistently and vocally are researchers who are interested in cultural differences in infants, families, and daily contexts of their interactions (e.g., Keller 2008; LeVine and Miller 1990; LeVine and Norman 2001; Weisner 2005). But these objections have not been persuasive in changing the course of research on attachment. The Strange Situation, used consistently and prolifically by Ainsworth and her colleagues, and to a lesser degree, the Q-sort, have become such dominant methodological paradigms, it is difficult for any study of attachment to gain traction that stands outside that paradigm.

There is a basic tension that exists in the current attachment paradigm—one that is shared by current approaches for studying many other developmental processes (Gaskins 2006a). First, there is Bowlby's central claim that attachment is a species-wide maturational process that is evolutionarily important and increases the chances of infants' survival. Second, there is Ainsworth's central claim that that process can be significantly molded through experience: how mothers interact with their infants influences the quality of attachment. If all mothers in the species treated their infants the same, this would be a consistent argument. But a tension arises because it is also well documented through ethnographies of childhood that there is a huge amount of variation across cultures in the care of infants and in the way those around them interact with them (e.g., Martini and Kirkpatrick 1981; Super and Harkness 1982; Chisholm 1983; Tronick, Morelli, and Ivey 1992; LeVine et al. 1994).

This, then, is the puzzle that researchers find so difficult: How can a process be universal if it is structured through experience, and that experience is itself variable? These three claims fit together like an Escher print of endlessly ascending stairs. Getting rid of any one of the three, and the puzzle untangles by itself:

1. Attachment could be based on experience, even if that experience is variable, if it is not theoretically required to be a universal.
2. Attachment could be universal, even in the face of cultural variation in infants' experiences, if it is not dependent on experience.
3. Attachment could be universal and dependent on experience, if the variation in experience is not central but only superficial.

While all three approaches to solving the puzzle are equally valid, most researchers from within the attachment paradigm have rejected both #1 (not universal) and #2 (not dependent on experience). That leaves only #3 as a viable option for a solution: Cultural variation is only superficial. Psychologists tend to see this solution to the puzzle as the easiest. For anthropologists, however, this is not an acceptable solution; they see the amount variation in infant experience as substantial and central to our understanding of infancy. And there is a growing literature, reviewed in the next section, which is providing evidence that such a solution leads to an inaccurate picture of the process of attachment.

Cultural Critiques of Attachment Theory

This brief review of cultural research on attachment will be presented in order of increasingly radical claims about the scope of the effect of culture on the attachment process.

Claim #1: Current Assessment Measures are Culturally Biased

Much of the critique of anthropologists and others has been focused on the cultural inappropriateness of the Strange Situation (and less commonly, the Q-sort) as an assessment measure (e.g., LeVine and Miller 1990). Since the overwhelming majority of research that has been done on attachment has been done using an artificial protocol (the Strange Situation or Q-sort) conducted in a laboratory setting, it is difficult to have any study focused on the ethnographic observations of daily life to be included as relevant evidence. Researchers interested in cultural influences on attachment have felt compelled to use the standard methodology in order for the findings to gain any traction in the literature on attachment.

But the Strange Situation involves a range of assumptions that have little face validity when used in other parts of the world (Takahashi 1990), especially (but not solely) in nonindustrialized groups such as peasants and hunter-gatherers. First, both exposure to novel settings (in this case, a research laboratory) and encounters with novel people (in this case a researcher) are common occurrences for most middle-class American infants. This is certainly not the case for many children in other cultures. Second, the protocol has the mother leave the infant under these novel circumstances—again a not uncommon occurrence for most American infants but for some other cultures, a decidedly uncommon experience. The level of stress that is induced by the Strange Situation, therefore, is not equal across cultures because of the differences in previous experiences and expectations that the infants and their caregivers bring to the task. (Undoubtedly, there are also individual differences among middle-class European and American infants as to how "familiar" the Strange Situation seems to them, as well as differences among subcultural groups, but the research tradition provides no framework for evaluating such differences.) Since one of Ainsworth's primary motives for developing the measure was to introduce a fixed amount of stress in a controlled way in order to insure an equal opportunity for the display of attachment behaviors across participants (Ainsworth et al. 1978), this is a central methodological problem.

In research on attachment in Japan, for instance, we can see some of the difficulties of being limited to a laboratory assessment with such significant cultural assumptions (Miyake, Chen, and Campos 1985). While about the same number of Japanese infants as American infants are categorized as "securely attached," Japanese babies are more likely to be assessed as "anxious/resistant" than American babies. In particular, they do not explore the room or the stranger with much distance from the mother, and they are quite upset when the mother leaves the room—so upset that researchers have felt compelled to reduce the length of time of the mothers' absence. (The mothers seem to be quite upset by leaving the child, as well.) Most Japanese infants are used to maintaining close physical contact with their mothers, often being carried on their mothers' backs throughout the day, and sleeping with their mothers at night. Even when the Strange Situation is carried out in exactly the same, carefully controlled way for Japanese and American infants, the experience of being separated from one's mother in the laboratory is in no way the same for infants from the two cultures, given the cultural differences in everyday caregiving.

Thus, the differences observed in the infants' behavior during the Strange Situation become problematic to interpret. Is the primary source of the differences the cultural bias in the procedure or a more fundamental difference in the nature of the infants' attachment? We cannot tell within the limitations of the laboratory setting. There is no easy solution to this problem. For instance, if the Strange Situation is modified to minimize the presumed increased stress on the Japanese infant (by shortening or eliminating mother's absence, for instance), it is no longer "the same" measure, and the benefit of a controlled measure to allow comparison across groups is lost. If it is not modified, then the amount of stress for one group of infants is greater than that for another. This methodological critique—that the assessment method is culturally biased—is an important challenge to the validity of the cultural work done on attachment, but it is the most conservative of the cultural critiques of the attachment paradigm.

Claim #2: Attachment Categories Have a Value System Built in that is Culturally Biased

There are several issues that go beyond the cultural appropriateness of the Strange Situation assessment measure. One of the most significant ones is that the four categories of attachment style are inadequate for capturing the range of normal variation in attachment across cultures. Ainsworth and her colleagues (Ainsworth et al. 1978) originally argued that three patterns of behaviors were consistently found, based on predictable clusters of a variety of behaviors, and they called these three types of attachment "secure attachment," "anxious/avoidant attachment," and "anxious/resistant attachment." Infants who are *securely attached* show initial shyness to the stranger and the new environment, staying close to their mothers, but they quickly warm up and play with the toys and the stranger, using their mothers as secure bases. They are upset when the mother leaves, go to her upon her return, and are easily consoled by their mothers (but not by the stranger). Infants who are *anxious/avoidantly* attached show a distinctly different cluster of behaviors. They do not use their mothers as secure bases; they rely little on the mother to mediate their interaction with novel objects and the stranger. They are not particularly upset when their mother leaves, and if they become upset about something, they can be comforted almost equally well by either the mother or the stranger. They often ignore their mothers when they return to the room. Infants who are *anxious/resistantly* attached seem highly stressed in the "Strange Situation" and stay close to their mothers. They become quite disturbed when their mothers leave, but they are also hard to console upon their mothers' return, often both seeking and resisting the mothers' efforts to calm them down.

Over two decades ago, Main and her colleagues (Main and Solomon 1986) argued that to explain all the types of reactions seen by children in the Strange Situation, a fourth category was needed—"disorganized attachment." Infants who are classified as disorganized show a pattern of behaviors that do not fall neatly into one of the original three clusters of behaviors and often display a series of behaviors that seem internally inconsistent from within the paradigm—for instance, crying loudly in the mother's absence but choosing to stay far away from her upon her return. This category has been interpreted as being of particular clinical concern (e.g., it is found fairly often in infants with mothers with a pattern of drug abuse (Rodning, Beckwith, and Howard 1991) and alcohol abuse (O'Connor, Sigman, and Brill 1987) or history of maltreatment (Carlson et al. 1989). It has come to be included in many studies as a meaningful category that identifies dysfunctional attachment systems. However, since the category is really just a residual one, designed to be applied to those infants who do not fit the other three categories, it might be seen more productively as evidence of the inadequacy of the three attachment classifications to explain the data in infants who do not come from mainstream European/American cultures (the group that was used for constructing the categories in the first place).

Among the populations that have been studied across cultures, there are both important similarities and differences in the distribution of attachment styles (Van IJzendoorn and Sagi-Schwartz 2008). For all the cultures studied using this paradigm so far, "securely attached" infants are the most commonly observed. From 45 to 75 percent of the infants in the various cultures studied show this type of attachment. But there are important differences, too. As mentioned earlier, Japanese infants are more likely to exhibit behaviors during the Strange Situation that lead to a classification of anxious/resistant attachment than are American infants (Rothbaum et al. 2000; Takahashi 1990); so are Chinese infants (Ding et al. 2012). In contrast, infants in northern European countries (North Germany, Sweden, the Netherlands, and Great Britain) are less likely than Americans to exhibit behavior classified as anxious/resistant (e.g., Grossman et al. 1985), and, in many of these societies, the infants showed a higher likelihood than American infants of being classified as anxious/avoidant.

Theoretically, working within the current paradigm of attachment classification, the normative value of the category of "secure attachment" could be abandoned, turning it into an empirical question to discover how the "proper" balance differs across various cultures between autonomy/exploration and connectedness/comfort. If one pictures these two goals as opposite ends of a single continuum, then we might say that for middle-class

Americans, the point along the continuum where the infant-caregiver dyad is considered to be in balance is somewhere near the middle, and that dyads are equally likely to stray in either direction from this ideal balance point. The results from studies from other industrialized societies suggest that cultures differ in terms of where the balance point is set along the continuum, and in particular in which direction it is likely to stray from the middle-class American norm. This difference is likely to be based on culturally specific parental goals for infants' development and caregiving practices with infants. Thus, we could conclude that parents from the Northern European countries studied set their ideal balance point closer to the autonomy/exploration end than American parents (e.g., LeVine and Norman 2001), while parents from the Asian countries studied set their ideal balance point closer to the connectedness/comfort end (Takahashi 1990). For each culture, infants and caregivers with "healthy" attachments are likely to cluster around the culture's ideal balance point. (From within a life history perspective, Chisholm [1996] has suggested that attachment should be viewed as a mechanism to help maintain a balance between survival and growth, and variation in attachment style could be conceived of as adaptations to the presence of differing risks and uncertainty.)

This, then, is the next most conservative argument about cultural differences in attachment: The current categories used to describe attachment are adequate, but it is culturally naive to assign a *moral* value of "best" to one point on this spectrum (i.e., secure attachment) when other set points appear to exist in other cultures (e.g., Japan and Northern Europe), especially when those differences appear to lead to well-functioning and healthy members of those societies.

Claim #3: Existing Attachment Categories Are Not Sufficient to Capture All Attachment Systems

The fourth style of attachment raises even more serious issues when applied across cultures. While it is called "insecure/disorganized," it is really made up of infants who do not fall neatly into any of the other three categories—so it should be labeled more accurately as "none of the above." It is, not surprisingly for a residual category, the least common style among American infants, often associated with neglect and abuse. But if in fact it is merely a flare announcing the inadequacy of the paradigm to capture other styles of attachment, the category should not have the same negative clinical interpretation when it is applied in other cultural settings that it has when applied in the culture where the paradigm was developed.

It has been found, for instance, to be a relatively common style of attachment in Israeli kibbutz infants (Sagi et al. 1995), actually being the most common type of attachment seen in infants who sleep in the infant-care centers (away from their parents) (44%) and still very high for those who sleep with their parents (32%). This finding, if interpreted from a cultural perspective, suggests that rather than being evidence that the Israeli infants' attachment is truly "disorganized" or that there exists more dysfunctional parenting or more infants at risk, it is evidence of the failure of the assessment classification system to identify and characterize those patterns of behaviors found in this population, patterns that clearly differ from those observed in American infants (i.e., the three clusters of behaviors, originally based on statistical analysis of factors [Ainsworth and Bell 1970], which have come to define the original three styles of attachment).

This leads to a more radical cultural argument: The current paradigm's classification system fails to capture the full range of qualitative differences found in healthy infants across cultures. In some (perhaps, even, *most*) cultures, beliefs and practices about social interaction and infant development lead to infant experiences organized in ways orthogonal to the continuum of autonomy and connectedness that has been found to capture European and European-American behaviors (e.g., Harwood, Miller, and Lucca Irizarry, 1995). In those cultures, infant attachment cannot be validly assessed by either the Strange Situation or Q-sorts, not only because of the cultural assumptions built into the administration of those measures, or because of an assumption about the "best" balance between connectedness and autonomy, but because there are cultural assumptions built into the operationalization of the theory itself into distinct categories.

Attachment could, this argument implies, be qualitatively different not just across individuals, but across cultures, and in ways that currently are not under the microscope, since the paradigm has been narrowed to look just for the three or four categories identified through work in the United States. But the lack of exploring the possibility of qualitative cultural differences in attachment systems comes not only from the dominance of a single approach to attachment. It has been difficult to gain traction for this more culturally radical theory because of the ethological basis of the theory itself: It is presumed that attachment, as a maturational process, is not very labile and therefore only minimally influenced by cultural differences. This is only exacerbated by the fact that the theory focuses on infants, an age-group that many researchers assume could not possibly be influenced by cultural differences on any count.

Conclusions: Cutural Critiques of Attachment

This final, most radical claim leads one straight back to the basic puzzle of attachment laid out in the introduction to this chapter—the underlying tension in a species-wide evolutionary process that gives an important role to experience. This tension already exists within the paradigm because of the individual variation found in attachment, although the tension is diffused in large part because of the existence of a value system—that only *one* kind of attachment is really *good* or *healthy*. Any individual deviation from that one type is evidence of less-than-optimal development for that individual.

But the tension is significantly increased by looking more open-mindedly at the diversity of children's experiences across cultures—where Boasian anthropology is unwilling to apply a value system to undermine the observed diversity. Thus, once you look across cultures and discover that there is variation in both caregiver behaviors and infant attachment behaviors, the fundamental logic of the basic argument collapses. How can a universal, evolutionarily based process that increases the likelihood of infant survival also be culturally constructed, vary across cultures, and produce healthy members of society? Any attempt to reconceptualize the field of attachment must address this puzzling question.

Unscrambling Maturational and Cultural Contributions to Attachment

The most elegant solution to this puzzle of attachment is to divide the concept into two kinds of elements: (1) those elements that are indeed universal and represent the basic process defining an emotional bond between infants and caregivers that leads them to seek and maintain proximity, and thus increase the likelihood of infant survival; and (2) those elements that are not *fundamentally necessary* as a part of that process, but in fact, occur in each culture as a set of adjustments in response to the universal developmental process of infants forming attachments colliding with culturally specific social understandings and practices.

Rather than looking askance at the inconvenience of significant cultural variation in a supposedly universal developmental process, researchers could embrace cultural differences as a method for testing the existing claims, since understanding the variation would allow them to distinguish between those elements in the current paradigm that are present in a wide range of cultures (and thus strong candidates for being part of the basic universal process) and those that appear to be culturally specific to infants of European heritage (and thus strong candidates for being culturally nearsighted overgeneralizations). Currently, the possibility that there might be two kinds of claims is unrecognized or overlooked. Moreover, the latter type of claims (those that have been overgeneralized) are tightly interwoven with the former into a single description of patterns of behaviors that is perceived to represent the species as a whole when in reality it represents a particular cultural synthesis of the two types of sources. American researchers have constructed a paradigm that matches their own understanding of attachment in infants and caregivers without recognizing that some of what they have inserted into their description of the general process is in fact culturally specific to the cultural understandings and practices that they themselves carry (often unknowingly) into their research.

As a result, at this point neither the strengths nor the limits of the theory are unambiguously clear. More about attachment is claimed to be universal than is congruent with cultural research on attachment, but by looking at a single culture, researchers cannot clearly identify their errors—what is species-wide and maturational versus what is error from sampling too narrowly.

And the theory as it stands is unable to deal with the increasingly rich array of cultural differences, as exemplified by the creation of a fourth kind of attachment that can be described, essentially, as "doesn't fit our paradigm." Ainsworth (1977) herself, from her perspective growing out of her work in Uganda, originally argued in favor of the methodological value of looking at attachment in multiple cultures to see both the sturdiness and the flexibility of the construct, but the field has long ago abandoned such an approach.

The remainder of this chapter will serve as a proposed model of how to address the puzzle of attachment with a more limited claim about universals and an expanded appreciation for variation in culturally organized infant social experiences. There are two sections. First, there is a summary of a cluster of maturational processes that appear about the same time as attachment bonds are formed, interact with attachment, and appear to be found in many cultures. One might conceive of this as the "skeletal frame" of attachment. I argue that attachment should be seen as a part of a more general developmental phenomenon that provides the infant with new capacities for entering into social engagement and understanding. While the research on the universality of these capacities is limited, there is increasing evidence that they are found in a wide range of cultures. In the second section, there is a review of known cultural differences in interaction and beliefs that have a direct influence on the particular behaviors that have been identified as being the key identifying characteristics of attachment. One might conceive of this section as demonstrating the variation in the "flesh" of attachment—how it works in the everyday world of infants and their caregivers. Taken together, the goal of these two sections is to begin to unscramble the two types of forces that act on infant development in order to understand both the skeleton and the flesh more accurately.

Attachment as Part of a General Maturational Process

There are a number of developmental milestones that have been identified in research on European and North American samples to occur around an infant's first birthday. Increasingly, there is evidence that these milestones are interdependent, and that they are found in a wide range of cultures. It may be productive to conceptualize this set of milestones as parts of a new generalized capacity in the infant to participate in social interactions with those around them. (Konner [2010] has developed a similar list of abilities that he has labeled *CAD: Cultural Acquisition Device.*) Such a capacity is necessary for infants in all cultures to enter into the specific social practices that allow them to become legitimate participants in their particular culture. Indeed, in many cultures, this new capacity is recognized by an increase or change in participation of infants in their social worlds as they become increasingly able to walk and talk, sometime around their first birthday.

The expression of this new capacity, and the feedback given from the infants' environments leads, then, to the beginning of the working model of social relations identified by Bowlby that allows full attachment bonds to develop. The working model, in turn, guides the infants' participation in increasingly culturally specific ways. Attachment in this model, then, could be considered one of an interrelated set of universal and evolved developmental milestones that serve as the foundation for cultural participation. The most profound characteristic of our species is how much each new infant must learn, and that learning must include what is locally needed to be an effective social member of a group. To do this, infants need some way into the cultural system. I would argue that, taken as a group, the milestones discussed here represent the first maturational watershed that allows the infant a way into the system, and that attachment is a critical component. In this section, a short review of each of the other milestones is given, along with what evidence there is about its universality and its connections to attachment.

Locomotion

While there is some cultural variation in age by which infants crawl/scoot and walk, the capacity to move independently is firmly established in most ethnographic reports of healthy infants by the first birthday, and walking is usually a developed skill by 15 months, despite cultural variation in practices surrounding motoric development. The developmental landmark of walking is reached somewhat earlier in cultures that give intentional practice in sitting, standing, and moving, and somewhat later in those cultures where the infant is confined and/or carried most of the time (Adolph and Robinson, 2013).

Locomotion holds an important place in attachment theory, since it is only when infants can move around on their own that they are at greater risk of encountering dangers and thus need the emotional bond of attachment to insure that they will actively seek the maintenance of proximity between infant and caregiver (Campos et al. 2000). Social referencing (checking with another person before engaging with a novel object or in a novel activity) is one example of an increased reliance on social partners that emerges along with locomotion.

Differentiating between Familiar People and Strangers

Infants also are developing an increased awareness of who is a known interlocutor and who is not, along with a strong preference for people who are familiar. Many ethnographers have reported that infants are more discerning about who interacts with them sometime before their first birthday—often recognized as a point when studying infants becomes problematic because of their new wariness of the researchers. For instance, Brazelton, in reporting on research he did in Chiapas, Mexico, among Tzotzil Indians, reported that he could only test infants up to 9 months, because by 12 months, he elicited too much stranger anxiety to allow him to interact with the infants (Brazelton 1977:159). In my own work, I have found that one-year-olds are more wary of a researcher than younger babies, but the strong reaction that Brazelton reports starts sometime between 18 and 24 months. I have found it impossible to observe (let alone interact with) two-year-olds in the Yucatec

Mayan village where I work; this limitation is gone again before the age of three years.

Stranger anxiety, which in the strongest cases is full-blown fear, is often used as one of the identifying behaviors of attachment. But it clearly indicates that infants recognize people they know and strongly prefer them over people they do not know. However, a recognition of someone as familiar, and a comfortableness to interact with them, is not unique to primary attachment figures, since it can be produced in other affiliative relationships as well.

There are two types of culturally constructed social experience that might further heighten or diminish what appears to be a universal response in infants. The first is the amount of exposure the infant has to strangers. Thus, an infant being raised in a small, face-to-face community, or one who is kept at home most of the time, is likely to have little exposure to true strangers, let alone experience in interacting with them. In contrast, in a large, urban setting, especially if infants are taken along to places their caregivers need to go, they will have a lot of exposure to strangers, and even have experiences interacting with them.

The second kind of experience is how many familiar people infants interact with during daily routines. The same rural infant who sees few strangers may see many people in the course of one day with whom they are familiar. One Yucatec Maya infant at 11 months, for instance, was observed interacting with 25 relatives during one day, none of whom were strangers, and all of whom were readily accepted by the infant as social partners (although they were arguably not all attachment figures) (Gaskins 2006b). Infants in isolated, small nuclear families with few children, in contrast, may have only two to three people they interact with regularly. We do not know how a rich social world might also contribute to infants' responses to strangers, but it is quite possible that strangers lose some of their positive appeal of offering variety to the infants' social world if it is already filled with lots of family members. Alternatively, it might be that infants who are comfortable with many social partners will actually be more flexible in accepting new social interlocutors and therefore find a stranger less intimidating.

It is only when an infant can differentiate cognitively between familiar people and strangers that they can identify appropriate partners in whom they make an emotional investment. Ainsworth (1977) argues that before this time, infants practice attachment-like behaviors (e.g., smiling, being soothed) with any available social partner, but once they make a distinction between familiar and unfamiliar people, they reserve them for those familiar people with whom they are forming attachment bonds.

Memory

The development of long-term memory (and the metacognitive skills to use it) is another candidate for a maturational milestone that is related to attachment. It is the foundation for discriminating between familiar and unfamiliar social partners, because to recognize someone as familiar, the infant must be able to consult stored memories of experiences. In particular, the application of object permanence in infants' everyday lives (Piaget 1954) is especially relevant for attachment. For infants to recognize that an attachment figure is absent, they must be able to remember the previous presence of that figure and compare it to the current situation in which the figure is absent, or, if they see the attachment figure leave, they must be able to remember that departure in order to be motivated to seek him or her or object to his or her absence. Before this skill is mastered, if caregivers are out of sight, they appear to be also out of mind. Without this increased capacity to recognize that objects and people continue to exist even when not present, infants cannot be disturbed by separation from an attachment figure, which is another key attachment behavior.

Memory is also likely to play a role in the enjoyment of attachment figures' company because knowledge about habitual routines are stored and brought up during interactions. Without a shared memory of routines and experiences, it is very difficult to take an active role in interactions or sustain an emotional closeness with another person (Gustafson, Green, and West 1979).

There are an increasing number of studies that look at infants' cognitive abilities in other cultures, including object permanence. For instance, Brazelton (1977) and Gaskins (1990) have found that object permanence (as measured by classic Piagetian tasks in the real world) is found in both Tzotzil and Yucatec Maya infants by the first birthday, if not before, providing the cognitive capacity for a negative emotional response to separation.

Understanding and Sharing Intentions and Attention

Tomasello and his colleagues (e.g., Carpenter, Nagell, and Tomasello 1998) have developed a list of social cognitive behaviors that they argue are the foundation for establishing and maintaining social interaction. Their research, focused on European and North American children, indicates that these behaviors develop between 9 and 15 months. These skills are hypothesized to be universal, since all infants must use other people to help them crack the code of the specific culture into which they are being socialized. Social learning is a particularly complex and sophisticated mechanism available uniquely to human children (Tomasello and Rakoczy 2003) in order that they may come to understand the particular practices and meanings they must master to be a functional adult in their culture.

Some of these behaviors provide evidence that the infant is able to recognize other people's intentions. Through controlled elicitations in a laboratory setting, Tomasello and colleagues have measured the infants' abilities to discriminate nonintentional action of other people from their intentional or goal-directed action, imitate goal-directed actions, and help others to attain their goals (Tomasello et al. 2005). For instance, when presented with a series of actions and given an opportunity to imitate them, infants will imitate those that appear to be intentional, but will not imitate those that appear to be accidental.

Also between 9 and 15 months, infants begin to demonstrate increased ability in and interest in understanding the directedness of others' attentions. They come to be able to follow the gaze direction of their social partners, including behind barriers. They also begin to follow others' points and to direct others' attentions by pointing themselves (Tomasello, Carpenter, and Liszkowski 2007).

In European and North American cultures, this new understanding moves seamlessly into sharing attention and intentions (Tomasello et al. 2005). Pointing is used by infants and caregivers as part of an arsenal of techniques for preverbal communication, including declarative pointing (i.e., pointing to comment on something). For instance, infants begin to check when they point to make sure that their interlocutors are looking at the item being pointed to, often accompanied by other actions to indicate the pleasure of shared attention, such as smiling, laughing, or vocalizing (Tomasello et al. 2007). Infants and their caregivers and other social partners also seem to enjoy engaging in joint activity such as pointing—pursuing a common goal—for its own sake (Liszowski et al. 2004). Thus, shared play with objects, sounds/words, and stylized social routines between infant and caregiver develop as pleasurable routines.

Until recently, while there is a wealth of ethnographic reports about infants interacting with others, there has been little systematic and quantitative study of such specific interactional behaviors in infants in cultures outside of Europe and North America. Happily, this is changing. Callaghan et al. (2011) looked at how the capacity for these behaviors develops in a range of non-Western cultures. This study shows that, in general, there is some continuity across cultures in the most basic social skills—understanding intentions and the attention of others. Other research suggests, however, that there are also cultural differences in how these skills are organized and practiced. For instance, Brown (2012) does a specific comparison of shared attention in two cultures where the rules of social engagement in infancy (and adulthood) differ dramatically: Tzeltal Maya of Chiapas and Rossell Islanders of Papua New Guinea.

Sharing attention and intentions are precisely those behaviors that humans can do but primates cannot do (Tomasello and Rakoczy 2003), so they are candidates for being uniquely human resources for socialization of social and communicative practices. But whether or not these are actually universal remains more of an open question than for understanding of intentions and attention. For instance, Brown (2012) reports that while Tzeltal Maya infants start pointing by 12 months, they do not socially reference their social partners to make sure that their attention has been drawn to the item being pointed at (a conclusion supported by more informal observations by me for Yucatec Maya and by DeLeon for Tzotzil Maya). And we know from the ethnographic literature (e.g., LeVine et al. 1994) that social play with infants (e.g., ritualized object sharing, peek-a-boo, and other similar games) is not common in many cultures, and perhaps absent all together in some.

Conclusions: Attachment as Part of a General Maturational Process

From this review, it appears that about the same time that attachment is established, infants demonstrate an expanded capacity for locomotion, differentiating familiar people and strangers, remembering, and understanding others' goals and attention. If the establishment of a commitment by the infant to attachment bonds is added to this list, then we can consider positioning the development of attachment bonds around the first year of life as part of a widespread (and perhaps universal) process in human infants that sets the stage for infants to become active social partners with others in their everyday lives, and thereby gives them the experiential information that they need in order to form culturally appropriate working models of their social worlds that they must master in order to participate in them. This time frame would fall within what Mead (1947) called "the knee infant"—an infant who is beginning to learn to get around independently but still fairly closely tied to caregivers; by the next stage, "the yard child" needs to have an adequate working model of the social world in order to participate in peer or sibling social interactions.

There is not a lot of specific documentation of whether or not the recognition of new social abilities around an infant's first birthday is culturally widespread. But there is some suggestion that it is. For instance, Bril, Zack, and Nkounkou-Hombessa (1989) asked French mothers and mothers in two West African cultures (Bakambo and Bambara) about developmental milestones and how they organized them in their own ethnotheories about child development. Physical milestones were used as primary anchors for the Bakambo and Bambara mothers (compared to chronological age for the French mothers), but the researchers converted their answers into age estimates for comparison. Two social abilities reported in their study that are relevant here were reported to develop at about the same age for all three cultures: "understanding" in the seventh or eighth month and "first words" in the month before infants' first birthdays. This generalization does not minimize the fact that various cultures might have widely different social expectations and limitations for infants at this age (Lancy, in press). Rather, what is suggested here is that there may be a universal maturational shift between 9 and 15 months that radically changes infants' capacities to pay attention to, initiate, sustain, and interpret social exchanges—a shift that is necessary for them to enter into the process of enculturation that will end in their becoming a legitimate member of the cultural group.

Cultural Differences in Beliefs about and Interactions with Infants

Finding evidence for a universal transformation in infants' capacity to engage in social interactions around their first birthday does not, however, demonstrate that all of these processes involved are exclusively maturational. Nor does it condemn us to dismissing as irrelevant cultural differences in infants' social worlds. While infants may have a significant universal maturational transformation around their first birthday, cultures may vary widely in how they respond to these new abilities. For some, they may leverage them to accelerate and expand the infant's more active participation in their social world; for others, they may not. How cultures use their infants' capacities is still not understood very well. What infants *can* do at age 1 in terms of understanding and acting on their social world may be shared across the species. What infants actually *do* do at age 1 and beyond will be dependent, in part, on the culturally organized everyday worlds they find themselves in. It is at the level of everyday activity that we would expect to find that cultural differences in understandings and practices are likely to influence the course of infant development in ways that are not universal (and not part of the species' evolutionary inheritance). The new maturational capacities provide a skeletal frame that must be fleshed out through experiences that will vary by culture. (Individual differences in infants—and caregivers—will, of course, also influence infants' everyday behavior in interesting ways, and in turn, caregivers' reactions to it. Such intracultural variation may obscure or complicate generalizations about cultural patterns, but the more robust ones should be discernible over such "noise.") This section will discuss just this sort of cultural variation for the set of behaviors that have been identified as being related to attachment: one primary attachment figure, sensitivity and responsiveness, crying and consolation, seeking and maintaining proximity, separation anxiety, fear of strangers, and exploration from a secure base. Examples of cultural influence will be drawn primarily from my own research with Yucatec Mayan families, along with evidence from related Mayan groups.

Single versus Multiple Attachment Figures

The expectation in attachment theory that there will be a single primary caregiver is multiply determined. First, Bowlby was working from both a psychoanalytic and evolutionary perspective. The privileged role of "mother" and the belief that emotional bonding would occur primarily with her, through the shared act of nursing, is well established in Freud's theory and in related theories (e.g., Winnicott 1971). Although Harlow (1958) demonstrated early on that emotional bonding could be separated from provision of food, the psychoanalytic perspective has retained a unique and central role for mothers.

In terms of his evolutionary perspective, Hrdy (2009) has argued that Bowlby was working with only partial knowledge about caregiving in other primates. At the time he was developing his theory, the accepted wisdom was that primates did not readily share caregiving with partners, other mothers, or other offspring. She argues that in fact, in many primate and great ape species, there is an established pattern of multiple caregivers. And she explicitly calls for a revision of the assumption of a single caregiver in attachment theory based on this evidence.

In addition, there is a plethora of ethnographic evidence that humans often distribute caregiving of children, including caregiving of infants who are still nursing, across multiple members of a family or a social group (see Hrdy 2009). Bowlby, however, was undoubtedly working on his theory of attachment without being aware of much of this evidence, under his own cultural assumption that it was normative for mothers, living in nuclear family units, to be the single or the dominant caregiver. This oversight has been a major critique of attachment theory by anthropologists. Bowlby also assumed that mothers would not be working outside of the home; thus they would be available throughout the day to take care of their infants. With the rise in the United States of institutional day care in the 1970s and 1980s, in response to increased employment of mothers with infants, a major argument against day care for infants was the damage that would be done to the primary attachment relationship between mother and infant (e.g., Belsky and Rovine 1988).

It is clear that our current understanding of who takes care of children, and who *should take care of children*, has changed dramatically since Bowlby developed his theory, but the conceptualization of mother as the attachment figure is firmly engrained in the tradition. There have been some studies of fathers as attachment figures (see Bretherton 2010 for review), with a few scattered studies of other distributive caregiver relationships (IJzendoorn, Sagi, and Labermon 1992; Sagi et al. 1995), including studies investigating the effect of day care on attachment and social development more generally (e.g., Howes et al. 1988). But the premise is so deeply embedded in attachment theory that simply adding auxiliary studies does not address the problem. The evidence from both primates and other cultures suggests that many if not most infants are cared for by more than one person and that mothers' roles in caregiving and in attachment bonds are, in fact, quite flexible.

In contrast to the dominant perspective that multiple caregivers place infants at risk of not forming deep and healthy attachments, there are some good arguments that, in fact, they offer infants a more resilient environment and thus put them less at risk than infants who receive the care exclusively from their mothers. Perhaps the primary advantage is that infants who are attached to multiple caregivers are at less risk for depression and anxiety if one caregiver (e.g., the mother) dies or is otherwise separated from the infant. Mothers' death has always been a legitimate concern, especially given the risks of childbirth. While those specific risks have decreased in many cultures over time, new threats to healthy mothers have taken its place (e.g., HIV, drug use, incarceration). In order to best serve infants who lose their mothers' presence, it is imperative that we better understand how multiple attachment figures work, and in particular, how they work to minimize distress in infants who lose or are separated from their mothers.

In addition, there are two other potential significant advantages for infants with multiple caregivers. The first is that by coming to place their trust in multiple people, they are more likely to generalize that the world is a benign and giving environment that they should explore. The second is that with multiple partners, they have to develop a much more complex working model of social relations, since people's interactions with them are quite different, based on personality, age, roles, status, and so forth. Thus, infants with multiple caregivers, as they are developing their first theories about how other people think, may be pushed to develop a more sophisticated theory that will accommodate a more complex set of experiences.

Sensitivity: Responsiveness and Consistency

One of the first and most robust findings from Ainsworth's research is that there are correlations between parental behaviors toward an infant and that infant's style of attachment (Ainsworth 1979). One of the central correlations that Ainsworth found in her original study of American children is that secure attachment is correlated with a high degree of maternal sensitivity to infants' communications (i.e., a mother who was judged to have heard and understood her infant and responded promptly and appropriately) (Ainsworth, Bell, and Stayton 1974). A more specific measure was responsiveness to crying in particular, and here, Bell and Ainsworth (1972) found that the mother's degree of responsiveness at one observation negatively correlated with the amount of crying seen three months later (i.e., mothers who were more responsive at Time 1 had infants who cried less at Time 2). Such time-lag correlations are usually interpreted as evidence that the first behavior is influencing the second.

One of the central claims of the attachment paradigm is that experience influences attachment formation. The basis for that claim is that everyday experiences stemming from the organization of caregiver behaviors have been found to influence the working model of social relations that infants develop and are used to negotiate interactions. But of course, which caregiver behaviors are consistently practiced will vary widely across cultures, based on cultural understandings about children, and daily patterns of work and social interaction. Those found by Ainsworth and Bell to correlate with their ideal type of attachment might not be relevant or central in some other system in establishing the infant's working model of the social world. This central claim, ironically, is also perhaps the strongest evidence from this tradition that cultural differences in attachment should be expected and studied.

Responsiveness is, however, a good candidate for a universal caregiver behavior, as long as it is understood that it needs to always be defined in local terms and include more than a single primary caregiver. Munroe and Munroe (1971) found, for instance, that in households with more potential caregivers, infants' cries were responded to more quickly and they were held more often (but the infants received less care from their mothers). The Yucatec Maya are highly responsive to their infants in just the way Ainsworth defines the concept: They pay close attention to the needs of the infant, are adept at interpreting their signals (even very subtle ones), and put a great deal of energy into responding promptly and appropriately. DeLeon (2012) has proposed that the extensive body contact that she observes occurring with Tzotzil Maya caregivers and infants provides additional channels of communication ("communication niches") that allow caregivers and infants to be aware of subtle information about each others' states.

Yet Mayan mothers look very different from the mothers that Ainsworth observed in America because while they are consistently responsive, their responses are designed to calm their infants, not stimulate them, and their responses often are relatively emotionally unexpressive. Their goal is a quiet infant, not an active one. Brazelton (1977) reports, for instance, that among the Tzotzil Maya he observed, infants' motor activity alone was enough to produce a milk "let-down" response in their nursing mothers, a response that for American mothers is more connected to their infants' cries.

Even if responsiveness turns out not to be a universally valued approach to infant care, consistency in care appears to be logically crucial in order to provide infants with the information they need to build an adequate working model of social relations. As Erikson (1950) proposed, infants need to have confidence that their needs will be met by other people in a predictable way in order for trust to be formed during the first year or two. It is difficult for that trust, or a working model of social relations, to be constructed in the face of inconsistent input from a caregiver. However, it is not necessary to have complete consistency across caregivers—in fact, as argued earlier, a variety of models of social interaction across caregivers might actually lead to a more complex and robust working model of social interaction.

Crying and Consolation

Infant crying is a complex phenomenon, and one that changes developmentally over time. A newborn cries because something is causing discomfort or pain. Bell and Ainsworth (1972) believe that at about the same time attachment bonds are formed, crying becomes more complex, with some infant cries more about communication than an unfiltered and direct expression of discomfort.

How caregivers respond to crying varies considerably across cultures. In cultures where mothers are often in proximity to their infants and their infants are nursing on demand, nursing is often used as a way to console a crying infant. Ainsworth argues that in these cases, nursing becomes an "integral part of the organization of his attachment relationship" (1977:128). In cases where infants are not nursed on demand, feeding becomes "splintered off" and is not integrated into the attachment relationship. Non-nursing mothers and other caregivers obviously have to use other methods to soothe an unhappy infant—holding, binding, rocking, jiggling, distraction—depending on their interpretation of what is making their infant cry at that moment.

One of the major goals of Yucatec Maya caregivers is to minimize infant crying, since they believe that when babies are upset, they are more at risk of getting ill. Their sensitivity to their infants' needs and their ability to anticipate them, coupled with nursing as a consoling activity, leads to relatively little crying among infants. Extended crying is so unusual that an infant who cannot be comforted is interpreted as being ill.

Some cultures let children cry without any caregiver response under certain circumstances, for example, when falling asleep or when a caregiver is temporarily busy or distracted. In such cases, when no consolation is forthcoming, it is not uncommon to find that infants develop their own methods for self-soothing, such as sucking a thumb or developing an emotional attachment to an object, like a security blanket or other "lovey." Such responses are not found in cultures, like the Yucatec Maya, where caregivers are consistently responsive to crying, especially if nursing for consolation is in practice.

Contact and Proximity Seeking (Especially with Locomotion)
Establishing and maintaining proximity (or other forms of contact) is at the heart of attachment behavior. It becomes particularly important as the infant becomes (and is allowed to be) mobile and begins to explore his environment. In Bowlby's (1969, 1988) conceptualization, it is as if the infant and caregiver become attached with an ever-lengthening piece of elastic, which, as the infant develops, allows the infant increasing distance to explore the world, but insures that the caregiver remains available for protection and comfort when needed and is consistently tuned in to the infant's activities. This "bungy cord" attachment is found more heavily in cultures where infants spend less of their time in direct body contact with their caregivers. With more distance, proximity seeking becomes elaborated to include not only moving toward the caregiver, but also in using distal nonverbal communication strategies, such as eye contact, smiling, crying, vocalizations, pointing, social referencing, and object exchange. Such behaviors are seen much less often in cultures where infants are carried most of the time (Keller et al. 2009). These distal ways of connecting appear to be compensatory behaviors to deal with the physical distance that caregivers impose on infants by taking them off their own bodies, especially if the infants are physically constrained, so that they cannot freely approach the caregivers.

Proximity seeking can be found not only when infants and caregivers have established some physical distance between them, but also when there is psychological distance or distraction. There appears to be a great deal of cultural variation in how caregivers' attention is distributed across competing foci (one of which is the infant). Chavajay and Rogoff (1999) have shown for Tzutujil Maya of Guatemala that caregivers (and infants) practice simultaneous attention, while American mothers practice sequential attention. This is in line with a kind of attention we have described as "open attention" (Gaskins and Paradise 2010), which is found in many indigenous communities in North and South America. With open attention, there is a diffusion of focus, such that a person's attention is both wide-angled and abiding, taking in the entire context on an ongoing basis. We argue that this is a unique way of attending to the world that can be culturally amplified, as with the Maya mothers studied by Chavajay and Rogoff. With open attention, infants do not have to compete with other events in the environment for caregivers' attention; their attention can be assumed (and in fact, is usually there). This has a profound effect on what kinds of proximity-seeking behaviors you might expect to see in infants. If they come to assume that caregivers are attending to them, then they need to spend much less time trying to secure or confirm their attention. The impact of this can be seen in Yucatec Maya infants, who explore their environment with little social referencing and little attempt to engage their caregivers' attention through vocalizations or instrumental crying (Gaskins 1990). If American standards were used to judge these infants' attachment, they might be classified as being detached, even though they demonstrate other strong attachment behaviors (like seeking consolation).

Separation Anxiety

Cultures vary dramatically in how much time infants spend with their mothers, based primarily on women's roles in the mode of production, the social organization of the household and community, and the amount of formal education available in the community. In contrast to the case where women work outside the home for wages (where they are unable to have their infants with them), women in cultures with other modes of production have more choices. If women are primarily responsible for farming, for instance, or gathering, they may be away from home much of each day. In such cases, mothers often take their infants with them to work, either with them strapped to their back, placed nearby in some kind of constraint, or under the care of a slightly older sibling (Weisner and Gallimore 1977). If their work does not take them too far from home, and an alternative caregiver is available, they may prefer to leave their infants at home and either return to nurse or have the hungry infant brought to them. If older children are at school during the day, then the number of available caregivers is considerably reduced, and the infant is more likely to stay with the mother.

As we saw with the Yucatec Mayan infant who interacted with 25 different people in one day, in many cultures, infants are never without a familiar caretaker around. In such cultures, separation anxiety is rarely triggered by circumstances. The density of households and the existence of multiple attachment figures virtually ensure that the infant does not experience separation. In the Yucatec Mayan case, even if no one is in the hut where the infant is (e.g., while the infant sleeps in one hut, members of the family are working in the yard or in another hut), the sounds and sights of the compound are readily available to the infant through porous walls. In contrast, in a nuclear household with a single caretaker and rooms that are self-contained, the infant may be left alone many times in the course of a single day.

Another time that infants in European and Northern American cultures often find themselves alone is at night and during naps. While in many other cultures mothers co-sleep with their infants, in these cultures it is culturally valued to teach infants how to sleep alone (and how to get to sleep alone) (Morelli et al. 1992). Parents in the United States reported that they believe that such training supports independence. A second motivation, less often invoked, is that parents feel that they need time and space away from their infants because taking care of them is so demanding and often stressful. When with their infants, these parents engage in face-to-face interaction and focused monitoring that interfere with their getting other work done or relaxing. Thus, they feel the need of a "break" from their infants to catch up on chores or "catch their breath."

Finally, cultures differ in how much attention they train their infants to expect. In child-centered cultures, infants learn to expect a lot of direct attention. These infants may feel a psychological separation if they cannot maintain their caregivers' attention. In response to that feeling, they may actively seek more attention as a tactic to increase psychological proximity. In other cultures, children, including infants, do not expect to be the center of caregivers' attention. Therefore, when adults are engaged in other activities, they do not feel ignored, but rather are content to observe what is going on or engage in their own, intrinsically motivated activities. In cultures like the Yucatec Maya, where caregivers are able to distribute their attention across many domains at once through open attention, this contrast does not even exist. I believe that Yucatec Maya infants are aware by the time they are one year old that they are being consistently monitored (for instance, they explore with little social referencing [Gaskins 1990]), even as their caregivers engage in work or other activities.

For infants, daily separations can be stressful and lead to the development of attachment to non-animate objects like pacifiers, blankets, and other objects (and also their own thumbs). Winnicott (1971) has termed such objects "transitional objects," in the sense that children use them as they move from total interconnectedness with the mother to more independence, which includes a full understanding of the social world as being made up of "me" and "not me." In a sense, caregivers as attachment figures serve the same role of soothing or reassurance, especially when infants can nurse on demand. In those cultures with co-sleeping (and otherwise few separations) and consolation through infant-initiated nursing, such emotional bonds with objects are unheard of; this is the case for the Yucatec Maya. Rather than being part of the normative process described by Winnicott, "lovies" appear to be an infant strategy to deal with and compensate for separation and isolation from their human attachment figures.

Fear of Strangers

As discussed earlier, fear expressed toward strangers is likely to be influenced by the amount (and kind) of experience with strangers infants have in their daily lives. Encounters with strangers can either be a regular event in infants' lives that they habituate to or a rare one. If the infant is regularly exposed to contexts (e.g., grocery stores, public parks) where other people are sharing the infant's space, the mere presence of an unfamiliar person (who is not trying to interact with the infant) is unlikely to produce any attachment response of communicating distress or seeking proximity. In contrast, for an infant who rarely sees an unfamiliar person, the mere presence of a stranger can easily invoke fear or anxiety.

Being willing to interact with strangers, while using attachment figures as a secure base, is clearly related to the general response to strangers' presence. If merely seeing strangers leads some infants to be afraid, it is unlikely that they will be comfortable interacting with them. In my experience working with infants in the Yucatan, one-year-olds are usually wary of strangers and disinclined to make eye contact or otherwise engage with them; however, two-year-olds are even less comfortable with strangers, often expressing strong fear and unable to be in the same room with them, even if being held by an attachment figure. However, because the emotion evoked by the stranger is so extreme, the failure of the attachment figure to act as a secure base in this case should not be seen as an indication of the quality of attachment.

Infants who are not bothered by the presence of strangers differ in their willingness to interact with them. The model of "secure attachment" expects that in the presence of an attachment figure, infants will be willing to engage with a friendly stranger, while being less willing to do so if the attachment figure is absent. It may well be that this expectation is based on the general attitude of some cultures that adult-infant interaction should be sought out as a positive activity, with the adult working on stimulating and amusing the infant. In contrast, if everyday adult-infant interaction is premised on responding to infants' needs and desires rather than stimulation, there is little motivation for infants to be interested in engaging in social interaction with strangers, who are unlikely to attend to their personal needs.

Exploration

Another measure of attachment in Ainsworth's paradigm is the infant's willingness, in the mother's presence, to explore the physical environment, especially a novel environment with interesting toys (Ainsworth and Wittig 1969; Main 1983). This is a particularly interesting item because it suggests that one effect of "secure" attachment is that the proximity-seeking behaviors may in fact *not* be invoked as often or as strictly as with less "secure" attachments. Rather, by using their attachment figure as a secure base, infants feel confident enough to leave that base, seeking distance rather than proximity for the sake of curiosity or stimulation, and relying on distal ways of communication to maintain a connection: eye contact, smiling, vocalizations, and social referencing.

One way in which cultures differ dramatically is the extent to which the infants' environment contains safe, interesting, and novel objects that are available for their exploration. In child-centered cultures, infants' homes are bursting with objects that have been manufactured and purchased with the single goal of stimulating and engaging infants. In many other cultures, there are *no* objects that fit that description. Likewise, the role of caregivers in exploration, whether they are viewed by infants as play partners or irrelevant, is also highly variable across cultures; and within a culture across types of caregivers. Such cultural diversity in infant exploration makes it a difficult basis by which to evaluate attachment behaviors. Since exploration is usually considered an "intrinsically-motivated" activity in children, most studies have assumed that it will be universal in character and have not considered how it might be organized by cultural values and practices.

In fact, if one looks at exploration through a cultural lens, it becomes obvious that it is highly organized by caregivers' priorities and by their ethnotheories about children's learning and development. For instance, for the Yucatec Maya in the 1970s and 1980s, infants' everyday environments were not constructed by caregivers to be interesting to them (Gaskins 1990). There were no toys bought or made for the infant, and no personal possessions of the infant, other than clothes. Their exploration focused on found items in the house and yard (e.g., rocks, discarded containers, ants). Interestingly, these infants spent as much time exploring objects as American children do, even though their actions toward those objects were less complex. Caregivers did little to mediate this exploration, either by demonstrating or engaging their infants, or even by providing objects for them to distract them. Infants did little to try to engage their caregivers, either, by pointing out or offering objects, or even by socially referencing their caregivers when encountering something novel. The effort to maintain safety through connectedness appeared to fall primarily on the caregivers, who consistently monitored their infants' exploration and removed either infant or object when that exploration was dangerous or inappropriate. Looking only at these infants' use of caregivers as a secure base for exploration, one would judge them to have little attachment to any of their caregivers, a conclusion that would be immediately discarded when their reactions to being hurt or scared were observed, where they readily sought comfort, often through nursing.

Conclusions: Cultural Contributions to Attachment

In the earlier discussion, it has been demonstrated that every behavior that has been used as an indication of attachment has some cultural organization to it, and as such, they are all suspected as unanalyzed variables in any study of attachment in other cultures. This is true not only for the structured assessments of the Strange Situation and the Q-sort, but also for more open-ended observations in everyday environments. None of these behaviors—one primary attachment figure, sensitivity and responsiveness, crying and consolation, seeking and maintaining proximity, separation anxiety, fear of strangers, and exploration from a secure base—is unproblematic for using as evidence of attachment across cultures.

A second and potentially more difficult problem to address is one that led Ainsworth herself to develop the Strange Situation in the first place. In her naturalistic home observations, she felt that the opportunity for observing attachment behaviors varied widely because the amount of stress infants faced also varied across households (and observations). Without stress, most attachment behaviors are not displayed. Her motivation in constructing the Strange Situation was to insure there was some stress (but not too much) in order to prompt the behaviors of interest and also to equalize the amount of stress across children.

While the second point is unlikely to be true across cultures—that the amount of stress experienced in the Strange Situation is the same for all children—the first is still a problem for looking at attachment in other cultures. For many cultures, infants are intentionally *not stressed* by their caregivers (e.g., the Yucatec Maya caregivers' goal to help the infant remain calm and quiet). For others, the infants are engaged less, and there is less expected of them than in the child-centered American homes in which Ainsworth observed. In many cultures, while the physical risks to the infants may be higher (snakes, open fire pits, uneven surfaces to walk on, heights), the level of tension and energy that goes into caretaking of infants is much lower.

Thus, one of the things that varies across cultures is the different demands each culture puts on the attachment system itself and on both the caregivers and the infants as participants in that system. The demands are different in both amount and quality if infants are strapped to the back versus free to roam. Likewise the demands differ depending on whether the infant is in a household with lots of people of multiple generations versus alone with mother. They also differ if caregivers give intense but sequential attention to infants versus consistent low-level attention. And they differ depending on whether they are encouraged to explore the world through highly mediated and scaffolded encounters versus given the responsibility to learn on their own through observation and exploration.

One way to address these problems would be to take the set of general attachment behaviors identified by the current paradigm, and make the goal of future investigations to be that of describing their lability and flexibility across cultures, along with the external factors that may color their display in infants and their caregivers. The examples given here, drawn largely from one culture, represent only a partial beginning. From this, we would have a better understanding of the complexity of determinants and affordances that contribute to infants' and caregivers' specific acts of displaying attachment behaviors. It may be the case that not all of the behaviors discussed here will hold up as useful, even as general categories, for identifying attachment across a diverse set of contexts. And undoubtedly, across all the behaviors, there will be a distribution of how central each is to attachment display across cultures and how varied those displays can be. But it is only by looking that we will be able to see the differences in the "flesh" of attachment across cultures.

General Conclusions

The puzzle of attachment is how a fundamental organizing system like attachment should best be understood, given the tension between three competing claims that have come to characterize the paradigm: (1) the system is evolutionarily important and universal; (2) the system is shaped by experiences in social interaction; and (3) there is significant variation in social interaction across cultures. This chapter works to solve the puzzle by reconceptualizing attachment as having two components, which one might think of as being like the skeletal system and the flesh.

The skeletal system is attachment as a universal emotional system that promotes survival by insuring that infants and their caregivers are motivated to seek and maintain proximity. This system matures around the same time as a number of other systems: locomotion, differentiation between familiar people and strangers, increased memory (including object permanence in the real world), and understanding and sharing attention and intentions. Together, these systems transform infants' capacities to engage in social interaction and to build a working model of social relations. The prediction is that in all cultures, there would be evidence of the formation of attachment bonds around infants' first birthdays.

Caregivers must integrate this new infant capacity into their own cultural system of understanding and practices about social interaction, the role of infants as social actors, and ethnotheories about learning and development. This process of integration leads the expression of attachment behaviors to be quite varied, and thus, each culture puts flesh on the bones of attachment in a distinct way. Whether or not there can be a list of specific attachment behaviors that accurately capture the attachment bond across cultures remains an open question, but it has been clear for some time that the current dominant descriptions of attachment behaviors and the ways of measuring them have been developed from culturally specific understandings about infants' places in their everyday worlds. Thus, while the general concept of attachment appears fairly robust, the description of details and the paradigm used to study the phenomenon appears quite restricted and culturally naive. As a result, we know less about the interaction between infant capacity and cultural practice than we should.

A number of categories were discussed here as potential starting points for a culturally informed catalog of attachment behaviors (i.e., number of attachment figures, sensitivity/responsiveness, crying/consoling, contact and proximity seeking, separation anxiety, fear of strangers, and exploration from a secure base). For each, examples were drawn from my own fieldwork and that of others to demonstrate the complex ways that cultures might support, augment, bend, or dampen the infants' emerging capacities. There are undoubtedly other cultural pathways to attachment than those covered here, but the discussion serves to illustrate that in order to understand how attachment bonds get expressed and practiced in everyday life, it will be necessary to interpret that behavior through a culturally informed lens. The capacity that all healthy infants display at one year of age can only blossom by taking root in the specific culturally organized context of social relations in which they are developing.

Margaret Mead (1963:187) made a useful distinction for this discussion, describing the difference between the process of socialization and the process of enculturation. Socialization is the general process that characterizes all humans' integration into their surrounding context. Enculturation is the specific process of becoming integrated into a particular world, one that comes with a need to accommodate to, master, and internalize the full complexity of a culture. She argued that while socialization was a useful theoretical construct, you could never observe it. The only process that was observable was enculturation. She thought that our task as researchers was to take a wide range of cases of enculturation and extract the commonalities in order to understand the more general process of socialization.

Similarly, we have the theoretical construct of attachment, a universal capacity that serves as opening for infants to enter into participation in the social world around them. But all we can ever observe is the particular attachment behaviors that have been organized by what a particular culture expects from and gives to infants. The difficult challenge that arises from this argument is to first distinguish and then integrate these two levels into a culturally informed theory of human attachment. But it is significant progress just to recognize that the two levels exist.

References

Adolph, Karen E., and Scott R. Robinson. 2013. "The Road to Walking: What Learning to Walk Tells Us about Development." In *Oxford Handbook of Developmental Psychology*, Phillip Zelazo, ed. New York: Oxford University Press.

Ainsworth, Mary D. Salter. 1967. *Infancy in Uganda*. Baltimore: Johns Hopkins.

Ainsworth, Mary D. Salter. 1977. "Infant Development and Mother-Infant Interaction among Ganda and American Families." In *Culture and Infancy*, P. Herbert Leiderman, Stephen R. Tulkin, and Anne Rosenfield, eds., pp. 119–148. New York: Academic Press.

Ainsworth, Mary D. Salter. 1979. "Attachment as Related to Mother-Infant Interaction." In *Advances in the Study of Behavior*, vol. 9. Jay S. Rosenblatt, Robert A. Hinde, Colin Beer, and Marie-Claire Busnel, eds., pp. 1–51. New York: Academic Press.

Ainsworth, Mary D. Salter, and Silvia M. Bell. 1970. "Attachment, Exploration, and Separation: Illustrated by the Behavior of One-Year-Olds in a Strange Situation." *Child Development* 41:49–67.

Ainsworth, Mary D. Salter, Silvia M. Bell, and Donelda J. Stayton. 1991. "Infant-Mother Attachment and Social Development: 'Socialisation' as a Product of Reciprocal Responsiveness to Signals." In *Becoming a Person. Child Development in Social Context*, vol. 1, Martin Woodhead, Ronnie Carr, and Paul Light, eds., pp. 30–55. Florence, KY: Taylor and Frances/Routledge.

Ainsworth, Mary D. Salter, Mary C. Blehar, Everett Waters, and Sally Wall. 1978. *Patterns of Attachment: A Psychological Study of the Strange Situation*. Hillsdale, NJ: Erlbaum.

Ainsworth, Mary D. Salter, and Barbara A. Wittig. 1969. "Attachment and Exploratory Behaviour of One-Year-Olds in a Strange Situation." In *Determinants of Infant Behaviour*, vol. 4. Brian M. Foss, ed., pp. 113–136. London: Methuen.

Bell, Silvia M. and Mary D. Salter Ainsworth. 1972. "Infant Crying and Maternal Responsiveness." *Child Development* 43(4):1171–1190.

Belsky, Jay, and Michael J. Rovine. 1988. "Nonmaternal Care in the First Year of Life and the Security of Infant-Parent Attachment." *Child Development* 59(1):157–167.

Berlin, Lisa J., Jude Cassidy, and Karen Appleyard. 2008. "The Influence of Early Attachments on Other Relationships." In *Handbook of Attachment: Theory, Research and Clinical Applications* (2nd edition), Jude Cassidy and Phillip R. Shaver, eds., pp. 333–347. New York: Guilford Press.

Bowlby, John. 1958. "The Nature of the Child's Tie to his Mother." *International Journal of Psychoanalysis* 39:350–373.

Bowlby, John. 1960. "Separation Anxiety." *International Journal of Psychoanalysis* 41:89–113.

Bowlby, John. 1969. "Attachment." *Attachment and Loss*. vol. I. London: Hogarth.

Bowlby, John. 1988. *A Secure Base*. New York: Basic Books.

Brazelton, T. Berry. 1977. "Implications of Infant Development among the Mayan Indians of Mexico." In *Culture and Infancy*, P. Herbert Leiderman, Stephen R. Tulkin, and Anne Rosenfield, eds., pp. 151–187. New York: Academic Press.

Bretherton, Inge. 2010. "Fathers in Attachment Theory and Research: A Review." *Early Child Development and Care* 180(1–2):9–23.

Bril, Blandine, Martine Zack, and Estelle Nkounkou-Hombessa. 1989. "Ethnotheories of Development and Education: A View from Different Cultures." *European Journal of Psychology of Education* 4(2):307–318.

Brown, Penelope. 2012. "The Cultural Organization of Attention." *The Handbook of Language Socialization*, Alessandro Duranti, Elenor Ochs, and Bambi B. Schieffelin, eds., pp. 29–55. Malden, MA: Wiley-Blackwell.

Callaghan, Tara, Henrike Moll, Hannes Rakoczy, Ulf Liszkowski, Felix Warneken, Tanya Behne, and Michael Tomasello. 2011. "Early Social Cognition in Three Cultural Contexts." *Monographs of the Society for Research in Child Development* 76(2):1–142.

Campos, Joseph J., David I. Anderson, Marianne A. Barbu-Roth, Edward M. Hubbard, Matthew J. Hertenstein, and David C. Witherington. 2000. "Travel Broadens the Mind." *Infancy* 1:149–219.

Carlson, Vicki, Dante Cicchetti, Douglass Barnett, and Karen Braunwald. 1989. "Disorganized/Disoriented Attachment Relationships in Maltreated Infants." *Developmental Psychology* 25:525–531.

Carlson, Elizabeth, and L. Alan Sroufe. 1995. "Contribution of Attachment Theory to Developmental Psychopathology." *Developmental Psychopathology, Vol. 1: Theory and Methods*, Dante Cicchetti and Donald J. Cohen, eds., pp. 581–617. Oxford, England: John Wiley and Sons.

Carpenter, Malinda, Katherine Nagell, and Michael Tomasello. 1998. "Social Cognition, Joint Attention, and Communicative Competence from 9 to 15 Months of Age." *Monographs of the Society for Research in Child Development* 63(4):1–175.

Chavajay, Pablo, and Barbara Rogoff. 1999. "Cultural Variation in Management of Attention by Children and Their Caregivers." *Developmental Psychology* 35(4):1079–1090.

Chisholm, James S. 1983. *Navajo Infancy: An Ethological Study of Child Development*. Hawthorne, NY: Aldine.

Chisholm, James S. 1996. "The Evolutionary Ecology of Attachment." *Human Nature* 7(1):1–37.

DeLeon, Lourdes. 2012. "Multiparty Participation Frameworks in Language Socialization." In *The Handbook of Language Socialization*, Alessandro Duranti, Elenor Ochs, and Bambi B. Schieffelin, eds., pp. 81–112. Malden, MA: Wiley-Blackwell.

Ding, Yan-hua, Xiu Xu, Zheng-yan Wang, Hui-rong Li, and Wei-ping Wang. 2012. "Study of Mother-Infant Attachment Patterns and Influence Factors in Shanghai." *Early Human Development* 88(5):295–300.

Erikson, Erik. 1950. *Childhood and Society*. New York: Norton.

Gaskins, Suzanne. 1990. "Mayan Exploratory Play and Development." PhD dissertation, Department of Education, University of Chicago.

Gaskins, Suzanne. 2006a. "Cultural Perspectives on Infant-Caregiver Interaction." In *The Roots of Human Sociality: Culture, Cognition, and Human Interaction*, Nick J. Enfield and Stephen Levinson, eds., pp. 279–298. Oxford, UK: Berg (Wenner-Gren Foundation International Symposium Series).

Gaskins, Suzanne. 2006b. "The Cultural Organization of Yucatec Mayan Children's Social Interactions." In *Peer Relationships in Cultural Context*, Xinyin Chen, Doran French, and Barry Schneider, eds., pp. 283–309. Cambridge, UK: Cambridge University Press.

Gaskins, Suzanne and Ruth Paradise. 2010. "Learning through Observation." In *The Anthropology of Learning in Childhood.* David F. Lancy, John Bock, and Suzanne Gaskins, eds., pp. 85–117. Lanham, MD: Alta Mira Press.

Grossmann, Karin, Klaus E. Grossmann, Gottfried Spangler, Gerhard Suess, and Lothar Unzner. 1985. "Maternal Sensitivity and Newborns' Orientation Responses as Related to Quality of Attachment in Northern Germany." In *Growing Points of Attachment: Theory and Research,* Inge Bretherton and Everett Waters, eds. *Monographs of the Society for Research in Child Development* 50(1/2):233–256.

Gustafson, Gwen E., James A. Green, Meridith J. West. 1979. "The Infant's Changing Role in Mother-Infant Games: The Growth of Social Skills." *Infant Behavior and Development* 2:301–308.

Harlow, Harry. 1958. "The Nature of Love." *American Psychologist* 13(12):573–685.

Harwood, Robin, Joan G. Miller, Nydia Lucca Irizarry. 1995. *Culture and Attachment: Perceptions of the Child in Context.* New York, NY: Guilford Press.

Howes, Carolle, Carol Rodning, Darlene C. Galluzzo, and Lisbeth Myers. 1988. "Attachment and Child Care: Relationships with Mother and Caregiver." *Early Childhood Research Quarterly* 3(4):403–416.

Hrdy, Sarah Blaffer. 2009. *Mothers and Others: The Evolutionary Origins of Mutual Understanding.* Boston, MA: Harvard University Press.

Karen, Robert. 1998. *Becoming Attached: First Relationships and How They Shape Our Capacity to Love.* New York: Oxford University Press.

Keller, Heidi. 2008. "Attachment—Past and Present. But What about the Future?" *Integrative Psychological and Behavioral Science* 42(4):406–415.

Keller, Heidi, Joern Borke, Thomas Staufenbiel, Relindis D. Yovsi, Monika Abels, Zaira Papaligoura, Henning Jensen, Arnold Lohaus, Nandita Chaudhary, Wingshan Lo, and Yanjie Su. 2009. "Distal and Proximal Parenting as Alternative Parenting Strategies during Infants' Early Months of Life: A Cross-cultural Study." *International Journal of Behavioral Development* 33(5):412–420.

Konner, Melvin. 2010. *The Evolution of Childhood: Relationships, Emotion, Mind.* Boston, MA: Harvard University Press.

Lancy, David F. In press. "'Babies Aren't Persons': A Survey of Delayed Personhood." In *Different Faces of Attachment: Cultural Variations of a Universal Human Need,* Heidi Keller and Hiltrud Otto, eds. Cambridge: Cambridge University Press.

LeVine, Robert A. and Patrice M. Miller. 1990. "Commentary, Sepcial Topic Issue: 'Cross-Cultural Validity of Attachment Theory.' " *Human Development* 33(1):73–80.

LeVine, Robert A. and Karin Norman. 2001. "The Infant's Acquisition of Culture: Early Attachment Reexamined in Anthropological Perspective." In *The Psychology of Cultural Experience,* Carmella C. Moore and Holly F. Mathews, eds., pp. 83–104. Cambridge: Cambridge University Press.

LeVine, Robert A., Suzanne Dixon, Sarah LeVine, Amy Richman, P. Herbert Leiderman, Constance H. Keefer, and T. Berry Brazelton. 1994. *Child Care and Culture: Lessons from Africa.* Cambridge: Cambridge University Press.

Liszowski Ulf, Malinda Carpenter, Anne Henning, Tricia Striano, Michael Tomasello. 2004. Twelve-Month-Olds Point to Share Attention and Interest." *Developmental Science* 7:297–307.

Main, Mary. 1983. "Exploration, Play, and Level of Cognitive Functioning as Related to Security in Infant-Mother Attachment." *Infant Behavioral Development* 6:167–174.

Main, Mary, and Judith Solomon. 1986. "Discovery of an Insecure-Disorganized/Disoriented Attachment Pattern." In *Affective Development in Infancy*, T. Berry Brazelton and Michael W. Yogman, eds., pp. 95–124. Nowrood, NJ: Ablex Publishing.

Main, Mary, Nancy Kaplan, and Jude Cassidy. 1985. "Security in Infancy, Childhood and Adulthood: A Move to the Level of Representation." In *Growing Points of Attachment: Theory and Research*, Inge Bretherton and Everett Waters, eds. *Monographs of the Society for Research in Child Development* 50(1/2):66–106.

Main, Mary and Jude Cassidy. 1988. "Categories of Response to Reunion with the Parent at Age 6: Predictable from Infant Attachment Classifications and Stable over a 1-Month Period. *Developmental Psychology* 24(3):415–426.

Martini, Mary and John Kirkpatrick. 1981. "Early Interactions in the Marquesas Islands." In *Culture and Early Interactions*, Tiffany M. Field, Anita M. Sostek, Peter Vietze, and P. Herbert Leiderman, eds., pp. 189–213. Hillsdale, NJ: Erlbaum.

Mead, Margaret. 1963. "Socialization and Enculturation." *Current Anthropology* 4(2):184–188.

Mead, Margaret. 1947. "Age Patterning in Personality Development." *American Journal of Orthopsychiatry* 17:231–240.

Miyake, Kazuo, Shing-jen Chen, and Joseph J. Campos. 1985. "Infant Temperament, Mother's Mode of Interaction, and Attachment in Japan: An Interim Report." In *Growing Points of Attachment: Theory and Research*, Inge Bretherton and Everett Waters, eds., *Monographs of the Society for Research in Child Development* 50(1/2):276–297.

Morelli, Gilda A., Barbara Rogoff, David Oppenheim, and Denise Goldsmith. 1992. "Cultural Variation in Infants' Sleeping Arrangements: Questions of Independence." *Developmental Psychology* 28(4):604–613.

Munroe, Ruth H., and Robert L. Munroe. 1971. "Household Density and Infant Care in an East African Society." *Journal of Social Psychology* 83:3–13.

O'Connor, Mary J., Marian Sigman, and Nancy Brill. 1987. "Disorganization of Attachment in Relation to Maternal Alcohol Consumption." *Journal of Consulting and Clinical Psychology* 55:831–836.

Piaget, Jean. 1954. *The Construction of Reality in the Child.* New York, NY: Basic Books.

Rheingold, Harriet L., and Carol O. Eckerman. 1973. "Fear of the Stranger: A Critical Examination." In *Advances in Child Development and Behavior*, vol. 8, Hayne W. Reese, ed., pp. 186–223. New York: Academic Press.

Rodning, Carol, Leila Beckwith, and Judy Howard. 1991. "Quality of Attachment and Home Environments in Children Prenatally Exposed to PCP and Cocaine." *Development and Psychopathology* 3:351–366.

Rothbaum, Fred, John Weisz, Martha Pott, Kazuo Miyake, and Gilda Morelli. 2000. "Attachment and Culture: Security in the United States and Japan." *American Psychologist* 55:1093–1104.

Sagi, Abraham, Marinus H. van IJzendoorn, Ora Aviezer, Frank Donnell, Nina Koren-Karie, Tirtsa Joels, and Yael Harel. 1995. "Attachments in a Multiple-Caregiver and Multiple-Infant Environment: The Case of the Israeli Kibbutzim." *Caregiving, Cultural, and Cognitive Perspectives on Secure Base Behaviors and Working Models: New Growing Points of Attachment Theory*, Everett Waters, Brian E. Vaughn, German Posada, Kiyomi Kondo-Ikemura, eds., *Monographs of the Society for Research in Child Development* 60(2/3):71–91.

Super, Charles, and Sara Harkness. 1982. "The Infant's Niche in Rural Kenya and Metropolitan America." *Cross-Cultural Research at Issue*, Leonore L. Adler, ed., pp. 47–55. New York: Academic Press.

Takahashi, Keiko. 1990. "Are the Key Assumptions of the 'Strange Situation' Procedure Universal?: A View from Japanese Research." Special Topic Issue, "Cross-Cultural Validity of Attachment Theory." *Human Development* 33(1):23–30.

Thompson, Ross A. 1999. "Early Attachment and Later Development." *Handbook of Attachment: Theory, Research, and Clinical Applications*, Jude Cassidy and Phillip R. Shaver, eds., pp. 265–86. New York: Guilford Press.

Tomasello, Michael, Malinda Carpenter, Josep Call, Tanya Behne, and Henrike Moll. 2005. "Understanding and Sharing Intentions: The Origins of Cultural Cognition." *Behavioral and Brain Sciences* 28:675–735.

Tomasello, Michael, Malinda Carpenter, and Ulf Liszkowski. 2007. "A New Look at Infant Pointing." *Child Development* 78(3):705–722.

Tomasello, Michael, and Hannes Rakoczy. 2003. "What Makes Human Cognition Unique? From Individual to Shared Collective Intentionality." *Mind and Language* 18(2):121–147.

Tronick, Edward Z., Gilda A. Morelli, and Paul K. Ivey. 1992. "The Efe Forager Infant and Toddler's Pattern of Social Relationships: Multiple and Simultaneous." *Developmental Psychology* 28(4):568–577.

van IJzendoorn, Marinus H., and Abraham Sagi-Schwartz. 2008. "Cross-cultural Patterns of Attachment: Universal and Contextual Dimensions." *Handbook of Attachment: Theory, Research, and Clinical Applications*, Jude Cassidy and Phillip R. Shaver, eds., pp. 880–905. New York: Guilford Press.

van IJzendoorn, Marinus H., Abraham Sagi, and Mirjam W. E. Labermon. 1992. "The Multiple Caretaker Paradox: Data from Holland and Israel." *New Directions for Child and Adolescent Development* 57:5–24.

Waters, Everett and Katherine E. Deane. 1985. "Defining and Assessing Individual Differences in Attachment Relationships: Q-methology and the Organization of Behaviors in Infancy and Childhood." In *Growing Points of Attachment: Theory and Research*, Inge Bretherton and Everett Waters, eds., *Monographs of the Society for Research in Child Development* 50(1/2):41–65.

Weisner, Thomas S. 2005. "Attachment as a Cultural and Ecological Problem with Pluralistic Solutions." *Human Development* 48:89–94.

Weisner, Thomas S., and Ronald Gallimore. 1977. "Child and Sibling Caretaking." *Current Anthropology* 18(2):169–190.

Winnicott, Donald W. 1971. *Playing and Reality*. London: Routledge.

Part II

Caregiving

Chapter 2

Cooperative Child Care among the Hadza: Situating Multiple Attachment in Evolutionary Context

Alyssa N. Crittenden and Frank W. Marlowe

Mainstream models of attachment theory are mother-centered and do not address the evolutionary underpinnings of attachment or cross-cultural variation. Recently, there has been a call to arms to adopt a new and less monotropic paradigm that incorporates cultural diversity. Here, we address the need of attachment theory to incorporate evolutionary perspectives and models of multiple attachment by exploring patterns of cooperative care among the Hadza hunter-gatherers of Tanzania. Data from small-scale foraging populations add to the rapidly expanding corpus of work that now views attachment as both culturally influenced and biologically based.

Challenges to Current Models of Attachment

Attachment, as defined by Bowlby and expanded by Ainsworth, is the process by which infants develop strong psychological and emotional bonds with their caregivers as an evolutionary adaptation for ensuring infant survival (Ainsworth 1967; Bowlby 1969). The Bowlby–Ainsworth model, which posits that attachment is mother-centered (Bowlby 1969; Ainsworth 1967, 1973), has been challenged on the grounds that it is limited in scope in that it primarily measures attachment in laboratory settings and focuses almost exclusively on the mother-infant dyad. Furthermore, critics have argued that this model suffers from an ethnocentric Western developmental bias and tends to view variation in attachment patterns as pathological (LeVine and Norman 2001; van IJzendoorn et al. 2008).

This "monocultural" approach makes a priori assumptions and value judgments about relational schemas that fall outside of the mother-centered model (Weisner 2005). Increasingly, however, mounting cross-cultural evidence suggests that secure attachment relationships can and do exist outside of the mother–infant dyad (Barlow 2001; Gottlieb 2004; Heinicke 1995; Howes and

Spieker 2008; Keller and Otto 2009; Kurtz 1992; Lamb and Lewis 2010; LeVine and Norman 2001; Mageo 1998; Mead 1928; Morelli and Rothbaum 2007; Tronick et al. 1987; Weisner 1987; Whiting 1941, 1963). Research is emerging showing that cooperative child care characterizes many (if not most) cultures around the world, cutting across geographic, economic, political, and social boundaries (Howes 1999; Hrdy 2009; Keller and Harwood 2009; Meehan and Hawks chapter 3; Rothbaum et al. 2000; Seymour, chapter 4, 2004; Weisner and Gallimore 1977). In addition to being a widespread model of child care, cooperative care may have been a key characteristic of our evolutionary past (Eibl-Eibesfeldt 1989; Hawkes et al. 1989; Hrdy 2009).

Back to Bowlby: Attachment Theory and Human Evolution

Attachment theory builds upon the framework provided by Bowlby. While Bowlby was explicitly evolutionary in his approach, contemporary attachment theory disregards natural selection, adaptation, and evolutionary theory. In order to more fully understand variation in attachment patterns and how this variation informs both human biology and culture, it is time to get back to Bowlby.

The initial iteration of attachment theory proposed by Bowlby laid the foundation for an evolutionary theory of human development. Drawing heavily on Darwinian natural selection, Bowlby viewed attachment through the lens of human evolution and outlined the selection pressures on attachment in the "environment of evolutionary adaptedness" (Bowlby 1969).

A shortcoming of Bowlby's evolutionary approach, however, was his failure to link attachment theory with reproductive success (Simpson and Belsky 2008). Attachment theorists are beginning to address this lacuna by focusing on the ways in which attachment in infancy and childhood may affect not only survival of offspring, but also reproductive strategies in adulthood (Belsky 1997; Chisholm 1999; Zeifman and Hazan 2008). The effects that the attachment process may have on a mother's reproductive success, however, remain largely overlooked.

Few attempts have been made to integrate life history with attachment theory and the evolution of cooperative care. The Cooperative Breeding Hypothesis (Hrdy 2005a,b, 2009) presents such a synthesis. This hypothesis predicts that a mother's best reproductive strategy is a flexible one in which she relies on various forms of social support to assist her with child care (Hrdy 2009; Sear and Coall 2011). Despite its clear relevance to understanding models of attachment, this hypothesis has not found traction in analyses and/or interpretations of attachment theory. If we are to fully understand attachment from a biological as well as cultural perspective, it is critical to address the evolutionary underpinnings of attachment, both from the infant's perspective and that of its mother.

The emerging interdisciplinary consensus is that a better understanding of the cultural *and* evolutionary correlates of cooperative care is necessary to further our understanding of the flexibility of the attachment process (Barlow, chapter 6; Chisholm 1996; Lewis 2005; Simpson and Belsky 2008).

Here, we outline the characteristics of female life history that may have necessitated the evolution of routine cooperative care among humans. Furthermore, we use naturalistic observations, often lacking from the attachment literature (see Meehan and Hawks, chapter 3, for discussion of why naturalistic observations are critical), to explore cooperative child-care patterns among the Hadza hunter-gatherers of Tanzania. Hunter-gatherer populations, although often overlooked in mainstream attachment literature, are ideal for exploring models of multiple attachment. They practice a nomadic foraging lifestyle that has characterized the bulk of human evolution and is the closest contemporary approximation to Bowlby's "environment of evolutionary adaptedness." The Hadza, although occupying a much smaller range than their ancestral territory and facing numerous geopolitical challenges to their hunting and gathering lifestyle, still forage for the majority of their diet and live in a communal setting (Marlowe 2010). Work among the Hadza, although they are certainly not a "model" population or evolutionary proxy, does allow us to make plausible predictions about the evolution of child-care patterns, attachment theory, and human reproductive evolution.

The Evolution of Human Life History in Comparative Perspective

Human life history has several unique characteristics that help to define humans. Understanding a human mother's unique reproductive tradeoffs and challenges in a comparative context will help situate female reproduction in an evolutionary framework and is the first critical step to understanding how attachment theory is linked with reproductive success and models of multiple child care.

In order to situate the human reproductive system in an evolutionary milieu, something Bowlby aimed to do at the outset, it is necessary to consider how human mothers are reproductively unique when compared to our closest living relatives, the great apes. Compared to apes, human females birth their first child at a later age, space their children more closely together (a shorter inter-birth interval—IBI), wean their infants earlier, and produce children with an extended period of juvenile dependence (Bogin and Smith 1995; Charnov and Berrigan 1993; Robson et al. 2006). Humans have a relatively slow life history—meaning slow development, low reproductive rates, and a life span that exceeds that of the great apes by decades (Charnov and Berrigan 1993). Species with slow life histories tend to wean later and have longer IBIs (Robson and Wood 2008), yet human reproduction is characterized by precisely the opposite pattern—the early weaning of infants before they are nutritionally independent and a short IBI (Hawkes et al. 1997; Kaplan et al. 2000, 2001). This pattern is not only novel among apes, but also differs from the typical mammalian pattern.

The majority of mammalian infants are weaned when they reach one-third of their mother's body weight or when their first permanent molar erupts (Charnov and Berrigan 1993; Lee et al. 1991). If humans followed this pattern, weaning would occur between the ages of 6 and 6.5 years (Smith 1991, 1992; Lee et al. 1991), rather than between 1.5 and 2.5 years of age, which is the typical pattern seen across human populations (Alvarez 2000; Kennedy 2005).

Human females, when compared to great apes, tend to have a relatively late age at first reproduction, ranging between 18 and 20 years of age. Cross-culturally, there appears to be only modest variation in age at first reproduction (Bogin 2008; Martin et al. 2003), which indicates limited flexibility in this human life history trait (Robson and Wood 2008). A late age at first reproduction permits slow growth over a longer period of development (Janson and van Schaik 1993; Purvis and Harvey 1994). Mammals with slow life histories also tend to have larger body sizes, which means that they can, in turn, produce larger and more energetically expensive infants (Stearns 1992; Hawkes 2006; Robson and Wood 2008).

The human life-history pattern is further unique in that it includes an extended period of dependence (Bogin 1997, 2008). Lengthened periods of juvenility in humans may be an evolutionary byproduct of selection on longer life spans in general (Charnov and Berrigan 1993; Jones and Marlowe 2002; Leigh 2001; Pagel and Harvey 1993) or may be linked to the increased demands of learning a wealth of information prior to adulthood (Bogin 1997; Kaplan et al. 2000). Regardless of the ontogenetic impetus for childhood, the end result is that human children require high levels of nutritional and behavioral investment over a very extended period of time.

A Human Mother's Unique Reproductive Challenge

All of the aforementioned life-history traits work in concert with one another to tell the story of human motherhood from a comparative evolutionary perspective. Human mothers wean their infants before they are nutritionally independent, allowing them to resume ovulation sooner and have subsequent offspring more rapidly, effectively shortening the IBI (Hawkes et al. 1997; Kaplan et al. 2000). A shortened IBI permits women to give birth to new infants while simultaneously providing care for existing children, allowing human females to have greater reproductive success than their ape counterparts (i.e., rear a greater percentage of children to adulthood) (Bogin 1997; Bogin and Smith 1995). Human children are energetically expensive, however, and require provisioning and other types of high-investment care for a decade or longer (Bogin 2008).

Young infants subsist entirely on mother's milk, and when an infant is weaning they must be provided with foods that are easily digestible and energetically rich (Bogin 2008; Sellen 2006). Older children, although they may eat some of the foods consumed by adults, are constrained by the type of food that their immature dentition and digestive systems can process (Kramer 2005a; Sellen 2006). It requires nearly 13 million kilocalories to raise a single infant from birth to nutritional independence (Kaplan 1994)—such requirements go far beyond what a mother can procure alone (Hrdy 2005b, 2009; Kramer 2005a). Mothers are, therefore, faced with the unique problem of providing care to unweaned infants while simultaneously maintaining their economic production to successfully feed older children (Hill and Kaplan 1988; Hrdy 1999, 2009; Kramer 2005a; LeVine et al. 1996; Panter-Brick 1989). Mothers accomplish the feat of provisioning multiple children by relying on other group members who care for and/or provision their infants (Bove et al. 2002; Hawkes et al. 1997; Hrdy 2005a; Ivey 2000; Kramer 2005 a,b; Meehan 2005). Investment from individuals other than the biological mother (allomothers[1]) increases a mother's fertility and/or the survivorship of her children (Bereczkei and Dunbar 1997, 2002; Crognier et al. 2001, 2002; Flinn 1989; Ivey 2000; Sear et al. 2000, 2002; Sear and Coall 2011; Turke 1998). It has been proposed that reliance on allomaternal support is a central characteristic of human life history and that humans evolved as cooperative breeders (Hrdy 1999, 2009).

"It Takes a Village to Raise a Child": Evolutionary Origins of Multiple Attachment

It has been recently suggested that allomaternal assistance, in the form of behavioral investment (e.g., child care) or food provisioning, is a derived characteristic of the genus *Homo* and was critical to both infant survival and reproductive success during the Pleistocene (Hrdy 2009). This system, which is markedly different from those of extant apes, would have allowed females to successfully produce multiple energetically costly infants without increasing the IBI (Hrdy 2009). Our hominin[2] ancestors lived under conditions of high mortality (Kurland and Sparks 2003) and children with access to allomaternal care would have been more likely to survive (Hrdy 2005a; Kennedy 2005). Shared care of young is also linked to the evolution of central place provisioning and the division of labor (Marlowe 2006), behavioral traits that would have allowed early hominins to effectively exploit new habitats and flourish.

Early members of the genus *Homo* migrated out of Africa between 2.5 and 1.5 million years ago. During this time, environmental changes resulted in a reduction of woodlands and resource availability (Bobe et al. 2002; Demenocal 1995; Potts 1998; Reed 1997). In order to adapt to this new environment, hominins may have expanded their home ranges in search of viable foods (Leonard and Robertson 1992). In addition to home range expansion, body size and daily energetic expenditure also increased, precipitating a dietary shift toward high-quality energy-rich foods (Aiello and Key 2002; Aiello and Wells 2002; Aiello and Wheeler 1995; Wrangham et al. 1999). Despite these increased energetic demands and shifting ecological conditions, *Homo* mothers were more reproductively successful than their Australopithecine counterparts and were able to produce more offspring at a lower energetic cost of gestation and lactation (Aiello and Key 2002).

During the Pleistocene, the availability of a wide range of helpers-at-the-nest offering support in the form of caregiving and/or provisioning would have allowed populations of early hominins to expand. A shift in subsistence behavior that included contributions of group members other than the mother would have been necessary to facilitate this system of cooperative care.

Using fossil evidence of tooth formation and eruption and endocranial volume, a pattern of life history similar to modern humans may have been present in early species of *Homo* (Robson and Wood 2008). Early weaning and late age at maturity may have allowed Pleistocene mothers to increase the number of offspring that they produced over a lifetime. Help from family and friends would have allowed for population growth that was not necessarily a rapid increase in numbers, but merely enough to allow groups to recover from population bottlenecks (Zeller 1987).

The theoretical explanation typically used to explain allomaternal investment is Hamilton's Rule, which states that an individual might be expected to help another whenever the benefit to the recipient is greater than the cost to the helper divided by the degree of relatedness between them, depicted as $B > C/r$ (Hamilton 1964). Allomothers, therefore, gain inclusive fitness benefits from helping their kin. Unrelated individuals may also be motivated to invest in young, thereby gaining potential benefits such as increased strength in social bonds or access to child care for their own offspring (i.e., reciprocity) (Clutton-Brock 2002; Emlen 1994; Hamilton 1964).

This flexibility in child-care patterning and subsistence behavior would permit a hominin mother to thrive in any ecological setting, a characteristic highlighting human behavioral diversity. The cooperative breeding system permits mothers to produce multiple dependent young at a faster rate by relying on the support of both kin members and unrelated helpers. In sum, humans have a slow life history coupled with a fast rate of reproduction; this could only have evolved in a setting where mothers could depend on reliable assistance in rearing their children. The old adage that "it takes a village to raise a child" appears to have roots in deep evolutionary time and may, indeed, be one of the bases for human reproductive behavior.

Hadza Hunter-Gatherers and Human Evolution

Studying cooperative care among hunting and gathering populations can provide unique insight into our evolutionary history. Such foraging populations are the most realistic models that we have for reconstructing the past lifeways of our Pleistocene ancestors. By studying multiple child care among nomadic small-scale hunters and gatherers, we are better able to "situate attachment processes in the environment that gave rise to them" (Chisholm 1996)—a critical component to understanding models of multiple attachment. Historically, the patterns of child care and attachment among the !Kung foragers of the Kalahari embodied the "hunter-gatherer" model in which mothers represented the primary caregiver (Konner 2005, 2010). Based on ethnographic data from various forager groups, this perspective is shifting and we now know that the "pan-forager" model of child care (Hewlett et al. 2000) involves a wide array of caregivers who routinely provide high-quality investment to infants and children (Hewlett 1991; Ivey 2000; Meehan 2005). Here, we add to this discussion by contributing detailed naturalistic observation data on multiple child care among the Hadza foragers of Tanzania.

The Hadza are an ideal population in which to study the evolution of cooperative care because they practice a lifestyle and subsistence regime that characterizes the bulk of human history and was similar to that of our hominin ancestors. The Hadza are a natural fertility population (i.e., practice no birth control), live in a communal setting, and rarely participate in a market economy.[3]

The Hadza occupy a 4000 km^2 region of Northern Tanzania, south of the Serengeti in a savanna woodland habitat around the shores of Lake Eyasi (Marlowe 2010). Approximately 300 individuals, out of a total population of 1,000, practice hunting and gathering as their primary means of subsistence. They live in camps with roughly 30 individuals with flexible residence patterns and fluid camp composition. This common pattern of frequent movement between camps is attributable to the fact that the Hadza do not traditionally recognize land rights and ownership of natural resources (Kaare 1994; Woodburn 1968). The average population size has not significantly grown in the last 100 years, although there has been a trend toward staying in larger camps for longer periods of time due to many areas being taken over by non-Hadza tribes (Crittenden 2013; Fosbrooke 1956; Marlowe 2002, 2010; McDowell 1981).

Camps move approximately every two months in response to the seasonal availability of water and foods (Marlowe 1999; Woodburn 1968). Distinct wet and dry seasons are linked with differential subsistence behaviors and social arrangements (Hawkes et al. 1989; Vincent 1985; Woodburn 1968). During the dry season, which lasts roughly from June through October, camp size is relatively large. The larger aggregation of people during the dry season may be due to limited availability of water and/or greater concentration of hunted animals near watering holes (Bunn et al. 1988; Woodburn 1968). During the wet season, which lasts roughly from November to May, camp size is smaller and may be linked to more freely available drinking water (Mabulla 2007; Woodburn 1968).

The Hadza diet consists of a wide variety of plant and animal foods and a distinct sexual division of labor characterizes their foraging. Men typically forage alone or in pairs, collecting baobab fruit and honey and hunting a wide variety of birds and mammals with bows and poisoned tipped arrows. Women forage in groups and primarily focus on gathering plant foods such as baobab fruit, berries, and tubers (underground storage organs). Female foraging may be constrained by the fact that they are carrying nursing infants, who accompany their mothers on daily foraging trips (Marlowe 2003). When a child is being weaned at approximately two to three years of age, he or she is typically left in camp with others, because they are too large to be carried easily and too young to walk long distances to berry or tuber patches. Children often remain in camp without any adult supervision but are also routinely left under the charge of at least one camp member, typically a grandparent or an older juvenile caregiver.

In addition to mothers, who are the primary caregivers (Crittenden and Marlowe 2008), a wide range of allomothers routinely contribute high-investment care to infants. Several group members, both related and unrelated, contribute to the care of a given child by way of nutritional or behavioral investment or both (Crittenden and Marlowe 2008; Hawkes et al. 1989, 1997; Marlowe 1999, 2003, 2005). Having others hold and carry an infant releases the mother from some of the high metabolic costs of infant transport (Gettler 2010; Wall-Scheffler and Myers 2013; Wall-Scheffler et al. 2007). Enumerating the caregivers that spend time holding infants, we can use this measure to determine whether or not an increase in the number of caregivers affects the time that mothers spend holding their infants. Such an effect would lend strong support to the notion that humans evolved as cooperative caregivers (i.e., cooperative breeders) and would have significant implications for the evolution of multiple attachment.

Child-Care Patterns among the Hadza

The constellation of allomaternal caregivers (both kin and non-kin) available to a Hadza infant include fathers, siblings, grandparents, cousins, aunts, uncles, distant relatives, and non-kin (Crittenden and Marlowe 2008; Marlowe 2005). Kin selection appears to strongly influence the amount of time that an individual spends holding an infant, yet unrelated individuals also spend considerable time participating in child care (Crittenden and Marlowe 2008). Our previous analyses have focused on holding from the perspective of the individual holding an infant. Here we focus on the perspective of the infant, giving a "child's-eye-view" (Fouts and Brookshire 2009) of allomaternal holding to determine the average number of caregivers available to an infant.

Data on holding and carrying infants were collected in 10 Hadza camps over 17 months of fieldwork between the years 1995 and 2004. Hourly in-camp scans were conducted on a daily basis, from sunrise to sunset, which measured the activity and location of every person present in camp. For each infant in the sample, we measured the number of holders during the study period. Hadza children above the age of four are rarely held (as they are too heavy); therefore we limited our sample to children four years of age and younger.

We measured each mother's frequency of holding by dividing the number of scans in which she was holding her infant by the total number of scans in which she was present in camp. We further limited our sample to residents only, which allowed us to exclude mother-infant pairs that appeared in less than ten scans. By removing these dyads, we were able to avoid inflation of maternal holding frequency; that is, if a visiting mother was present in two scans and was holding her infant in both, it would appear that she was holding her infant 100 percent of the time.

Our sample of 42,031 person scans represented a total population of 470 residents (n_1 = 234 females; n_2 = 236 males), which included a total of 69 children (n_1 = 35 females; n_2 = 34 males), four years of age and younger, who were held. Among these children, 3 were held exclusively by their mothers, 17 were held exclusively by allomothers, and 49 were held by a combination of their mother and allomothers. During the time of our observations, each infant was cared for by an average of 2.3 different allomothers, with the number of allomaternal caregivers ranging from 1 to 17.

We have previously shown that a Hadza child's age is a strong predictor of the frequency with which they are held, with younger infants being held significantly more than their older counterparts (Crittenden and Marlowe 2008). Interestingly, here we find that the *number* of different caregivers does not increase with the infant's age ($\beta = -0.558$, $p = 0.391$, df = 69, $R2 = -0.012$). Above the age of weaning, we find that a decrease in the frequency of maternal holding correlates with a higher rate of allomaternal holding ($\beta = 0.256$, $p = 0.04$, permutation test with 10,000 simulations on weighted linear regression). These results suggest that a wide range of caregivers is available to an infant immediately after birth and continues past weaning. In addition, the care provided by allomothers decreases the amount of time that mothers spend holding their child, thus releasing her to perform other activities.

The data presented here demonstrate that Hadza children are held by a wide range of caregivers and participate in a system of cooperative child care. Our results are in agreement with the cross-cultural data on small-scale societies showing that a greater number of helpers available to a mother decreases her investment in child care (Munroe and Munroe 1971). Among the Hadza, this form of social support releases the recipient mother from some of the energetic burden of child care, which may function to reduce metabolic costs and help mothers return to ovulation more quickly (Ellison 2003). These data add to the growing body of work that is beginning to view attachment as biologically based yet culturally influenced (Keller and Otto 2009). A more thorough understanding of the ways in which culture and evolution interact in a system of cooperative care will enhance our understanding and appreciation of the flexibility of the attachment process.

Cooperation, Cognition, and Sociality: Toward an Evolutionary Synthesis of Multiple Attachment

The flexibility provided by models of cooperative child care may have been one of the keys to the success of early members of the genus *Homo*. During the Pleistocene, shifting ecological conditions necessitated the exploitation of new resources (Aiello and Key 2002; Aiello and Wheeler 1995; Leonard and Robertson 1992; Wrangham et al. 1999). A wide range of allomothers who offered child care and/or provisioning would have allowed populations to expand into these new habitats. Help from family and friends would have permitted *Homo* mothers to wean earlier and return to ovulation sooner, successfully increasing their lifetime reproductive success.

If humans evolved as cooperative breeders, infants would not only take cues from their mothers on how the world worked, but would also glean critical information from their allomothers. Infants, then, must be able to successfully elicit care from a range of caregivers (Hrdy 2005). Human infants are uniquely qualified to elicit such care, as they have the sociocognitive ability to monitor the thoughts and intentions of others (Tomasello 1999). As Hrdy compellingly argues, a permanent move away from cooperative networks of care may have dire consequences for our children (Hrdy 2009). If our species' typical ability to empathize and cooperate with others is developed early in life and is based, even partially, on routine interaction with a constellation of caregivers, we must give serious credence to the importance of models of multiple attachment. This paradigm shift in attachment theory, still largely viewed as controversial, would move away from viewing mother-centered models of attachment as universal and would begin incorporating models with developmental, ecological, and cross-cultural variability.

Acknowledgments

This research was supported by National Science Foundation grants #9529278 and #0544751 (to FWM) and grants from the University of California, San Diego (to ANC). The authors would like to thank Naomi Quinn, Jeanette Mageo, and Courtney Meehan for helpful comments on earlier drafts of this chapter. We would also like to extend thanks to Lene and Johannes Kleppe for their generous hospitality, Dr. Audax Mabulla and our Tanzanian assistants (Happy Msofe, Golden Ngumbuke, Danny Ngumbuke, and Ephraim Mutukwaya) for research support, Dave Zes for assistance with R, and the Hadza—not only for welcoming us into their lives, but also for making this type of work so enjoyable.

Notes

1. Given that some human populations have pair bonds and fathers in many cultures routinely provide a significant amount of high-quality investment, the term "alloparent" is often used. Here, however, we use the term "allomother" to remain consistent with the biological literature and to discuss the evolutionary significance of non-maternal investment.
2. The term hominin refers to the taxonomic group including extant humans (*Homo sapiens*) and fossil human ancestors (members of the genera *Homo* and *Australopithecus*) after the split with chimpanzees (genus *Pan*).
3. Hadza ethnotourism is becoming increasingly commonplace and many camps located close to villages are now participating in wage labor (Crittenden 2013; Marlowe 2010). The data used for this study were collected in bush camps where individuals did not engage in wage labor and foraged for approximately 90 percent of their diet.

References

Aiello, Leslie C., and Cathy Key. 2002. "Energetic Consequences of Being a *Homo erectus* Female." *American Journal of Human Biology* 14(5):551–565.

Aiello, Leslie C., and Jonathan C. K. Wells. 2002. "Energetics and the Evolution of the Genus *Homo*." *Annual Review of Anthropology* 31:323–338.

Aiello, Leslie C., and Peter Wheeler. 1995. "The Expensive-Tissue Hypothesis: The Brain and the Digestive System in Human and Primate Evolution." *Current Anthropology* 36(2):199–221.

Ainsworth, Mary D. 1967. *Infancy in Uganda*. Baltimore, MD: Johns Hopkins University Press.

Ainsworth, Mary D. 1973. "The Development of Infant-Mother Attachment." In *Review of Child Development Research—Volume 3*, Bettye M. Caldwell and Henry N. Ricciuti, eds., pp. 1–94. Chicago, IL: University of Chicago Press.

Alvarez, Helen Perich. 2000. "Grandmother Hypothesis and Primate Life Histories." *American Journal of Physical Anthropology* 113(3):435–450.

Barlow, Kathleen. 2001. "Working Mothers and the Work of Culture in a Papua New Guinea Society." *Ethos* 29(1): 78–107.

Belsky, Jay. 1997. "Attachment, Mating, and Parenting: An Evolutionary Interpretation." *Human Nature: An Interdisciplinary Biosocial Perspective* 8:361–381.

Bereczkei, Tamás, and Robin I. Dunbar. 1997. "Female-Biased Reproductive Strategies in Two Gypsy Populations." *Proceedings of the Royal Society of London Series B* 264: 17–22.

Bereczkei, Tamás, and Robin I. Dunbar. 2002. "Helping-at-the-Nest and Reproduction in a Hungarian Gypsy Population." *Current Anthropology* 43:804–809.

Bobe, Rene, Anna K. Behrensmeyer, and Ralph E. Chapman. 2002. "Faunal Change, Environmental Variability, and Late Pliocene Hominin Evolution." *Journal of Human Evolution* 42(4):475–497.

Bogin, Barry. 1997. "Evolutionary Hypotheses for Human Childhoods." *Yearbook of Physical Anthropology* 40:63–89.

Bogin, Barry. 2008. *Patterns of Human Growth*. London: Cambridge University Press.
Bogin, Barry, and B. Holly Smith. 1995. "Evolution of the Human Life Cycle." *American Journal of Human Biology* 8(6):703–716.
Bowlby, John. 1969. *Attachment and Loss: Volume 1 Attachment*. New York: Basic Books.
Bove, Riley B., Claudia R. Valeggia, and Peter T. Ellison. 2002. "Girl Helpers Time Allocation among the Toba of Argentina." *Human Nature: An Interdisciplinary Biosocial Perspective* 13(4): 457–472.
Bunn, Henry, Laurence E. Bartram, and Ellen M. Kroll. 1988. "Variability and Bone Assemblage Formation from Hadza Hunting, Scavenging, and Carcass Processing." *Journal of Anthropological Archaeology* 7:412–457.
Charnov, Eric L., and David Berrigan. 1993. "Why Do Female Primates Have Such Long Lifespans and So Few Babies? Or Life in the Slow Lane." *Evolutionary Anthropology* 1:191–194.
Chisholm, James. 1996. "The Evolutionary Ecology of Attachment Organization." *Human Nature: An Interdisciplinary Biosocial Perspective* 7(1): 1–37.
Chisholm, James. 1999. *Death, Hope and Sex: Steps to an Evolutionary Ecology of Mind and Morality*. New York: Cambridge University Press.
Clutton-Brock, Tim H. 2002. "Breeding Together: Kin Selection and Mutualism in Cooperative Vertebrates." *Science* 296:69–72.
Crittenden, Alyssa N. 2013. "The Hadza Hunter-Gatherers of Tanzania: Ethnography, Demography, and Importance for Human Evolution." In *Cradle of Humanity*. Monograph of the Museo Nacional de Antropología: Madrid, Spain.
Crittenden, Alyssa N., and Frank W. Marlowe. 2008. "Allomaternal Care among the Hadza of Tanzania." *Human Nature: An Interdisciplinary Biosocial Perspective* 19(3): 249–262.
Crognier, Emile, Abdellatif Baali, Mohamed-Kamal Hilali. 2001. "Do 'helpers at the nest' increase their parents' reproductive success?" *American Journal of Human Biology* 13(3):365–373.
Crognier, Emile, Mercedes Villena, and Enrique Vargas. 2002. "Helping Patterns and Reproductive Success in Aymara Communities." *American Journal of Human Biology* 14(3):372–379.
Darwin, Charles. 1871. *The Descent of Man*. London: Gibson Square Books.
Demenocal, Peter B. 1995. "Plio-Pleistocene African Climate." *Science* 270(5233):53–59.
Eibl-Eibesfeldt, Irenäus. 1989. *Human Ethology*. New York: Aldine de Gruyter.
Ellison, Peter T. 2003. "Energetics and Reproductive Effort." *American Journal of Human Biology* 15(3):342–351.
Emlen, Stephen T. 1994. "Benefits, Constraints, and the Evolution of the Family." *Trends in Ecology and Evolution* 9:282–285.
Flinn, Mark V. 1989. "Household Competition and Female Reproductive Strategies in a Trinidadian Village." In *The Sociobiology of Sexual and Reproductive Strategies*, Anne E. Rasa, Christian Vogel, and Eckart Voland, eds., pp. 206–233. London: Chapman and Hall.
Fosbrooke, Henry A. 1956. "A Stone Age Tribe in Tanganyika." *The South African Archaeological Bulletin* 11(41):3–8.
Fouts, Hillary N., and Robyn A. Brookshire. 2009. "Who Feeds Children? A Child's-Eye-View of Caregiver Feeding Patterns among the Aka Foragers in Congo. *Social Science & Medicine* 69: 285–292.

Gettler, Lee T. 2010. "Direct Male Care and Hominin Evolution: Why Male-Child Interaction is More Than a Nice Social Idea." *American Anthropologist* 112(1): 7–21.

Gottlieb, Alma. 2004. *The Afterlife is Where WE Come from: The Culture of Infancy in West Africa*. Chicago, IL: University of Chicago Press.

Hamilton, William D. 1964. "The Genetical Evolution of Social Behaviour." *Journal of Theoretical Biology* 7: 1–18.

Hawkes, Kristen. 2006. "Slow Life Histories and Human Evolution." In *The Evolution of Human Life History*, Kristen Hawkes and Richard R. Paine, eds., pp. 95–126. Santa Fe: School of American Research Press.

Hawkes, Kristen, James F. O'Connell, and Nicholas G. Blurton-Jones. 1989. "Hardworking Hadza Grandmothers." In *Comparative Socioecology of Humans and Other Mammals*, V. Standen and Robert Foley, eds., pp. 341–366. London: Basil Blackwell.

Hawkes, Kristen, James F. O'Connell, and Nicholas G. Blurton-Jones. 1997. "Hadza Women's Time Allocation, Offspring Provisioning, and the Evolution of Long Postmenopausal Life Spans." *Current Anthropology* 38(4):551–577.

Heinicke, Christoph. 1995. "Expanding the Study of the Formation of the Child's Relationships." *Monographs of the Society for Research in Child Development* 60(2–3):300–309.

Hewlett, Barry S., Michael E. Lamb, Birgit Leyendecker, and Axel Schölmerich. 2000. "Internal Working Models, Trust, and Sharing among Foragers." *Current Anthropology* 41(2):287–297.

Hill, Kim, and Hillard Kaplan. 1988. "Tradeoffs in Male and Female Reproductive Strategies among the Ache: Part 1." In *Human Reproductive Behaviour: A Darwinian*, eds., pp. 277–289. Cambridge: Cambridge University Press.

Howes, Carolee. 1999. "Attachment Relationships in the Context of Multiple Caregivers." In *Handbook of Attachment: Theory, Research, and Clinical Applications*, Jude Cassidy and Phillip R. Shaver, eds. New York: Guilford Press.

Howes, Carollee, and Susan Spieker. 2008. "Attachment Relationships in the Context of Multiple Caregivers." In *The Handbook of Attachment: Theory, Research, and Clinical Applications*. 2nd edition, J. Cassidy and P. Shaver, eds., pp. 317–332. New York: Guilford.

Hrdy, Sarah Blaffer. 1999. *Mother Nature: A History of Mothers, Infants, and Natural Selection*. New York: Pantheon Books.

Hrdy, Sarah Blaffer. 2005a. "Comes the Child Before the Man: How Cooperative Breeding and Prolonged Post-weaning Dependence Shaped Human Potentials." In *Hunter Gatherer Childhoods*, Barry S. Hewlett and Michael E. Lamb, eds., pp. 65–91. Piscataway: Aldine Transaction.

Hrdy, Sarah Blaffer. 2005b. "Evolutionary Context of Human Development: The Cooperative Breeding Model." In *Attachment and Bonding: A New Synthesis*, Carol Sue Carter, Lieselotte Ahnert, Karin E. Grossman, Sarah Blaffer Hrdy, Micheal E. Lamb, Stephen W. Porges, and Nobert Sachser, eds., pp. 9–32. Cambridge: MIT Press.

Hrdy, Sarah Blaffer. 2009. *Mothers and Others: The Evolutionary Origins of Mutual Understanding*. Cambridge, MA: Harvard University Press.

Ivey, Paula K. 2000. "Cooperative Reproduction in the Ituri Forest Hunter-Gatherers: Who Cares for Efe Infants?" *Current Anthropology* 41:856–866.

Janson, Charles H. and Carel van Schaik. 1993. "Ecological Risk Aversion in Juvenile Primates: Slow and Steady Wins the Race." In *Juvenile Primates: Life*

History, Development and Behavior, Michael E. Pereira and Lynn A. Fairbanks, eds., pp. 57–76. New York: Oxford University Press.

Jones, Nicholas G. Blurton, and Frank W. Marlowe. 2002. "Selection for Delayed Maturity: Does it Take 20 Years to Learn to Hunt and Gather?" *Human Nature: An Interdisciplinary Biosocial Perspective* 13(2):199–238.

Kaare, Bwire. 1994. "The Impact of Modernization Policies on the Hunter-Gatherer Hadzabe: The Case of Education and Language Policies of Post independence Tanzania." In *Key Issues in Hunter-Gatherer Research*, Ernest S. Burch and Linda J. Ellanna, eds., pp. 315–331. Oxford: Berg Publishers.

Kaplan, Hillard. 1994. "Evolutionary Wealth Flows Theories of Fertility: Empirical Tests and New Models." *Population and Development Review* 20:753–791.

Kaplan, Hillard. 1997. "The Evolution of the Human Life Course." In *Between Zeus and Salmon: The Biodemography of Longevity*, Kenneth W. Wachter and Caleb Ellicott Finch, eds., pp. 175–211. Washington, DC: National Academy of Sciences.

Kaplan, Hillard, Kim Hill, Jane Lancaster, and A. Magdalena Hurtado. 2000. "A Theory of Human Life History Evolution: Diet, Intelligence, and Longevity." *Evolutionary Anthropology* 9(4):156–185.

Kaplan, Hillard, Kim Hill, Jane Lancaster, and A. Magdalena Hurtado. 2001. "The Embodied Capital Theory of Human Evolution." In *Reproductive Ecology and Human Evolution*, Peter T. Ellison, ed. Hawthorne, NY: Aldine de Gruyter.

Keller, Heidi, and Robin Harwood. 2009. "Culture and Development Pathways of Relationship Formation." In *Pathways on Human Development, Family, and Culture*, S. Beckman and A. Aksu-Koc, eds. Cambridge, England: Cambridge University Press.

Keller, Heidi, and Hiltrud Otto. 2009. "The Cultural Socialization of Emotion Regulation during Infancy." *Journal of Cross-Cultural Psychology* 40(6):1006–1011.

Kennedy, Gail E. 2005. "From the Ape's Dilemma to the Weanling's Dilemma: Early Weaning and Its Evolutionary Context." *Journal of Human Evolution* 48:123–145.

Konner, Melvin. 2005. "Hunter-Gatherer Infancy and Childhood." In *Hunter-Gatherer Childhoods: Evolutionary, developmental and cultural perspectives*, Barry S. Hewlett and Michael G. Lamb, eds., pp. 19–46. New Brunswick, NJ: Transaction Publishers.

Konner, Melvin. 2010. *The Evolution of Childhood: Relationships, Emotion, Mind.* Cambridge, MA: Harvard University Press.

Kramer, Karen L. 2005a. *Maya Children: Helpers at the Farm.* Cambridge, MA: Harvard University Press.

Kramer, Karen L. 2005b. "Children's Help and the Pace of Reproduction: Cooperative Breeding in Humans." *Evolutionary Anthropology* 14: 224–237.

Kurland, Jeffrey A., and Corey S. Sparks. 2003. "Is There a Paleolithic Demography? Implications for Evolutionary Psychology and Sociobiology." Paper presented at the 15th Annual Meeting of the Human Behavioral and Evolution Society Meetings, Lincoln, Nebraska: January 4–8, 2003.

Kurtz, Stanley N. 1992. *All the Mothers Are One: Hindu India and the Cultural Reshaping of Psychoanalysis.* New York: Columbia University Press.

Lamb, Michael E., and Charlie Lewis. 2010. "The Development and Significance of Father-Child Relationships in Two-Parent Families." In *The Role of the Father in Child Development.* 5th edition, Michael E. Lamb, ed., pp. 94–153. Hoboken, NJ: Wiley and Sons.

Lee, Phyllis C., Patricia Majluf, and Iain J. Gordon. 1991. "Growth, Weaning, and Maternal Investment from a Comparative Perspective." *Journal of Zoology* 225:99–114.

Leigh, Steven R. 2001. "The Evolution of Human Growth." *Evolutionary Anthropology* 10:223–236.

Leonard, William R., and Marcia L. Robertson. 1992. "Nutritional Requirements and Human Evolution: A Bioenergetics Model." *American Journal of Human Biology* 4(2):179–195.

LeVine, Robert, and Karin Norman. 2001. "The Infant's Acquisition of Culture Early Attachment Reexamined in Anthropological Perspective." In *The Psychology of Cultural Experience*, Carmella C. Moore and Holly F. Mathews, eds., pp. 83–104. Cambridge, England: Cambridge University Press.

LeVine, Robert Alan, Sarah Levine, Suzanne Dixon, Amy Richman, P. Herbert Leiderman, and T. Berry Brazelton. 1996. *Child Care and Culture: Lessons From Africa*. New York: Cambridge University Press.

Lewis, Michael. 2005. "The Child and Its Family: The Social Network Model." *Human Development* 48:8–27.

Mabulla, Audax Z. 2007. "Hunting and Foraging in the Eyasi Basin, Northern Tanzania: Past, Present and Future Prospects." *African Archaeological Review* 24:15–33.

Mageo, Jeannette Marie. 1998. *Theorizing Self in Samoa: Emotions, Genders, and Sexualities*. Ann Arbor, MI: University of Michigan Press.

Marlowe, Frank W. 1999. "Male Care and Mating Effort among Hadza Foragers." *Behavioral Ecology and Sociobiology* 46(1):57–64.

Marlowe, Frank W. 2000. "Paternal Investment and the Human Mating System." *Behavioural Processes* 51:45–61.

Marlowe, Frank W. 2002. "Why the Hadza are Still Hunter-Gatherers." In *Ethnicity, Hunter Gatherers, and the "Other": Association or Assimilation in Africa*, Susan Kent, ed., pp. 247–275. Washington, DC: Smithsonian Institution Press.

Marlowe, Frank W. 2003. "A Critical Period for Provisioning by Hadza Men: Implications for Pair Bonding." *Evolution and Human Behavior* 24(3): 217–229.

Marlowe, Frank W. 2005. "Who Tends Hadza Children?" In *Hunter-Gatherer Childhoods*, Barry S. Hewlett and Michael E. Lamb, eds., pp. 177–190. Piscataway: Aldine Transaction.

Marlowe, Frank W. 2006. "Central Place Provisioning: The Hadza as an Example." In *Feeding Ecology of Apes and Other Primates: Ecological, Physiological, and Behavioural Aspects*, Gottfried Hohmann, Martha Robbins, and Christophe Boesch, eds., pp. 359–377. Cambridge: Cambridge University Press.

Marlowe, Frank W. 2010. *The Hadza Hunter-Gatherers of Tanzania*. Berkeley, CA: University of California Press.

Martin, Joyce A., Brady E. Hamilton, Paul D. Sutton, Stephanie J. Ventura, Fay Menacker, and Martha L. Munson. 2003. *Births: Final Data for 2002*. National Vital Statistics Reports 52. Hyatsville, MD: National Center for Health Statistics.

McDowell, William. 1981. "A Brief History of the Mangola Hadza." Mbulu District Development Directorate, Mbulu District, Arusha Region.

Mead, Margaret. 1928. *Coming of Age in Samoa*. New York: William Morrow.

Meehan, Courtney L. 2005. "The Effects of Residential Locality on Parental and Alloparental Investment among the Aka Foragers of the Central African Republic." *Human Nature: An Interdisciplinary Biosocial Perspective* 16(1):58–80.

Morelli, Gilda, and Fred Rothbaum. 2007. "Situating the Child in Context: Attachment Relationships and Self- Regulation in Different Cultures." In *Handbook of Cultural Psychology*, S. Kitayama and D. Cohen, eds., pp. 500–527. New York: Guilford Press.

Munroe, Ruth H., and Robert L. Munroe. 1971. "Household Density and Infant Care in an East African Society." *Journal of Social Psychology* 83(1):3–13.

Pagel, Mark D., and Paul H. Harvey. 1993. "Evolution of the Juvenile Period in Mammals." In *Juvenile Primates: Life History, Development and Behavior*, Michael E. Pereira and Lynn A. Faribanks, eds., pp. 28–37. New York: Oxford University Press.

Panter-Brick, Catherine. 1989. "Motherhood and Subsistence Work: The Tamang of Rural Nepal." *Human Ecology* 17(2):205–228.

Potts, Richard. 1998. "Environmental Hypotheses of Hominin Evolution." *Yearbook of Physical Anthropology* 41:93–136.

Purvis, Andy, and Paul H. Harvey. 1994. "Mammalian Life History Evolution: A Comparative Test of Charnov's Model." *Journal of Zoology* 237:259–283.

Reed, Kaye E. 1997. "Early Hominin Evolution and Ecological Change through the African Plio-Pleistocene." *Journal of Human Evolution* 32(2–3):289–322.

Robson, Shannen L., Carel P. van Schaik, and Kristen Hawkes. 2006. "The Derived Features of Human Life History." In *The Evolution of Human Life History*, Richard L. Paine and Kristen Hawkes, eds., pp. 17–44. Santa Fe: School of American Research Press.

Robson, Shannen L., and Bernard Wood. 2008. "Hominin Life History: Reconstruction and Evolution." *Journal of Anatomy* 212:394–425.

Rothbaum, Fred, Martha Pott, Hiroshi Azuma, Kazuo Miyake, and John Weisz. 2000. "The Development of Close Relationships in Japan and the United States: Paths of Symbiotic Harmony and Generative Tension." *Child Development* 71(5):1121–1142.

Sear, Rebecca, and David Coall. 2011. "How Much Does Family Matter? Cooperative Breeding and the Demographic Transition." *Population and Development Review* 37 (Supplement):81–112.

Sear, Rebecca, Ruth Mace, and Ian A. McGregor. 2000. "Maternal Grandmothers Improve Nutritional Status and Survival of Children in Rural Gambia." *Proceedings of the Royal Society London Series B* 267:1641–1647.

Sear, Rebecca, Fiona Steele, Ian A. McGregor, and Ruth Mace. 2002. "The Effects of Kin on Child Mortality in Rural Gambia." *Demography* 39:43–63.

Sellen, Dan. 2006. "Lactation, Complementary Feeding, and Human Life History." *The Evolution of Human Life History*, Kristen Hawkes and Richard R. Paine, eds., pp. 155–196. Santa Fe, New Mexico: SAR Press.

Seymour, Susan. 2004. "Multiple Caretaking of Infants and Young Children: An Area in Critical Need of a Feminist Psychological Anthropology." *Ethos* 32(4):538–556.

Simpson, Jeffry A., and Jay Belsky. 2008. "Attachment Theory within a Modern Evolutionary Framework." In *Handbook of Attachment: Theory, Research, and Clinical Applications*, Jude Cassidy and Phillip Shaver, eds., pp. 131–157. New York, NY: Guilford Press.

Smith, B. Holly. 1991. "Dental Development and the Evolution of Life History in *Hominінae*." *American Journal of Physical Anthropology* 86:157–174.

Smith, B. Holly. 1992. "Life History and the Evolution of Human Maturation." *Evolutionary Anthropology* 1:134–142.

Stearns, Stephen. 1992. *The Evolution of Life Histories*. Oxford: Oxford University Press.

Tomasello, Michael. 1999. "Having Intentions, Understanding Intentions, and Understanding Communicative Intentions." In *Developing Theories of Intention: Social Understanding and Self-Control*, Philip David Zelazo, Janet Wilde Astington, and David R. Olson, eds, pp. 63–75. Mahawah, NJ: Lawrence Erlbaum Associates Publishers.

Tronick, Edward Z., Gilda Morelli, and Steven Winn. 1987. "Multiple Caretaking of Efe (Pygmy) Infants." *American Anthropologist* 89(1):96–106.

Turke, Paul. 1998. " 'Helpers at the Nest': Childcare Networks on the Ifaulk." In *Human Reproductive Behaviour: A Darwinian Perspective*, Laura Betzig, Monique Borgerhoff-Mulder, and Paul Turke, eds., pp. 173–188. Cambridge: Cambridge University Press.

van IJzendoorn, Marinus H., and Abraham Sagi-Schwartz. 2008. "Cross-Cultural Patterns of Attachment: Universal and Contextual Dimensions." In *Handbook of Attachment: Theory, Research, and Clinical Applications (Second Edition)*, Jude Cassidy and Phillip R. Shaver, eds., pp. 713–734. New York: Guilford Press.

Vincent, Anne. 1985. "Plant Foods in Savanna Environments: A Preliminary Report of Tubers Eaten by the Hadza of Northern Tanzania." *World Archaeology* 17(2):131–148.

Wall-Scheffler, Cara M., K. Geiger, and Karen L. Steudel-Numbers. 2007. "Infant Carrying: The Role of Increased Locomotory Costs in Early Tool Development." *American Journal of Physical Anthropology* 133(2):841–846.

Wall-Scheffler, Cara M., and Marcella J. Myers. 2013. "Reproductive Costs for Everyone: How Female Loads Impact Human Mobility Strategies." *Journal of Human Evolution* 64(5):448–456.

Weisner, Thomas S. 1987. "Socialization for Parenthood in Sibling Caretaking Societies." In *Parenting across the Life Span*, Jane Lancaster, Alice Rossi, Jeanne Altmann, and Lonnie Sherrod, eds., pp. 237–270. New York: Aldine Press.

Weisner, Thomas S. 2005. "Attachment as a Cultural and Ecological Problem with Pluralistic Solutions." *Human Development* 48:89–94.

Weisner, Thomas S., and R. Gallimore. 1977. "My Brother's Keeper: Child and Sibling Caretaking." *Current Anthropology* 89:97–106.

Whiting, Beatrice B. 1963. *Six Cultures: Studies of Child Rearing*. New York.

Whiting, John W. M. 1941. *Becoming a Kwoma: Teaching and Learning in a New Guinea Tribe*. New Haven, CT: Yale University Press.

Woodburn, James. 1968. "Stability and Flexibility in Hadza Residential Groupings." In *Man the Hunter*, Richard B. Lee and Irven DeVore, eds., pp. 103–110. Chicago, IL: Aldine.

Wrangham, Richard W., James H. Jones, Greg Laden, David Pilbeam, and Nancy Lou Conklin-Brittain. 1999. "The Raw and the Stolen: Cooking and the Ecology of Human Origins." *Current Anthropology* 40(5):567–594.

Zeifman, Debra, and Cindy Hazan. 2008. "Pair Bonds as Attachments: Reevaluating the Evidence." In *Handbook of Attachment: Theory, Research, and Clinical Applications*, Jude Cassidy and Phillip R. Shaver, eds., pp. 436–455. New York: Guilford Press.

Chapter 3

Cooperative Breeding and Attachment among the Aka Foragers

Courtney L. Meehan and Sean Hawks

While attachment research has generally been situated and understood within the confines of the mother-child dyad, there is an increasing call to examine the "constellation of relational influences" on children's attachment security (Thompson 2000:147). In addition, some attachment theorists have begun to argue that a focus on the mother-child dyad significantly decreases predictive power when examining the effects of attachment on child development (van IJzendoorn et al. 1992). These calls to incorporate other caregivers in our understanding of children's attachments stem from a growing understanding of the extent and nature of children's broader social relationships—specifically, that the mother-child dyad does not exist in isolation. Mothers and children are situated within large social networks and these networks affect the formation and security of children's attachments with mothers and others (Ahnert et al. 2000; Jacobson and Frye 1991; Spieker and Bensley 1994; Tronick et al. 1992). Unfortunately, research on children's attachments to non-maternal caregivers (Howes and Spieker 2008), and attachment in cross-cultural perspective (van IJzendoorn and Sagi 2008) is limited. There continues to be an emphasis on the mother-child dyad and research is predominately conducted in Western cultures, where mothers and children are more isolated from assistance than what is typically found throughout most of the world.

We have three main goals in this chapter. First, we seek to illustrate the cooperative nature of child care among the Aka tropical forest foragers of the Central African Republic (CAR). Cross-cultural studies that document the extent of multiple caregiving are essential as they show that mothers and children are embedded in extensive social networks and rely on care and investment by others. Examining the holistic nature of children's social worlds firmly places the mother-child dyad in its appropriate and larger social context. Second, we identify that not only are mothers and children embedded in dense social networks, but children form meaningful attachment relationships with some, but not all, of their non-maternal caregivers. As discussed later, investment by others in child care has a long evolutionary history among humans and is tied to successful child development. Thus, we should expect that the formation of close attachment relationships with non-maternal caregivers enhances a child's sense of security and increases the level of physical, social, and emotional investment they receive. Third, we argue that it is essential for attachment theorists to explore and identify the consequences of multiple attachments on children's development. While the potential for children to form multiple attachments has been documented, relatively few cross-cultural studies move beyond simply acknowledging these relationships.

Throughout the chapter we draw attention to the need for naturalistic observational data, something that Ainsworth (1977b) strongly urged. Naturalistic observations allow us to examine not only whether children form attachments to non-maternal caregivers, but also to explore attachment in a culturally relevant manner. Naturalistic observations enable investigations into the cultural context of early childhood experiences (i.e., maternal–child separations, the effect of caregivers on children's reactions to maternal separations and reunions, and the effects of caregivers on children's emotional states) that are not possible to explore using traditional measurements. Consequently, these data offer insights into the cross-cultural applicability of traditional measures of attachment security (e.g., the Strange Situation Procedure [SSP]), particularly when examining multiple attachments.

Human Cooperative Breeding

Humans have multiple life history traits that suggest a long history of cooperative child rearing. First, human ontogeny requires that mothers invest heavily in their offspring (Blurton Jones and Marlowe 2002; Hrdy 2009), both calorically (Kaplan 1994) and through caregiving (Hewlett and Lamb 2002; Hrdy 2009). Additionally, human children remain dependent for an extended period of time (Bogin 1999). Intensive investment in each child and the propensity for human females to have multiple dependents at one time are also complicated by a reduction in subsistence activities during the early postnatal period and lactation (e.g., Hurtado et al. 1992). Females face increasing reproductive costs throughout their reproductive stage of life. Without the assistance of others, it would be unlikely that human mothers could successfully meet the demands of multiple dependents simultaneously. To maintain high fertility and to reduce child mortality throughout our evolutionary history, females needed assistance. Hrdy (2009 and references therein) argues that allomaternal (non-maternal) assistance alters female life-history trade-offs, enabling women to produce more costly, more dependent, and more closely spaced offspring than they would be able to sustain on their own. Cooperative breeding—broadly defined as caregiving and provisioning by others—is argued to buffer maternal trade-offs and increase female fertility and child survivorship. Thus, throughout our evolutionary history allomothers (non-maternal caregivers) and alloparents (non-parental caregivers) were essential to child survivorship and reproduction. The cooperative nature of human child rearing is evident cross-culturally (e.g., Crittenden and Marlowe 2008; Gottlieb 2004; Lancy 2008; Meehan 2005) and, beyond direct caregiving, research indicates that allomaternal care has significant positive and long-lasting effects on child health (e.g., Hawkes et al. 1997; Sear and Mace 2009), child stress responses (Flinn and Leone 2009), and maternal responsiveness (Hrdy 2007; Olds et al. 2002).

Our emphasis on allomothers should not insinuate that mothers are not important or that they are not primary in attachment. On the contrary, as Hrdy (2009:68) notes, "Of all the attachments mammalian babies form, none is more powerful than that between baby primates and their mothers." Additionally, despite recent interest in documenting and exploring the significance of allomaternal investment in child physical, social, and emotional development, cross-cultural data continue to support maternal primacy in child care and rearing. Mothers offer more care to offspring than others and offer children their introduction to the social world in which they will develop (Hrdy 2009). Even among foragers, where allomaternal care is often ubiquitous, infants still receive the majority of their care from their mothers (Crittenden and Marlowe 2008; Konner 2005; Meehan 2005). However, as Konner (2005) has noted over the years, the mother-child dyad does not exist in isolation but functions within its larger social network. Consequently, the focus on the mother-child dyad has not been misguided, but rather, it has limited our ability to understand the multiplicity of factors that contribute to child attachment in a cross-cultural perspective.

Multiple Attachment and Internal Working Models

As developed by Bowlby (1969) and furthered by Ainsworth (1977a), attachment theory argues that children's attachment systems promote proximity to specific, preferred caregivers as a means to enhance infant survivorship. Attachment is a dynamic process where children's felt security, their sense of safety and protection, will develop through caregiver responsiveness (Ahnert 2005; Bretherton 1985; Chisholm 1996). It is through repeated child-caregiver interactions that children learn about their social and caregiving environment. Through this process, children develop internal working models of others and self (Ahnert 2005; Bowlby 1973). When caregivers respond appropriately, promptly, and with warmth, children will develop "secure" trusting internal working models (Ahnert 2005; Bowlby 1973; Hewlett et al. 2000; Lamb et al. 1984). For example, Hewlett and colleagues (2000) argue that among foragers, constant physical contact and affectionate and immediate response to infants' demands and needs promote children's felt security. Specifically, the socio-emotional experience that these children have with their caregivers leads to the development of "secure" internal working models.

While internal working models likely develop through early attachment relationships, the effects of these models extend beyond interpersonal relationships (Hewlett et al. 2000). As Hewlett and colleagues argue, the felt security experienced in early childhood among foragers leads to the development of an internal working model in which the individual's environment is safe and giving. For example, although there is tremendous cultural diversity among extant foragers, pan-forager characteristics emphasize sharing, cooperation, and trust (Bird-David 1990; Hewlett et al. 2000). The Aka, Nayaka, Mbuti, and Batek view others and their environments as giving, in spite of frequent food shortages and clear risk factors, and they trust that their environment will provide for them (Bird-David 1990; Hewlett et al. 2000).

Because forager children, and children around the world for that matter, rely on care and provisioning from individuals other than their parents, the formation of internal working models is likely a consequence of the overall social environment. However, despite the well-documented role of allomothers throughout the world and even early claims that care can be distributed (Bowlby 1969:303), attachment theory is still very much focused on the mother-child dyad and based on Western perceptions of the mother-child dyad and child rearing practices (LeVine 2004; Rothbaum et al. 2000; Takahashi 1990; Weisner 2005). As mothers, children, and investment strategies evolved in environments where families were part of larger social networks and offspring received significant investment from others, it is logical to assume that allomothers not only contribute to physical well-being, but are attachment figures and have clear effects on children's socio-emotional development (Kermoian and Leiderman 1986; Sagi et al. 1995; Sagi-Schwartz and Aviezer 2005; van IJzendoorn et al. 1992). Yet, the social environment and the role of multiple attachment figures have not been fully integrated into attachment theory.

It is important to note that anthropologists and psychologists have long noted that children outside of many middle-class, white, Western populations are engaged in multiple attachment relationships and that a sole focus on the mother-child dyad is inappropriate in most cultural contexts (Gottlieb 2004; Howes and Spieker 2008; Kermoian and Leiderman 1986; Lamb and Lewis 2010; Sagi et al. 1995; Seymour 2004; Tronick et al. 1992; True 1994; van IJzendoorn et al. 1992; van Ijzenoorn and Sagi 2008). Thus, the social environments in which many infants and young children are raised are relevant to attachment theory. Dense social and caregiving environments, common among foragers (e.g., Tronick et al., 1992), can encourage close, trusting relations with multiple individuals (Tronick et al. 1992). However, it is important to note, that non-maternal care in small-scale societies is not limited to forager populations. Research among the Hausa, a Nigerian population, suggested that children have three to four attachment figures and that the primary attachment figure is not even always the child's biological mother (Marvin et al. 1977).

Unfortunately, because the vast majority of attachment research continues to be conducted in laboratory settings and focused on the mother-child dyad, the role of non-maternal caregivers in children's attachment formation and emotional development is still not well understood. Therefore, it is essential to situate attachment investigations within children's larger social framework; so we may begin to investigate and document the breadth, depth, and quality of non-maternal attachment relationships, as well as their effects on children's behavior and developmental outcomes.

Cross-cultural Applicability of the SSP

In our opinion, the frequent omission of non-maternal caregivers is often due to the difficulty in determining the extent of a child's social network, children's engagement with non-maternal caregivers, and the quality of those relationships. Specifically, it has proven difficult to measure, classify, or analyze children's attachment to allomothers. The difficulty often arises from the methodology employed. Ainsworth's contributions, particularly in terms of evaluating sensitivity (Bell and Ainsworth 1972) and the SSP, are inherently focused on the mother-child dyad (Ainsworth and Bell 1970) and thus ignore the role of others, even when that role is prominent. We suggest that naturalistic observations, which capture the cultural context of child rearing, are essential in explorations, assessments, and categorizations of children's attachment relationships.

Additionally, albeit not exclusively, the SSP is often conducted without regard to cultural variation in child-rearing practices. As more thoroughly outlined in the introduction to this volume, LeVine and Miller (1990) argue that while the SSP is suitable to accessing attachment in "middle-class" American society, the test is less suitable in cultures where children have different experiences. If children rarely experience separation, we should expect their reactions to the SSP to be in excess of mild stress, and assessments of reunion episodes difficult to assess.

Due to children's expectations of care and separation, the senior author found it problematic to assess attachment utilizing the SSP among the Aka. As part of a larger project on parenting and non-maternal caregiving, she recorded a culturally modified SSP. While she could serve the role of the stranger in the procedure, a variety of children's caregivers were always close by and often within the visual range of the focal child during the procedure. Isolating Aka children with her or a field assistant was not always an option. During the recordings there were often multiple individuals present and children crawled, scooted, or walked over to another caregiver; others stayed and signaled for someone to come to them. These experiences led her to question whether children's responses to their mothers during reunions were the result of their interaction histories with their mothers, or because their grandmother, for example, was in camp and they were reacting to her presence, sensitivity, and their interaction history with her? It was clear that children's larger social environments and the cultural practice of cooperative child rearing were significant factors in children's attachment formation.

Ethnographic Background

The Aka tropical forest foragers reside in the Congo Basin Rain Forest. They practice a flexible postmarital residence pattern, where personal preference and/or family needs dictate where the families live (Meehan 2005). Camps are comprised of 6–8 huts and average 25–35 people (Hewlett 1991). Similar to other foraging populations in the region (Fouts et al. 2005), the Aka emphasize egalitarianism and sharing. Sharing occurs on a daily basis between households in camps. With few exceptions, food items from a hunt and/or a gathering expedition are shared widely among camp members. This extensive sharing pattern is expected considering the high level of cooperation needed between individuals participating in a foraging lifestyle (Hewlett 1991), and an extension of this sharing pattern can be seen in allomaternal caregiving.

Early infancy is characterized by intense caregiving. Infants and young children are held in a sling on the side of their mother or other caregiver. Children breast-feed on demand and sleep with their parents, which enables continuous night-time breast-feeding as well. Over 50 percent of Aka infants are breast-fed by other women, in addition to their mothers (Hewlett and Lamb 2002). Allomothers do approximately one-quarter of all caregiving (Meehan 2008b). Allomaternal care is undertaken by multiple individuals and caregivers span age, sex, and kin and non-kin categories (i.e., juvenile females/males, adult females/males, and elderly males/females) (Meehan 2005, 2008b).

Methods

Quantitative data were collected through a focal sampling technique (Altmann 1974). This naturalistic observation procedure, modified from Belsky et al. (1984), has been used successfully in multiple child-focused studies in recent years (e.g., Fouts et al. 2005; Hewlett et al. 2000; Meehan 2005, 2008a, 2009). The procedure requires the researcher to observe and follow a focal individual over several days covering all daylight hours (6 a.m.–6 p.m.). Observations occur in four-hour intervals from 6 a.m. to 10 a.m., 10 a.m. to 2 p.m., and 2 p.m. to 6 p.m. Observations start at the top of each hour and last for 45 minutes. This allows a 15-minute break at the end of each 45-minute segment, prior to commencing the observation again (e.g., observe and record from 6:00:00 a.m.–6:44:59 a.m., break from 6:45:00 a.m.–6:59:59 a.m., observe and record from 7:00:00 a.m. to 7:44:59 a.m., etc.). Due to the 15-minute breaks, all infants were observed for 9 of the 12 daylight hours. Observers carried tape-recorded timekeepers with earphones that directed the observer when to observe and when to record child and caregiver behavior. Observations were divided into 30-second intervals. The 30-second observations yielded 1,080 observations per child or 31,320 observations for the 29 children included in this sample.

We also conducted maternal-focal observations, following the same procedure described earlier. Behavioral observation data were collected on all but one focal child's mother.[1] Since child-care behaviors were also recorded during these observations we use both sets of observations, doubling the number of observations used in the analysis (18 hours of observation per child). Thus, data presented on maternal interactions with their children are the mean of two sets of observations and the result of 2,160 observations per child or 61,560 observations for the entire sample.

Observers were trained in the methodology in the United States at local day-care centers prior to departing for the CAR. Observers met interobserver reliability at ≥90 percent for all behavioral categories with the exception of proximity and vocalization, for which inter-reliability scores were ≥80 percent.

Behavioral variables discussed in the following analyses include infant state (i.e., crying or fussing), child attachment behaviors, caregiver behaviors, and responses to distress and/or attachment bouts, and maternal presence/absence. *Fussing* was coded if the child was awake and showed signs of agitation—emitting whining sounds or moans, but was not crying. *Crying* was recorded if a child was visibly agitated and had tears. The specific attachment behaviors include the child: *approaching* a caregiver (with clear intent to gain proximity to caregiver); *seeking* to be held through gestures or vocalizations; *reaching* for a caregiver; *touching* a caregiver (if the child is touching to maintain physical contact after seeking or reaching for a caregiver—not coded in the case of passive or accidental touching); *proffering* toward a caregiver; *crawling into the lap* of a caregiver, *kissing*, *hugging*, or *nuzzling* a caregiver; *burying his or her face* into the caregiver's lap or body; *following* a caregiver (as a means to maintain proximity—not coded if the child is simply walking behind their caregiver); and *clinging* to the body or clothing of a caregiver.

Mothers and fathers discussed in the analysis are the biological parents of the focal children. Adult females and males are those who are married, or have children, or who are beyond the age of 18 years. Juveniles are children between the ages of 4 and 18 years. While children under four have been observed performing allomaternal care, we do not consider them to be allomothers due to the difficulty in determining motivation in a three-year-old allomother and their lack of physical strength to engage in allocare.

Sample

Data were collected over two field seasons in 2009 and 2010. The total sample consists of 29 focal children between 2 weeks and 32 months old (Table 3.1). The Aka do not keep track of birth dates; therefore, age was determined by ascertaining the child's season of birth and then relative aging the child to all other children in the vicinity. Analysis describing the social world of infants and their interactions with caregivers will include all 29 children.

Table 3.1 Sample description

Age category in months	N	*Min age*	*Max age*	*Mean number of caregivers*[a]
0–6	7	.5	6	17.9
6.5–11	6	7	11	19.3
12–23	10	12	23	24.0
24–32	6	25	32	19. 7

[a]The mean number of caregivers is the total number of caregivers who care for or interact with a child over the 12-hour focal child observation period.

Age categories are: (1) 0–6 months; (2) 6.5–11 months; (3) 12–23 months; and (4) 24–32 months. We broke the first year of life into two categories because there is a clear and dramatic increase in attachment behaviors at 6.5 months—the frequency of attachment displays at 6.5 months is similar to the frequency of displays of older infants. Therefore, analyses that focus directly on attachment displays and caregiver responsiveness comprise a subsample of 22 children between 6.5 and 32 months (32 months being the upper age limit in the sample of children observed to date).

The sample is heavily biased toward males (males = 20; females = 9). This sample is part of a longitudinal study in which recruitment is continuing over the next five years. Children and their families were recruited based on availability and willingness to participate. Their participation was not declined based on the sex of their child. Whether sex plays a role in attachment displays and caregiver responsiveness will be investigated with a more sex-balanced sample in the future.

Results

As outlined at the start of the chapter, our goals are to: (1) illustrate the pluralistic nature of Aka child care; (2) investigate whether children form multiple attachments outside of the mother-child dyad; and (3) identify potential consequences of multiple attachments on child behavior. To achieve the first goal, we present data on the nature of both maternal and allomaternal child care among the Aka. We document the frequency of maternal and allomaternal care over the first three years of children's lives. To achieve the second goal, we analyze children's attachment behaviors to determine whether Aka children form multiple attachments with non-maternal caregivers. Specifically, we present data on children's behaviors meant to promote or maintain proximity to a caregiver. We also describe child and caregiver interactions during attachment bouts (defined later). Moreover, we analyze maternal and allomaternal responses to children's attachment bouts to identify the characteristics of those relationships. In particular, we examine whether allomothers are sensitive and responsive caregivers and thus whether they might be contributing to secure emotional development in infancy and early childhood. To achieve the third goal, examining the consequences of multiple attachments, we present data on the cultural context of the maternal-child relationship, specifically focusing on maternal-child separation. We describe the frequency and length of typical Aka mother-child separations, as well as maternal and child behaviors as separations occur and during the subsequent reunions. Through the use of naturalistic observational data, we seek to offer insights into the cultural context of the Aka mother-child relationship and the cultural pattern of mother-child separation. Additionally and directly related to our third goal, these data allow us to gauge children's attachment to non-maternal caregivers during moments when their primary attachment figure is not present. We investigate whether the highly sensitive and intimate care that Aka children receive from their mothers primes children to expect constant maternal care. Alternatively, we explore whether their experience with non-maternal caregivers mediates stress during maternal separations. The naturalistic data and following analyses provide a much needed cultural framework to explore the effect of allomothers on children's behaviors during maternal-child separations and reunions.

Aka Maternal and Allomaternal Caregiving in Infancy and Early Childhood

Mothers do the majority of caregiving throughout early childhood. Figure 3.1 illustrates the average frequency with which mothers held, touched, or were in proximity (within a forearm's distance) to their children over the course of daylight hours. As children develop, specific categories of care (e.g., holding) may become less essential, but physical contact and access to caregivers remains important. Figure 3.2 illustrates the composite variables of physical contact and access to mothers. Physical contact with mothers is high in infancy, yet during the second and third years, mothers are in physical contact with their children less than half the day. While forager mothers are characterized as highly indulgent, as their children age and mothers begin to reproduce again, they face energy expenditure trade-offs, which can result in less energy devoted to older children (Hawkes et al. 1997; Kramer 2010). This reduction in care by mothers and access to mothers occurs earlier than we expected. Child age (in months) is negatively correlated with maternal holding (Pearson's $r = -0.629$, $p = 0.000$) and proximity (Pearson's $r = -0.480$, $p = 0.008$). Furthermore, the composite variables of maternal physical contact (the total frequency of holding and touching) (Pearson's $r = -0.559$, $p = 0.002$), and access (the total frequency of physical contact and proximity) (Pearson's $r = -0.481$, $p = 0.008$) with children also show a highly significant decline over the first three years of life. In sum, children experience intensive maternal care during infancy, but mothers significantly reduce the amount of time and frequency of contact with their children thereafter.

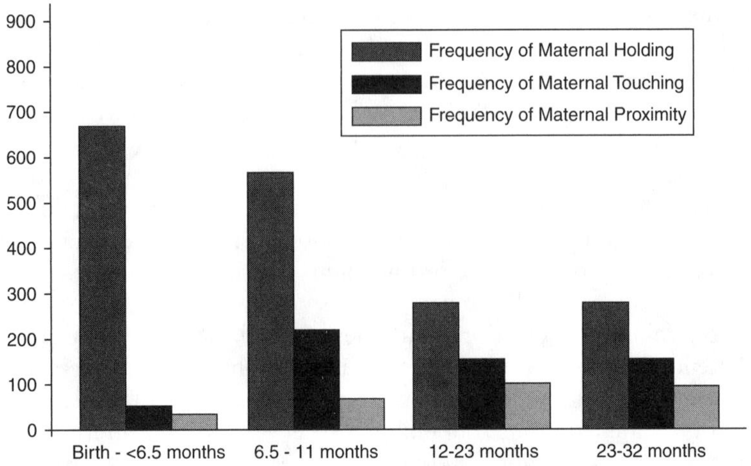

Figure 3.1 Mean frequency of maternal holding, touching, and proximity. The frequency of intervals caregivers engaged the focal child, rather than the number of minutes, is displayed to illustrate the depth of care. A mother can hold, touch, or be in proximity to a child during an interval, but there can be multiple allomothers engaged with a child in one interval. The frequency of interactions enable a better comparison between maternal care and allomaternal care.

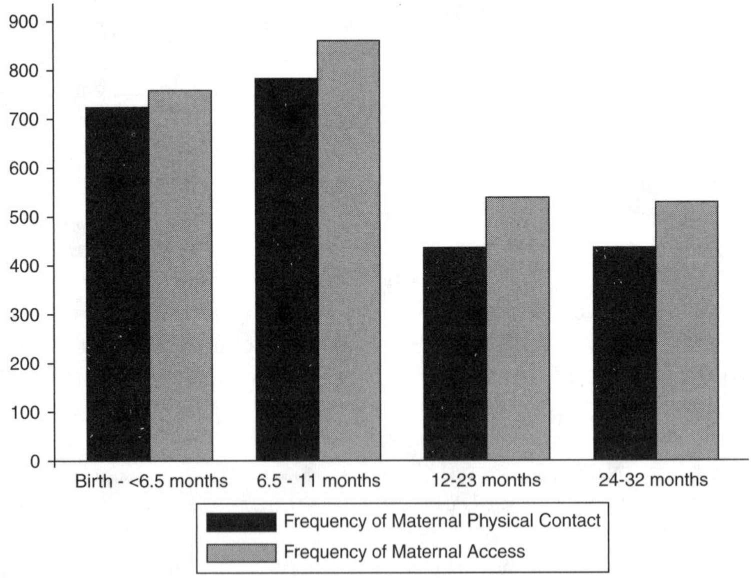

Figure 3.2 Mean frequency of maternal physical contact and access. The frequency of intervals caregivers engaged the focal child, rather than the number of minutes, is displayed to illustrate the depth of care. A mother can hold, touch, or be in proximity to a child during an interval, but there can be multiple allomothers engaged with a child in one interval. The frequency of interactions enable a better comparison between maternal care and allomaternal care.

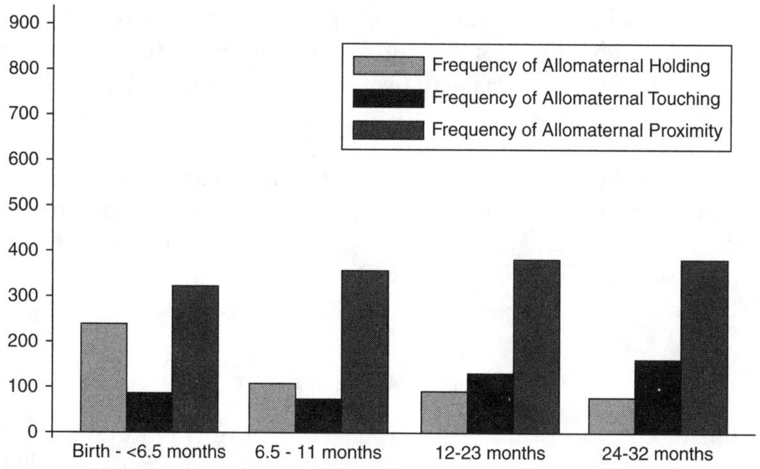

Figure 3.3 Mean frequency of allomaternal holding, touching, and proximity. The frequency of intervals caregivers engaged the focal child, rather than the number of minutes, is displayed to illustrate the depth of care.

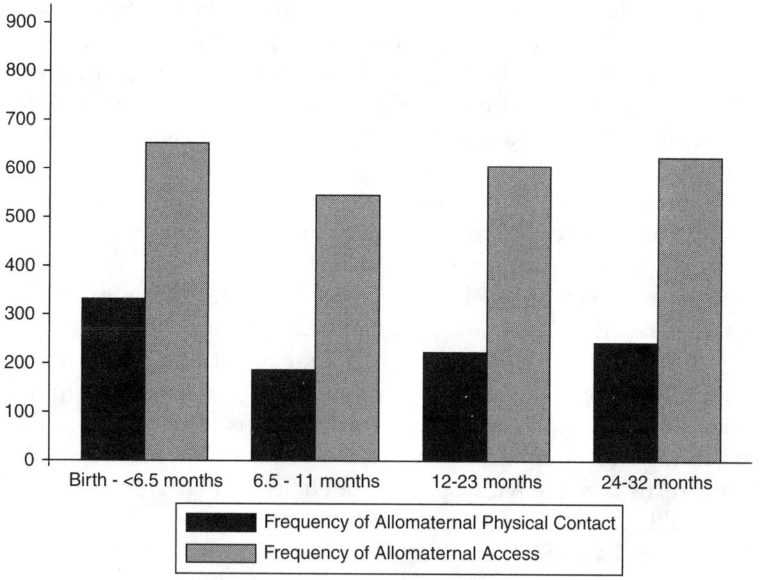

Figure 3.4 Mean frequency of allomaternal physical contact and access. The frequency of intervals caregivers engaged the focal child, rather than the number of minutes, is displayed to illustrate the depth of care.

Data demonstrate that while mothers are primary caregivers, offering the majority of care, allomothers frequently also contribute to child care. Figures 3.3 and 3.4 illustrate the mean frequency of allomaternal contact with children. Similar to mothers, allomothers significantly decrease the frequency of holding as children age (Pearson's $r = -0.487$, $p = 0.007$). This reduction in holding is not surprising—children become heavier, more mobile, and physically independent over time. However, in contrast to mothers, allomothers demonstrate a statistical trend toward increased touching of children (Pearson's $r = 0.340$, $p = 0.071$) and show no significant reduction in the frequency of proximity, or the composite variables of physical contact (holding and touching) or access (holding, touching, and proximity). Therefore, while maternal investment significantly decreases over the first three years, allomaternal investment, with the exception of holding, stays stable or increases.

Multiple Attachments

As shown, mothers are primary caregivers (i.e., they offer more direct care and provisioning than other caregivers), yet they are not the only individuals to offer investment to children. We recognize that allomaternal investment may not necessarily result in secure and trusting attachment relationships—not all individuals in a child's social network are attachment figures (Thompson 2005). Yet, we predict that the frequency of allomaternal-child contact encourages the formation of strong and trusting relationships with others and hypothesize that Aka children form multiple attachment relationships. We take attachment behaviors to be a measure of such trusting relationships and predict that children will display attachment behaviors to multiple individuals over the course of a day. The attachment behaviors recorded are characterized by actions in which the child sought to maintain or establish contact and/or proximity. As already indicated by our descriptions of how these behaviors were coded, they are not passive interactions, such as being held, general physical contact, visual and/or verbal contact. Because of this, we argue that when displayed to caregivers they illustrate not simply common caregiver-child interactions, but significant relationships.

Table 3.2 shows the mean number of attachment bouts (continuous displays of attachment behaviors) by age category. The number of individuals to whom children display attachment behaviors is relatively small in comparison to the size of children's caregiving network. As noted in Table 3.1, children are in contact with approximately 20 caregivers across daylight hours. Notably though, not all allomothers are attachment figures—children display these behaviors to only a small subset of individuals. On average, children direct attachment behaviors to six different caregivers (including mothers) each day. Allomothers are the object of approximately one-third of all attachment displays. Additionally, over 60 percent of caregivers who had attachment behaviors directed toward them receive multiple attachment displays from a focal child over one 12-hour observation period. Attachment displays are also not directed to specific categories of caregivers (i.e., only adults).

Table 3.2 Child attachment bouts, mean number of responders, and percentage of attachment bouts directed toward mothers, fathers, adult allomothers, and juvenile allomothers

Age category (months)	N	*Mean number of attachment bouts*	*Min*	*Max*	*SD*	*Mean number responders*	*Min*	*Max*	*SD*	*% of attachment behaviors directed toward*				
										Mothers	*Fathers*	*Adult allomothers*	*Juvenile allomothers*	*Allomothers (total)*
6.5–11	6	53.5	3	102	40.6	4.5	1	8	2.9	74.4	0.0	7.3	18.4	25.6
12–23	10	45.4	18	98	23.7	6.5	3	11	2.9	62.7	3.9	18.3	15.1	37.3
24–32	6	40.7	30	58	10.7	6.7	2	13	3.9	61.4	13.8	14.1	10.7	38.6
All children 6.5–32 months	22	46.3	3	102	26.2	6	1	13	3.2	65.5	5.5	14.1	14.8	34.5

Maternal and Allomaternal Responsiveness and Sensitivity

While the data presented earlier show that children are in contact with multiple caregivers across daylight hours and that they are attached to a subset of these caregivers, they offer little illustration regarding the characteristics of these relationships. For example, children spend the majority of time in close physical contact or proximity to their mothers in early childhood, yet allomothers provide approximately one-quarter of child care (Meehan 2005) and those who are providing the care may approach child care with differing skill levels, knowledge, motivation, emotional connection, and even physical strength. Thus, it is possible that while children are surrounded by multiple caregivers, these relationships are not equal. The mere presence of—and investment by—multiple caregivers may not equate to sensitive care. As discussed earlier, sensitive and responsive care among foragers has been associated with the development of trusting relationships and secure internal working models (Hewlett et al. 2000). Yet if one-quarter of the care that children receive is nonresponsive, insensitive, or rejecting, it is essential to identify and explore the effects of such care. For that reason, we examine and compare maternal and allomaternal responsiveness and sensitivity, investigating two relevant components of child care. The first, response to distress, is culturally relevant as forager child-care patterns are in part characterized by quick responsiveness to children's needs (Hewlett et al. 2000). Second, we investigate caregiver responses to attachment displays.

Caregiver Responsiveness to Crying and Fussing

Distress is relevant because soothing a fussing or crying child requires not only sensitivity, but the trust of the child. A young child who is already in an agitated state will not likely be soothed by an incompetent or unfamiliar caregiver, one that the child does not trust. Distress displays and responses to them are a good measure of both allomothers' willingness to invest and the children's trust in these caregivers. Our results indicate that mothers are primary responders to young children's distress displays, responding to over half (51.2%) of the displays. A non-maternal caregiver is the sole responder to approximately 18 percent of all distress displays. Only 2.5 percent of distress displays are not responded to by caregivers. The remaining approximately 29 percent of responses are comprised of simultaneous responders (e.g., an aunt and a mother) to the same distress bout. Distress displays, unlike attachment bouts, are not necessarily directed at a particular individual. When multiple individuals responded it was not possible to determine who responded first and which caregiver was successful at soothing the child. Therefore, in order to determine caregiver success at soothing a distressed child, bouts that included multiple responders have been eliminated from our analysis.

There is no significant difference in response time between mothers and allomothers to child distress displays (mean number of intervals – mothers = 0.118; allomothers = 0.123; $t = 0.0514$, $p = 0.959$). Additionally, there is no significant difference in the mean number of intervals it took mothers and allomothers to soothe a fussing or crying child (mothers = 1.616; allomothers = 1.443; $t = -1.176$, $p = 0.240$). Allomaternal success in soothing is particularly impressive considering that allomothers in this sample never nursed, a typical maternal response to children's distress displays. We argue that this demonstrates that allomothers respond promptly and appropriately to children's cues, which defines sensitive care (Ahnert 2005).

Caregiver Responsiveness to Attachment Displays

In our analyses regarding caregiver responsiveness and sensitivity to attachment bouts we predicted that because allomothers are highly invested in caregiving, as well as responsive and successful in soothing child distress, they will be responsive, sensitive, affectionate, and rarely rejecting of children's attachment bouts. Additionally, juveniles are highly engaged in child care among the Aka and the quality of their responsiveness is of particular importance. They represent half of all allomothers and receive approximately 15 percent of attachment displays to all caregivers, or over 50 percent of attachment displays to allomothers. Due to the frequent contact with and investment by juvenile allomothers, we predict that they will be equally responsive, sensitive, and affectionate as adult allomothers in response to child attachment displays. If juveniles are not responsive, offer insensitive care, and are more rejecting, infants and young children will experience inconsistent care across the day, influencing their overall sense of security.

In order to evaluate our hypotheses regarding variation in maternal and allomaternal sensitivity and responsiveness to attachment bouts, principal components analysis (PCA) was conducted. PCA is a data reduction method that condenses a large number of variables into a few compact "latent" variables, called components. These components contain all of the information from the original variables, but they are more easily employed in more common statistical techniques, such as *t*-tests or linear regression. The technique constructs these latent variables by determining which of the original variables are closely related to one another. These variables have certain correlations with the new latent variables, called loadings. A variable is said to "load highly" on a component if its loading is above 0.3. Variables that load highly on a component define the component, and the component can then be named (Kline 1994).

In this analysis, watch/check, general care, feed, nurse, vocalize, and physical contact load together on the first component (see Table 3.3). These behaviors demonstrate sensitive, attentive care. Accordingly, we call component 1 "sensitive responses." Rejecting and ignoring behaviors, "negative affect," loaded highly on component 2. Soothing and affectionate behaviors, "positive affect," loaded highly on component 3.

Table 3.4 shows the mean PCA component scores for maternal and allomaternal responses to child attachment bouts. Maternal PCA scores are significantly higher for sensitivity (comp 1: $t = -9.78$, $p < 0.001$, $df = 120$) and

Table 3.3 Component loadings for responses to attachment behaviors

Sensitive responses (variance explained = 45.7%)		*Negative affect (variance explained = 15.6%)*		*Positive affect (variance explained = 15.6%)*	
Nurse	0.466	Reject	0.656	Affection	0.703
Feed	0.439	No response	0.633	Soothe	0.646
Watch/check	0.423				
Vocalize	0.396				
Physical contact	0.372				
General care	0.340				

Table 3.4 Mean component scores[a] for mothers and allomothers

Attachment figures	*Sensitive responses*	*Negative affect*	*Positive affect*
Mothers[b]	3.02	1.01	1.23
Allomothers[c]	−0.67	−0.22	−0.27

[a] Component scores have a mean of zero across the entire sample. A negative score indicates that caregivers had less than the mean of the sample on that component.
[b] $n = 22$.
[c] $n = 100$.

positive affect (comp 3: $t = -5.74$, $p < 0.001$, $df = 120$) than allomothers. However, mothers are also significantly more likely to respond negatively to their children (comp 2: $t = -4.52$, $p < 0.001$, $df = 120$). Mothers are more likely to either physically or verbally reject and ignore their child's attachment displays than allomothers. It may appear counterintuitive for mothers to be both more affectionate and high investing on one hand, and more rejecting or aloof on the other. However, closer contact presents more opportunities for emotional ambivalence. Moreover, as Hewlett (1991:113) has noted, mothers attempt to balance work and child care and so are more likely to be impatient with older children.

To investigate variation in allomaternal responsiveness, we compared juvenile and adult allomothers on the three components listed in Table 3.3. Adults trend toward showing more positive affect than juveniles (juveniles = −0.403; adults = −0.133; $t = -1.88$, $p = 0.06$), but are not significantly more sensitive or more negative than juveniles in their responses to child attachment displays directed at them. In other words, adults show more positive affect, but juveniles, whom readers will remember are the objects of 50 percent of allomaternal attachment bouts, are equally as sensitive and are just as unlikely to be rejecting to children.

Results indicate that mothers and allomothers are similar in terms of their responses and success in soothing a distressed child. Mothers have significantly higher PCA scores for sensitive and positive affect in response to attachment bouts, but they were also significantly more rejecting to their children's attachment bouts. In many respects, the higher loading on sensitive care by mothers is expected. While not dismissing the higher scores for sensitive responses, it is important to note that mothers received and responded to more bouts and that many (but not all) of the attachment behaviors recorded are mother-centered (Field 1996:544). Additionally, nursing, which loaded the highest in PCA analysis under sensitive care, was only performed by mothers in response to attachment bouts. Because nursing was a fairly typical maternal response to an attachment bout, and allomothers did not nurse, allomothers could not score as high on sensitive care as did mothers. As discussed, allomaternal nursing does occur among the Aka, but is limited to early infancy (Hewlett and Lamb 2005), outside of the age range of our analysis on attachment. Considering the similarities between mothers and allomothers in response to and success at soothing a distressed child, and the lower rejection score for allomothers, non-maternal caregivers prove to be engaged and responsive attachment figures. Mothers may be more sensitive, but that does not mean that allomothers are unresponsive or insensitive toward children, or that they reject them. Adult alloparents were significantly more affectionate in response to children's attachment bouts, but there was no difference between adult and juvenile sensitivity and rejecting behaviors.

The Context of Mother-Child Separations

The Aka represent an important case study in which to examine maternal-child separation and its cross-cultural applicability for assessing attachment for two reasons. First, based on the current and previously published data on maternal care, Aka children spend the majority of the day in contact or at least within eyesight of their mothers, and young children are never left alone (Meehan 2005, 2008b). Children are often held while sleeping and if placed down, they are within eyesight or hearing range of their caregivers. Therefore, much like what was reported among the Ganda (Ainsworth 1977b), and to a lesser extent among the Japanese (Takahashi 1990), we should expect that children will experience maternal-child separation as unusual and potentially stressful. However, because allomaternal care is so pervasive and children form multiple attachment relationships, we might alternatively predict that children would not be stressed during separations, as they have additional attachment figures to rely on. Ainsworth (1977b) described Ganda children being left with allomothers during separations and, in spite of the presence of familiar caregivers, those children loudly protested maternal separations. The presence of allomothers among the Ganda did not seem to mitigate child stress during separations. Thus, in the following analyses, we seek to tease apart the multiple factors that might influence maternal and child behaviors and responses to separations. These analyses are targeted toward understanding the cultural context of maternal-child separations, children's reactions to such separations, and how or whether a multiple caregiving environment might affect children's sense of security during separations.

We calculated the number of 30-second intervals in which the focal children's mothers were coded as *not present*. As predicted, Aka mother-child separations are infrequent. On average mothers only leave their infants and young children 2.9 times per day (min = 0; max = 8). Therefore, maternal–child separations are less frequent than what is found among both the Baltimore sample and the Ganda sample (Ainsworth 1977b). The average length of the separation is 19.48 minutes (min = 30 seconds; max = 3 hours). Approximately 55 percent of maternal-child separation bouts lasted 5 minutes or less, 25 percent lasted between 6 and 10 minutes, 9.4 percent lasted between 30 and 60 minutes, and 10.9 percent lasted over 1 hour.

Despite the infrequency of maternal-child separations, Aka infants and children rarely displayed strong reactions to maternal separations. In only 3 out of the 58 separations did we observe a child cry during or immediately following a separation from his or her mother. Children fussed in 12 out of the 58 separations, but children did not display any distress (fussing and/or crying) in approximately 74 percent of the separations. As expected, they were always in the physical company of or near an allomother.

It is possible that there are specific maternal behaviors or child characteristics that may affect children's responses to maternal separation. Thus, we tested whether Aka maternal behavior (the length of separations) is associated with their child's age. We assumed that mothers would be less likely to leave younger children and/or they would alter the length of the separation according to their child's age. Surprisingly, the frequency of separation is not significantly associated with the child's age (Pearson's $r = 0.1907$, $p = 0.395$), nor is the age of the child positively associated with the minimum (Pearson's $r = 0.2206$, $p = 0.3791$) or maximum (Pearson's $r = 0.1955$, $p = 0.3834$) length of separation.

During reunion episodes, close to 35 percent of the infants did not immediately respond to their mother's presence. Even after 3 minutes, approximately 25 percent of the infants still had not visually, verbally, or physically engaged with their mothers (see Table 3.5). Infants were observed looking at their mothers in the first 3 minutes following a reunion in only 17.3 percent of the reunion bouts recorded. Twenty-one percent of the infants fussed, but only 3.9 percent cried during the first 3 minutes. As with most Aka child fussing and/or crying episodes, they ended quickly. Additionally, in only 30 percent of the reunion episodes did children display attachment behaviors that sought to gain or maintain proximity to their mother.

A mother's attention after arriving in camp, particularly during the first minute, is directed toward placing her baskets or other containers on the ground, although this activity rarely takes more than 30 seconds. As seen in Table 3.6, approximately 35 percent of mothers did not engage their child during the first minute after they returned. Only 32 percent commenced physical contact with their child within the first minute, with that number rising to just over 50 percent within the first 3 minutes. However, approximately 25 percent of mothers did not verbally, physically, or even visually engage their children during the first 3 minutes of a reunion.

Table 3.5 The percentage of child responses to their mother in the first minute and the first three minutes following a separation

Behavior[a]	*Reunion—minute one*	*Reunion—minute zero–three*
No response	34.7	25.0
Fuss	17.3	21.2
Look at mother	15.4	17.3
Vocalize to mother	7.7	13.5
Approach mother	7.7	15.4
Sleep	3.9	3.9
Kiss/hug/nuzzle	1.9	1.9
Cry	1.9	3.9
Smile at mother	1.9	1.9
Follow mother	0	1.9
Touch mother	0	9.6
Crawls in mother's lap	0	1.9
Reach for mother	0	0
Proffer to mother	0	0
Buries face in mother	0	0
Cling to mother	0	0

$n = 52$.
[a] The percentage total to more than 100 percent. Infants often display multiple behaviors toward their mother during one reunion episode.

In sum, despite the infrequency of maternal-child separations, the majority of children do not display strong reactions to these separations. In addition, response to reunions is muted. Even in this physically intimate caregiving environment, children are not necessarily focused on gaining proximity to their mothers during a reunion. We argue that the pluralistic nature of children's attachments allows them to feel secure in the absence of their mothers.

Maternal Effects on Children's Emotional States

In the following analysis we explore whether children's experiences with their mothers affect children's stress levels during separations. Bell and Ainsworth (1972) suggest that infants whose mothers respond promptly to their crying begin to cry much less between six and nine months. Therefore, we test whether their experiences with maternal care will result in less need to "proceed directly to higher arousal level manifestations" (Konner 1977:319). If children have highly sensitive mothers, we predict that even

Table 3.6 The percentage of maternal responses to their child in the first minute and the first three minutes following a separation

Behavior[a]	*Reunion—minute one*	*Reunion—minute zero–three*
No response	34.6	25.0
Proximity	19.2	23.1
Vocalize	19.2	28.9
Hold	17.3	26.9
Touch	15.4	25.0
Nurse	3.9	15.4
General care	7.7	9.6
Watch/check	7.7	17.3
Soothe	3.8	7.7
Affection	1.9	1.9
Feed	1.9	7.7
Play	0	1.9
Reject child	0	0

$n = 52$.
[a] The percentage total to more than 100 percent. Mothers often display multiple behaviors toward their children during one reunion episode.

during separations they will be less likely to become aroused as they have experience and know that their mothers will return and provide for them.

There are three potential confounds to the following analysis that need to be addressed. First, three of our focal mothers never left their children during the entire observation period. These children may have been fussier than other children, making it difficult for their mothers to leave them. For example, Winn et al. (1989) found that Efe 4.5-month-olds who cried more were likely to be closer to their mothers because allomothers were unable to soothe them. The three infants in our sample whose mothers never left them may have been fussier on average and this made it difficult for their mothers to leave them in the care of others. However, the mean difference between the number of intervals these children cried ($n = 3$, mean = 41) compared to those children whose mothers did leave them ($n = 19$, mean = 54.2), was not significant ($t = -0.793$, $p = 0.4371$, $df = 20$). Second, children's age might explain some of the variation in their frequency of crying during maternal absence. While children statistically trend toward reducing their frequency of crying from 6.5 to 32 months (Pearson's $r = -0.3694$, $p = 0.09$), age is not a significant factor in distress signaling when mothers are absent (Pearson's $r = -0.0863$, $p = 0.68$). Third, because there is variation in how often mothers left their young children in the care of others, we examine whether children cry and fuss more if their mothers are gone for a greater percentage of the day. Again, there is no association. The percentage of the day that mothers are absent does not increase external signals of distress (Pearson's $r = -0.1991$, $p = 0.3$).

As these confounds do not appear to affect our analyses we examined whether maternal sensitivity is associated with child distress across the day or during separations. Contrary to our prediction, we found that maternal sensitivity is not associated with the frequency of crying across the entire day (Pearson's $r = 0.111$, $p = 0.623$). Furthermore, maternal sensitivity is not associated with the frequency of distress signaling during mother-child separations (Pearson's $r = -0.2803$, $p = 0.245$).

Allomaternal Effects on Children's Emotional States

As neither a child's mother-child interaction histories nor a mother's sensitivity seem to affect child distress, we next examine whether children's experiences with allomaternal attachment figures may be mitigating children's stress responses during maternal-child separations. Considering that these attachment figures offer sensitive and responsive care to children, we predict that the level of children's distress in the absence of their mothers will be negatively associated with allomaternal sensitivity. Specifically, maternal absence will prove to be less stressful, as there are likely several individuals present with whom the infant or young child has a strong attachment. We found a correlation between the mean principal component score of sensitive care for all of a child's allomothers with the frequency of child crying (during

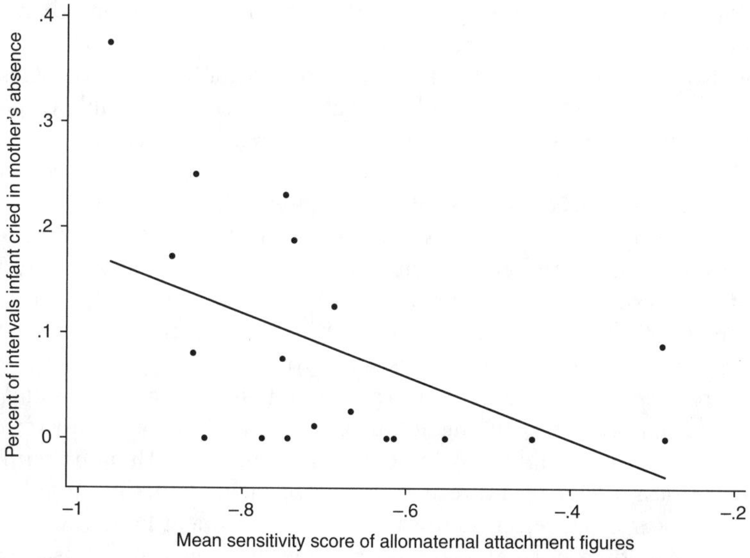

Figure 3.5 Relationship between child distress and allomaternal sensitivity during mother-child separation. Pearson's $r = -0.505$, $p = 0.0274$.

mother absence). There is a significant negative association between allomaternal sensitivity and children's distress signaling (Figure 3.5). Children with highly sensitive allomothers fuss and cry less during mother-child separations than do children with less sensitive allomothers. As mentioned, these analyses indicated that this effect is not the result of maternal sensitivity affecting child behavior during her absence or even across the day. Children's distress displays during separation bouts are associated with allomaternal sensitivity scores, but not with maternal sensitivity scores.

Discussion

Children receive the majority of their care from their mothers; however, allomaternal care is extensive among the Aka. Allomaternal investment commences early and, with the exception of holding, the frequency of care and interaction with others remains stable or increases over children's first three years. While not all caregivers are attachment figures, children display attachment behaviors to an average of six individuals. Because the coding of attachment behaviors excluded passive interactions, these attachment displays signal that these individuals are attachment figures. Support for multiple attachment relationships is also seen in our results regarding caregiver-child interactions during attachment displays. Beyond children displaying attachment behaviors to multiple individuals, children's displays are almost always responded to by the object of the attachment display, indicating that these particular caregivers are sensitive to children's cues. Mothers supplied the greatest number of responses to their children's attachment behaviors (and were the focus of the greatest number of bouts); however, allomothers were the object of over one-third of all attachment bouts.

We also examined caregivers' responses to children's distress displays and attachment bouts to determine whether children receive variable responses and/or quality of responses from the wide range of caregivers to whom they displayed attachment behavior. Mothers and allomothers are equally responsive to and successful at soothing children's distress displays. Mothers scored higher than allomothers in terms of sensitivity and positive affect when responding to attachment behaviors. However, as mentioned, nursing loaded highest on the sensitivity score and is a response that only mothers performed. Mothers were also more likely to be rejecting to their infants than were allomothers. In sum, as is seen cross-culturally, mothers are primary caregivers. They interact with their infants more than others and they have more opportunities to engage in sensitive, affectionate, and rejecting behaviors with their children. Allomothers are sensitive, although their interactions are less frequent and responses do not include nursing. In addition, they are almost never rejecting toward infant attachment bouts.

We also explored normal, everyday mother-child separations as a way to examine children's attachments and felt security. The majority of children did not display strong reactions to their mothers' departure, although variation exists. Consequently, we examined whether maternal sensitivity was associated with children's emotional state during separations. Aka mothers are well-documented as sensitive and responsive caregivers. A child's interaction history with his or her mother may result in children not feeling distress during separations. However, maternal sensitivity scores are not associated with the frequency of children's distress behaviors during naturalistic separations.

We then examined whether non-maternal attachment figures mitigated children's distress response during separations. Results indicated that children with sensitive allomothers are less distressed during maternal absence. Specifically, there is a significant negative association between allomaternal sensitivity and the frequency of fussing and crying during mother-child separations. It is possible that children who do not display external distress signals may be internalizing stress (Bensel 2009). However, we argue that in this cultural context—high levels of allomaternal care, quick responses to children's attachment displays, and the sensitive nature of responses—Aka children are not internalizing stress during maternal separation episodes. Rather, sensitive allomaternal responses to distress and attachment bouts mean that a child's physical and emotional needs are often met by multiple individuals. Our results support Hewlett and colleagues (2000) who argued that Aka children's early experiences prime them to trust others. However, our study also uncovers significant intra-cultural variation in this population.

We recognize that a limitation of the current study is the small sample size, although the detail provided through the observational method is robust. As data collection on the larger research project is ongoing, future research, with a larger sample, will enable us to examine the intra-cultural variability in maternal and allomaternal sensitivity and whether there is concordance in caregiving and response styles between mothers and allomothers. As demonstrated, while most Aka children do not experience distress during separations and reunions, the pattern was not universal. Understanding child temperament and dyadic interaction histories between children and their caregivers will enable us to tease apart variation in children's attachment security and the socioecological factors underlying such diversity.

These results offer insights into the methods utilized to examine children's security classifications. Aka children will not likely ever experience a situation similar to the SSP. If we were to conduct a traditional SSP with infants, it could be the first time in an infant's life that they were alone and not able to at least have visual contact with a familiar face. Even in Japan, where mothers told researchers that they had only left their infant a few times in the past few months with another caregiver (Takahashi 1990), it seems reasonable to assume that a middle-class Japanese mother might have placed her infant on the floor or in a bed and left the room, where a child would not be able to see or hear his or her mother. This is not likely to happen among the Aka. Considering the cultural context of child rearing, the senior author's previous experience with the SSP, and the infrequent occurrence of maternal-child separations, we feel that the use of a traditional SSP would be so novel and so stressful as to limit its explanatory power. However, given the physically close and intimate relationship children have with their mothers and the fact that mother-child separations occur infrequently, it was possible for children to experience mild stress during separations.

Our findings suggest that among the Aka and potentially in other cultures with child-rearing systems defined by dense social networks, children will not only have multiple attachments, but their expectations of their primary attachment figure might be diffused. In the West, the majority of children develop their primary attachment to their mother, and possibly their father, but most additional attachment figures are subsequently developed in infancy or when children enter day care or school (Howes and Spieker 2008). Aka children, on the other hand, are integrated into the social fabric of Aka life from the moment of birth. It is more likely that multiple attachments form simultaneously rather than sequentially, as they do in Western populations, and children's expectations regarding who will care for and protect them is naturally more distributed. Thus, children's responses to separations and reunions will not fit Western models of child behavior. Classifying these responses in light of the mother-child relationship only may be unreliable. If children do not visually or physically seek out their mother upon her return, which we found to be common, is it because they are demonstrating an avoidant/insecure attachment to their mother, or is it because they are content in their knowledge that other individuals are always ready, able, and willing to attend to them? In Western contexts, where children have few caregivers outside of their immediate family, "others" may be less likely to be emotionally invested and less likely to be seen by a child as responsive to his or her needs. Unease during maternal absence and the presence of a stranger and related responses to reunions with mothers make sense and are expected for these children, given their cultural experiences. However, we should expect this pattern to vary cross-culturally. Future research that explores how caregiving practices in diverse contexts enhance or diminish the formation of multiple attachments and their significance in child development is clearly needed.

Finally, our results emphasize that the focus on the mother-child dyad, particularly in non-Western contexts is limited in scope and has underrepresented the role of others in attachment theory. We suggest that naturalistic observations of children in their day-to-day social environments around the world may shed light on the cultural context of children's attachments. There are a wide variety of child-care arrangements throughout the world and the SSP is not appropriate in all cultural contexts. While it may remain challenging to incorporate naturalistic observations and elucidate the cultural context of parenting and child rearing into current attachment research, it is a promising and worthwhile avenue to pursue.

Acknowledgments

The research reported in this chapter was supported by a grant from the Leakey Foundation and a National Science Foundation CAREER Award

(BCS-9055213). The authors would like to thank Naomi Quinn and Jeannette Mageo for their thoughtful and helpful comments on earlier drafts. We would also like to thank the Aka families who have so generously shared their lives with us, Courtney Helfrecht, Mark Caudell, Jennifer Wilcox Roulette, and Michelle Dillon for assistance with data collection, Robert Quinlan for statistical review on an earlier draft, and our local field assistants, Eduard Mboula, Francis Aubin Moboulou, Guy Alain Kolet, Matthieu Banzengola, Hervé Dopeningue, and Mesmin Dopeningue.

Note

1. One child's mother left unexpectedly during the observation period. Therefore, we only collected child focal observations on that subject. Data for that child's interactions with his mother are based on the child focal observations only and not an average.

References

Ahnert, Lieselotte. 2005. "Parenting and Alloparenting: The Impact on Attachment in Humans." In *Attachment and Bonding: A New Synthesis*, C. Sue Carter, Lieselotte Ahnert, Klaus E. Grossmann, Sarah B. Hrdy, Michael E. Lamb, Stephen W. Porges, and Norbert Sachser, eds., pp. 229–244. Cambridge, MA: The MIT Press.

Ahnert, Lieslotte, Tatjana Meischner, and Alfred Schmidt. 2000. "Maternal Sensitivity and Attachment in East German and Russian Family Networks." In *The Organization of Attachment Relationships: Maturation, Culture and Context*, Patricia M. Crittenden and Angelika H. Claussen, eds., pp. 61–74. New York: Cambridge University Press.

Ainsworth, Mary D. Salter. 1977a. "Attachment Theory and Its Utility in Cross-Cultural Research." In *Culture and Infancy: Variations in the Human Experience*, P. Herbert Leiderman, Steven R. Tulkin, and Anne Rosenfeld, eds., pp. 49–67. New York, NY: Academic Press.

Ainsworth, Mary D. Salter. 1977b. "Infant Development and the Mother-Infant Interaction among Ganda and American Families." In *Culture and Infancy: Variations in the Human Experience*, P. Herbert Leiderman, Steven R. Tulkin, and Anne Rosenfeld, eds., pp. 119–149. New York: Academic Press.

Ainsworth, Mary D. Salter, and Silvia M. Bell. 1970. "Attachment, Exploration, and Separation: Illustrated by the Behavior of One-Year-Olds in a Strange Situation." *Child Development* 41:49–67.

Altmann, Jeanne. 1974. "Observational Study of Behavior: Sampling Methods." *Behavior* 49:227–267.

Bell, Sylvia M., and Mary D. Salter Ainsworth. 1972. "Infant Crying and Maternal Responsiveness." *Child Development* 42(4):1171–1190.

Belsky, Jay, Michael Rovine, and Dawn G. Taylor. 1984. "The Pennsylvania Infant and Family Development Project, III: The Origins of Individual Differences in Infant-Mother Attachment: Maternal and Infant Contributions." *Child Development* 55(3):718–728.

Bensel, Joachim. 2009. "Separation Stress in Early Childhood: Harmless Side Effect of Modern Care-giving Practices or Risk Factor for Development?" In *Substitute Parents: Biological and Social Perspectives on Alloparenting in Human Societies*, Gillian Bentley and Ruth Mace, eds., pp. 287–303. Oxford, UK: Berghahn Books.

Bird-David, Nurit. 1990. "The Giving Environment: Another Perspective on the Economic System of Gatherer-Hunters." *Current Anthropology* 31(2):189–196.

Blurton Jones, Nicholas G., and Frank W. Marlowe. 2002. "Selection for Delayed Maturity: Does it Take 20 Years to Learn to Hunt and Gather?" *Human Nature* 13(2):199–238.

Bogin, Barry. 1999. *Patterns of Human Growth*. Cambridge: Cambridge University Press.

Bowlby, John. 1969. *Attachment and Loss Volume 1: Attachment*. New York, NY: Persus Books.

Bowlby, John. 1973. *Attachment and Loss, Volume 2: Separation*. New York: Basic Books.

Bretherton, Inge. 1985. "Attachment Theory: Retrospect and Prospect." *Monographs of the Society for Research in Child Development* 50(1/2):3–35.

Chisholm, James, S. 1996. "The Evolutionary Ecology of Attachment Organization." *Human Nature* 7(1):1–37.

Crittenden, Alyssa N., and Frank W. Marlowe. 2008. "Allomaternal Care among the Hadza of Tanzania." *Human Nature* 19(3):249–262.

Field, Tiffany. 1996. "Attachment and Separation in Young Children." *Annual Review of Psychology* 47:541–561.

Flinn, Mark V., and David V. Leone. 2009. "Alloparental Care and the Ontogeny of Glucocorticoid Stress Response among Stepchildren." In *Substitute Parents: Biological and Social Perspectives on Alloparenting in Human Societies*, Gillain Bentley and Ruth Mace, eds., pp. 212–231. Oxford: Berghahn Books.

Fouts, Hillary N., Barry S. Hewlett, and Michael E. Lamb. 2005. "Parent-Offspring Weaning Conflicts among the Bofi Farmers and Foragers of Central Africa." *Current Anthropology* 46(1):29–50.

Gottlieb, Alma. 2004. *The Afterlife is Where We Come From: The Culture of Infancy in West Africa*. Chicago, IL: University of Chicago Press.

Hawkes, Kristen, James F. O'Connell, and Nicholas G. Blurton Jones. 1997. "Hadza Women's Time Allocation, Offspring Provisioning, and the Evolution of Long Postmenopausal Life Spans." *Current Anthropology* 38(4):551–557.

Hewlett, Barry S. 1991. *Intimate Fathers: The Nature and Context of Aka Pygmy Paternal Infant Care*. Ann Arbor, MI: The University of Michigan Press.

Hewlett, Barry S., and Michael Lamb, eds. 2005. *Hunter-Gatherer Childhoods: Evolutionary, Developmental and Cultural Perspectives*. New Brunswick, NJ: Aldine Transaction.

Hewlett, B. S., and Michael E. Lamb. 2002. "Integrating Evolution, Culture, and Developmental Psychology: Explaining Caregiver-Infant Proximity and Responsiveness in Central Africa and the USA." In *Between Culture and Biology: Perspectives on Ontogenetic Development*, Heidi Keller, Ype H. Poortinga, and Axel Schölmerich, eds., pp. 241–269. Cambridge: Cambridge University Press.

Hewlett, Barry S., Michael E. Lamb, Birgit Leyendecker, and Axel Schölmerich. 2000. "Internal Working Models, Trust, and Sharing among Foragers." *Current Anthropology* 41(2):287–297.

Howes, Carollee, and Susan Spieker. 2008. "Attachment Relationships in the Context of Multiple Caregivers." In *Handbook of Attachment: Theory, Research, and Clinical Applications*, Jude Cassidy and Philip R. Shaver, eds., pp. 317–332. New York, NY: The Guilford Press.

Hrdy, Sarah Blaffer. 2007. "Evolutionary Context of Human Development: The Cooperative Breeding model." In *Family Relationships: An Evolutionary Perspective*, Catherine A. Salmon, and Todd K. Shackelford, eds., pp. 39–68. New York, NY: Oxford University Press.

Hrdy, Sarah Blaffer. 2009. *Mothers and Others*. Cambridge, MA: The Belknap Press of Harvard University Press.

Hurtado, A. Magdalena, Kim Hill, Ines Hurtado, and Hillard Kaplan. 1992. "Trade-Offs between Female Food Acquisition and Child Care among Hiwi and Ache Foragers." *Human Nature* 3(3):185–216.

Jacobson, Sandra W., and Karen F. Frye. 1991. "Effect of Maternal Social Support on Attachment: Experimental Evidence." *Child Development* 62(3):572–582.

Kaplan, Hillard. 1994. "Evolutionary and Wealth Flows Theories of Fertility: Empirical Tests and New Models." *Population and Development Review* 20(4):753–791.

Kermoian, Rosanne, and P. Herbert Leiderman. 1986. "Infant Attachment to Mother and Child Caretaker in an East African Community." *International Journal of Behavioral Development* 9:455–469.

Kline, Paul. 1994. *An Easy Guide to Factor Analyses*. New York, NY: Routledge.

Konner, Melvin J. 1977. "Infancy among the Kalahari Desert San." In *Culture and Infancy: Variations in the Human Experience*, P. Herbert Leiderman, Steven R. Tulkin, and Anne Rosenfeld, eds., pp. 287–328. The Child Psychology Series, David S. Palermo, ed. New York: Academic Press, Inc.

Konner, Melvin J. 2005. "Hunter-Gatherer Infancy and Childhood: The !Kung and Others." In *Hunter-Gatherer Childhoods: Evolutionary, Developmental and Cultural Perspectives*, Barry S. Hewlett and Michael E. Lamb, eds., pp. 19–64. New Brunswick, NJ: Transaction Publishers.

Kramer Karen L. 2010. "Cooperative Breeding and Its Significance to the Demographic Success of Humans." *Annual Review of Anthropology* 39:417–436.

Lamb, Michael E., Ross A. Thompson, William P. Gardner, Eric L. Charnov, and David Estes. 1984. "Security of Infantile Attachment as Assessed in the 'Strange Situation': Its Study and Biological Interpretation." Behavioral *and Brain Sciences* 7:127–171.

Lamb, Michael E., and Charlie Lewis. 2010. "The Development and Significance of Father-Child Relationships in Two-Parent Families." In *The Role of the Father in Child Development*, Michael E. Lamb, ed. Hoboken, NJ: Wiley and Sons.

Lancy, David F. 2008. *The Anthropology of Childhood: Cherubs, Chattel, Changelings*. Cambridge: Cambridge University Press.

LeVine, Robert. 2004. "Challenging Expert Knowledge: Findings from an African Study of Infant Care and Development." In *Childhood and Adolescence: Cross-Cultural Perspectives and Applications*, U. P. Gielen and J. Roopnarine, eds., pp. 149–165. Gusii, Kenya: Praeger.

LeVine, Robert A., and Patrice M. Miller. 1990. "Commentary." In "Special Topic: Cross-Cultural Validity of Attachment Theory." *Human Development* 33:73–80.

Marvin, R. S., T. L. VanDevender, M. I. Iwanaga, S. LeVine, and R. LeVine. 1977. "Infant-Caregiver Attachment among the Hausa of Nigeria." In *Ecological*

Factors in Human Development, Harry McGurk, ed., pp. 247–259. New York, NY: North-Holland Publishing Company.

Meehan, Courtney L. 2005. "The Effects of Residential Locality on Parental and Alloparental Investment among the Aka Foragers of the Central African Republic." *Human Nature* 16(1):58–80.

Meehan, Courtney L. 2008a. "Allomaternal Investment and Relational Uncertainty among Ngandu Farmers of the Central African Republic." *Human Nature* 19(2):211–226.

Meehan, Courtney L. 2008b. "Cooperative Breeding in Humans: An Examination of Childcare Networks among Foragers and Farmers." Paper presented at the Annual Meeting of the American Anthropological Association. San Francisco.

Meehan, Courtney L. 2009. "Maternal Time Allocation in Cooperative Childrearing Societies." *Human Nature* 20:375–393.

Olds, David L., Charles R. Henderson Jr., Robert Chamberlin, and Robert Tatelbaum. 2002. "Preventing Child Abuse and Neglect: A Randomized Controlled Trial." *Pediatrics* 110:486–496.

Rothbaum, Fred, Martha Pott, Hiroshi Azuma, Kazuo Miyake, and John Weisz. 2000. "The Development of Close Relationships in Japan and the United States: Paths of Symbiotic Harmony and Generative Tension." *Child Development* 71:1121–1142.

Sagi, Abraham, Marinus H. van IJzendoorn, Ora Aviezer, Frank Donnell, Nina Koren-Karie, Trista Joels, and Yael Harl. 1995. "Attachments in a Multiple-Caregiver and Multiple-Infant Environment: The Case of the Israeli Kibbutzim." *Monographs of the Society for Research in Child Development* 60(2–3):71–91.

Sagi-Schwartz, Abraham, and Ora Aviezer. 2005. "Correlates of Attachment to Multiple Caregivers in Kibbutz Children from Birth to Emerging Adulthood: The Haifa Longitudinal Study." In *Attachment from Infancy to Adulthood*, Klaus E. Grossmann, Karin Grossmann, and Everett Waters, eds., pp. 165–197. New York: Guilford Press.

Sear, Rebecca, and Ruth Mace. 2009. "Family Matters: Kin, Demography and Child Health in a Rural Gambian Population." In *Substitute Parents: Biological and Social Perspectives on Alloparenting in Human Societies*, Gillian Bentley and Ruth Mace, eds., pp. 50–76. Studies of the Biosocial Society. Oxford: Berghahn Books.

Seymour, Susan. 2004. "Multiple Caretaking of Infants and Young Children: An Area in Critical Need of a Feminist Psychological Anthropology." *Ethos* 32(4):538–566.

Spieker, Susan J., and Lillian Bensley. 1994. "Roles of Living Arrangements and Grandmother Social Support in Adolescent Mothering and Infant Attachment." *Developmental Psychology* 30(1):102–111.

Takahashi, K. 1990. "Are the Key Assumptions of the 'Strange Situation' Procedure Universal? A View from Japanese Research." *Human Development* 33:23–30.

Thompson, Ross A. 2005. "Multiple Relationships Multiply Considered." *Human Development* 48:102–107.

Thompson, Ross A. 2000. "The Legacy of Early Attachments." *Child Development* 71(1):145–152.

Tronick, E. Z., Gilda A. Morelli, and Paula K. Ivey. 1992. "The Efe Forager Infant and Toddler's Pattern of Social Relationships: Multiple and Simultaneous." *Developmental Psychology* 28(4):568–577.

Tronick, Edward Z., Gilda A. Morelli, and Steve Winn. 1987. "Multiple Caretaking of Efe (Pygmy) Infants." *American Anthropologist* 89(1):96–106.
True, Mary M. 1994. "Mother-Infant Attachment and Communication among the Dogon of Mali." Ph.D. dissertation. University of California, Berkeley.
van IJzendoorn, Marinus H., and Abraham Sagi-Schwartz. 2008. "Cross-Cultural Patterns of Attachment: Universal and Contextual Dimensions." In *Handbook of Attachment: Theory, Research, and Clinical Applications*, Jude Cassidy and Philip R. Shaver, eds., pp. 880–905. New York, NY: The Guilford Press.
van IJzendoorn, Marinus H., Abraham Sagi, and Mirjam, W. E. Lambermon. 1992. "The Multiple Caretaker Paradox: Data from Holland and Israel." *New Directions for Child and Adolescent Development* 1992(57):5–24.
Weisner, Thomas S. 2005. "Commentary: Attachment as a Cultural and Ecological Problem with Pluralistic Solutions." *Human Development* 48:1/2:89–94.
Winn, Steve, Edward T. Tronick, and Gilda A. Morelli. 1989. "The Infant and the Group: A Look at Efe Caretaking Practices in Zaire." In *The Cultural Context of Infancy, Volume One: Biology, Culture, and Infant Development*, J. Kevin Nugent, Barry M. Lester, and T. Berry Brazelton, eds., pp. 87–109. Norwood, NJ: Ablex.

Chapter 4

"It Takes a Village to Raise a Child": Attachment Theory and Multiple Child Care in Alor, Indonesia, and in North India

Susan C. Seymour

Introduction

The African proverb, "It takes a village to raise a child,"[1] expresses an underlying truth. Most societies around the world do not expect mothers, or parents, to rear children alone. Mothers and their young children are usually enmeshed in larger kinship groups and communities that help with child care and other tasks. Dating at least back to Margaret Mead's (1974) 1928 groundbreaking study of adolescence in Samoa, sociocultural anthropologists have been documenting multiple child care and discussing some of its probable effects upon children's emotional bonds with their caretakers and other people. The bias toward exclusive mothering that has dominated much of Western psychology—including John Bowlby's (1969) theory of attachment—has been evident to anthropologists for a long time.

It is ironic that Bowlby's theory of attachment has become so mother-centered because he acknowledged, in the first volume of *Attachment and Loss* (1969), that infants and young children could become attached to a variety of caretakers in their environment. "It is evident," he (1969:305) wrote "that whom a child selects as his principal attachment-figure, and to how many other figures he becomes attached, turn in large part on who cares for him and on the composition of the household in which he is living." Theoretically, according to Bowlby, attachment was a process that would vary cross-culturally depending upon the child's home and community environment, but this is not how it has come to be characterized.[2] Due initially to Mary Ainsworth's (e.g., Ainsworth et al. 1978) experimental work with mothers and infants in laboratories, the focus of attachment theory became more one of clinically measuring the "security" or "insecurity" of *mother*-child attachment, primarily in laboratory settings, than one of examining the cross-cultural variability of attachment figures and processes. This, too, is ironic in that Ainsworth (1967) was also well aware of cross-cultural variability in infant-caretaker attachments from her own systematic observations of Gusii caregivers and infants in Africa.

In this chapter I want to bring attention back to the widespread phenomenon of multiple child care[3] and to some of its potential effects upon children's emerging emotions and cognitive models for social relationships. It is an opportune moment for such a reanalysis due to the recent interdisciplinary consensus about cooperative breeding and shared child care that is emerging among biological and evolutionary anthropologists, psychological anthropologists, and some child development psychologists. Sarah Blaffer Hrdy's recent book, *Mothers and Others: The Evolutionary Origins of Mutual Understanding* (2009), for example, makes a strong argument that humans evolved as cooperative breeders with mothers who had to rely upon others, especially nonreproductive grandmothers, to help with child care. Alloparenting, or multiple child care, Hrdy (2009:66) argues, is associated with early hominids' increased capacities for "mindreading"—for improved "decoding [of] the mental states of others, and figuring out who would help and who would hurt." Similarly, in his recent book, *The Evolution of Childhood*, Melvin Konner (2010:447) addresses cooperative breeding, writing: "Phenomenologically and psychologically, we can no longer believe, as many psychodynamic theorists did, that there is one basic relationship—that with the mother—from which all others are derived." "Multiple caregiving," Konner (2010: 449) continues, "is very widespread cross-culturally, and it persisted after the hunting-gathering era."

In recent years, some child development psychologists have also been rethinking and broadening the Bowlby–Ainsworth mother-centered model of attachment. For example, Michael Lamb (1998:74), in his review of the US non-parental child-care literature, acknowledged that multiple child care is "a universal practice with a long history, not a dangerous innovation." Carolee Howes and Susan Spieker (2008:317), in their chapter on attachment and multiple caregivers in the *Handbook of Attachment*, have noted, "There are practical reasons to consider children as having a network of attachment figures." However, the discussion that follows this assertion is oriented to US-based research, to day-care studies rather than familial arrangements, and to the issue of attachment "security." In contrast, some other child development psychologists (e.g., Keller and Harwood 2009; Keller and Otto 2009; Morelli and Rothbaum 2007) have begun to address more diverse models of attachment, including cross-cultural studies of multiple child care and attachment. For instance, in a recent study of Cameroonian Nso children, Otto and Keller (2011:14) have noted, "All mothers wanted their children to grow up with many different caretakers, not with only one or [a] few primary attachment figures." In other words, these researchers had learned that the Nso not only practiced multiple child care but that they *valued* it and wanted their children to develop multiple attachments.

This chapter has several goals: to argue (1) that not only is multiple child care, with resulting multiple attachments, *widespread* and *normal* but that it takes different forms that are adaptive to local environmental and cultural conditions; (2) that these different forms of multiple child care help to shape attachment in culturally variable and distinct ways, all of which are within the realm of human normality; and (3) that "mothering"—that is, the care by a birth mother or primary caretaker—must be examined *within* these specific conditions of multiple child care. I shall address these issues by using two strikingly different case studies from Asia—Cora Du Bois's (1944) classic study of Alor, a small island in the eastern part of the Indonesian archipelago, and my own longitudinal research of children and families in North India.

Alor: It *Does* Take a Village to Raise a Child

Background

Du Bois's pioneering study of Alor was carried out in 1937–1939 when the island was part of the Netherlands East Indies. She selected it as a site to test out theories emerging from the early Culture and Personality "movement" of the 1930s, specifically to examine the relationship of cultural institutions to personality development, with child-rearing practices presumed to be the significant mediating factor. Thus, *The People of Alor: The Psychosocial Study of an East Asian Island* (1944) became one of the early full-scale psychocultural studies within anthropology,[4] and it has continued to be cited by anthropologists and psychologists interested in the cross-cultural study of socialization and personality development (e.g., Munroe and Gauvain 2010).

On Alor, Du Bois selected a remote mountain village—well away from the only Dutch settlement on the coast—in which to reside for 18 months of research. At the time, the village of Atimelang had a population of about 180 inhabitants, with another 300 persons living nearby. The Alorese were small-scale horticulturists who, until recently, had been engaged in chronic warfare and headhunting. The Dutch had tried to pacify them and had resettled them in a valley just below their former settlements on mountain spurs and crests. Du Bois was, therefore, observing a society that had been adapted to warfare conditions where men still gathered in Male Houses and in patrilineage ceremonial houses, participated in a complex wealth/prestige system, and dressed in warfare regalia for ceremonial purposes. The culture of warfare had not disappeared with the next generation, either, because Du Bois observed boys occasionally dressing up and engaging in mock battles with weapons that they had created.

Women, on the other hand, constituted the principal workforce. They left their villages daily to tend gardens where they raised a variety of fruits and vegetables. This sexual division of labor had a major impact upon the care of infants and young children. New mothers remained in seclusion for only one or two weeks after giving birth and then returned to their fields, leaving infants in the care of others for long periods of time—a practice that may have been adapted to their former village locations where excursions to fields were long and safety was an issue. The Alorese, accordingly, practiced multiple child care, but their family structure and households, which were highly variable in make-up, did not provide a set of reliable in-house mother-surrogates. Du Bois described them as mostly nuclear in structure, but her household census indicates that there was everything from single mother-child households to extended households with two couples, widowed mothers or mothers-in-law, and children residing together.[5] Also, due to a high divorce rate, households were not stable, and people moved about among different sets of relatives in other villages. Women also kept field houses near some of their gardens where they would sleep during harvesting periods, a practice that also took them away from young children.

Infancy (Birth to One-and-a-Half to Two Years)

Infancy is a dangerous time when the child is completely dependent upon others for its survival.[6] In Bowlby's model of attachment, infants are born to seek proximity to others and, hence, safety. Those who respond also elicit emotional bonds. During the early months of life, "[t]he emotion is positive but impersonal; anyone can elicit it and—despite its favoring primary caretakers—strong emotional bonds, which will prove vital to survival, do not yet exist" (Konner 2010:227). In many foraging societies (see chapters 2 and 3), mothers share child care with one another, holding and nursing each other's infants. The Alorese also relied on other mothers for some help with early child care. In their kinship terminological system any woman of the first ascending generation was addressed as "mother," and any lactating woman could pick up and nurse a hungry infant. Du Bois (1944:33) reported that everyone in the community, including young boys, was "entranced" by infants and wanted to hold, fondle, and mouth (caress with mock bites of the lips) babies. In their pre-walking phase, young children were continually carried about in shawls next to a person's body, for to place them on the ground was viewed as "gross neglect." At night they slept with their mothers on mats.

Despite such attention from all members of the community, Alorese infants experienced periods of hunger and frustration when their mothers were away and no lactating woman was available to nurse them. During such periods, infants would attempt to suckle from the nipples of fathers or older children who would try to assuage their hunger with premasticated foods (including rat), which the infant usually spat out. Thus, Alorese infants experienced variable degrees of hunger and frustration depending upon how frequently, and for how long, their mothers were away gardening. Alorese mothers recognized these feeding problems and told Du Bois, "when we are pregnant a lot, we have to work in the fields all the time or our children get thin."[7] This dilemma that Alorese mothers voiced is one that we now know is a universal problem for our species. In their discussion of attachment and human evolution, Crittenden and Marlowe (chapter 2) point out that human mothers, unlike other primates, "are faced with the unique problem of providing care to unweaned infants while simultaneously maintaining their economic production to successfully feed older children."

Du Bois also stressed the problem of inconsistency of child care. "A whole series of parent surrogates may care for the child during this period after the mother goes out to work in the fields. It is important to note that the mother surrogate is not always the same person, it may be one person after another in the course of days...There are long periods when particularly the older sibling's care is extremely haphazard and casual."[8] Adult men and women who, in their life histories, volunteered memories of being sibling caregivers, substantiated this latter observation:

> On the way [to the fields] Maliema cried a lot, so I put her down and slapped her. Then I talked nicely to her, and we went on when she was quiet...When Maliema was a little older, she would cry to go to the fields with me. If I was not angry with her, I would take her along to dig sweet potatoes. I would give her the big ones and keep the small ones...[I was angry] because she was always crying. She cried to go places; she cried to be fed. I hit her on the head with my knuckles and then I would feed her. She cried because she was hungry (Du Bois 1944:421–422).

Or:

> Once mother and I were living in a field house near our gardens. She told me to carry Senmani [younger brother] while she worked. At noon he was hungry and wanted to nurse. I gave him food but he only vomited it. He cried and cried and wouldn't stop. I cried too. Finally I went and told mother to come and nurse him but she wouldn't. So I took Senmani, laid him down on a mat in the house and ran off to Folafeng [a nearby community]. There from the ridge I shouted, "Mother, your child lies in the house. If you want to care for it good. If you don't want to, that is also good. I am going to Atimelang to play." (Du Bois 1944:251)

These two accounts of sibling child care, the former from an adult woman and the latter from a man, are striking in that they were unsolicited. They just emerged as part of these individuals' memories of their own childhoods—the frustration and resentment they experienced as caregivers of younger siblings. Alorese children received little training in responsibility and were rarely supervised in the care of younger siblings. In fact, as one peruses Du Bois's fieldnotes, it becomes clear that, in Alor, it really *did* take an entire village to raise a child.[9] (Mageo makes a similar observation for Samoans, chapter 7.) The village of Atimelang was small and safe and, once mobile, young children were allowed to wander about, being taken care of by anyone who was available. Below is an illustrative excerpt from Du Bois's fieldnotes:

> Pedafani (18 months) is the first and only child of Djetmani and Mallemai who have had violent quarrels about Djetmani's other wives. Since he has no older

> sibling to care for him, he is often left to shift for himself. His father is off about other affairs and stays home very little. Altho' he seems very fond of his son, he does not care for him as some fathers do for their children. Today the mother was off in the fields all afternoon and Pedafani was left to crawl about by himself. He was on the dance place and all the other women and children keep an eye out for him. He seems thoroughly placid and contented about the state of affairs. He practically never cries and is a general village favorite.[10]

As we shall see, Pedafani's placidity changed during toddlerhood.

Toddlerhood (Two to Five Years)

Although caretaking of infants may have been highly dispersed among caregivers and somewhat inconsistent, it was not negligent. Alorese children learned, during the first year of life, that they had numerous caregivers and potential attachment figures who provided them with lots of physical contact and some food. Only mothers, however, could fully satisfy their hunger. That young children had become emotionally attached to their mothers—or, in two cases, their grandmothers[11]—was evident when, as toddlers, they tried to follow their mothers (or grandmothers) to the fields, only to be rebuffed. Temper tantrums resulted. "Rages are so consistent, so widespread, and of such long duration among young children," Du Bois (1944:51) wrote, "that they were one of my first and most striking observations." These emotional outbursts, usually instigated by the departure of a child's mother for her gardens, lasted anywhere from a few minutes to as many as 20 minutes. (See Mageo, chapter 7, for a discussion of tantrums among Samoan toddlers.)

Alorese toddlers were pushed into self-reliance early and had multiple reasons to be dissatisfied with this stage of life. Their daily baths were now in cold water rather than the pre-warmed water prepared for infants. They were no longer carried about in shawls and given lots of physical comfort by an array of caregivers while their mothers were away. Instead, they were left largely on their own to wander about the village, hoping that someone might offer them food when they were hungry. As Du Bois (1956:244) astutely noted, "after the child learns to walk, his frustrations with respect to hunger are increased, and simultaneously he loses the constant handling and support he had during the first stage of life in the carrying shawl." Unlike the Murik (Barlow, chapter 6), however, there were no rules that stipulated that older children should share food with younger children, so Alorese toddlers had to scrounge and beg for food. Even the placid Pedafani, described earlier, began having temper tantrums at age two years.

Most toddlers were not hesitant to express emotions of protest and anger during this stage of development. Attachment theory predicts that infants will have formed emotional bonds with their caretakers during the first year of life and will respond to any perceived disruptions to them—in this case, the departure of the mother, the child's most reliable source of food, and the decreased attention of surrogate mothers. Young children's tantrums were not consistently responded to—sometimes they were ignored, while other times the mother or someone else would pick up an unhappy child and try to placate her. Thus, tantrums were inconsistently reinforced.

Unlike in some societies, such as the Cameroonian Nso where there is a belief that young children should remain calm and quiet (Keller and Otto 2009), Alorese adults not only tolerated emotional outbursts from young children, but they helped to incite them. Toddlers were often the targets of teasing, threats, ridicule, and intentional scare tactics. If a child became mildly irritable or aggressive during such attacks, people would laugh and encourage greater displays of anger by saying to the child, "Hit him!" "Kill him!" (Du Bois 1944:8). In other words, young children were being intentionally socialized into an emotionally turbulent culture where, although warfare had recently been quelled, interpersonal squabbles and fights were not uncommon.

Later Childhood (Six to Ten Years)

The violent tantrums of toddlerhood began to disappear by five to six years of age, although Du Bois's fieldnotes include the observation of an eight-year-old boy who was trying to accompany his father on a trail to another village. His father did not want the son to come because it was to be a long excursion and, as he told the boy, he would not be able to keep up. The boy began crying and "yelling bloody murder" and refused to be consoled by a village woman who happened to arrive on the scene.[12]

Having been pushed into an early stage of self-reliance, most boys by this age had formed play groups and had begun to roam in small groups, hunting and cooking rats, sometimes growing their own sweet potatoes, but most often pilfering vegetables and fruits from other people's gardens. They were learning to feed themselves and to explore their environment. Gradually, they would begin attaching themselves to older men from whom they could learn the skills of the political and economic negotiations required for acquiring a wife and beginning to build up capital. Clearly, in the aforementioned incident, the father did not yet consider his son old enough to participate in such a venture.

In contrast, girls of nine or ten years began to accompany their mothers to their fields where they became helpers in growing food and, accordingly, had more direct access to it. They were also expected to run errands and help care for younger siblings, but as we have seen, they and their brothers did not always do this responsibly.

Older girls and boys, Du Bois (1944:78) emphasized, experienced "inconsistency in adult behavior toward them" and learned "to assert themselves by running off, by seeking the protection of other kin, and by vigorous and often violent resistance." For example, in the second sibling child-care case cited earlier, the boy (Ripalda) provocatively called to his mother, saying, "Mother, your child lies in the house. If you want to care for it good. If you don't want to, that is also good. I am going to Atimelang to play." In response, his mother threatened him, saying, "All right, you have thrown away your younger brother. Tomorrow you will die." Ripalda ran off and stayed at the house of his maternal grandparents that night, but the next day his mother came to punish him. She tied his hands behind his back and removed his loincloth—the sign of his physical maturity as a male—saying, "You wear a loincloth but you aren't old enough to wear a loincloth." Ripalda's grandfather came to his grandson's rescue by splitting his own shawl and giving half of it to his grandson to cover his private parts. He also chastised his daughter, saying, "You hit him [Ripalda] and opened his loincloth, so now go cut your weeds with your right hand and care for your infant with your left hand" (Du Bois 1944:251). Irregular punishment of children, including intrafamilial disputes over them, were not uncommon among the Alorese. In this case, Ripalda stayed with his grandparents for a month until his mother came and asked him to return home and resume caring for his younger brother. The autobiographies that Du Bois collected are full of stories of older children going off to spend time with relatives in other villages—something for which their own early multiple child care had prepared them.

Attachment

How might this case study help to expand our understanding of attachment? Western theorists who are focused on the importance of exclusive mothering could easily view the Alorese as a case of maternal neglect and unstable mother-child attachment. According to Munroe and Munroe (1975), "Only one society, the Alorese of the former Dutch East Indies, has received a score of very low infant satisfaction in all the cross-cultural ratings thus far compiled (Barry, Bacon, and Child 1967; Barry and Paxson 1971; Whiting and Child 1953) as well as a low score on the acceptance-rejection scale (Rohner 1975)." These studies led Munroe and Munroe (1975:41) to conclude, "by any definition, the Alorese child is rejected." The cross-cultural scoring procedures, however, have tended to be biased against highly dispersed child care. For example, the Alorese were ranked low on "constancy of presence of nurturing agent" and even on "protection from environmental discomforts" by Barry, Bacon, and Child (1967) even though Du Bois makes it clear that infants were constantly carried about and could be nursed by any lactating woman. Furthermore, "display of affection toward infant" was also marked low for the Alorese despite Du Bois's report that everyone was "entranced" by infants. In the absence of quantitative data, however, it is easy to overemphasize the qualitative information that Du Bois provides about the unsatisfactory daytime feedings of infants and the painful transition into toddlerhood. With respect to infant attachment, however, the Alorese satisfied Bowlby's two primary criteria—physical safety and tactile comfort. And it is important to note that in this context of village-wide child care, infants displayed neither stranger anxiety (except initially with the anthropologist) nor separation anxiety from their mothers during the first year of life. It took a significant reduction in multiple child care sometime during the second year of life, combined with the child's enhanced cognitive and motor skills, to set off Alorese children's emotional outbursts at being left behind during the day by their mothers.

If part of the attachment process involves a child developing a working model of social relationships in his or her immediate cultural environment, then many Alorese children may have become disillusioned during their second year of life when they experienced a sudden decline in village-wide nurturing, combined with the regular absences of their mothers and the uncertainty that they would be fed. At this point their initial working models of social relationships had to be revised. Positive attention from others became less frequent and hunger a reality when mothers were away, so toddlers were highly motivated to follow their mothers. (Alorese children were not weaned for the first two years.) In addition, they became subject to teasing, ridicule, and other aggressive tactics by adults and older siblings. The trust in others that had developed during the first year of life was gradually transformed into fear, anger, and distrust—the prevalent adult personality characteristics that Du Bois's ethnographic and psychological data depict. Du Bois's observational insights were confirmed by independent analyses of the autobiographies, Rorschach tests, children's drawings, and other psychological materials that she collected. These analyses, made by a variety of different experts, all pointed to the same conclusion—the Alorese were, in general, suspicious and distrustful of one another and fearful.[13] Du Bois was careful to emphasize, however, that there was great variability in child-care practices and in adult behavior. Accordingly, she used the term "modal personality"—a statistical concept that recognized individual variability around a mean—to describe some of these predominant features of adult Alorese personality.

The frequent marital and non-marital disputes that children witnessed undoubtedly reinforced their working models of interpersonal relationships as being unreliable. One of Du Bois's early assessments was that Alorese adults were emotionally brittle and easily provoked into anger and that this affected the stability of marriages. Some of her first observations in Atimelang were of marital disputes or disputes between jealous wives. (Men had their own frequent disputes over trade objects and debts.) These disputes regularly occurred in public where everyone might observe them, including children. The following is a description of such an event from one of Du Bois's early letters to Abram Kardiner, her psychoanalyst collaborator:

> Again, the woman took the initiative in overt aggression. In the middle of the dance place she began to hit and berate her husband. He was angry but also embarrassed and sheepish. He simply warded off her blows until she spat at him and then he gave her a push which sat her down pretty emphatically... When a row of this sort is going on, it is the woman who talks and complains to all who will listen. The men simply stand by, interestedly enough, but saying nothing. The female audience usually says little but nods sympathetically with

> the woman's tale. *Of course all the children cluster around and listen to such tales of woe. There is no attempt to keep anything from them.*[14]

Not only were infants and young children witnesses to marital disputes, but the high rate of divorce also affected many of them. During the course of her fieldwork, Du Bois learned that Atimelangers averaged two divorces apiece, with some experiencing as many as six divorces (Du Bois 1956:248). "Divorce is easy and usually a woman takes the initiative," she wrote in the same letter to Kardiner. "This is simply a matter of returning to live in her father's or brother's house." At an early age, therefore, Alorese children experienced not only variable nurturance from others and food deprivation, but also the emotional and angry outbursts of adults that often led to shifting household arrangements. The autobiographies that Du Bois collected are filled with informants' memories of the comings and goings of mothers, fathers, siblings, and other relatives. Mobility of residence and shifting personnel may have contributed to a child's sense of emotional instability and distrust.

The distrust that tended to characterize Alorese interpersonal relationships was also reflected in their conceptions of the supernatural. Supernatural agents were viewed as capable of both good and evil deeds and were, accordingly, not considered trustworthy. Since they were believed to inhabit all corners of villages and fields and could be harbingers of ill health, hunger, and death, they needed to be regularly placated. This was done by feeding them ceremonial foods—rice and sacrificed pigs (Du Bois 1956). Similarly, the dead were believed to be sources of malignant power—that is, negative affect—and had to be placated with numerous burials and feasts. According to Du Bois, ceremonial feedings had great salience to the Alorese for whom early childhood was associated with irregular feedings, hunger, and frustration. "The motif of sacrifice [of pigs and chickens] or feeding occurs over and over again, not only in relation to the dead but in relation to the supernatural beings. Feeding is the chief cultural tool for symbolizing social euphoria and for placating supernatural beings" (Du Bois 1944:162). Without using the terminology, "culturally constituted defense mechanisms," Du Bois was making an argument similar to that of Mageo (chapter 7) and Quinn (chapter 8): that is, there can be societal-level resolutions to tensions produced in individuals by the attachment process. For the Alorese, these centered upon ceremonial foods and feedings, symbolically important components of attachment in some societies (a topic discussed in the introduction and in Barlow's discussion of the Murik, chapter 6).

The Alorese are an interesting case study for examining multiple child care and attachment because they practiced an unusually dispersed form of cooperative child care that ended abruptly with the child's ability to walk. There is no doubt that during their first 18 months of life Alorese children experienced bouts of hunger during their mothers' absences, but they also experienced continuous tactile comfort and attention from a variety of people in their close-knit village. They learned to trust others and clearly exhibited emotional attachment to their mothers. Although renowned in the cross-cultural literature as having unusually low "infant satisfaction" scores, Alorese children's experiences are vividly different from the emotionally deprived institutionalized children whom Bowlby observed following World War II and who inspired his thinking about attachment. Nor do they resemble the postinstitutionalized Romanian orphans who, in the 1990s, were adopted into American families and have subsequently been treated by Attachment Centers in the United States for severe emotional and cognitive deficits (Talbot 1998).[15]

The Alorese case study challenges us to think beyond Western stereotypes of "secure" and "insecure" attachment in an effort to try to understand how the attachment process operates in very different cultural settings with different models of virtue (see introduction). Jean Briggs (1998), in her in-depth exploration of morality play among the Inuit, has demonstrated how complex the attachment process can be and how young children must learn, as the Alorese did, how to navigate between affection and hostility. As Thomas Weisner (2005) has recently argued, communities have different perceptions of what is satisfactory attachment behavior and promote different kinds of trust and emotional bonding. Consequently, we must learn to think more broadly about human attachments and their cross-cultural variability. The Alorese of the 1930s valued early self-reliance, the open expression of anger and hostility, and male competition over women and resources. These traits were associated with low interpersonal trust and high interpersonal aggression, characteristics that tended to produce unstable marriages but that, in all likelihood, were adaptive to conditions of endemic warfare.

North India: The Diffusion of Affect

Background

India provides a dramatic contrast with Alor in almost all respects. Rather than being a small island characterized by tribal groups that practiced horticulture, India is a large, highly populated agrarian state that is rapidly urbanizing and industrializing. Also, unlike Alor, India has a long history of literacy and cultural coherence. It is also a complex, socially stratified society with overlapping caste and class systems. Unlike the relatively small, flexible—even unstable—families that Du Bois observed in Alor in the 1930s, the predominant Indian family system, known as "the joint family," is highly structured and remarkably stable (Seymour 1999). It is a multigenerational extended family system characterized in the north of India, and in some parts of the south, by such patriarchal principles as patrilocal residence, patrilineal descent and inheritance, control of female sexuality and reproduction through the practices of purdah and arranged marriage, and a gender-differentiated authority system and ideology that give same-generational males authority over socially equivalent females.

Bhubaneswar, Odisha, India, has been the locus of my own research since 1965. Formerly a small Hindu temple town (the "Old Town") with a rice-growing agricultural base, Bhubaneswar became the site of a new planned administrative center (the "New Capital") when, following India's independence from Great Britain in 1947, it was selected as the capital city for the new state of Odisha. In a 20-year period Bhubaneswar's population jumped from an estimated 10,000 people to over 50,000. (Today the population is approaching one and one-half million.) Two different sets of people became juxtaposed—the long-term residents of the Old Town who lived in densely populated, caste-based neighborhoods, clustered around medieval temples, with the newly arrived government servants who resided in dispersed Western-style houses and neighborhoods in the New Capital. Because of Bhubaneswar's new status, it also became the locus for educational development. Schools from the kindergarten level to postgraduate studies were established. Thus, Bhubaneswar was an ideal setting to examine some of the forces of change in post–World War II, postcolonial India.[16]

From 1965 to 1967, I studied a sample of 24 families that represented the caste system in the Old Town and the emerging class system in the New Capital. Using the Whiting (1963) Six Culture Study model, I made timed observations of caregiver-child interactions in homes during different periods of the day. Most households[17] had infants, and all of them had at least two children under the age of five years. Timed observations were supplemented with extensive participation in each family's daily life and in all ceremonial occasions over that two-year period. Subsequently, I have remained in touch with 23 of the 24 families. I have visited them with some regularity and have been able to follow 128 children from my original sample of 130 into maturity, including marriage and the production of the next generation of children.

Child-Care Practices

In all Bhubaneswar households that I have studied, mothers were never left alone to care for children. In the New Capital, where families had moved to take up new government jobs, there were rarely full-fledged joint families residing together. However, in all instances women had mothers or mothers-in-law staying with them, and/or full-time servants, to help with child care and other household chores. Older siblings were also expected to help with child care. In the Old Town, traditional patrifocal joint families were predominant. In these households mothers had a variety of other adults—mothers-in-law, sisters-in-law, husbands, fathers-in-law, brothers-in-law, and other children (patrilineal nieces and nephews)—to help with child care, although child care was principally the responsibility of women. In other words, households were organized around a set of patrilineally related males whose wives moved in from the outside at the time of marriage and collaborated in household chores with one another under the supervision of their mothers-in-law. Middle- and upper-status women of childbearing age were in purdah, which meant that they were not free to leave the house without the supervision of a male relative. Lower-status women in both sides of town worked outside the home to help support their families. They had to rely upon one another, especially grandmothers and older children, to care for infants and young children.

In this family system multiple child care was, and continues to be, not only the norm but also the culturally valued expectation. Depending upon their class/caste status and their rank within the household, mothers were expected to return to household chores soon after childbirth. In high-status Brahmin households, new mothers were considered polluting and were kept separate from others for some days or weeks after giving birth. During this period of pollution, other women in the family cared for new mothers and their infants. (In some cases new mothers were allowed to return to their natal families to give birth and be cared for by their own mothers and sisters rather than by in-laws.) Like Alorese women, low-status mothers returned to work outside the home almost immediately after giving birth. Even in Brahmin households, soon after her period of pollution ended, a new mother was expected to return to her household chores that might include preparing meals for as many as 25 family members. She could not be a full-time caretaker to her new infant and other children, nor was she expected to be.

Infancy (Birth to Two Years)

There were many hands to care for infants and young children in this family system, and cultural taboos reinforced the principle of multiple child care and impeded exclusive mothering. For example, focusing too much attention on a newborn infant—even gazing lovingly at it—was believed to attract the evil eye and to endanger an infant's survival. Therefore, a new mother (or the anthropologist) would endanger a baby if she held it or looked at it for extended periods. Although nursing was exclusive to the birth mother, periods of nursing tended to be brief and intermittent. Someone would pick up a crying infant, hold it and try to comfort it, or hand it to its mother to be nursed. The mother would nurse it briefly, setting the infant down again or handing it to another person. Then the infant would cry again, and the same routine would follow. Infants were rarely nursed to satisfaction at one sitting; rather, a system of intermittent crying and nursing would ensue. Even as newborn infants, children were encouraged to look to others for comfort and attention, but caregiving was more regular and distributed across fewer caretakers than in Alor.

Infants in Bhubaneswar were never put into cribs, cradles, or other containers where they might be left alone. As in Alor, they were carried everywhere by a variety of caretakers, and when it was time to sleep, someone would lie down on a mat or bed with them. At night, they slept next to their mothers who could easily nurse them. After being weaned, they might continue to sleep with their mother or be shifted to a grandparent or father. Thus, infants and young children were assured of almost continual physical contact—one means of establishing interpersonal trust and attachment. The following is a characteristic example of multiple child care in action:

> Older Sister (child's paternal aunt) left the room and returned carrying Bapu, a one-month-old boy. Two neighbor girls (aged 16 & 18) came in and sat down. Older Sister lay Bapu on his back on the wooden platform on which she was seated. Bapu, undiapered, urinated and began to cry. Older Sister ignored him. One of the neighbor girls picked him up and held him for a moment, and Bapu stopped crying. Then she passed him to the other neighbor girl. They took turns bouncing him on their laps. Bapu's mother came in, took him from the girls and held him for a moment. Then she handed him back to one of the neighbor girls and left the room. Bapu did not cry or object to his mother's departure. A moment later Grandmother came in carrying Rabi (Bapu's 2-year-old brother), who was half asleep in her arms. She told him to greet me, which he did, holding his hands together in the approved fashion. She left the room but returned with him a moment later, setting him down on the floor and asking him where his brother was. Rabi pointed to Bapu. Grandmother nodded, picked him up, and carried him out of the room. (Seymour 1999:81)

The mother in this episode appears only briefly. Her new baby is being looked after by her sister-in-law and two neighbor girls while her mother-in-law (Grandmother) is watching over her two-year-old son. The only verbal interaction was to teach the older boy greeting behavior and to have him acknowledge his new brother. On the average, mothers in these joint households performed only half of all nurturing acts directed to their infants and young children. The nature of mothering in such households was clearly a group endeavor, and children learned from infancy on to accept, trust, and seek nurturance from a variety of persons in the house and immediate neighborhood.

Low-status infants, whose mothers were employed away from the house, were left in the care of aging grandmothers and older siblings (mostly, but not exclusively, females) for extended periods of time. Children as young as six or seven years were considered competent to care for babies, even newborns, under the supervision of a grandmother. Like Alorese babies, these infants sometimes suffered from hunger and were given bottles of sugar water to keep them somewhat satisfied until their mothers returned home and nursed them. Usually, a designated older sibling carried, fed, and slept with such an infant during its mother's absence. When ready for solid foods at about one year, infants were handfed by their surrogate mothers. Perhaps because the caretaking was so regularized and the personnel limited to a set of family members, Alorese-style temper tantrums did not occur when low-status mothers went off to work. Also, once on solid food, infants and young children were assured of being fed. In fact, by age two years they began learning how to participate in the preparation of food.

In these intimate family and neighborhood settings infants had little experience with strangers. The only stranger anxiety that I witnessed was when mothers and other caretakers would hold out an infant to me and say,

"Take her. Take her home to America with you." When the young child responded by crying in fear, the mother and others present would laugh hilariously and repeat the action. Over time, young children came to find these teasing threats amusing as well and would pretend to come with me, but initially they were frightened. Such teasing of infants and young children seemed to be another means of creating some degree of frustration with the infant's initial attachment to its mother or primary mother-surrogate that would encourage the child to reach out to other family members for support.

Toddlerhood (Two to Five Years) and Later Childhood (Six to Ten Years)

Infants in Bhubaneswar were introduced to rice and other solid foods at one year. In higher-status families the first rice feeding was a ritually celebrated event. However, infants and toddlers would continue to be nursed for at least two years and often up to four or five years if no new sibling came along. A toddler would simply crawl or walk over to her mother and take her mother's breast in her hands and nurse, even when the mother was busy cooking. Nursing was not a time of intimacy. Similarly, being fed solid foods was a perfunctory matter. Mothers—or grandmother and older siblings in low-status households—would make balls of rice and lentils or curried vegetables and hand-feed toddlers. In upper-status Old Town households, this routine continued throughout childhood. Children up to eight to ten years were hand-fed and hand bathed by their mothers—one of the few means mothers had for focusing attention upon their own children. New Capital mothers tended to allow children, by the age of four or five years, to help feed and bathe themselves. Whereas in Old Town households the physical dependency of children was extended throughout early childhood, it was gradually reduced in New Capital households where there was greater allowance for some degree of self-reliance. In low-status households, in contrast, the physical dependence of young children abruptly ended at about two years when toddlers could begin to take care of themselves. By six or seven years such children were put in charge of younger siblings, food preparation, hauling water, and other household chores.

Toddlers and young children, although enjoyed and nurtured by a variety of family members, continued to be subject to teasing. Teasing games of repeated asking and receiving, such as the offering and denying of food and comfort, were common and have been observed by researchers in other parts of India (e.g., Beals 1962; Maduro 1976; Minturn and Hitchcock 1966; Trawick 1992). Such practices probably helped to keep young children actively engaged in dependent seeking-type activities with others until they were old enough to reverse roles and become the teasers/givers. In this manner an active form of interdependence among family members was inculcated. Similarly, children who had initially been the receivers of care and nurturance by mothers and other caregivers became, over time, the active nurturers of younger household members.

By five or six years, all upper- and middle-status children had begun school, so their worlds were no longer limited to the home. Most low-status children were not enrolled in school because they were needed at home to help with the care of younger siblings and other household tasks.

Attachment

In joint households in Bhubaneswar and elsewhere in India, children are encouraged to have many objects of emotional attachment. Early on they learn not to rely solely on their birth mother, who is often preoccupied with other chores and for whom it is dangerous to focus too much attention upon them. Accordingly, they accept and then learn to request caregiving from a variety of other people. This does not produce what Western attachment theorists might label "insecure" attachment but rather *a diffusion of affect* and multiple bonds of attachment. (See Meehan and Hawks, chapter 3, for a discussion of multiple attachments among the Aka and Barlow, chapter 6, for a discussion of "diffuse attachment" among the Murik.) As I have argued elsewhere (Seymour 1983), it is this diffusion of affect among family members that—like glue—helps bind together the joint family. Since there is no *one* object of attachment for infants, there are few, if any, expressions of distress when a particular caregiver is absent. Children learn at an early age to trust other family members and close neighbors, and this intergenerational trust that multiple child care engenders is, in turn, critical to the maintenance of joint families. Ideally, under these circumstances children will grow up wanting to put the welfare of the family above their own more individualistic desires.

Dyadic bonds, while not entirely absent in such households, are considered dangerous because they might motivate sets of individuals to break away from the extended family. Thus, a mother—especially under the eyes of her mother-in-law—pushes her infant away from an exclusive attachment by nursing the child intermittently and withholding empathic attention. The message to the child is to seek emotional satisfaction in other relationships, and other persons are there to nurture, tease, and play with the child. The child is, accordingly, encouraged to sacrifice his or her initial emotional attachment to the mother for a more generalized attachment to the whole family and acceptance into that larger group. The more intimate dyadic relationship between mother and child, often assumed by Western psychologists to be critical to the child's healthy attachment, is controlled and muted in this joint family environment.

As Margaret Trawick has noted in her book about a South Indian Tamil family, *Notes on Love in a Tamil Family* (1992), dyadic bonds—whether between mother and child or husband and wife—must be controlled. She writes as follows about the family with whom she lived and became intimately involved:

> [T]he great danger to a joint family was that it would fracture along the dividing nuclear units—each pair of spouses with their respective children. Love,

> which naturally *(iyatkaiyãka)* was given to one's own, had to be redirected across those lines. The stronger the love the stronger the force that had to be exerted against it, to drive it outwards. Consequently, in our family, mothers deliberately spurned or mistreated their own children, forcing their own and their children's affection away from the closest blood bond. (Trawick 1992:103)

While I never observed overt mistreatment or spurning of children by mothers, Bhubaneswar mothers did convey mixed messages to their children about positive affect and dyadic attachments. For example, while a mother's milk is believed to contain her "love," it must not be given freely. Thus, nursing periods were brief, and mothers rarely sat and cuddled or played with their children. They were busy and somewhat emotionally distant mothers who knew that their children needed to learn interdependence, not an exclusive dependence on and attachment to them. Perhaps for this reason, in the cross-cultural socialization literature Indian mothers have tended to be ranked high on control and low on warmth (Minturn and Lambert 1964; Rohner 1975; Whiting and Whiting 1975; Whiting and Edwards 1988). But it is not just emotional displays of affection and warmth toward one's children that should be restrained but also any public displays of affection between husbands and wives. In this cultural context, dyadic bonds are considered dangerous.

Some Developmental Outcomes

Contrary to much of the Western attachment literature, emotional interdependence and intergenerational trust, rather than a sense of autonomy and independence, are the culturally desired outcomes for children and young adults in Bhubaneswar as in other parts of India. (Interdependence does not, as I have argued elsewhere [Seymour 1999:278], preclude "intrapsychic autonomy"—the kind of autonomy that Chapin discusses for Sri Lankan children in chapter 5.) Young people are not expected to make their own decisions about how much schooling to have, what subjects to study should they go on into higher education, what professions to pursue, or whom to marry. These are all considered family affairs.

For Westerners, perhaps the most dramatic example of this familial interdependence and intergenerational trust is the institution of arranged marriage, which has remained strong in most parts of India and even in some Indian communities abroad. Most young adults *trust* their parents and other extended kin to help select a suitable spouse for them and *distrust* marriage based upon romantic love and self-choice. As one highly educated, employed daughter from a New Capital family put it:

> My parents have left me free...But I have left the responsibility to them [of finding a suitable husband]. I don't want to take any such project on for myself because I know my parents are very capable in this matter. (Seymour 1999:197)

This family was unusual in giving their daughter a choice, but Laxmi did not want the responsibility of finding a husband. Generally, self-chosen unions are considered individualistic and antisocial in character, even in large, contemporary, urban centers like Kolkata [Calcutta] (Donner 2008). Not only do young people generally accept the authority of their elders in this seemingly grave and personal matter but, consistent with their early childhood experiences and learned cultural models, they believe that marriage is not necessarily the most crucial relationship in adult life. This was made clear to me during my first fieldwork in India when two adolescent girls were querying me about divorce in the United States, something they had heard about but could not understand.

> "Why," Mita and Sita asked, "would anyone want to leave one's husband or wife?" I tried to explain that husbands and wives are sometimes very unhappy with one another. They responded, "But you're part of a joint family." [The idea that the husband-wife relationship could be central to one's happiness made little sense to them.] As a woman, they explained, one's relationships are primarily with other women, and the source of one's unhappiness is more likely to be other women than one's husband. (Seymour 1999:59)

This conversation helped jolt me into a new understanding of interpersonal relationships in Indian joint families. Unlike in much of the United States (see Quinn, chapter 8), the dyadic bond between husband and wife was not expected to be the paramount one, and *prem* (unselfish love) was expected to emerge slowly out of that union in a manner that would not jeopardize the stability of the joint family. In North Indian languages *prem* is distinguished from *kam* (a dangerous form of love that includes the selfish lust and desire for another person). The former is the kind of emotional attachment that should characterize familial relationships, and early in childhood young people learn to distinguish the safe from the dangerous kind of emotion by listening to and then reading the Hindu epics.

Within Hindu India there is, therefore, a recognized tension between these two kinds of affect just as there is a tension between exclusive and multiple mothering, and they are played out in Hindu mythology and drama as well as in contemporary literature, film, and television shows. Properly reared children should be prepared to sacrifice the one for the other—the son, his lust or desire for a particular woman; and the mother/daughter-in-law, her devotion to her own child. In my longitudinal study of children and families in Bhubaneswar, only two in my sample of 130 children have had love marriages, and these two to the great distress of their parents. (Both were sons who were studying and working abroad.) All other marriages have been arranged, although with greater or lesser participation by the young people whose fates were being determined.[18]

As one might expect in this system of patrifocal households, with its emphasis upon the well-being of the extended family over the personal interests of the individual, divorce is unusual. Sons remain under the authority of parents well into adulthood, and daughters marry out into their husbands' families where they are expected to submit to the authority of their mothers-in-law. They have been reared with this cultural expectation and with the belief that it is their duty to sacrifice on behalf of their husband's family and for the sake of their children. In contemporary Kolkata, according to Henrike Donner (2008), young middle-class, educated women favor joint family residence with their in-laws. Donner (2008:11) writes:

> Many young married women and middle-aged mothers were proud of the way their in-laws' family reflected what they saw as "traditional Bengali culture." While the nuclear family provides a solution to those who want to leave the tensions of joint living behind, it also gives rise to particular anxieties: first, the fear of abandonment in old age and, second, fear of violence from outsiders, in particular from people working in the house.

Furthermore, for those who have been reared in a joint or extended household where they have experienced multiple child care, have formed multiple attachments, and have developed a sense of self characterized by interdependence—what Alan Roland (1988) has called a "we-self"—nuclear family life will seem strange and lonely.

Finally, while it is tempting to try to relate Indian joint family life, with its multiple child care and multiple attachments, to Hindu theology and practices, that is a daunting project which cannot be undertaken here.[19] One distinctive aspect of Hinduism is that it provides its followers with a multitude of male and female deities to worship, especially mother goddesses. There is a large array of mother goddesses, with great powers of both positive and negative affect, to be supplicated just as one may have experienced an array of mother-surrogates with different emotional attributes. Instead of *being offered* milk and food, however, one *offers* them milk and food as part of one's worship. As with the Alorese, feeding is an important way of relating to the deities, and elaborate feasts are part of all religious and life-cycle events in India.

Some Conclusions

This chapter had several goals: (1) to begin normalizing multiple child care in the attachment literature and to demonstrate how it can vary in response to different environmental and cultural conditions; (2) to illustrate how different forms of multiple child care help to shape attachment in children in culturally distinct ways; and (3) to argue that mothering, or the primacy of the biological mother, must be examined within specific conditions of multiple child care. Contrasting Cora Du Bois's data from Alor, Indonesia, with my own research in North India has enabled me to illustrate how differently multiple child care can operate and the kinds of consequences there can be for early attachment in children, as well as for adult attachments.

In Alor, where multiple child care was highly dispersed across many caretakers and somewhat inconsistent, and where mothers were gone for long periods of the day leaving infants without a good source of nourishment, children had difficulty developing trusting relationships with others. Bowlby's conditions for attachment—that the infant have proximity to others and be kept safe—were satisfied because infants were looked after and carried about by many members of the village, but hunger was a real issue. Mobility during the second year of life only made young children more frustrated and angry because they were not allowed to follow mothers to their fields. In addition, they became subject to intense teasing by older children and adults. Alor, in the 1930s, was not a highly nurturing society but rather one that had recently emerged from chronic warfare and that emphasized independence, competition, and interpersonal distrust. Furthermore, as Quinn and Mageo point out in the introduction to this volume, "attachment theory gives us a rosy version of human development and a benign vision of society" that is not cross-culturally valid at either the individual or the societal level. The underside of positive attachment is some degree of inner conflict, fear, anger, and distrust.

In contrast with Alor, in North India there was a highly structured family system that produced stable and consistent multiple child care, and children learned—and were even overtly encouraged—to trust a variety of caregivers and family members. Infants and young children's attachment behaviors were distributed among a variety of household members—the people who were available to them to respond to their requests for nurturance and attention. Although Old Town children had a greater range of caretakers than did New Capital ones, children in all households had mother surrogates—grandmothers, aunts, older siblings, and servants—with whom they could and did establish emotional bonds. This diffusion of affect helped to produce interpersonal trust and interdependence, two of the desired outcomes of this child-care system. Middle- and upper-status mothers participated in this system by withholding empathic attention and by nursing infants casually and intermittently. Lower-status mothers were simply absent most of the time, which forced infants and young children to rely on others. As Mageo argues (chapter 7), "distancing" practices were used to undercut disfavored forms of attachment. In other words, dyadic bonds of attachment were intentionally muted in favor of diffused affect among a larger group of family members.

In both societies infants and young children were, nonetheless, clearly attached to their mothers (or, in the absence of mothers, to their grandmothers), the persons who were primarily responsible for feeding and sleeping with them. But mothers were just one of the many caregivers and objects of attachment. For the Alorese, mothers also became objects of overt frustration and anger. Within Indian joint families, what frustration infants may have experienced was muted by the constant availability of other responsible caregivers. As Hrdy (2009) has theorized, postmenopausal women—grandmothers—played an important role in both societies, although in Alor most grandmothers were still engaged in horticultural work and were rarely available for full-time child care. In Bhubaneswar, India, grandmothers played a significant role in child care in both the Old Town and the New Capital, although statistically, female siblings were even more frequent caregivers of infants and young children than grandmothers.

Finally, there is evidence that these two versions of multiple child care had differential effects upon children's working models of interpersonal relationships and their adult capacities for attachment to others. The balance of trust and distrust in the two societies was strikingly different. Alorese children came to view others as relatively unreliable and untrustworthy—probably a realistic assessment for the kind of society into which they were being socialized. Again, it is important to emphasize that in no way should their experience be compared with that of the emotionally deprived children from post–World War II (Bowlby 1969) or, in more recent times, from Romanian orphanages (Talbot 1998). But we do know that the Alorese of the 1930s had difficulty establishing stable marital relationships. In contrast, Indian children, growing up in large, stable joint households, developed a high degree of trust in others that included allowing elders to arrange their marriages—marriages that were very infrequently broken. It is important to note, however, that Hindu culture also emphasized personal sacrifice and the muting of dyadic bonds in favor of the well-being of the familial group. The two different systems of multiple child care and attachment were enmeshed within very different cultural contexts and expectations for adult behavior.

Acknowledgments

First, I want to thank Naomi Quinn for stimulating my interest in attachment theory several years ago by organizing a session, "Rethinking Attachment and Separation," in which I participated at the 2009 biennial meeting of the Society for Psychological Anthropology. That session led to an interdisciplinary conference on attachment theory that Naomi Quinn and Jeannette Mageo organized in 2011 (see introduction). I want to thank them both not only for organizing that excellent conference, for which a draft of this chapter was prepared, but for their support and suggestions for improving it. Finally, I want to thank my two Pitzer College colleagues, Robert L. Munroe and Claudia Strauss, for their invaluable comments upon several different versions of this chapter.

Notes

1. Hillary Rodham Clinton's book, *It Takes a Village: And Other Lessons Children Teach Us* (1996), has most recently popularized this proverb that seems to have African origins.
2. Early on Margaret Mead (1962) criticized Bowlby's theory of attachment for focusing too much on the "natural mother" and for inadequately recognizing

that mothering "can be safely distributed among several figures [quoted in Bowlby 1969:303, footnote 2]." Bowlby responded, "No such views have been expressed by me."

3. From a cross-cultural perspective, exclusive mother caretaking is rare. Weisner and Gallimore (1977), using holocultural ratings for 150 small-scale societies, found that in only 3 percent of the cases were infants exclusively nurtured by mothers.
4 Du Bois learned and transcribed the Alorese language (Abui), observed caregiving practices and parent-child relationships, collected genealogies in order to understand the kinship system, and participated in everyday life as well as in the ceremonial life of the village. In addition to her ethnographic research, Du Bois collected a large amount of psychological data from samples of men and women: eight in-depth autobiographies; 54 Porteus Maze tests (problem-solving intelligence tests); 36 word association tests; 55 children's drawings; and 37 Rorschach tests.
5. Du Bois (1944:20) described Alorese households as generally nuclear, although "supplemented from time to time by other kin, bilaterally reckoned." In fact, her census data indicate that for Atimelang's 16 households, 4 were nuclear in structure, 9 were extended, 3 were single-parent households (either a single mother or grandmother with children), and 1 had a maternal grandmother, mother, and children residing together. Cora Alice Du Bois Papers, 1903, Tozzer Library, Harvard College Library, Harvard University, Box 52.
6. The ages cited here for childhood maturational periods in Alor are the ones that Du Bois used, and they closely resemble the ones I have used in India.
7. Cited from Du Bois's Alorese fieldnotes, Cora Alice Du Bois Papers, op. cit., Box 46.
8. An excerpt from Lecture #9, Washington School of Psychiatry, 1952, Cora Alice Du Bois Papers, op. cit., Box 67.
9. I have examined all of Du Bois's fieldnotes from Alor in the process of researching and writing a biography about her. They reside in the Cora Alice Du Bois Papers, op. cit.
10. Cited from Du Bois's Alorese fieldnotes, Cora Alice Du Bois Papers, op. cit., Box 52.
11. Du Bois's Alorese census and fieldnotes indicate that in one case a grandmother was the sole caregiver for her daughter's two children. The children's mother and father had died. In another case, an infant was given to the full-time care of a maternal grandmother. Cited from Du Bois's fieldnotes, Cora Alice Du Bois Papers, op. cit., Box 52.
12. Cited in Du Bois's Alorese fieldnotes, Cora Alice Du Bois Papers, op. cit., Box 52.
13. The psychoanalyst Abram Kardiner analyzed the autobiographies. Emil Oberhozer, a psychiatrist who had helped Hermann Rorschach develop the Rorschach test, analyzed the set of Rorschachs that Du Bois collected. And the children's drawings were analyzed by Mrs. Schmidl-Waehner, an Austrian artist with psychoanalytic training.
14. April 12, 1938, letter to Abram Kardiner (emphasis added). Cora Alice Du Bois Papers, op. cit., Box 23.
15. A recent report indicates that some of these children who spent the first two years or more in a Romanian orphanage have brain abnormalities (Sanders 2012).

16. In 1961, Cora Du Bois, then the Zemurray Professor of Anthropology at Harvard University, selected Bhubaneswar, Odisha, India, as the site for a 12-year study of socioeconomic and cultural change. Some 14 Harvard, MIT, and Indian graduate students participated in the study.
17. I use the word "household" to distinguish the portion of a joint family that resided together under one roof. Sometimes families became too large to live under one roof or, in the case of the New Capital, not all government servants had been able to move with their extended families to their new residences in Bhubaneswar.
18. It has become increasingly common for prospective grooms and brides to meet and to have a veto power over their parents' selection of a spouse for them.
19. Stanley Kurtz, in his ambitious book, *All the Mothers are One: Hindu India and the Cultural Reshaping of Psychoanalysis* (1992), has tried to relate Indian child-rearing practices and child development to a revised psychoanalytic understanding of adult personality and Hindu practices of mother goddess worship in India.

References

Ainsworth, Mary D. Slater. 1967. *Infancy in Uganda: Infant Care and the Growth of Attachment*. Baltimore: Johns Hopkins Press.

Ainsworth, Mary D. Slater, Mary C. Belher, Everett Waters, and Sally Wall. 1978. *Patterning of Attachment*. Hillsdale, NJ: Erlbaum Press.

Barry, Herbert III, Margaret K. Bacon, and Irvin L. Child. 1967. "Definitions, Ratings and Bibliographic Sources of Child-Training Practices of 110 cultures." In *Cross-Cultural Approaches*, C. S. Ford, ed., pp. 293–331. New Haven, CT: HRAF Press.

Barry, Herbert, III, and Leonora M. Paxson. 1971. "Infancy and Early Childhood: Cross-Cultural Codes 2." *Ethnology* 10:466–508.

Beals, Alan. 1962. *Gopalpur: A South Indian Village*. New York: Holt, Rinehart, & Winston.

Bowlby, John. 1969. *Attachment and Loss Vol. 1: Attachment*. New York: Basic Books.

Briggs, Jean L. 1998. *Inuit Morality Play: The Emotional Education of a Three-Year-Old*. New Haven, CT: Yale University Press.

Donner, Henrike. 2008. *Domestic Goddesses: Maternity, Globalization and Middle-Class Identity in Contemporary India*. Burlington, Vermont: Ashgate Publishing.

Du Bois, Cora. 1944. *The People of Alor: A Social-Psychological Study of an East Indian Island*. Minneapolis, MN: The University of Minnesota Press.

Du Bois, Cora. 1956. "Attitudes toward Food and Hunger in Alor." In *Personal Character and Cultural Milieu*, Douglas G. Haring, ed., pp. 241–253. New York: Syracuse University Press.

Howes, Carolee, and Susan Spieker. 2008. "Attachment Relationships in the Context of Multiple Caregivers." In *Handbook of Attachment: Theory, Research, and Clinical Applications*, Jude Cassidy and Phillip R. Shaver, eds., pp. 317–332. New York: Guilford Press.

Hrdy, Sarah Blaffer. 2009. *Mothers and Others: The Evolutionary Origins of Mutual Understanding*. Cambridge, MA: The Belknap Press of Harvard University Press.

Keller, Heidi, and Robin Harwood. 2009. "Culture and Development Pathways of Relationship Formation." In *Pathways on Human Development, Family, and Culture*, S. Beckman and A. Aksu-Koc, eds., pp. 157–177. Cambridge, England: Cambridge University Press.

Keller, Heidi, and Hiltrud Otto. 2009. "The Cultural Socialization of Emotion Regulation during Infancy." *Journal of Cross-Cultural Psychology* 40(6): 996–1011.

Konner, Melvin. 2010. *The Evolution of Childhood: Relationships, Emotion, Mind.* Cambridge: The Belknap Press of Harvard University Press.

Kurtz, Stanley. 1992. *All the Mothers Are One: Hindu India and the Cultural Reshaping of Psychoanalysis.* New York: Columbia University Press.

Lamb, Michael E. 1998. "Nonparental Child Care: Context, Quality, Correlates, and Consequences." In *Handbook of Child Psychology*, vol. 4, Irving E. Sigel and K. Anne Renninger, eds., pp. 73–133. New York: Wiley.

Maduro, Renaldo. 1976. *Artistic Creativity in a Brahmin Painter Community.* Berkeley, CA: Center for South and Southeast Asia Studies, University of California.

Mead, Margaret. 1962. "A Cultural Anthropologist's Approach to Maternal Deprivation." In *Deprivation of Maternal Care: A Reassessment of Its Effects.* Public Health Papers 14. Geneva: World Health Organization.

Mead, Margaret. 1974 [1928] *Coming of Age in Samoa.* New York: Morrow.

Minturn, Leigh, and William W. Hitchcock. 1966. *The Rajputs of Khalapur, India.* New York: Wiley.

Minturn, Leigh, and William W. Lambert. 1964. *Mothers of Six Cultures.* New York: Wiley.

Morelli, Gilda A., and Fred Rothbaum. 2007. "Situating the Child in Context: Attachment Relationships and Self-regulation in Different Cultures." In *Handbook of Cultural Psychology*, S. Kitayama and D. Cohen, eds., pp. 500–527. New York: Guilford Press.

Munroe, Robert L., and Mary Gauvain. 2010. "The Cross-cultural Study of Children's Learning and Socialization: A Short History." In *The Anthropology of Learning in Childhood*, David F. Lancy, John Bock, and Suzanne Gaskins, eds., pp. 35–63. Lanham, MD: Alta Mira Press.

Munroe, Robert L., and Ruth H. Munroe. 1975. *Cross-Cultural Human Development.* Prospect Heights, IL: Waveland Press.

Otto, Hiltrud, and Heidi Keller. 2011. "A Good Child is a Calm Child: Mothers' Social Status, Maternal Conceptions of Proper Demeanor, and Stranger Anxiety in One-Year Old Cameroonian Nso Children." Unpublished paper prepared for the Lemelson/Society for Psychological Anthropology Conference, "Rethinking Attachment and Separation Cross-Culturally," Washington State University, Spokane, May 19–21, 2011.

Rohner, Ronald P. 1975. *They Love Me, They Love Me Not: A Worldwide Study of the Effects of Parental Acceptance and Rejection.* New Haven, CT: HRAF Press.

Roland, Alan. 1988. *In Search of Self in India and Japan: Toward a Cross-Cultural Psychology.* Princeton, NJ: Princeton University Press.

Sanders, Laura. 2012. "Scars from Harsh Early Years Linger: Brain Changes Seen among Kids from Grim Orphanage." *Science News*, March 10, 2012:9.

Seymour, Susan. 1983. "Household Structure and Status and Expressions of Affect in India." *Ethos* 11:263–277.

Seymour, Susan. 1999. *Women, Family, and Child Care in India: A World in Transition.* Cambridge: Cambridge University Press.
Talbot, Margaret. 1998. "Attachment Theory: The Ultimate Experiment." *New York Times Magazine*, May 24:24–30, 38, 46, 50, 54.
Trawick, Margaret. 1992. *Notes on Love in a Tamil Family.* Berkeley, CA: University of California Press.
Weisner, Thomas S. 2005. "Attachment as a Cultural and Ecological Problem with Pluralistic Solutions." *Human Development* 48:89–94.
Weisner, Thomas S., and Ronald Gallimore. 1977. "My Brother's Keeper: Child and Sibling Caretaking." *Current Anthropology* 18(2):169–190.
Whiting, Beatrice B. 1963. *Six Cultures: Studies of Child Rearing.* New York: Wiley.
Whiting, Beatrice B., and John W. M. Whiting. 1975. Children of Six Cultures: A Psycho-Cultural Analysis. Cambridge: Harvard University Press.
Whiting, Beatrice B., and Carolyn P. Edwards. 1988. *Children of Different Worlds: The Formation of Social Behavior.* Cambridge, MA: Harvard University Press.
Whiting, John W. M., and I. L. Child. 1953. *Child Training and Personality.* New Haven, CT: Yale University Press.

Part III

Autonomy and Dependence

Chapter 5

Attachment in Rural Sri Lanka: The Shape of Caregiver Sensitivity, Communication, and Autonomy

Bambi L. Chapin

The goals of attachment theory are, in some key ways, very close to my own as a researcher and psychological anthropologist. Attachment theory, as established within developmental psychology, seeks to identify the kinds of care that human infants need and to understand how the provision of that care shapes people over their life course. Psychological anthropologists like myself also take seriously the question of what capacities, inclinations, and needs human infants share. As John Bowlby did in his original formulations of attachment theory, we too assume that these pan-species characteristics have been arrived at through processes of natural selection and adaptation. We recognize that key among these characteristics are the relatively long period of utter dependency on others and the mental plasticity of human infants, features of human development that lead to deep shaping through early social interaction.[1] Most importantly, we too look to the patterns of behavior, personnel, and emotion in these early interactions to see how it is that people are formed.

There are significant departures, though, between the approaches generally taken by attachment psychologists and those taken by psychological anthropologists, as the contributions to this volume make clear. The biggest of these differences lies in the cultural contexts in which data are collected and in the interest (or absence of interest) in determining which developmental paths are optimal. Despite initial research based in diverse culture groups (see Mary Ainsworth's 1967 work in Uganda) and occasional applications to non-US groups, attachment theory has largely grown out of examinations of patterns of child care and personhood specific to groups in the United States.[2]

Attachment theory holds that human infants display biologically-based behaviors designed to maintain proximity to attachment figures, principally their mothers.[3] Mothers' responses to these behaviors, the working models children develop out of these experiences, and the ways the attachment system interacts with other systems are thought to pattern children's future emotional orientations, relationships, and senses of themselves. Children whose mothers are available and responsive in infancy develop secure views of the world that allow them to explore and express themselves in positive ways, leading them to establish a solid sense of their own autonomy as they grow up. Children who do not receive responsive care from consistent attachment figures are, according to the standard view within attachment theory, likely to be anxious and clingy, aggressive, or unable to connect with others.

This theory reflects a particular twentieth-century, middle-class, US style of parenting and set of personhood goals, which it then uses to determine optimal child rearing and outcomes. The kinds of interaction between mothers and children that this theory describes, measures, and assesses are purported to reflect universal patterns of human development, evolved as adaptations during our species' past. However, ethnographic observations of caregiving practices and relationships in other communities are often at odds with this theory, as this volume and previous research demonstrate (Harwood et al. 1995; Keller and Harwood 2009; LeVine 2004; LeVine and Norman 2001; Mageo 1998; Morelli and Rothbaum 2007; Rothbaum et al. 2000; Weisner 2005). As LeVine and Norman point out in their analysis of German infant-care practices, this research suggests that "there is a wider range of pathways to normal emotional development than has been imagined in attachment theory" (2001:101).

In my own long-term ethnographic fieldwork with Sinhala families in rural Sri Lanka, I observed patterns of child care, relationships, and valued ways of being that complicate the picture of attachment offered by current theories within developmental psychology. In their responsiveness to children's needs, the infant-care practices I observed were very much in keeping with the kinds of care that attachment theory says lead to "secure" attachment. However, in these interactions needs were signalled and responded to in a largely non-verbal manner, which is at odds with the verbal expressiveness and open communication thought to be part of secure attachments in the United States. Furthermore, the ways that Sinhala children are expected to be as they grow up, the goals for mature personhood, look very different from the ways a "securely attached" individual is expected to look according to the attachment literature. In Sri Lanka, maturity is judged by an increasing sensitivity and deference to the preferences of parents and other senior figures, rather than increasing self-assertion and independence. As I will argue, this does not mean that "autonomy" is not part of Sri Lanka-style maturity; rather, it is required by it. Taken together, these observations suggest that the particular ways that caregivers respond to infants shape the ways that autonomy is experienced and manifested in later life. This suggestion is in keeping with the general propositions of attachment theory but requires a broadening of the conception of caregiving responsiveness, of autonomy, and of how these might be related in different cultural circumstances.

In this chapter, I will begin by describing the patterns of child care I observed in Sri Lanka, focusing especially on how caregivers typically responded to infants' needs and the signals of those needs. I will describe the kind of parent-child relationships valued by the people whom I knew there and the kinds of behavior and emotion that were expected within these relationships, explaining how children internalize this relationship model through everyday interactions with caregivers and use it as a template for subsequent hierarchical relationships. I will discuss the increasing deference to authority and self-control demonstrated by Sinhala adolescents and young adults and the limited communication between them and their parents, contrasting this with the kind of communication and autonomy-seeking expected from US teens. In the end, I will argue that, although this developmental path appears to diverge in crucial ways from the path of "secure" development mapped by attachment theorists, it also shares key elements regarding the establishment and mastery of one's self and self-expression. Throughout, I will demonstrate the centrality of attachment relationships in Sinhala child rearing, culture transmission, and the shaping of culturally consonant people.

Child Care in a Sinhala Village

I have been conducting research over the last decade in a village I call "Viligama." Viligama is in the center of Sri Lanka, about a half-hour's bus ride from the provincial capital, Kandy. The residents of this village are primarily Sinhala speakers and mostly identify as Buddhist. In 1999, just over half of the households in Viligama were nuclear and neolocal; most of the rest were composed of parents and their married children, often with children of their own. Generally, newly married couples hoped to move into their own homes where they would raise their children. Although mothers were typically the primary caregivers, it was not unusual for fathers and other relatives, especially grandmothers and aunts, to care for children. This was generally made easy since households tended to be situated adjacent to or very near close relatives, particularly on the father's side. However, ties with the mother's side of the family were also important, as reflected in and supported by bilateral kinship and inheritance practices, as well as a preference for bilateral cross-cousin marriages.

Although the ideal in Viligama as in other Sinhala areas was for new couples to move into their own homes, when a new baby was born, the mother and baby typically returned to the mother's own mother's home, where they stayed for the baby's first three months. During this time, the mother's relatives would care for her and the baby, doing their laundry, cooking for her, and sparing her from her usual household chores. When I visited new mothers during this early period, they were always in their housedresses and usually lying in bed with the baby who dozed and nursed as it wished. Both babies and mothers slept as much as they liked.[4] As new mothers began to feel stronger, they would get up more frequently, often leaving the baby on its back on a cloth on the bed, awake or asleep. When visitors came, they would lean over the baby, smiling exaggeratedly and cooing "uu-kuu, uu-kuu" (which one person translated for me as being a form of a word for "milk"). Seldom did children cry, and mothers too seemed relaxed and well cared-for during this period.[5]

Caregiver Sensitivity: Accessible and Responsive

In this time of togetherness for mother and baby, a time of touching and gazing and the establishment of "attunement," we see the kind of behaviors thought by attachment theorists to promote the development of a strong and secure attachment bond from the infant to the mother. It is a time when the mother is close by, laying the groundwork for the infant to develop a working model of the caregiver as available and responsive, which presumably will then allow the child to explore the world confidently and with increasing independence (Weinfield et al. 2008:79). Indeed, this intense togetherness is far more powerfully supported by social arrangement and expectations in Viligama than is typical in the United States, and not only during the first three months but for a long time afterward, as children continue to sleep next to their parents and other family members and continue to nurse on demand for several years.

As attachment theorists point out, "accessibility is not enough to establish security for the child...The child needs to experience a parent who is not only accessible but also *responsive*" (Kobak and Madsen 2008:30, emphasis in original). What is key in convincing infants of their caregivers' accessibility and responsiveness, according to Ainsworth, is the "sensitivity" of those caregivers to infants' signals (Kobak and Madsen 2008:30). In Viligama, typical child-rearing methods not only entail a great deal of proximity but also require a great deal of sensitivity to infants' signals, thus giving children ample opportunities to become "securely attached."

Typically, Sri Lankan adults are attentive and responsive to subtle signs of infants' needs. This is particularly evident in the ways that elimination is handled. In my own observations, those who cared for children treated urine and feces casually, with only the minimum of off-handed concern that a child might soil something or someone. Babies in this warm climate were left bottomless or dressed in panties and laid on towels or cloths, all of which were replaced as necessary throughout the day. Only when traveling did people seem to be concerned. My questions about these processes were not very interesting to people; it all seemed quite obvious to mothers, as well as to the others I asked. People reported that by the time babies are around ten months old, they no longer have accidents but use a toilet or other appropriate spot.[6] Children learn to eliminate in the proper place and manner, I was told, by being placed repeatedly astride the in-ground toilet by their mothers or other caregivers.

What allows this training to succeed is keen attention and responsiveness to the subtle physical signs that children display when they are about to urinate or defecate. Although mothers told me that babies just learn to control their bladder and bowels on their own, my observations led me to make a slightly different sense of this matter. First, there were frequent "accidents" beyond the first year, but these did not excite the attention or concern of anyone. Second, it seemed to be the adults who were being successfully trained rather than the children. Parents and others who held babies were particularly motivated to notice small signs that indicated a child might be about to evacuate bladder or bowels, and they quickly held the child away from their own bodies, usually without drawing verbal attention to it. When babies were able to stand on their own, mothers and others swiftly removed them to a more appropriate place, positioning them over one of the gutters that ran around the houses or down the edges of the streets.

In this, as in most parent-child interactions, the child is not encouraged to recognize and intentionally express his or her needs. Instead, the parent recognizes the child's need and acts to meet it, providing direction by physical manipulation without verbal instruction, all the while conceptualizing this development as something the child is just ready to do, the parents only having provided the opportunity. Rather than using toilet training as an opportunity to encourage children to verbalize their internal states and to make choices about what they want to do about them, as is common in the contemporary United States, Sri Lankan adults see children as autonomously developing control over their own bodily processes.[7] Toilet training demonstrates the contrast between the kinds of autonomy children were encouraged to develop in this Sri Lankan village and the kinds of autonomy vaunted in attachment theory—something I will return to later in this chapter. For now, I want to call attention to ways that these practices around elimination demonstrate the attentiveness and responsiveness of Sri Lankan caregivers. This same style of interaction can be seen in countless other daily interactions between children and older, more fully socialized people, including the kinds of feeding practices I will describe in the next section.

Communication, Choice, and Self-expression

Seldom do Sri Lankan parents ask their children of any age what they want, nor do they aim to encourage children to express their opinions or exercise their choices. Good children wait patiently and uncomplainingly, taking what they are given. Good parents provide for their children what they need, without consulting the children about those needs or preferences. This is evident in the toilet training that I just described.

A similar pattern is evident in the ways that children are fed. In Viligama, children were typically fed by hand from a plate their mother prepared. Each day at meals with children of all ages, mothers and grandmothers massaged together bits of rice and curry then popped the little balls into their waiting children's mouths. Siblings might be fed one at a time or together from the same plate. In contrast, these same mothers looked on bemused as I haggled with my four-year-old son over which foods he wanted to try, encouraging and negotiating with him to try more of what I thought good for him and praising him for his choices. In this basic, everyday child-rearing task, the ways that we thought we should interact with our children and the ways we wanted our children to be diverged sharply. Our children's expectations also diverged, showing that they were already learning what to expect from their caregivers and how they should behave with others. The Sri Lankan children were learning that when they waited passively, their caregivers would identify and provide what they needed.

It is not that young children in Viligama never expressed their wishes—they did and often quite vehemently. However, parents did not enter into negotiation over these demands. As I have discussed at length elsewhere, if attempts to ignore, distract, lie to, or slap at children failed to get them to desist from their demands, most people simply gave into those demands, no matter how outrageous (Chapin 2010). But these outbursts of desire were expected to—and usually did—dissipate as children grew older and came to "understand" (*tērenavā*). What exactly children were supposed to understand was hard for people to articulate but generally had to do with recognizing the consequences of their actions—especially the social consequences. This general capacity for understanding was thought to develop as a child matured, beginning around age five and being well-established by age ten. One of the principal ways that a maturing understanding manifests itself is in increasing compliance with social norms, deference to elders, and self-denial, all of which require a kind of self-control and autonomy that looks very different from the self-expression central to the definition of autonomy in mainstream attachment theory.

In contrast, the kind of expressive training that is posited by attachment theorists to be required for the confident self-expression central to the achievement of "autonomy" was largely absent in child-caregiver interactions I observed in Sri Lanka. Children were not encouraged to express themselves in words, and caregivers did not model verbal expressiveness when they interacted with children. Rather, Sri Lankan caregivers relied on nonverbal cues and physical structuring to indicate to children behaviors that were appreciated and ones that were undesirable.

This generalization was illustrated one day during a play interview I was conducting with a four-year-old girl. The girl was not paying much attention, picking up dolls at random and trying to pull off their hair. The mother, visibly embarrassed by her daughter's behavior, said nothing to her daughter. Instead, while laughing nervously, she physically restrained and repositioned her daughter throughout the interview, pulling and pushing her into some semblance of poses the mother thought appropriate. Earlier, on that same day, when the girl had hurt herself and was crying loudly, this same mother had clamped her hand over the child's mouth and pushed her head into her lap, saying that it was nothing. At the end of the interview, when it was time for them to go, the girl burst into angry sobs, although she made no effort to verbally communicate what had upset her. I was alarmed and asked what the matter was, but her mother kept saying it was nothing, while dragging her daughter to the door. Finally, in response to my apologies, the mother admitted that, in order to get her daughter to cooperate with the play interview, she had told her daughter that she would get to play with (or maybe that I would give her) my computer when we were finished. I was alarmed and felt terrible that the girl had been coerced into the interview with false promises. Insisting that they stay a bit longer, I quickly grabbed an electronic game belonging to my son that looked something like a computer and brought it out for the girl to play with, something her mother indulged but seemed to find totally unnecessary—even funny. Since the little girl did not yet have the capacity for understanding, it did not really matter what people said to her. The purpose of the mother's promise had been to make her daughter behave properly, not to give her accurate information about our session so she could decide whether or not to participate.

Before children reached the age at which they could understand things, it was considered foolish to explain things to them or to reason with them about their desires. Children were not encouraged to articulate their perspectives, desires, ideas, or feelings, nor did parents model this for children themselves. When there was verbal communication from the parent (as in the promise of the computer), its value was in its efficacy rather than its accuracy. While parents often verbalized threats or promised treats, these did not necessarily represent events actually anticipated by the parent as consequences of children's behavior.

This pattern of communication also informs culturally standardized approaches to widely shared mothering tasks, such as weaning. Conventionally in Sri Lanka, when a mother is ready to stop breast-feeding—typically when the child is between two and four years or when another baby is coming along—she will apply a bitter oil to her nipples to discourage the child from nursing. If the child objects, the mother will not explain the reason for the bitter taste or discuss with the child why he or she should stop breast-feeding. Instead, she will continue to apply the oil surreptitiously until the child no longer attempts to nurse.

These patterned interactions contain important features that resonate with a more general cultural model of hierarchically ranked relationships, which I will describe in the next section. In these caregiving interactions, the person in the superior role determines what is to be done without soliciting or attending to the expressed wishes of the subordinate. The verbal communication from senior to junior is minimal and void of explicit rationales. This departs from what in attachment theory is seen as the kind of training in verbal expression considered necessary for the achievement of autonomy; it also precludes the exercise of a junior person's autonomy as this is defined within attachment theory. Yet, throughout, the parent does not overtly interfere with the child's continuance of the relationship; the child is allowed to continue nursing until he or she decides to stop, a piece of the pattern and a kind of autonomy I will return to later.

Attachment Theory on Sensitive Care and Self-expression

What I observed in this Sri Lankan village was a pattern of caregiving in which mothers and other caretakers were attuned and responsive to children but did not encourage verbal expression. While this pattern contrasts with the recommendations of attachment theorists that caretaking be both responsive and expressive, it resonates with caregiving patterns that are normative and valued in other parts of the world. For instance, Fred Rothbaum and his colleagues (2000) have observed that Japanese caregivers prefer to respond to babies' needs before they express them, helping them with stress management and emotional regulation rather than facilitating the babies' expression and pursuit of their own needs. Robert LeVine (2004) describes the Gusii mothers whom he observed in Kenya as very sensitive and responsive to children's distress signals but relatively unresponsive to children's non-distress vocalizations, in contrast to American mothers who were "moderately responsive to both kinds of signals" (160).

I am not suggesting that we interpret these data to mean that there are two alternative patterns of "sensitive parenting"—one that encourages verbal expression and another that does not. The other behaviors and emotions in which these caregiving behaviors are nested, the theories about parenting and the goals for personhood that parents and others in these various societies hold, and the kind of relationships that are valued and taught differ significantly across these and other cultural contexts. However, these observations do support LeVine's (2004) suggestion that the various components of "maternal sensitivity," as it is discussed in attachment theory, may in fact vary independently of each other and be incorporated differently in specific cultural contexts. The ways that children experience their needs being responded to and the ways they are being taught to communicate may both be significant components in the development of children's expectations of those around them, their models of how to participate in relationships, and their senses of themselves. However, there is not necessarily one particular configuration of these factors or outcomes that is universally optimal as implied by the standard version of attachment theory.

Working Models of Relationships

The ways that Sri Lankan parents responded to their children's needs sensitively but without encouraging verbal expression of those needs reflects one of their central cultural models of relationships. These interactions display a cultural model of hierarchically ranked relationships that implicitly guides the actions and options of fully acculturated caregivers in Viligama. These patterned caregiving interactions also convey that model of hierarchy to the children involved. As children participate in these salient interactions with important others to get the things they need and want, they are assembling their own "working models"—to use Bowlby's phrase (1982:354)—of the world, of others, of relationships, and of themselves.[8] These models form templates for subsequent interactions not only with these particular caregivers but with other superiors, juniors, and peers in a range of settings over the life course, with each enactment potentially reinforcing, altering, or adding to the models. Because children's experiences are patterned by social arrangements and the understandings held by their caregivers, the working models that children are developing are also likely to be shared with others. To the extent that they are shared with others, these are "cultural models" (see D'Andrade 1995, Strauss and Quinn 1997).

In the Sinhala cultural model of hierarchically ranked relationships that is brought to life and conveyed in early parent-child interactions, good superiors (principally mothers, at least at first) provide children what they need, without consulting those children about their needs or preferences (see Table 5.1). Good juniors, like good children, wait patiently and uncomplainingly, accepting what they are given. Experiences like the ones I have described of remaining passive while being directly cared for by someone who does not expect input or choice from the child are repeated throughout the life course in relationships between superiors and subordinates. These primary experiences of hierarchical relationships with sensitive, responsive caregivers are infused with nurturance, trust, and dependence, coloring the Sinhala model of hierarchy as it is enacted and internalized within these early attachment relationships. Through these interactions children come to

Table 5.1 Sinhala model of hierarchically ranked relationships

The Superior	
Obligations	Identifies and provides for subordinate's needs
Proscriptions	Does not solicit verbal input from subordinate
	Does not justify or explain actions
Emotional orientation	Kind, caring, and committed
	Confident and powerful
	Restrained and judicious
The Subordinate	
Obligations	Offers compliance, passivity, service, respectfulness
Proscriptions	Does not question or offer opinions
	Does not discuss thoughts and experiences
Emotional orientation	Acquiescent, expectant, and patient
	Shy/properly ashamed, a little afraid
	Deferential and respectful
	Admiring and trusting

know, feel about, and value relationships of dependence and hierarchy—knowledge, feelings, and values that will inform their hierarchical relationships outside the family as well as their own future parenting.

Adolescence in a Sinhala Village

By adolescence, most children in Viligama demonstrate that they have fully internalized the model of hierarchy as experienced within the family and reinforced by other social interactions. They not only understand and perform the roles, expectations, and possibilities of these relationships as entailed in the model, but they have come to feel about these relationships in ways appropriate to the model. When I asked parents in Viligama to describe what happens as children grow up, they also emphasized both cognitive and affective dimensions of this developmental process as demonstrated in proper relationship behavior. They described these changes within a distinctive, if implicit, cultural theory of development. As Sinhala children entered adolescence, their understanding was said to be more fully developed. This did not, however, lead to greater independence from parental supervision, more of a say in the decisions that affected them, or greater information exchange between parents and children. Instead, as children in Viligama grew, they were expected to be more rather than less deferential to their elders, more sensitive to hierarchy, more confident that their elders know what is best for them, and less assertive about their own needs and opinions. And indeed, that is what I observed.

In what follows, I will describe the behaviors and emotions that are expected of adolescents and young adults as they act within this model, as well as the importance of consent. I will then discuss how those behaviors and emotions contrast with what is expected of securely attached and increasingly autonomous young people within attachment theory. However, as I will argue, the ways that Sinhala young people participate within hierarchical relationships does not, as attachment theory might see it, demonstrate lack of a secure and autonomous self; instead, proper participation in these ranked relationships requires autonomy and demonstrates its achievement.

Increasing Dependence and Deference

Adolescence is a time in a Sinhala person's life that requires intensive supervision and guidance, particularly for Sinhala girls. Several of the mothers in the village worked abroad while their children were young, leaving them in the care of fathers and extended kin, but returned when their daughters neared puberty because the mothers felt that their daughters were entering a period in which a mother's guidance and protection were essential.[9] Instead of leading to more autonomy, the adolescent's developing understanding leads to a fuller sense of shame, respect, and social propriety and a greater trust of and compliance with the dictates of one's parent, an internalization of the Sinhala model of hierarchically ranked relationships and the subordinate role within that model. My limited observations of older boys' interactions with their parents make me think that they also internalized the basic frame of this model; however, since most of my direct interviewing and social contact was with women, girls, and little boys, the material about adolescent boys' development that would round out this picture is not available to me.

As girls entered puberty, they were not only expected to act in ways that demonstrated their virtue and a properly disciplined self, but they also reported feeling the emotions that were understood to prompt those actions. They said that, following the "big girl" ceremonies that marked their first menstruation, they felt increasingly uncomfortable and shy around their fathers.[10] Although they used to sit on their fathers' laps, now they would leave the room if their fathers came in. They said that they did these avoidance and distancing actions because they respected and loved their fathers so much that they felt *lajja* (shy/embarrassed/ashamed) in their presence. They also reported that they could not ask their mothers about what was happening to their bodies because they knew it was not appropriate and felt shy to do so, all of which they reported proudly as it demonstrated their understanding and their virtue. It is not just that these young women had learned to perform their roles with greater aptitude and completeness but that they had come to feel toward their parents in ways that motivated them to enact those performances.

With increased understanding also came fuller feelings of trust in the decisions of parents and a fuller commitment to follow their directions. At a time when there were major life choices to be made, adolescents and young adults in Viligama waited patiently for their parents to make these decisions for them, just as they had waited to have food placed in their mouths as young children. By their teen years, it was clear that they had internalized an expectation that their parents would willingly and ably manage their lives. While for major life decisions, such as those regarding marriage, education, and employment, the young person's consent is required, the pressure of parental desires and expectations is strongly felt. This is evident in the following excerpt from an interview with Shanthi, a 22-year-old woman who had just started attending the prestigious and selective Peradeniya University.

Excerpt from Interview with Shanthi

(NOTE: Unlike most of my interviews in the village, this was conducted in English so that, at Shanthi's request, she could practice her language skills.)

Bambi: Why did you choose to go to university?
Shanthi: I didn't choose.
B: You didn't choose? Who chose?

S: My mother. She very [much] likes [for me] to go—but I don't like.
B: So you're only going because your mother wants you to?
S: I like to learn but I... (pause).
B: If you got to decide by yourself — your mother said "Oh, I don't care"— what would you choose? What would you do?
S: I would dancing choose.

In making decisions, elders do not solicit young people's opinions, desires, and feelings, but it would be incorrect to say that adolescents did not have any opinions, desires, or feelings about these decisions.[11] Privately, they could articulate their own preferences even when these conflicted with their elders', but they generally planned to follow the expectations of their parents as they understood them. When I asked young women whether they would like to have their parents arrange a marriage for them or choose their own husband—both of which were practiced with equal frequency in the village[12]—they consistently said they preferred for their parents to find a husband for them. While there were certainly many reasons for giving this answer, not the least of which was to show their own virtue and modesty, these young women explained that their parents would know what match was best for them, who would make a good husband, who was from a good family. One girl, exasperated with my denseness in not seeing the advantage parents had in making this decision, told me, "I would just choose someone handsome!"—clearly a poor criterion on which to hang one's future.[13]

Their own specific preferences did not seem salient or motivating, nor were they especially troubling when unfulfilled. Although important exceptions emerged, what most adolescents may have wanted for their own lives was relatively hypocognized in comparison to the commitment to stay in the relationship with the parents, a relationship that necessarily entailed deference to the parents' will. It is only with the consent of the junior person that these relationships continued, a topic that I will take up in the next section. In keeping with this requirement for consent, we will see that, while young people were unlikely to speak to their elders about their particular wishes, they might raise objections when confronted with the plans made for them.

Marriage is one of the most important decisions Sri Lankan parents make for their children, although there is a range of ways families are involved, from arranging marriage proposals to supporting one with someone the child met on his or her own. In the most formal arrangements, young women have no role in initiating or directing the search for a husband. When I first asked about this, my assumption that the girls themselves might have talked to their parents about undertaking this process produced confusion and then shocked laughter. No girl would be so shameless as to ask to be coupled—but no parent should be so dim or uncaring as to not recognize that, after completing their schooling, girls would of course be waiting for a marriage. That parents should be sensitive, caring, and responsive to their children's needs is part of the basic model of child care in the village and part of the expectations for the way seniors should behave within the Sinhala hierarchy model.

Even in the most formal marriage arrangements, consent is required from both partners for an engagement to proceed. This is classically conveyed during the visit of a potential bridegroom and his family to a potential bride's family by the emergence of the prospective bride from the back rooms of the house, where she has been eavesdropping on the proceedings, with a glass of water for the young man. If she does not emerge, the families can part, claiming this was nothing more than a friendly visit. While she may not select the candidates nor be consulted about her preferences in a match, she has the right to refuse a suitor for any reason, as does the groom. While I was living in the village, a young woman in her mid-twenties, with two sisters behind her in line for marriages, rejected a man because he was shorter than she. A bachelor in his mid-thirties rejected a series of women because they were not pretty enough. Parents react to these refusals with amused resignation, almost proud that their children are not too eager to be married, a reaction similar to that displayed by parents when a younger child refuses food at a relative's house, claiming not to be hungry. Not only do individuals have the right to refuse a marriage proposal, but they have the right to leave unhappy marriages, an option considered scandalous but one that is supported by law as well as by a social structure of bilateral descent in which women retain ties to their natal families and control over their dowries.

Consent and Choice

This requirement for consent from subordinates is a crucial element of the Sinhala hierarchy model and a key way that the autonomy of children and other junior people is recognized and evidenced. In all kinds of ranked relationships in Sri Lanka—whether between parent and child, employer and employee, doctor and patient, guru and novice—the junior person is understood to consent to the relationship if it continues, and it is the junior person rather than the senior who has the option of ending it.

Entailed in this model of hierarchy is not only what is expected from the participants but what counts as a violation and what may be done about it. Juniors—even very young ones—who feel that their superiors are not attending to their needs, thus violating their obligations as superiors, may employ two main cultural strategies in response. The first is to convey distress in a variety of nonverbal ways, from moping and illness behavior to possession or suicide. Because parents themselves have powerful emotional commitments to their children, these behaviors on the part of their children can be very persuasive. Such actions may also have the flavor of retaliation when the junior person's actions involve refusal to work, costly remedies, or shame to the family. Eventually, if the parents do not provide their children with what the children feel they need, children may take up the second strategy available to them: They have the right to sever the relationship, typically attaching themselves to a new superior.

Two of the 13 women with whom I conducted intensive person-centered interviews used this second strategy, leaving their parents in order to pursue unsupported "love matches."[14] Both Jayanthi and Kumari eloped with boyfriends because they could not get their parents' permission to marry. Jayanthi eloped with her cross-cousin, whom she feared her parents would forbid her to marry; although a cross-cousin is an ideal marriage partner, he had been raised in her home since he was a boy and so was more of a brother. Without telling anyone, they ran away to the village of a distant relative where they were married and lived for several years until they were reunited with her parents. Kumari also eloped with her boyfriend. Unlike Jayanthi, who merely assumed her parent's would disapprove of her marriage, Kumari knew that her parents disapproved. After her father discovered the relationship, a terrible fight ensued between father and daughter, culminating in him beating her and her running away to her boyfriend's elder brother's home where she lived until they were married. She had no contact with her parents until after the birth of her first child, at which point her father let it be known that he would like to see her, and she began visiting her natal home. Like Jayanthi, Kumari had ascertained that her parents would not provide what she felt she needed, and so she left the relationship. In keeping with the shape and importance of ranked relationships in this context, both of these young women entered the care of another senior relative, in this case from their husbands' sides.[15] For both women, it is important to note, the relationships with their parents were eventually reestablished, albeit with continuing strain, when the parents let it be known that they would accept their children back and then the children initiated the reunion. This demonstrates the strength of the ties between parents and children in this cultural context and reinforces the importance of consent from the junior person.

It is not only grown children who have the option to leave the relationship with their parents if their parents are not meeting their needs. Even young children may leave their parents to find new caregivers if they choose. Another two of the women I interviewed had left their parents' homes in early childhood to live with other relatives. Nirmala, the oldest daughter in her family, went to live with her grandmother when she was two years old and her younger sister was born. In her own report and that of her sister, this move is considered to have been Nirmala's own choice, although not wholly arranged by her. While her age at the time makes me wonder whether she was fully aware of making this choice or whether she came to think of the move in this way at a later time, the explanation made sense to the participants now, fitting into their shared model of parent-child relationships and the possibility of the subordinate person leaving a relationship that is unsatisfactory, as when a new baby displaces the young child from her mother's side. Manjula had a similar story to tell. She said that when she was about three years old, she went to visit an aunt and stayed with her after her parents and siblings returned home. Although Manjula does not remember the reasons herself, she understands from what others in her family have said that she was very unhappy at her own parents' home, being frequently and inexplicably tearful and difficult. At her aunt's house she was happier, so she stayed there. While it seemed to me, from other things that both Nirmala and Manjula said, that they harbored some hurt and anger against their own parents, everyone seemed satisfied with the explanation that a child might be unhappy in her own home and so choose another caregiver. That hierarchically ranked relationships continue only with the consent of the subordinate is a key feature of the Sinhala model of hierarchical relationships.

Autonomy, Self-Expression, and Attachment Theory

Ideal adolescent behavior within these relationships in Sri Lanka looks very different from the kind of behavior expected of a "securely attached" teen in the United States, the kind of secure adolescent described in the literature on attachment theory. Secure, Western adolescents are expected to be working to achieve autonomy from their parents, struggling against their attachments to parents to find their own identity, make their own choices, express their own opinions, and function independently.[16] In contrast, well-raised young people in Sri Lanka are expected to recognize and defer to the wisdom and wishes of their parents and other hierarchical figures, understanding that their own identity is inextricably intertwined with their family, caste, class, ethnicity, and region.[17] They are not expected to express their specific feelings or ideas to parents or other superiors but to have the respect and good judgment to keep these to themselves or only share them with peers.

However, it would be wrong to interpret the ideal Sri Lankan or most actual Sri Lankan adolescents and young adults as lacking autonomy, as I indicated earlier. Rather, performing as they are expected to within these relationships *requires* autonomy. Sinhala young people evidence their maturity, independent good judgment, and capacity to make good choices not by differing from their parents and other hierarchical figures but by complying with them. It requires a kind of autonomy to recognize the wishes of others even though they might differ from one's own inclinations, to judge those wishes of others as worth following, and to defer to them. This exercise of discernment and self-control, and the feelings of shame when one is seen to have failed to demonstrate these capacities, display a young person's capability for independent evaluation, choice, action, and self-government. This deference and self-control also afford repeated experiences of the distance between one's own inclinations and those of one's family and other seniors, making the separateness and distinctions between self and other impossible for most young people to miss.

The point I am making about Sri Lankan young people having achieved a kind of internal autonomy that allows them to function in social appropriate ways that defer to the wishes of their elders is similar to the one made by Katherine Ewing (1991). In her analysis of the experiences of Pakistani women adjusting to their new positions in the families into which they married, Ewing distinguishes between interpersonal autonomy and intrapsychic autonomy, a distinction she borrows from Cohler and Geyer (1982). Ewing says that, although a Pakistani woman "typically spends her whole life firmly embedded in interpersonal dependency relationships," (1991:132) her ability to function within these relationships requires intrapsychic autonomy, particularly as she must move into and adapt to her husband's family and establish satisfactory relationships there. Ewing sees this intrapsychic autonomy as evidenced by a capacity for self-comfort and adaptability and as opposed to intrapsychic enmeshment. She observes that, for those women who have not developed intrapsychic autonomy, the stress of the transition into a new family at marriage leads to signs of psychological distress such as depression, expressed in culturally patterned ways. Ewing argues against Western psychologists and anthropologists who have asserted that South Asians are less autonomous, more interdependent, and have more porous boundaries between persons than do Westerners, who are more individualistic and autonomous. She says that position results from confusing what people say about themselves and do by social convention with how they are psychologically organized.[18]

This distinction is helpful in thinking about autonomy in terms of attachment theory and how the concept of autonomy might be broadened to apply cross-culturally. Currently, attachment theory sees autonomy as one of the goals of and criteria for secure early attachments. It recognizes this autonomy in self-reliance, self-expression, independence from caregivers, and confident exploration, which are culturally valued ways of behaving in the contemporary United States, as well as other places and times. This is not, however, the only kind of social behavior or emotional orientation that is encouraged or valued in Sri Lanka, and still less so for the young Pakistani women Ewing describes or the young Indian women Susan Seymour describes (chapter 4). Even so, in each of those examples from South Asia—and possibly elsewhere—where attunement to the wishes of others is given primacy, a kind of intrapsychic autonomy is required for this arrangement to work smoothly. As Seymour and Ewing have both described, a maturing person is expected to exercise self-control and self-regulation as she or he defers to the larger social group. While these are quite different manifestations of autonomy than are described in the literature on attachment, self-control and self-regulation are indeed experiences, exercises, and evidence of autonomy. Thus, we are led to ask if autonomy in its intrapsychic form is a definitive part of psychological maturity everywhere and, if so, how it is related to early attachment experiences.

Attachment Theory and the Sinhala Case

This set of observations of caregiving and growing up in a Sinhala village highlights features that are both important in this cultural context and relevant to attachment theory, particularly the features related to caregiver sensitivity and children's achievement of self-governance. However, even these key aspects take different cultural shapes and have different effects than in the standard attachment theory narrative. In this village, it is a social, cultural, and personal priority that mothers and other caregivers be available and responsive to infants and young children, and this is so to an even greater degree, I have argued, than it is for middle-class mothers in the contemporary United States. However, this sensitivity is largely and by preference nonverbal. Children are not encouraged toward the kind of self-expression and "open, full dyadic communication" understood by attachment theorists to be optimal and necessary for the achievement of autonomy (Allen 2008:424). However, the achievement of autonomy does appear as a crucial, if quite different-looking, expectation and experience for Sinhala young people. It seems to me that this way of interacting with young children so that their needs are met quickly and satisfactorily but without the children themselves having to recognize, articulate, or advocate for ways to meet those needs may lead to a kind of autonomy that is more about self-control than about self-assertion.

This analysis suggests several candidates for universal features of human attachment, which—as Suzanne Gaskins points out in chapter 1—is part of the promise of the kind of cross-cultural work presented in this volume. It contributes to the case Gaskins makes for "responsiveness," in whatever local terms that is defined, as "a good candidate for a universal caregiver behavior" (chapter 1). Like the Yucatec Maya Gaskins describes, the Sinhala caregivers I observed were "highly responsive to their infants in just the way Ainsworth defines the concept: They pay close attention to the needs of the infant, are adept at interpreting their signals (even very subtle ones), and put a great deal of energy into responding promptly and appropriately" (chapter 1). Further, as I have argued intrapsychic autonomy is something we might look for as a potentially universal feature and an outcome of good-enough attachment relationships. However, it remains to be discovered whether even this kind of autonomy is part of a human maturational process that we should expect to find everywhere—comparable to the maturational processes that produce the capacities for locomotion and memory Gaskins (chapter 1) suggests are universal for one-year-olds. Alternatively, is what we are more broadly construing as autonomy a product of culturally specific practices only in some contexts but not in others? What further remains to be determined is to what extent—and through what mechanisms—early caregiving practices and styles may be causally related to the particular cultural shape of autonomy children achieve.

The Sinhala case demonstrates the promise of cross-cultural, ethnographically rich examinations of child care and development for crafting a better, more universal theory of attachment. As Heidi Keller notes, if this kind of research were taken seriously within attachment theory, "it would imply a serious shift from the view of attachment as a universal human need that has the same shape and emerges the same way across cultures to attachment as a universal human need, which looks differently and has different developmental trajectories across cultural environments" (2011:2). However, there is another benefit of developing a better, more universal theory of attachment, for anthropologists and others interested in the workings of culture. By identifying key features of attachment processes and their dynamic interplay, we will have a better understanding of how diversity comes about—diversity among individuals and diversity across and within groups. It is through the attachment capacities of children and reciprocal caregiving behaviors that children come to learn and care about particular cultural forms of attachment-caregiving relationships and to become particular kinds of selves within them.

Acknowledgments

The field research presented in this article was assisted by Inoka Baththanage and funded, in part, by the United States–Sri Lanka Fulbright Commission, the University of California, San Diego's Department of Anthropology and Friends of the International Center, and a National Institute of Mental Health's Postdoctoral Training Grant to the University of Chicago's Department of Comparative Human Development under the sponsorship of Rick Shweder. The research was conducted with the approval of the Internal Review Boards at the University of California, San Diego and the University of Chicago. I am grateful to the people of Viligama for allowing me into their homes and sharing their perspectives with me. Earlier versions of this chapter were presented in 2011, first as part of the Lemeson/Society for Psychological Anthropology Conference "Rethinking Attachment and Separation Cross-Culturally" and then as part of an SPA Invited Session, "Cross-Cultural Challenges to Attachment Theory," at the American Anthropological Association Meeting in Montreal in November. The responses of the participants in these conferences and of my fellow contributors to this volume have been indispensable in helping me develop this analysis. Naomi Quinn's insights have been especially helpful, as has editorial advice from John Wentworth Chapin and an anonymous reviewer. A version of this argument and a fuller description of my research can be found in *Childhood in a Sri Lankan Village: Shaping Hierarchy and Desire* (Chapin, forthcoming).

Notes

1. See Crittenden and Marlowe (chapter 2) and Meehan and Hawks (chapter 3) for their discussions of the evolutionary context of human development.
2. Although key theorists, including Bowlby who was British and Ainsworth who was Canadian, have come from a range of countries, the foundational research has been conducted primarily been conducted in the United States, along with studies in Western Europe and English-speaking countries. See Ijzendoorn and Sagi-Schwartz (2008) for a review of the non-Western evidence.
3. Attachment theory was initially developed by Bowlby and Ainsworth in the 1950s and '60s (see Ainsworth and Bowlby 1991). See Suzanne Gaskins's summary in chapter 1.

4. Early in my fieldwork I would ask new parents if they were getting any sleep, expecting that they were not. They were consistently confused by my question. Babies and young children were never made to sleep alone or on a strict schedule, so the sleep struggles so common among parents of young children in the contemporary United States were not something I could intersubjectively share with these parents.
5. In Baker's ethnography of life in a rural community in the south of the island, she also observed that, "It is rare to hear an infant cry in the village" (1998:100).
6. The teachers at one of the preschools in town expressed dismay to a fellow foreign researcher whose child was still wearing diapers at nearly three years of age. Apparently finding it incomprehensible that these parents were putting diapers on such an old child, the teachers approached the mother to find out if there was something wrong with the child.
7. This style of toilet training in the United States is in accord with the dominance-dependence pattern Quinn discusses in chapter 8, following B. Whiting and Weisner, in which American children are encouraged to assert their desires in ways that demand the attention and assistance of their caregivers. In these interactions the US child is explicitly encouraged toward independence and simultaneously toward a kind of bossy dependence.
8. For a review of Bowby's development and use of the concept of internal working models, see Bretherton and Munholland (2008). See also Quinn (chapter 8) for a more explicit discussion of how "Bowlby's concept of working models translates into" the more contemporary terms of cognitive schemas used by cognitive anthropologists.
9. Providing for children was a central part of a Sinhala mother's role and something that drove many women to seek employment abroad, especially as housemaids in the Middle East. For an intimate portrait of Sri Lankan women's experiences working abroad and the effects on their families, see Gamburd (2000).
10. For a comparative description of these first menstruation rituals in different ethnic groups in Sri Lanka and the concepts of womanhood they convey, see Winslow (1980).
11. For a similar formulation of hypocognized desires in deference to parental expectations with Vietnamese immigrants, see Leininger (2001).
12. Within the 71 households I surveyed on a single day in Viligama in 2001, there were 43 arranged "proposal" marriages and 43 "love-match" marriages, as well as three marriages of older family members about which the respondents did not know.
13. See Seymour's discussion in chapter 4 of a similar trust in parents to make important decisions, particularly regarding marriage, for young people in neighboring India.
14. Not all "love matches" face parental disapproval. This option for marriage pairings is supported by economic factors involving diminished costs to parents, who are not expected to provide dowry in this case, as well as the prestigious association with being modern.
15. It could be argued that both women also entered the charge of their new husbands, although relationships between spouses in Sri Lanka is not a straightforwardly hierarchical one. As it is usually discussed in Sri Lanka, marriage is a ranked relationship with the husband in the senior position. There is a preference for husbands to be older than their wives, hence having more authority. However, there are ways in which husbands are dependent on their wives,

particularly in regard to food preparation. In still other ways, the spousal relationship is conceived of as one between peers. Cross-cousins are not only the preferred marriage partners but the only colloquial kin terms that do not indicate elder-younger relationship.

16. See Allen (2008) for a discussion of attachment in adolescence that entails these features.
17. Since Mead's (1928) work in Samoa, anthropologists have been pointing out that adolescence is not universally or necessarily filled with *Sturm und Drang*, nor is it even consistently marked out as a developmental period.
18. In chapter 7, Mageo points out that the US emphasis on self-reliance—what people say about themselves—may be a defensive reaction to internal experiences of and anxieties about dependency and a lack of autonomy.

References

Ainsworth, Mary D. Salter. 1967. *Infancy in Uganda: Infant Care and the Growth of Love*. Baltimore: Johns Hopkins University Press.

Ainsworth, Mary D. Salter, and John Bowlby. 1991. "An Ethological Approach to Personality Development." *American Psychologist* 46(4):333–341.

Allen, Joseph. 2008. "The Attachment System in Adolescence." In *Handbook of Attachment Theory, Research and Clinical Applications*, 2nd edition, Jude Cassidy and Phillip R. Shaver, eds., pp. 419–435. New York: The Guilford Press.

Baker, Victoria J. 1998. *A Sinhalese Village in Sri Lanka: Coping with Uncertainty*. Fort Worth, TX: Harcourt Brace College Publishers.

Bowlby, John. 1982. *Attachment, 2nd ed. Vol. 1, Attachment and Loss* (first published 1969). New York: Basic Books.

Bretherton, Inge, and Kristine A. Munholland. 2008. "Internal Working Models in Attachment Relationships: Elaborating a Central Construct in Attachment Theory." In *Handbook of Attachment Theory, Research and Clinical Applications*, 2nd edition, Jude Cassidy and Phillip R. Shaver, eds., pp. 419–435. New York: The Guilford Press.

Chapin, Bambi L. 2010. " 'We Have to Give': Sinhala Mothers' Responses to Children's Expressions of Desire." *Ethos* 38(4):354–368.

Chapin, Bambi L. Forthcoming. *Childhood in a Sri Lankan Village: Shaping Hierarchy and Desire*. New Brunswick, NJ: Rutgers University Press.

Cohler, Bertram, and Scott Geyer. 1982. "Psychological Autonomy and Interdependence within the Family." In *Normal Family Processes*, F. Walsh, ed., pp. 196–228. New York: Guilford.

D'Andrade, Roy. 1995. *The Development of Cognitive Anthropology*. Cambridge, England: Cambridge University Press.

Ewing, Katherine P. 1991. "Can Psychoanalytic Theories Explain the Pakistani Woman? Intrapsychic Autonomy and Interpersonal Engagement in the Extended Family." *Ethos* 19(2):131–160.

Gamburd, Michele Ruth. 2000. *The Kitchen Spoon's Handle: Transnationalism and Sri Lanka's Migrant Housemaids*. Ithaca, NY: Cornell University Press.

Harwood, Robin L., Joan G. Miller, and Nydia Lucca Irizarry. 1995. *Culture and Attachment: Perceptions of the Child in Context*. New York: Guilford Press.

Keller, Heidi. 2011. "Attachment as a Biocultural Construct: Taking Biology and Culture Seriously." Manuscript in circulation for the Lemelson/Society for Psychological Anthropology Conference "Rethinking Attachment and Separation in Cross-Cultural Perspective," Washington State University, Spokane, May 19–21, 2011.

Keller, Heidi, and Robin Harwood. 2009. "Culture and Developmental Pathways of Relationship Formation." In *Perspectives on Human Development, Family, and Culture*, S. Bekman and A. Aksu-Koç, eds., pp. 157–177. Cambridge, England: Cambridge University Press.

Kobak, Roger, and Stephanie Madsen. 2008. "Disruptions in Attachment Bonds: Implications for Theory, Research, and Clinical Intervention." In *Handbook of Attachment Theory, Research and Clinical Applications*, 2nd edition, Jude Cassidy and Phillip R. Shaver, eds., pp. 23–47. New York: The Guilford Press.

LeVine, Robert. 2004. "Challenging Expert Knowledge: Findings from an African Study of Infant Care and Development." In *Childhood and Adolescence: Cross-Cultural Perspectives and Applications*, Uwe P. Gielen and Jaipaul Roopnarine, eds., pp. 149–165. Westport, CT: Praeger Publishers.

LeVine, Robert A., and Karin Norman. 2001. "The Infant's Acquisition of Culture: Early Attachment Reexamined in Anthropological Perspective." In *The Psychology of Cultural Experience*, Carmella C. Moore and Holly F. Mathews, eds., pp. 83–104. Cambridge, England: Cambridge University Press.

Leininger, April. 2001. "Culture and Cognitive Psychodynamics in Vietnamese-American Families." University of California, San Diego, dissertation.

Mageo, Jeannette Marie. 1998. *Theorizing Self in Samoa: Emotions, Gender, and Sexualities*. Ann Arbor, MI: University of Michigan Press.

Mead, Margaret. 1928. *Coming of Age in Samoa: A Psychological Study of Primitive Youth for Western Civilization*. New York: Marrow.

Morelli, Gilda A., and Fred Rothbaum. 2007. "Situating the Child in Context: Attachment Relationships and Self-regulation in Different Cultures." In *Handbook of Psychology*, S. Kitayama and D. Cohen, eds., pp. 500–527. New York: Guilford Press.

Rothbaum, Fred, John Weisz, Martha Pott, Kazuo Miyake, and Gilda Morelli. 2000. "Attachment and Culture: Security in the United States and Japan." *American Psychologist* 55(10):1093–1104.

Strauss, Claudia, and Naomi Quinn. 1997. *A Cognitive Theory of Cultural Meaning*. Cambridge, England: Cambridge University Press.

van Ijzendoorn, Marinus H., and Abraham Sagi-Schwartz. 2008. "Cross-cultural Patterns of Attachment: Universal and Contextual Dimensions." In *Handbook of Attachment Theory, Research and Clinical Applications*, 2nd edition, Jude Cassidy and Phillip R. Shaver, eds., pp. 880–905. New York: The Guilford Press.

Weinfield, Nancy S., L. Alan Sroufe, Byron Egeland, Elizabeth Carlson. 2008. "Individual Differences in Infant-Caregiver Attachment: Conceptual and Empirical Aspects of Security." In *Handbook of Attachment Theory, Research and Clinical Applications*, 2nd edition, Jude Cassidy and Phillip R. Shaver, eds., pp. 23–47. New York: The Guilford Press.

Weisner, Thomas S. 2005. "Attachment as a Cultural and Ecological Problem with Pluralistic Solutions." *Human Development* 48:89–94.

Winslow, Deborah. 1980. "Rituals of First Menstruation in Sri Lanka." *Man* 15(4):603–625.

Chapter 6

Attachment and Culture in Murik Society: Learning Autonomy and Interdependence through Kinship, Food, and Gender

Kathleen Barlow

Bowlby (1969) argued that infants become attached to their caregivers through an adaptive behavior system that establishes their capacity for social relationships. He and others after him described attachment as a universal developmental process leading to stable personality and competent adult functioning (Cassidy 2008).[1] By about one year of age, infants seek proximity to a specific caregiver in times of stress, and, when not under stress, use the caregiver as a secure base from which to explore and learn about their environment (Ainsworth 1969). Bowlby (1969) considered attachment relations[2] to be the source of "internal working models" of self and other that support and shape each individual's social relationships and are integral to coping with separation and loss throughout a lifetime.

The theory privileges a pattern of "secure" attachment that has been criticized as historically and culturally limited (e.g., LeVine and Miller 1990; LeVine 1995; Rothbaum et al. 2000; Weisner 2005). It valorizes the exclusive mothering prevalent among the middle class of post–World War II America and Europe and the achievement of individual autonomy characteristic of nuclear families living within capitalist economic systems (Keller and Harwood 2009). A recent convergence of data and theory from multiple disciplines (see Seymour, chapter 4) demonstrates the need for substantial revisions of attachment theory to account for the broad range of developmental pathways known to exist in human societies and among primates.[3] Evolutionary anthropologists have argued for the evolutionary value of shared caregiving in human childrearing (Hrdy 1999; Konner 2011). Hrdy (2009) has gone on to argue that humans are part of a small subset of primates called cooperative breeders that require support from others to care for infants, and that humans' communicative competence and capacity for empathy may be evolutionary results of this adaptation. Cultural anthropologists (see Seymour 2004 for a review) have provided much evidence that a strategy of multiple mothering is more often the norm for humans than the exclusive mother–child dyad of attachment theory. Studies of infancy and childhood across cultures provide evidence that many developmental pathways are adaptive and functional within particular cultural contexts (LeVine 2004:151).

Bowlby's goal was to bring developmental theory into line with evolutionary theory and scientific evidence. Some of the ethnocentric biases in attachment theory result from his determination to break from psychoanalytic interpretations based on drive theory and Oedipal motivations. He relied instead on behavioral data from ethological studies of mammals, other primates, and humans (Bowlby 1969:155–157). Ethology and psychology tend to exclude the world of cultural meaning and symbols and to de-emphasize the role of language in early childhood development (birth to three years). Language has a major impact on social relationships because it brings children into a world of cultural meanings and provides symbolic and communicative resources for maintaining attachment relations at a distance from or in the absence of caregiver(s).

Critics of the ethnocentrism of attachment theory (see Gaskins, chapter 1) urge researchers to explore variations in cultural contexts and experiences that shape attachment behaviors, attachment relationships, and their outcomes in later experience. As Gaskins points out, a whole suite of developmental capacities converge around the age of one year that enable infants to identify specific caregivers, communicate with these caregivers, and explore their environment. Because these capabilities are embedded in and shaped by cultural contexts of practice and meaning, they require us to explore cultural influences on development.

The analysis presented here is based on ethnographic work on how children learn cultural meanings through social relationships in a marine foraging society, the Murik of Papua New Guinea. The case study draws attention to four ways in which attachment is culturally informed and thus culturally variable. These include culturally desirable form(s) of attachment; cultural models of self and person; material forms and practices through which attachment emotions are evoked and communicated; and cultural models of relationship based on age, gender, and kinship. (1) Attachment theory assumes that the most valuable form of attachment is secure attachment to a primary other, leading to individuation and autonomy. In contrast, Murik child rearing develops and values both independence/autonomy and interdependence/identification with group(s). (2) The qualities of a "good" person are developed through cultural forms of discipline that shape attachment orientations in support of cultural values. Negative and positive emotions are instrumental in producing culturally good persons (Keller and Harwood 2009; Mageo 1991, 1998, and chapter 7; Quinn 2001). For example, Murik punish sibling rivalry in older siblings in order to instill caregiving qualities that extend to all senior-junior relationships. (3) In Murik culture, food and feeding are a crucial material basis for conveying and shaping the emotional commitments of attachment. Giving food expresses maternal caregiving, while going without food expresses feelings of separation and loss. (4) Murik cultural concepts of gender deeply inform relatedness, including when and how attachment-related emotions are activated across the life cycle and within particular relationships. Attachment emotions and behaviors are differentiated by gender in cross-sex sibling relationships and in romantic, marital ones.

I first describe the Murik environment and general features of culture in terms of Weisner's (1996) concept of an ecocultural niche adapted to child care, and of LeVine and Norman's (2001) suggestion that every culture guides children toward a cultural model of virtue. I then discuss each of the four dimensions of attachment theory presented earlier in relation to Murik cultural shaping of (1) independent and interdependent forms of attachment; (2) disciplinary practices and concepts of self and person; (3) food and feeding as material expressions of attachment; and (4) gendered relationships and adult expressions of attachment-related emotions.

The Ecological and Cultural Environment of Caregiving and Childhood

The cultural dimensions of attachment in Murik culture are partial solutions to subsistence in a mangrove environment and the challenges it poses for caregivers and children. Weisner (1996) proposes an ecocultural approach to understanding how subsistence requirements and work allocations are organized to provide an adequate context for children's development. All societies must solve the problem of nurturance and support for their members and must provide affection, physical comfort, assistance in tasks and problem-solving, provision of food and resources, and protection against harm and aggression (Weisner 1993). These needs are met through the routines of daily life and must fit the competencies of the members of family and community in ways that are meaningful and valued (Weisner 1996:296). As children's needs, understandings, and capabilities change, family and community adjust. Early attachment to caregivers eventually takes on the contours of cultural competence, membership in family and community, and commitment to cultural values. Meehan and Hawkes (chapter 3) and Morelli and Rothbaum (2007) underscore the organization of daily work, especially mothers' work, as a crucial variable in how opportunities for attachment and separation are organized.

The Murik ecocultural niche is demanding. Murik are marine foragers living in five villages (total population ~1,200) on the edge of mangroves at the mouth of the Sepik River. They exploit the mangrove environment for fish and shellfish—highly valued protein resources that they trade and sell throughout the region. The environment lacks any staple carbohydrate such as tubers or grains and there is little capacity for garden crops. Murik depend on trade with inland groups to obtain sago, and in the dry season trade with coastal and island groups for garden produce, such as fruits, vegetables, nuts, and pigs. Men and women fish, but shellfish is gathered by women. Women are absent working in the mangroves for hours at a time, all day and even longer. Processing, mostly women's work, is done as needed, day or night. Trade is mainly conducted by men who also fish with nets to accumulate the surplus of fish needed for trade.

Intermittently since the 1920s, Murik have acquired mission churches, schools, government aid posts, and trade stores. They have become accustomed to outboard motors, and to trade store commodities and clothing, and now need cash to pay school fees for children and to buy fuel for outboard motors. Despite hopes for development and greater prosperity, to this day they rely on fishing as their main source of food and income. Although a financial hardship, many Murik live in town for periods of time so that their children can go to school or family members can get medical treatment. My analysis is based mainly on village life.

The villages and mangroves are a high-risk environment because of physical dangers, endemic malaria, and seasonal shortages of food and fresh water. Prior to Australian colonial government, there was also endemic raiding and warfare throughout the region. Village houses are built on stilts and several villages flood twice a day at high tide.[4] In order to access food resources, individuals must be intrepid about going into the mangroves to fish and gather shellfish and traveling long distances in canoes and small boats, often alone, day or night. As traders Murik actively seek new trade partners and relationships with neighboring groups through marriage, adoption, and extended visiting. They view all kinds of property as potentially alienable through trade, and use hospitality and generosity to create indebtedness that can be called in when help is needed.

As an environment for raising children, these physical circumstances and this lifestyle necessitate vigilance about dangers to young children. The division of labor requires separations between mothers and their young children, leading to early training for older siblings as caregivers and domestic helpers. Children encounter many people in the course of daily life, as child care is distributed through the extended family and community. Older children accompany kin beyond the villages to travel and trade in town and throughout the wider region. Their safety and security depend on being embedded in networks of supportive relationships (Weisner 2005:92).

LeVine and Norman (2001:84) assert that the cultural context of early childhood encourages children to develop according to values and models of relationships that define a good person. From the point of view of outsiders, children may appear precocious in just those ways that cultural norms prioritize as virtuous. Thus, ethnotheories of personhood and development shape the course of attachment and its consequences.

The Murik model of virtue calls for people who are willing explorers, take initiative, have confidence in their abilities to manage in their environment, and are highly social, taking responsibility for others, and getting through lean times by relying on social networks. A senior woman proudly described her granddaughter (~eight years old), who had lived with her since she was a baby. Her idealized version of the good child emphasizes fearlessness, independence, and self-directed behavior combined with caring for others and helpful participation in the household.

> Carol is not afraid. I have taught her this, and if we go anywhere at night and she wants to go to sleep, she will go back home by herself and go to bed. Even when we lived in Kreer [a settlement outside of Wewak] and she was much younger, she would get up [at night] to go to the toilet [across the road from the houses] by herself. When I heard her come back I would ask where she was and finding out she had been out alone, I told her to wake me next time and the two of us would go together.
>
> The same thing if she is hungry. She knows how to cook and make a fire and I will say, "All right, you go to the house and cook," and she will make some rice and tin fish or sago bread and eat. If there are people visiting she knows to cook and serve them, to ask how many want Milo or coffee and make it and serve it. I have taught her that the house is a woman and a woman gives food. When someone comes you feed them. Also, there is no reason to be afraid at night. If you hear a rat or a noise, you stand up and say, "*Yu kam, bai mi lukim pes bilong yu.*" [Tok Pisin, you come, let me see your face] If the other children try to scare her, she tells them this and is not spooked. The woman [spirit] of the house accompanies you and keeps you safe.
>
> When two women eat together, the women of each one's house sit behind them, just as a shadow does, and they eat, too... When I come back from fishing, she carries the clams [which are very heavy]. She will come to my canoe when I come back from fishing and carry things, so that all I have to do is bring my paddles and small basket. If I say, "I have to clean the canoe," Carol offers to do it for me. (Field Notes:7–18–81)

In actuality, young girls may be shy and retiring, timid about venturing forth, or adept at being elsewhere when their help is needed with chores. This senior woman's description presented a model to me, an outsider, and to young girls who might be encouraged to emulate the values she admired.

Similarly, a young firstborn man who had returned from high school to visit in the village was lauded for his generosity and caregiving, which demonstrated leadership qualities that bade well for the future of his descent group. Younger children in his kin group followed him around, and he played with them, cooked for them, and held them on his lap. My notes describe how his mother enthused that he was "just like her real father, who even used to let them suck his nipples to console them when he looked after them while their mother went into the mangroves to fish" (Field Notes:9–29–81). The maternal qualities of caregiving and nurturance are valued and intensively cultivated in men and women.

Independent and Interdependent Attachment Orientations

One glaring ethnocentrism of attachment theory as first formulated is its emphasis on independence/autonomy as the optimal outcome of secure attachment (Gaskins 2006; LeVine 2004; Weisner 2005). Many societies do not emphasize or value autonomy and independence, but socialize children to be sensitive to the needs of the larger group (e.g., family, band, community, etc.) and to identify with it (Keller and Harwood 2009). Seymour (2004), Mageo (1998), Lutz (1988), Miyake et al. (1985), and Takahashi (1990) show how very different societies (India, Samoa, Ifaluk, and Japan) prioritize interdependence, in contrast to the individualistic orientation that seems consistent across Euro-American cultures. Initially, cultural challenges to attachment theory led to the formulation of a dichotomy between independent and interdependent social orientations to account for cultural variation in preferred outcomes (Keller and Otto 2009). Inspired by the analysis of Kağitçibaşi, Keller and Harwood (2009) now consider the range of variation evidenced by the cross-cultural record to be greater than can be accounted for by a simple dichotomy. In every society individuals are required to develop a sense of separate identity and to participate in social life as members of a group or groups in culturally appropriate ways (McCollum 2001; Quinn, chapter 8). Murik strongly socialize for both orientations.

Interdependence/Autonomy in Foraging Adaptations

Foragers, it is sometimes argued (Crittenden and Marlowe 2008; Konner 2005), represent the "environment of evolutionary adaptedness," identified by Bowlby as the environment in which attachment first evolved. If so, then these rapidly disappearing societies are a preferred context for examining cultural contributions to attachment. This claim deserves careful scrutiny. Some research suggests that foraging societies (Morelli and Rothbaum 2007; Shostak 1981) combine strong interdependent orientations with a high tolerance for individual independence. It is hypothesized that interdependence may be in part an outcome of shared caregiving practices (Hrdy 2009). A pan-forager cognitive model of sharing, cooperation, and trust based on "secure" attachment to the group has been proposed as the product of a social environment that includes high rates of physical contact, multiple caregivers, and the constant presence of others (Hewlett et al. 2000; Meehan and Hawkes, chapter 3). How independence in adults among foragers correlates with care by mother and others is only beginning to be studied (Crittenden and Marlowe, chapter 2).

Inferences about the evolutionary past based on Murik foraging may not be warranted (Roscoe 2006). It is unlikely that Murik have always lived in their current and historical foraging adaptation. Their origin story describes their migration down the Sepik River from an area characterized by fishing and gardening and agnatic social organization (associated with clan-based ownership of garden land). Murik similarities to foragers of other types (land-based hunters and gatherers) in other regions (e.g., Central Africa) are most likely the more recent effects of the work requirements of subsistence foraging. In contrast to their gardening neighbors, they do exhibit features common among foragers, such as bilateral social organization, flexible residence and household composition, egalitarian gender roles, and emphasis on both individual autonomy and interdependence on the group. Their political organization is based on primogeniture among groups of siblings, and is less egalitarian and more hierarchical than is characteristic of foragers. Both women and men occupy leadership statuses, which include substantial authority and power. In spite of this hierarchy, the need for flexible adaptation to a difficult environment often overrides rules about status and leads to strong reliance on group membership for help and protection.

Socialization for Independence: Primary Attachment to a Single Mothering Figure

Murik practice intense early mothering by a primary figure, thought by attachment theorists to support both a sense of security and a growing autonomy (independence). They also supplement mothers' caregiving with care distributed among maternal relatives and siblings and value strong loyalty to kin and community (interdependence).

Attachment theorists emphasize that attachment is person-specific and the primary attachment figure is a preferred source of security (Bowlby 1969; Cassidy 2008). Based on interactions with a sensitive and responsive caregiver, a child develops a sense of trust and security on which he or she can base confident exploration of his or her world (Ainsworth 1969). Murik children's earliest experience provides for a strong primary bond with a specific person—usually, but not always, the biological mother. [5] A new mother is secluded in the birth house with her infant, breast-feeding on demand and paying close attention to her baby's comfort and cleanliness. Traditionally, new mothers stayed in the birth house for several months, cared for by female relatives who kept them company; offered advice; and supplied food, firewood, and basket-weaving materials. More often, a new mother moves to her parents' house a few days after giving birth, and her own mother and sisters care for her and help her husband care for their other children, as do the husband's female kin. Infant care conforms to the requirements for secure attachment to a primary mothering figure as originally formulated by Bowlby. Meanwhile, a new mother is the object of diffuse caregiving by others.

When a baby is about six months of age, mothers and other familiar caregivers introduce him or her to the community. As mothers rejoin the community, they carry their babies in a sling, nursing them on demand and whenever they need soothing. When others carry a child around the community, every effort is made to make it an enjoyable and playful experience of interaction with admiring others. If a child fusses even mildly, it is rushed back to its mother. The transition from mother to others is as seamless as possible.

Once a child begins to be mobile, he or she continues to be in almost constant physical contact with a caregiver, with whom he or she also sleeps. The physical environment is not safe with its many sharp objects, fires, places from which to fall, and water hazards. Houses have gaps in the flooring, cooking hearths, and open doorways and ladders. Caregivers hold crawling infants by an arm or leg to prevent them from approaching the hearth, doorway, or holes in the flooring. Familiar others in the household include parents, siblings, grandparents, and mother's sisters, but young children are mainly in their mothers' care.

Socialization for Interdependence/Diffuse Attachment

Over time, children become increasingly immersed in an environment that Keller and Harwood (2009) describe as fostering interdependence. They are constantly in the presence of social activity, though not necessarily the center of attention. By about six months of age babies begin to cope with their mother's absence as mothers resume their work provisioning the household. When and how this takes place is quite variable. For first-born children the shift is gradual and begins after six months or more of near-exclusive care. For women who do not have many younger kin to help them or who have several children, pressure to resume other work may begin within a few days of giving birth. Their babies are stressed by their absence, and primary attachment is lessened in favor of more diffuse attachment to several caregivers, usually mother's mother and sisters. Eventually children enter a larger realm of maternal figures (from both mother's and father's side of the family), older siblings (classificatory and directly related), and peers. In all relationships, seniority connotes obligatory maternal behavior—giving, protecting, and teaching. For each individual the community becomes encoded as caregiving others who are senior, and juniors to whom caregiving must be extended.

By age three years, a child spends most of his or her time circulating through households and community immersed in groups. Even within children's peer groups, relationship dyads are organized according to who is senior/maternal to whom. Older children are accountable for the welfare of their juniors. A common scene is for children to remain in one household, play group, or venue until something makes it less rewarding, hospitable, or interesting. Then they move elsewhere or find other companions. When asked why they left a particular situation, children and adults often respond, "*Mi les*" (I was tired of it), or "*Skin bilong mi i no isi*" (I felt uncomfortable). Diffuse attachment to the larger group of maternal others and siblings/peers means rather easy shifting of personnel and context.

The Relationship of Primary and Diffuse Attachment

Equipped with the security of primary attachment to an indulgent mother figure and the diffuse interdependence of secondary attachment to caring others, Murik children negotiate ongoing challenges to their sense of security and growing expectations of responsibility for others. First, they adjust to their mother's absences for work, which become longer and more frequent as their tolerance grows and others, especially mother's mother and younger sisters, become more familiar. Eventually, most children are displaced from their mother's focus of attention by newborn siblings. Mothers tolerate older children clinging to them or hovering over them while they nurse or hold a younger child, as long as the older one is solicitous toward the younger one. Mothers say to an older child, "you are the mother, s/he is the child." Acting like caregivers helps older children maintain proximity to their mothers and encourages positive identification with and internalization of caregiving.

Weisner (2005:92) describes sibling caregiving as an arena for learning about the benefits of reciprocity in larger social networks. Sibling caregiving from an early age might qualify as one of LeVine and Norman's (2001) "precocities" that indicate culturally valued qualities of the person. Murik children learn that mothering behavior is an aspect of being a good person and internalize/identify with mothering figures. Their reward is their own mother's continued approval and pride in them.

As George and Solomon (2008) describe, initially children's caregiving behavior is partial, inconsistent, and subject to distraction. When Murik women leave babies or toddlers with younger caregivers, they are under the oversight of another adult, often their grandmother. These "supervisors" often remind older children what their responsibilities are and how to gain cooperation from a younger child. Strategies include modeling—"lie down and sleep, so he will nap," doing—"take her home, don't tell her to go home," and distraction—"hand her the shell (and take the knife away)."

As older siblings become skilled caregivers, they learn to manage feelings of rivalry and aggression. Consider the layers of positive and negative emotions in the following incident in which an older sibling policed his younger sister's aggression toward their younger brother.

> Jason (~5 yrs.) hit Donna (~14 yrs.) with a stick, to which she responded by picking up the stick and hefting it in her hand. Afraid of her, Jason collapsed in a dejected heap on the ground. Their older brother Andrew (~18 yrs.) observed this as he approached their house and ran over to Donna and held her by the wrists, saying to Jason, "Get up. Hit her. Hit her." Jason remained where he was. Andrew took the stick and went up the house ladder. Donna gave Jason a half-hearted shove with her foot as she walked away. (Barlow 1985:365)

Overtly, Andrew enforced the proscription against aggression toward a younger sibling by restraining Donna, but perhaps it also allowed him to act out repressed aggression toward his younger sister by encouraging their younger brother to hit her. Having already learned that even though she was older Donna might not refrain from hitting him back, Jason ignored Andrew's exhortation. Donna reluctantly conformed to expectations, but registered her displeasure with Jason as she left. Such interactions lay emotional groundwork for later complaints among siblings that older ones share grudgingly rather than generously, and that younger ones are slow to offer help when they should.

My hypothesis is that as children become immersed in larger social networks, they identify seniority with protection, caregiving, and feeding in a basic schema of relatedness that informs many relationships (Barlow 2010). They expect individuals whose roles and/or behaviors mark them as maternal to help and protect them. Yet they have experienced lapses such as the interaction described earlier where antagonism breaks out; and they have seen and experienced the sometimes harsh discipline used to contain it. Along with strong bonds of attachment come occasional experiences to the contrary that warn of repressed anger or resentment.

Discipline and Caregiving

Murik closely monitor each other to maintain maternal and sibling caregiving that accords with cultural values of generosity and reciprocity. They demand and model appropriate behavior and move to redirect and correct undesirable impulses and actions. In so doing, they encourage the maintenance and transference of attachment emotions in and to particular relationships and contexts.

Attachment theorists warn that abandonment, rejection, or threats of desertion by a primary attachment figure are damaging (Bowlby 1973), but they say little about ordinary discipline that guides attachment emotions and behavior along cultural norms. Quinn (2001) lays out the case for a universal project of child rearing that uses different strategies for different ends according to cultural concepts of person and moral ideology (2001:494). By creating heightened emotional awareness, events of teasing, shaming, frightening, or beating selectively sensitize children to cultural values and associated emotional states (Quinn 2001:498).

Mageo (chapter 7) points out that theorists working within Western cultural paradigms and focusing on secure attachment have missed at least half the story—the cultural uses of insecurity and negative emotion to motivate and shape culturally competent persons. Using examples from three Pacific societies, she notes that, across cultures, scaring, teasing, and punishment inculcate inhibitions that support culturally valued behavior (Mageo 1991). She develops these insights in her analysis of the psychodynamics of person and self in Samoa, where distancing strategies encourage children to perform service for high-status others in order to regain the acceptance and admiration that they lose soon after infancy (Mageo 1998).

Murik use multiple strategies to develop caregiving behavior and other valued qualities in children. Two stand out as especially prominent and consistent, and each is associated with idealized expectations of maternal behavior and its generalization to many other relationships. The first is direct punishment by the primary attachment figure for failure to give to younger siblings. The second is punishment by someone other than the primary attachment figure, including a bogey called Gaingeen, potentially displacing the child's anger over being punished onto someone else. The primary attachment figure then acts as a safe refuge, even when she (or he) may have overtly or covertly instigated the punishment.

Direct punishment by mothers is reserved almost exclusively for enforcing the expectation that older siblings give to younger ones. They move quickly, often silently, to land a blow on a child who is making a younger sibling cry, refusing to share, or taking something away. The extreme consistency of this enforcement eventually makes giving to younger siblings an immediate and habitual response—though never so firmly established that younger siblings are entirely safe from an older one's aggression or withholding, as in the incident mentioned. Firstborns and their immediate juniors are the most experienced at taking on the caregiver role and perhaps most strongly internalize it. As adults their protection and generosity toward younger siblings are strongly rewarded in terms of inheritance, authority, and prestige. Middle children become adept at the back and forth of giving and receiving, at sizing up a situation and acting accordingly. They may be inconsistent about enacting the obligations of seniority, as they switch from generosity toward their juniors based on positive identification with nurturing attachment figures to seeking either dependent gratification as younger siblings or diffuse support from extended kin and peers. Lastborn children are described as open about wanting what others have. This stereotype is partially true, but they are often helpful and generous, and are praised for these highly valued qualities. However, they do enjoy a privileged role as recipients of prolonged indulgence by their parents, extended kin, and siblings.

The second strategy of discipline is that others (not the primary attachment figure) shame or discipline a child who misbehaves (Barlow 2010). The caregiver recruits a child's cooperation by saying (falsely), "Look, she is angry. We have to leave now." Mothers and others call for the bogey, Gaingeen, who occasionally does appear. By displacing disapproval and discipline onto others, mothers act as a safe refuge for a child whom others have corrected (see examples in Barlow 2010). Mothers refer discipline to others by inviting their critique of a child's actions. They often used me in this role, saying such things as, "Ketty, tell him to stop nursing or you will bring the shot to immunize him!" Or they would say to the child, "If you don't stop, I'll ask her [the nursing sister] to give you a shot!" Then they would hold the child close and comfort him or her. Perhaps this successfully directs the child's resentment over being corrected onto others. Publicly, it preserves a certain image of the parent, even if the child eventually realizes that its mother solicited and/or allowed the punishment to take place.

The bogey Gaingeen comes unannounced to punish children for unspecified misbehavior. He is the most junior of a large complex of masked figures that emerge from the men's house, all of whom have disciplinary functions. The Gaingeen costume is made and worn by young men in the most junior age grade, who emerge to chase and throw sticks at children. Young children respond to him as monstrous, shrieking in fear, and clinging to their caregivers. One mother instructed her young child, hiding behind her skirts, in how to respond to Gaingeen by deferring retribution. She advised him, "Tell Gaingeen that he can chase you now, but when you are Gaingeen you will chase his children." Older children run away from him, but in keeping with general encouragement to overcome fear and stand up to aggression from others, the Gaingeen figure is soon demystified. Children discuss who is wearing the costume and may recognize his feet. They come close to taunt him, and gauge their escape based on knowledge about the wearer's swiftness and accuracy with a fishing spear.

Gaingeen and the more senior figures represent diffuse retribution for unspecified misbehavior, but most of all they express the authority of seniority relations within the community. Each age grade controls one or more figures that belabor all those junior to them when they appear in the village. The positive leadership expressed in food giving, protection, and care is backed by the threat of angry and powerful spirit figures who arrive unannounced to discipline subordinates. The most senior figures appear during food shortages in the form of giant open-mouthed fish and go from house to house collecting food that is redistributed later to the entire community.

One other powerful disciplinary force is a set of joking relationships that begin when a child is about six months old and continue throughout a lifetime. These joking partners (designated by the prefix *mwara*, Murik, valuable) are classificatory father's sisters for women, and classificatory mother's brothers for men. The mwara kin are both hostile and caring, and they play on the conversion of needy attachment to competent independence. They mock need and dependency and require that one stand up to them. Parents and others coach a child to respond to joking partners, until gradually he or she learns how to reply or to initiate these interactions on his or her own. The joking is about wanting, first food, then more and more (even with six- and seven-year-olds) about wanting food and sex and the many double entendres that can be generated around hunger, eating, and sex. The mwara kin demand an outward persona of competence and assertiveness by escalating their taunting and mockery until the junior partner stands up to them. To be a senior joking partner is to exhibit independence and competence and to demand it in others.

Through specific disciplinary tactics, Murik insist that individuals be competent and confident—persistent, assertive, and wary of potentially dark consequences of needy dependence. Others are likely to be angry and resentful of those who demand too much or fail to fulfill obligations. These resentments are the suspected cause of misfortune or illness, whether those others are known individuals, spirit entities, ancestors, or distant trade partners.

Particular forms of discipline shape attachment relations into competence and caregiving abilities that fit the Murik cultural model of a good person. These forms include displacing anger and punishment away from primary attachment figures, and demanding caregiving behavior from senior to junior without exception. Joking relations underwrite these expectations. Murik adults may behave in competent and self-confident ways because of the supportive environment provided by primary caregivers. They may exhibit these qualities because group membership provides many arenas for rehearsing the values of the primary caregiving relationship in diffuse form; or perhaps they perform these qualities because the relentless surveillance of joking partners does not let them act otherwise. All of these are possible and probable variations across times and contexts. Attachment relations in infancy by themselves do not explain adult competence or the symbolic logic of adult personhood and its emotional commitments. Disciplinary strategies and practices guided by cultural models of virtue do provide insights into the cultural shaping of attachment dispositions as children become enculturated persons.

Food and Attachment

Many of the most highly valued qualities of a good person in Murik culture are expressed through the production and sharing of good food. Actions related to food evoke attachment emotions and are integral to cultural practices that express separation and loss. Attachment theory gives scant attention to this important domain of symbolic activity. Bowlby rejected psychoanalytic arguments that a child's need for proximity to its mother (or mothering figure) was a direct result of its need for food, or of its need to reduce the tension of primary drives through access to her care (feeding, bathing, holding, soothing). He insisted that "food plays only a marginal part in the development and maintenance of attachment behavior" (1969:224). Ainsworth (1969), based on her work in a society where most women breast-fed their babies, the Ganda of Africa, took a less exclusionary stance. She suggested that food and feeding vary in the extent to which they are involved in attachment.

> Under circumstances in which an infant through his own active attachment behavior, including sucking and rooting and also reaching, grasping, and approaching, can gain contact with an actual or potential attachment figure who is also his food source, his feeding behaviors become an integral part of the organization of his attachment relationship. The circumstances under which this integration is possible are: (1) when the baby is fed contingent on his own behavior, including both his signaling behavior and his more active contact-seeking behavior, as in thoroughgoing demand feeding; (2) when the baby is breast-fed, so that the food-providing source and the attachment figure are one and the same; and (3) when weaning is deferred until after an attachment has already been established. Under these circumstances, feeding behavior is so enmeshed in the organization of the attachment relationship that weaning may threaten the whole relationship. (Ainsworth 1977:128)

All of these conditions are met in the Murik case, and feeding and attachment behavior have much to do with each other. Rather than weaning jeopardizing the mother-child relationship, the attachment of nursing children over time is referred into other relationships and activities having to do with food. Giving and receiving food are symbolic elaborations of maternal care. Food is the quintessential expression of relatedness, caring, and belonging. Unless otherwise explained, open expressions of anger are assumed to be about being refused food. When amends have to be made, aggression averted, status acknowledged or restored, plates of good food are the means to these ends. It would be hard to overestimate the importance of this theme in Murik culture, so pervasive are the occasions, emotional components, and explicit maternal associations of food.

Mothering is defined more by the social act of feeding than by giving birth, and children are said to "belong" to those who feed them. Nursing on demand goes on for two years and more. Mothers use their breast as a way to recall an adventurous child by calling, "*Susu, susu*!" (Tok Pisin, suck, or breast) or the child's name and showing him or her their breast. During the stressful period of weaning and learning to eat solid food, children's association of their mothers with satisfying food is challenged. Many of them do not like sago, which can smell vinegary and have a sour taste. These children are often hungry, somewhat undernourished, and vulnerable to malaria and other illness.[6] Mothers do not refuse to let children nurse, but do go to great lengths to find rice or other food.

Mothers distribute food in their households and make sure that those who work to support the household are well fed. Work is rewarded with food and becomes a way of gaining maternal approval. As children begin to perform useful work, their mothers acknowledge their effort by cooking things especially for them (Barlow 2001).

The same pattern is evident in many other events and potentially draws on both primary and diffuse attachment orientations. Teaching via apprenticeship such as learning to carve, build a canoe, and weave baskets, is reciprocated with plates of food. Group work, such as house-building, repairing nets, and washing sago is acknowledged with a shared meal. Someone who has been away from the village for work or trade is received home with a special event (Murik, *bas*), a meal shared village-wide at which news and accomplishments are discussed.

Separation and loss are expressed by going without food. When someone does not return from a trip or from work in the mangroves when expected, his or her mother endeavors to "pull" her child back. She wraps her stomach tightly and sits by the fire, but does not cook or eat. When a death occurs, the most bereaved are watched carefully and fed by hand if necessary because their grief may cause them to starve themselves. To repair a break in relationships or to end a period of mourning, plates of food must be given.

Food carries with it the emotional power of primary attachment and is explicitly and consistently associated with mothering. To give food is to be powerful and resourceful like a mother, while to receive is to be indebted, weak, and dependent like a child, but also gratified. The emotional power of attachment, the security it provides, and the competence and initiative it fosters inform cultural practices of giving food and hosting feasts as expressions of leadership, power, and community.

Bowlby rejected the argument that food was the reason for attachment. Using the research of ethologists, such as Lorenz on imprinting and the Harwoods on infant monkeys, he argued that attachment as proximity seeking has direct adaptive value (Bowlby 1969:157). On the other hand, food and access to food are also adaptive, necessary, and emotionally charged. As

Ainsworth insightfully noted, when the attachment figure is also a food giver, the two adaptive systems become enmeshed. They do so in culturally constituted ways. Cross-culturally, it may be more common than not for attachment and food to be intertwined and mutually influential.[7] Understanding specific cultural configurations of these two culturally constructed systems may shed light on how attachment becomes transformed into caregiving behavior and how it informs other relationships and activities, such as cultural norms of giving and receiving food.

Attachment and Gender: Managing Sex and Aggression

The course of Murik relational development draws our attention to the cultural shaping of gender as a crucial dimension of the consequences of attachment in later life. Perhaps because of his concern to move away from psychoanalytic drive theory Bowlby paid little attention to gendered developmental processes that organize sexuality and aggression. He, Ainsworth, and others noted differences in the attachment behavior of boys and girls, but seldom interpreted or analyzed them. Neither universalizing (e.g., biologically based pair-bonding) (Zeifman and Hazan 2008) nor Western culture-bound theories of adult attachment (e.g., stable monogamous marriage as an outcome of secure attachment) (Feeney 2008; Roisman et al. 2002; Sroufe and Fleeson 1986) provides an adequate theoretical framework for understanding the role of attachment in adult relationships in different cultures. Relational outcomes of early attachment experiences "make sense" only in light of cultural systems of meaning that organize gender and sexuality.

For Murik, cultural meanings around gender, sexuality, food, and attachment are dense and multifaceted. Gender and sexuality draw emotional force from attachment relationships, both primary (individuated/one-on-one) and diffuse (interdependent/group). Here I outline in simplified form some dimensions of Murik gender roles, adult romantic relationships, and psychodynamic processes that shape them.

Gender Roles

The Murik cultural construction of gender emphasizes maternal qualities for males and females. Not only do Murik men value and express maternal qualities of caregiving and feeding others, men and women alike consider the caregiver role to be one of power, independence, and resourcefulness. In adulthood, influence over others comes from having the resources to feed them generously, whether as part of the daily life of the household, as compensation for work, or on the many ritual occasions that require presentations of food. Men and women speak of giving food in terms of proximity-seeking, the hallmark of attachment behavior. Being fed evokes the emotion of a child wanting to be near its mother, and giving food to others "pulls" them into one's sphere of influence. Within this common core of personhood, gender roles are differentiated in contexts where maternal qualities and the positive and negative emotions they evoke are salient or suppressed.

Girls identify with their mother(s) as women who feed others and exercise power over them. They are expected to take up a consistently maternal role, helping their mothers. Their daily life is filled with instances of others' need for them. Taking on the role of a caregiver gradually enables a conversion (perhaps through reaction formation, as Quinn also argues in the case of Ifaluk Islanders, in chapter 8) of their own attachment needs as they become attachment figures to others. In their extended family and peer group relationships they receive and offer caregiving and contribute to the more diffuse attachment bonds of larger groups.

Boys are expected to take responsibility for their younger siblings and to be able to care for children, but they do not usually cook for or feed them. They are seldom asked to serve as caregivers on a daily basis, but they are always expected to be responsible for children around them. As adults, older siblings and fathers, men are competent caregivers and welcome children's presence in most activities. Away from the domestic household, for boys same-sex peer groups are a refuge of diffuse attachment, as is the men's house where food is often distributed and mother's brothers can be counted on to share.

As girls become women and mothers[8] through identification, they achieve the competence and ability to take charge as adult women. They achieve a fair amount of independence in organizing their own activities and work. Boys identify with caregiving in senior to junior relationships and, as adults, act out dominance by giving food to others in the men's house. Nevertheless, they remain dependent on women to provide cooked food, and expect to be fed in contexts of primary attachment (by mother and wife) and diffuse ones as well (sibling group, men's house). Resentment of this dependence sometimes emerges domestically as anger over not being fed, a lapse for which men and women agree that a man should beat his wife—reiterating the emotional dynamic of a senior/maternal role against which juniors/dependents may act out aggressively.

Men also act out the punitive and authoritative dimensions of "bad" mother figures—symbolically removed from idealized, nurturing mothers through displacement and perhaps splitting—in the form of age-graded bogey figures characterized as masculine or as gendered parental pairs. These figures, deployed exclusively from the men's house, signal the predominant association of masculinity with aggression.[9] The figures are split off images of maternal punishment, aggression, and the power to take food away and to enforce sharing.

Rituals of the men's house contain and deploy aggression in the form of war spirits whose handling requires assiduous separation from maternal influences. Women are thought to become ill from contact with homicidal war spirits; hence reproductive women must avoid the men's house and the area around it. If young men are preparing for a raid or fight, they seclude themselves in the men's house and eat only food prepared by non-maternal women—postmenopausal and unrelated to them. Aggression and violence are the antithesis of maternal caregiving and attachment. When they erupt, embodied as male aggression, senior women, the most powerful maternal presences, can and do wade into the middle of a fight and stop it by holding up their hands. Heavy compensation then has to be paid to them in the form of pigs—an expensive prestige food obtained through trade—and a large feast. Good relations are restored through gifts of food. Then maternal solidarity returns to the community.

Cross-Sex Relationships and Adult Attachment

Many situations of paradox and contradiction are generated by the combination of gender and seniority embodied in particular individuals and relationships. Some of the most interesting relationships for revealing the role of attachment in the transition to adulthood are those of cross-sex siblings and spouses.

Cross-sex sibling relationships are organized around seniority relations of birth order and prohibitions on sexuality and aggression. Young girls learn caregiving behavior by imitating their mothers, with one important exception. Mothers sometimes pat and stroke their small son's genitals while they are nursing or bathing them; and while the boys are still young and run around naked, a mother may playfully and even aggressively reach out to give her little son's penis a tug. Daughters may not imitate their mothers' behavior in this regard. They are instructed not to touch their brothers in this way. The prohibition on sexuality between brothers and sisters varies in how it is experienced and expressed. Sometimes it develops into extreme caution and shame, or fuels teasing between siblings about flirtatious behavior, or infuses physical competition and playful wrestling.

Brother-sister pairs ideally involve mutual caregiving (maternal behavior). The two should not argue or fight. Neither sex nor aggression should be directly expressed in these relationships. An important myth describes the disastrous consequence of a brother's anger toward his sister, and the close association of (perhaps jealous) anger with sexuality. The story also underscores an expectation of both sex *and* aggression in marital relationships.

> Maeb beat his younger sister, Debwa, repeatedly. In despair she went to her boyfriend to ask him to save her, but he refused, saying "You already have a husband—your brother!" She hanged herself from a tree near where her elder sister went to bathe. When the sister found her body, she called her husband to cut her down and carry her back to the village. The brother fled in disgrace.

Based on Maeb's aggression, Debwa's lover (and potential husband) refused to believe that Maeb was her brother. The brother's aggression implied sexual jealousy, and an incestuous relationship. Debwa committed suicide in despair over the brother who behaved like a husband. The story is a cautionary tale about the disastrous consequences of aggressive (and by implication sexual) behavior from brother to sister. Women are assumed to be always desirable. Brothers must protect their sisters from others' desire, and their own desire must be inhibited, repressed.

Romantic relationships for young adults in Murik culture are notoriously tumultuous and fragile (Ledoux 1936; Lipset 1997; Schmidt 1922–1923). They are riven by affairs, suspected and real, and often partners fight over infidelities but continue to return to each other. Each partner seemingly invests attachment emotions in the other. The liaisons are like brother-sister relationships in terms of mutual helpfulness and loyalty, but include prohibited behavior. Removing the prohibition on sexuality effectively invites the other prohibited behavior, aggression. Hence the common Murik saying, "Fight and marry."[10] My guess is that romantic relationships arouse the full force of primary attachment, expectations of caregiving and indulgence that are difficult to sustain between two young adults. When these expectations are not met, the dissatisfied partner resorts to an alternative strategy. A casual sexual encounter provides solace, just as in childhood resorting to the peer group provided a substitute for mother's attention. Infidelity inspires jealous aggression from men and women, the return of repressed anger at displacement from the caregiver's focus of attention. Nevertheless, partners often reunite following brief relationships with others, reiterating the childhood pattern of going from primary attachment figure to substitute ones or peers and back to "mother."

To men, women are the powerful other in sexual relationships, just as they are in primary attachment. When confronted about why they had an affair, men say, "Well, she asked me." One old man, anticipating the excitement and affairs that often take place at an intervillage end of mourning celebration, described the coming event in terms that evoked not just the image of an amorous lover, but also that of a nursing male child. He said, "Tomorrow we will go to Big Murik [for the celebration] and hold the breasts of their women." The eroticism of mother-son attachment informs later romantic attraction. At the same time, expectations of maternal care inform husband-wife relationships. An adult man, worrying after his angry wife had taken her canoe paddle and left, exclaimed that he now had no one to feed him, even though he had another wife and several grown daughters present in the village at the time. For him, attachment to his wife was inextricably bound up with food. Although most marriage partners seem to be fairly close in age, sometimes a wife is senior in age and status to her husband. Then he works on behalf of her leadership obligations.[11]

Stable long-term marriages draw on the strength of primary attachment bonds in which the woman is the (maternal) source of security and sustenance, and the man is the helpful junior partner (child). Long-term marriages are considered so emotionally all-encompassing that the death of one spouse could lead the surviving one to despair and die of grief. The loss of a primary attachment figure is traumatic, but in the Murik view, the more so the longer the relationship has endured.

Romantic liaisons sometimes allow women to indulge their desire to be the center of another's attention, as they were in infancy. A husband easily becomes a dependent other, and women sometimes refer to men waiting to be fed in the men's house as the "old" children. That this identification with the maternal role does not completely satisfy women's desire for someone who provides them with security and affection is revealed in songs sung by initiated women in secluded circumstances and on exclusively female ritual occasions. The songs describe desertions of child and husband for a lover who was completely irresistible. The urge to be with the lover cannot be suppressed, delayed or re-directed. One of the most poignant of these songs was composed by a mother about her daughter. The daughter was so overcome with longing for her lover in another village that she abandoned her newborn baby and left in her canoe in the middle of the night to go to the next village and find him. The mother/grandmother discovered the baby alone in its bed and immediately understood where her daughter had gone. The song epitomizes the dependent proximity seeking characteristic of attachment, recognizable to the woman's mother because it overwhelmed her care for her own baby. In this song the woman's actions entirely reverse the self-control, abstinence and caregiving behavior expected of a new mother, as she gives in to her wish to be loved, held, and cared for by another.

Attachment in Relation to Cultural Meanings: Seniority, Siblingship, Food, and Gender

Murik cultural orientations related to emotions generated by attachment highlight features of attachment theory that need to be expanded and revised in light of cross-cultural variation. Rather than a single orientation toward a specific other person, Murik attachment takes at least two forms—one focused and person-specific, and another more diffuse and role oriented. Each provides a basis for forms of cultural competence and personhood. Primary attachment underwrites strong paired relationships, in which expectations are organized according to senior/independent/resourceful and junior/dependent/in need. Primary attachment becomes a model for dyadic interactions associated with fundamental cultural activities of food and work. Diffuse attachment provides multiple contexts in which security and acknowledgment can be found. The Murik ecocultural adaptation requires highly flexible work regimes in which household composition and caregiving personnel change constantly to accommodate weather, tides, resource exploitation, and trade in a precarious environment. Children and adults endure long separations from those most dear to them, and participate in work, travel, and trade groups that involve many participants, including strangers. They rely on the flexibility and adaptive strengths of dual attachment orientations. Nevertheless, primary and diffuse attachment are not always compatible or complementary. Challenges and tensions generated by contradictions and incompatibilities generate expressive culture—including joking, songs, myth, and ritual—about tensions, disappointments, and longing of unmet needs or failed expectations.

Disciplinary strategies redirect attachment emotions to siblings, other senior/junior relationships and larger groups. Mothers consistently exact proper sibling behavior from young children. In most other situations, negative emotions are displaced from primary attachment figures onto others, including aggressive joking and diffuse retribution by ritualized spirit figures. Through these strategies competence and caregiving are demanded and reinforced, as is acknowledgment of the power of senior others and the danger of their anger and resentment.

Whereas attachment theory was formulated in contexts that did not include nursing, the Murik case builds strong associations among breastfeeding, maternal care and protection, and the meaning of food. Food expresses attachment emotions, and is a vehicle for conveying these emotions in a broader range of contexts and relationships. Giving and receiving food are culturally elaborated as pervasive and emotionally powerful elements of social relationships in which participants alternately take the role of powerful and resourceful giver and dependent and gratified taker. An attachment theory that does not investigate the cultural relationship of attachment and food is likely to miss a critical area of symbolic activity that expresses and draws emotional power from attachment dynamics.

Sexuality and aggression are organized through cultural concepts of gender and seniority, and managed in terms of respect or joking in daily interactions. Where impulses and rules of relationship contradict each other, play and joking erupt spontaneously and often moderate the resulting tensions. At other times, loss, anger, and despair break out when personal wants and needs or other role obligations overwhelm the self-control and generosity of maternal ("attachment") figures. At such times, individuals experience agonizing personal choices and/or others feel let down in their hopes for care from parents, senior siblings, spouses, and senior men and women.

If we accept that attachment relations are an adaptive system integral to the definition of self, other, and relatedness, then it is crucial that we understand it in terms of our most important adaptive resource—culture. The Murik case demonstrates how thoroughly intertwined these developmental processes are with cultural systems of meaning. Cultural forms of attachment include independent and interdependent orientations in dynamic relation to each other. Cultural regimes of discipline are an important means of molding attachment orientations to cultural models of self and person. The cultural uses of food and feeding express attachment through material forms and practices. Finally, the Murik case directs our attention to gender as a defining factor in attachment relations throughout the life course. A culturally sensitive theory of attachment must attend to cultural meanings and practices that shape forms of attachment, models of self and person, material expressions of attachment, and forms of identity and relatedness.

Acknowledgments

This work is based on research supported by The Institute for Inter-cultural Studies, Wenner-Gren Foundation for Anthropological Research, The

Australian Museum, and the Department of Anthropology and Museum Studies, Central Washington University. I am especially grateful to Naomi Quinn and Jeannette Mageo for their thoughtful responses to an earlier draft and to the other participants of the Lemelson/SPA Conference at which it was presented for their interest and ideas.

Notes

1. Ainsworth identified some dimensions of cultural variation that eventually would need to be explored. Bowlby (1969, 1973) often noted that his use of the term "mother" referred to the primary caregiver, who might or might not be a child's natural mother. And he noted that attachment to father and others was not only possible but likely. LeVine (2004) points out that subsequently, rather than pursuing these leads, attachment theorists have muddied the waters by conflating an ideological project to improve child-rearing practices within Western society with the scientific project of understanding attachment relations and their role in development.
2. Note that he distinguished and preferred the term "attachment," which he considered adaptive and active in different forms throughout the life of an individual, from "dependency," which in psychoanalytic theory was associated with immaturity and incompetence at meeting needs (Bowlby 1969:228).
3. From the point of view of anthropology, culture is our adaptation. In other words, our innate genetic and biological endowment is a set of general and flexible capacities completed through experience in a specific cultural environment; just as a general capacity for linguistic communication is completed (and specified) by learning a particular language or languages.
4. Quinlan and Quinlan (2007) predict a high mating strategy under these circumstances, but Murik prefer to space births up to three years apart, a high parenting strategy. Seymour (chapter 4) argues for Alorese, that a high mating strategy and "insecure" attachment are adaptive to a high-risk environment developed under historical conditions of endemic warfare. For Murik, the predicted suspicion and "insecurity" associated with a high-risk environment are present alongside high levels of confidence and trust, which leads to situations of emotional ambivalence and cognitive paradox.
5. It is considered inappropriate for a younger sibling to bear a child before an older one, especially a firstborn sibling. Such a child is often given to the older sibling.
6. When a child is ill, its mother's attention becomes focused on its care as in infancy. I have seen mothers offer their breast to children who are ten years old and more out of desperate concern that they are not eating during an illness.
7. Kahn (1986) describes a society in which refraining from consuming food has a high cultural value, and fosters a different emotional cathexis with respect to attachment, food, and feeding from Murik indulgence.
8. If a woman is not a biological mother, she is by kinship a mother to others and symbolically a mother to those whom she feeds.
9. Women who act aggressively in their maternal role are severely criticized, but there are occasions and roles when aggression by women is approved or at least expected behavior.

10. Another conjunction of aggression and appetite is the "desire" to eat one's enemies in fighting—Murik warfare included taking the heads of enemies and symbolically eating the victim. Aggression is a means to acquire the object of one's desire and is also a response to thwarted desire.
11. In one particularly volatile breakup, a woman used her senior status to take away a young and junior woman's husband. Following a public discussion of his infidelity, the younger woman confided, "What can I do? She is an initiated woman. If she wants him, I can't say anything."

References

Ainsworth, Mary Salter. 1969. "Object Relations, Dependency, and Attachment: A Theoretical Review of the Infant-Mother Relationship." *Child Development* 40(4):969–1025.

Ainsworth, Mary Salter. 1977. "Attachment Theory and Its Utility in Cross-Cultural Research." In *Culture and Infancy: Variations in the Human Experience*, ed., P. Herbert Leiderman, et al. New York: Academic Press, Inc.

Barlow, Kathleen. 1985. "Learning Cultural Meanings through Social Relationships: An Ethnography of Childhood in Murik Society, Papua New Guinea." PhD Dissertation. Ann Arbor, MI: University Microfilms International, No. 3592.

Barlow, Kathleen. 2001. "Working Mothers and the Work of Culture in a Papua New Guinea Society." *Ethos* 29(1):78–107.

Barlow, Kathleen. 2010. "Sharing Food, Sharing Values: Mothering and Empathy in Murik Society." *Ethos* 38(4):339–353.

Bowlby, John. 1969. *Attachment and Loss: Vol. I. Attachment.* New York: Basic Books, Inc.

Bowlby, John. 1973. *Attachment and Loss: Vol. II. Separation: Anxiety and Anger.* New York: Basic Books, Inc.

Cassidy, Jude. 2008. "The Nature of the Child's Ties." In *Handbook of Attachment: Theory, Research, and Clinical Application*, 2nd edition, eds., Cassidy, Jude and Phillip R. Shaver, pp. 3–22. New York: Guilford Press..

Crittenden, Alyssa N., and Frank W. Marlowe. 2008. "Allomaternal Care among the Hadza of Tanzania." *Human Nature* 19:249–262.

Feeney, Judith A. 2008. "Adult Romantic Attachment: Developments in the Study of Couple Relationships." In *Handbook of Attachment: Theory, Research, and Clinical Application*, 2nd edition, Cassidy, Jude and Phillip R. Shaver, eds., pp. 456–482. New York: Guilford Press.

George, Carol, and Judith Solomon. 2008. "The Caregiving System." In *Handbook of Attachment: Theory, Research, and Clinical Application*, 2nd edition, Cassidy, Jude and Phillip R. Shaver, eds, pp. 833–856. New York: Guilford Press.

Hewlett, Barry S., Michael E. Lamb, Birgit Leyendecker, and Axel Scholmerich. 2000. "Internal Working Models, Trust and Sharing among Foragers." *Current Anthropology* 41:287–297.

Hrdy, Sarah Blaffer. 1999. *Mother Nature: A History of Mothers, Infants, and Natural Selection.* New York: Pantheon.

Hrdy, Sarah Blaffer. 2009. *Mothers and Others: The Evolutionary Origins of Mutual Understanding.* Cambridge, MA: Harvard University Press (Belknap).

Kahn, Miriam. 1986. *Always Hungry, Never Greedy: Food and the Expression of Gender in a Melanesian Society*. Prospect Heights, IL: Waveland Press, Inc.
Keller, Heidi, and Robin Harwood. 2009. "Culture and Developmental Pathways of Relationship Formation." In *Perspectives on Human Development, Family, and Culture*, S. Bekman and A. Aksu-Koç, eds. Cambridge: Cambridge University Press.
Keller, Heidi, and Hiltrud Otto. 2009. "The Cultural Socialization of Emotion Regulation during Infancy." *Journal of Cross-Cultural Psychology* 40(6):996–1011.
Konner, Melvin. 2005. "Hunter-Gatherer Infancy and Childhood: The !Kung and Others." In *Hunter-Gatherer Childhoods*, B. S. Hewlett and M. E. Lamb, eds. Piscataway, NJ: Aldine Transactions.
Konner, Melvin. 2011. *It Does take a Village*. Review of *Mothers and Others: The Evolutionary Origins of Mutual Understanding*. Harvard University Press (Belknap). New York: New York Review of Books.
Ledoux, Louis Pierre. 1936. "Murik Fieldnotes." Unpublished. American Museum of Natural History.
LeVine, Robert A. 2004. "Challenging Expert Knowledge: Findings from an African Study of Infant Care and Development." In *Childhood and Adolescence: Cross-Cultural Perspectives and Applications*, U. P. Gielen and J. Roopnarine, eds., pp. 149–165. Westport, CT: Praeger.
LeVine, Robert A., and Patrice M. Miller. 1990. "Commentary. IN Special Topic: Cross-Cultural Validity of Attachment Theory." *Human Development* 33(1):73–80.
LeVine, Robert A., and Karin Norman. 2001. "The Infant's Acquisition of Culture: Early Attachment Reexamined in Anthropological Perspective." In *The Psychology of Cultural Experience*, C. C. Moore and H. F. Mathews, eds., pp. 83–104. Cambridge, England: Cambridge University Press.
Lipset, David. 1997. *Mangrove Man: Dialogics of Culture in the Sepik Estuary*. Cambridge, UK: Cambridge University Press.
Lutz, Catherine. 1988. *Unnatural Emotion: Everyday Sentiments on a Micronesian Atoll and Their Challenge to Western Theory*. Chicago, IL: University of Chicago Press.
Mageo, Jeannette Marie. 1991. "Inhibitions and Compensations: A Study of the Effects of Negative Sanctions in Three Pacific Cultures." *Pacific Studies* 14(3):1–40.
Mageo, Jeannette Marie. 1998. *Theorizing Self in Samoa: Emotions, Genders, and Sexualities*. Ann Arbor, MI: University of Michigan Press.
McCollum, Chris. 2002. "Relatedness and Self-Definition: Two Dominant Themes in Middle-Class Americans' Life Stories." *Ethos* 39(1/2):113–139.
Miyake, Kazuo, Shing-jen Chen, and Joseph J. Campos. 1985. "Infant Temperament, Mother's Mode of Interaction, and Attachment in Japan: An Interim Report." In *Growing Points of Attachment: Theory and Research*, I Bretherton and E. Waters, eds. *University of Chicago Press Monographs of the Society for Research in Child Development* 50(2/2):276–297.
Morelli, Gilda A., and Fred Rothbaum. 2007. "Situating the Child in Context: Attachment Relationships and Self-regulation in Different Cultures." In *Handbook of Psychology*, S. Kitayama and D. Cohen, eds., pp. 500–527. New York: Guilford Press.

Quinlan, Robert J., and Marsha B. Quinlan. 2007. "Parenting and Cultures at Risk: A Comparative Analysis of Infidelity, Aggression, and Witchcraft." *American Anthropologist* 109(1):164–179.

Quinn, Naomi. 2005. "Universals of Childrearing." *Anthropological Theory* 5(4):477–516.

Roisman, Glenn I., Elena Padrón, L. Alan Sroufe, Byron Egeland. 2002. "Earned-Secure Attachment Status in Retrospect and Prospect." *Child Development* 73(4):1204–1219.

Roscoe, Paul B. 2006. "Fish, Game, and the Foundations of Complexity in Forager Society: The Evidence from New Guinea." *Cross-Cultural Research: The Journal of Comparative Social Science* 40:29–46.

Rothbaum, Fred, John Weisz, Martha Pott, Kazuo Miyake, and Gilda Morelli. 2000. "Attachment and Culture: Security in the United States and Japan." *American Psychologist* 55(10):1093–1104.

Schmidt, Joseph S. V. D. 1922–1923. "Die Ethnographie der Nor-Papua (Murik-Kaup-Karau) bei Dallmannhafen, New Guinea." *Anthropos* 18–19:700–732.

Seymour, Susan. 2004. "Multiple Caretaking of Infants and Young Children: An Area in Critical Need of a Feminist Psychological Anthropology." *Ethos* 32(4):538–556.

Shostak, Marjorie. 1981. *Nisa: The Life and Words of a !Kung Woman*. Cambridge: Harvard University Press.

Sroufe, L. Alan, and June Fleeson. 1986. "Attachment and the Construction of Relationships." In *Relationships and Development*, William Hartup and Z. Rubin, eds. Hillsdale, NJ: Erlbaum.

Takahashi, Keiko. 1990. "Are the Key Assumptions of the 'Strange Situation' Procedure Universal? A View from Japanese Research." *Human Development* 33:23–30.

Weisner, Thomas S. 2005. "Commentary: Attachment as a Cultural and Ecological Problem with Pluralistic Solutions." *Human Development* 48:89–94.

Zeifman, Debra, and Cindy Hazan. 2008. "Pair Bonds as Attachments: Reevaluating the Evidence." In *Handbook of Attachment: Theory, Research, and Clinical Application*, 2nd edition, Cassidy, Jude and Phillip R. Shaver, eds. New York: Guilford Press, pp. 436–455.

Part IV

Childhood-Adulthood Continuities

Chapter 7

Toward a Cultural Psychodynamics of Attachment: Samoa and US Comparisons

Jeannette Marie Mageo

Attachment theorists see a capacity for close one-to-one bonding and autonomy as ideal developmental outcomes and tend to see early distrust as the inevitable consequence of largely unavoidable separation anxieties that are part of physical and emotional weaning—a consequence mitigated by secure attachment. For Freud ([1930] 1964), in contrast, socialization creates individual anxieties to syphon energy away from personal fulfillment and redirect it toward socially valued behaviors. A psychodynamic account of development, then, would question if one-to-one bonding and autonomy are really ideal or only normative and would ask if separation anxieties are somehow intrinsic to norms and to their reproduction.

This chapter is a comparison of development in Samoa and the middle-class Northwestern United States that aims to explore what a truly psychodynamic theory of attachment might resemble. The data from these two locals come from very different periods of my work and intellectual life and so are in many ways disparate but both supply significant information about attachment relationships in these cultures and their emotional effects. In the next section I present three interrelated ideas, further explained and supported in the course of the chapter, about how attachment and psychodynamics vary across cultures. These ideas draw on assumptions fundamental to attachment theory and psychoanalysis: that early bonding affects adult psychology and that people have phantasies, compulsions, and defenses. The seminal psychoanalytic theorist of infancy and pre-Oedipal childhood is Melanie Klein. This chapter first briefly considers attachment theory from the perspective of Klein's psychoanalysis, building on the fresh look at insecurity in infancy that results to formulate my three ideas. I then go on to support these ideas through ethnographic and historical presentations of my two cases.

Attachment Theory and Klein's Psychoanalysis

While Bowlby (1969) originated the concept of attachment, Ainsworth (1973) was the first to measure it. Her measure was "the Strange Situation" (SS) in which a mother accompanied her infant into a room and left. Ainsworth identified three responses. A "securely attached" infant became upset, then calmed down and explored the room, and when mother returned was happy to see her. An "insecurely attached" infant behaved ambivalently when mother returned, clinging and/or resisting, or was simply withdrawn. Ainsworth classified the first of these insecure responses, and their long-term relational manifestations, as ambivalent/resistant (hereafter simply called ambivalent) and the second as avoidant.[1]

Klein (1988) argues that weaning and separation incite infants' rage toward a mother figure, which they cannot bear and so project onto her, making her scary like the witches and ogresses that haunt children's tales in so many cultures (Bettelheim 1976; Lehmann, Myers, and Moro 2005:258–304). If all infants experience not only love but also rage, it follows that all infants are ambivalent; if all infants project their rage and become afraid, they would tend to withdraw from the frightening person. What one sees in those infants whom attachment theory classifies as ambivalent and avoidant, I suggest, are simply the common emotions of infancy experienced to more intense degrees. In "ambivalent attachment" separation rage, fear, and subsequent mistrust prevent children from relating positively to mother upon her return in the SS, while in "avoidant attachment," these emotions compel children to act as if it had no personal relationship to mother.

Two emotions are entwined in Klein's portrait of separation: dependency and rage. Before weaning, the infant is more or less comfortably dependent on its caretaker; it has needs, which its caretaker fulfills. With separation need fulfillment declines, which would make the nursling's dependency more frustrating: I need her and she is not here! It is this frustration that leads to rage. In Klein's view (1988) the enraged little one wants to destroy its object. At this stage, moreover, the infant does not differentiate between wishing and doing. Inasmuch as the infant fears its rage will destroy mother, I further suggest, rage too is likely to intensify dependency feelings: I need her and she is gone for good!

What then are the implications of Klein's psychoanalysis for our understanding of attachment and for the categories used by attachment theorists? First, if dependency, rage, and projection are likely to undermine early attachments, the question of emotional development might better be conceived as one of how elders foster what I call *resilient security*: security that survives these challenges. Relatedly, for Ainsworth attachment is narrowly defined as a bond between individuals: "One can be attached to more than one person," Ainsworth says, "but one cannot be attached to many people" (1973:1). Resilient security is a potentially more encompassing term than "secure attachment" referring to all forms of attachment that help the infant maintain trust in others in face of inevitable threats to this trust. In Samoa and the middle-class Northwestern United States, I will show, pleasurable forms of skin and eye contact, and also of communing and regard, help infants and children develop resilient security in culturally privileged early relationships, which become models for emotional bonding. In Samoa these are group bonds and in the middle-class Northwestern United States individual-to-individual bonds. These are not the only important types of relationship in either society but these types take their emotional strength from early attachments.

My second idea is that culturally shared *distancing practices* (namely, painful forms of skin and eye contact and also of regard, the absence of a person or persons to whom the infant or child is attached, along with isolation) amplify the dependency and rage intertwined in separation. Some distancing practice, however, may accentuate one of these feelings more than the other.

Samoan distancing practices feature elders' refusal to pay attention to youngsters, a refusal enforced through shaming and punishing. Inattention, shaming, and punishing powerfully reinforce the rage that Klein describes. This rage is projected back on mother and other individuals who participate in these practices and undermine one-to-one bonding thus producing what attachment theorists label "insecure attachment." This form of insecurity, I suggest, might more precisely be termed *interpersonal insecurity* when this term is taken to mean insecurity in relations between individual persons. Indeed, I believe this is one of the major confusions in the literature: Attachment theorists often correctly identify interpersonal insecurity in cultures and classes other than the US middle class but they mistake it for insecurity in a general sense and see it only as disadvantageous. In Samoa, interpersonal insecurity helps direct children away from personal relationships toward group bonds. Those behaviors that attachment theorists call ambivalent and avoidant are common and can help us identify stages in the Samoan child's successful enculturation.

Attachment theorists routinely assume that interpersonal insecurity tends to create maladjusted adults and assume that it is by far the most significant insecurity in human development. While my Samoan data lead me to question this first assumption, my Northwestern data lead me to question the second. Northwestern distancing practices, practices common in the United States throughout the mainstream white middle class, feature a primary caretaker's intermittent absence. If one credits Bowlby's (1969) hypothesis, that proximity-seeking/maintenance needs are rooted in human evolution, then a culturally shared attachment system that focuses these needs primarily on one person and is punctuated by periods during which that person is absent, would leave primal needs unsatisfied, amplifying infants' frustrated dependency. Dependency feelings tend to undermine emotional separation and result in insecure personal boundaries, a form of insecurity that, I will show, is as compelling as interpersonal insecurity. My Northwest data imply, then, that the predominant feature of the Western self famously portrayed by Geertz (1984:126) as a "bounded...more or less integrated motivational...universe," is the opposite of what many middle-class infants and toddlers are likely to feel: namely, needy and blurred.

Neither Samoan nor Northwestern caregivers consciously intend to exacerbate infants' insecurities nor are these practices indicative of elders' hostility or lack of care. Rather, Samoan elders distance children because conventional wisdom counsels this treatment as the way to prevent them becoming self-centered and aggressively individualistic. Northwest mothers, on the other hand, feel that they need to be intermittently absent either for labor in a capitalist system that demands it or for relief from the burden of narrow dependency in a mother-centric child care system (cf. Hays 1996; McCollum 2002).

My third idea is that, while pleasurable forms of contact and regard help children become resiliently secure within the confines of certain relationships, the insecurities distancing practices amplify often remain troubling. In order for children to mature into stable adulthood, they need ways to manage these insecurities, which they find in what I call "culturally constituted reaction formations." In psychoanalytic theory, *reaction formation* is a defense in which people dissociate and deny feelings they might naturally express through a censured behavior, but beneath the level of their awareness go on expressing through the opposite behavior (Freud 1925 [1926]:77–178). This substitution works because the unconscious operates via association: there, thoughts that are associated as opposites serve as synonyms for one another (Freud 1900). One might mask for oneself and another one's latent resentment with overly considerate behavior, for example, to the point of being annoying or overbearing. *Culturally constituted reaction formations*, in contrast, manage children's dependency and rage by allowing symbolic expression of these feelings through shared and valued behaviors that are opposites of censured behaviors through which these feelings might more naturally be, and initially are, expressed. Expression via an opposite serves to disguise, deny, and dissociate socially unacceptable feelings.

Thus, in Samoa, developing youngsters at first tend to express rage at elders' refusal to pay attention to them by disrespectful behavior but gradually come to express/deny this feeling by attending on elders, *tautua* in Samoan terms, which means to obediently serve. In the Northwestern United States, middle-class youngsters tend to express dependency on mother and her later substitutes by attention seeking but come to express/deny dependency through autonomous action and achievement. These shared reaction formations are examples of what Spiro (1961:482–490) calls "culturally constituted defenses," by which he means defenses institutionalized within a culture.

Culturally constituted reaction formations are particularly useful in managing rage and dependency because the behaviors by which these feelings are expressed/denied are normative and even ideal, as service is in Samoa and individual achievement is in the middle-class Northwest. Yet, many do not manage the transformations of sentiment and behavior predicated by such defenses, or they manage them only to a degree—which in the Samoan case leads to shirking service and in the Northwest case means remaining emotionally or financially dependent on others. And there are intercultural variations in these defenses, most significantly gender variations, explored in the course of the chapter. I turn first to Samoa to develop and illustrate my three ideas in depth.

Resilient Security in Samoa

I draw the following account of Samoan socialization from my own long-term research on socialization in Samoa (1989, 1991, 1998:3–118, 2001) as well as from the writings of nineteenth-century missionaries and ethnologists and other contemporary ethnographers. Again, Samoans forge resilient security in group relations by way of ubiquitous forms of pleasurable contact and regard. Mead observes that women in the household other than the mother "succor and breastfeed the child" (1959a:61). Everyone, old and young, carries and cares for the baby. In turn, toddlers constantly touch, groom, or lean against other family members (Gardner 1965:146–47, Sutter 1980, Odden 2009:169, 171). Children continue this contact, walking hand-in-hand and sleeping in one another's arms. I call these expectations about communal child care the Devoted Kin model.

Kinship understandings support this model: Samoans use a cognatic system in which all aunts and uncles are "mothers" and "fathers." Family elders' constant injunction to juniors is to "take care of your *tei*," a term of affection for all younger relatives. The "child of three," Mead ([1928] 1961:41–42) tells us, can wander safely among the adjacent households of its various mothers, fathers, and elder siblings, "sure of finding food and drink, a sheet to wrap herself up in for a nap, a kind hand to dry casual tears and bind up her wounds." Samoan babies and toddlers bask in their family's attention. In old Samoa and still today, elders gaily applaud when the baby first crawls, stands, walks, dances, and sings (Kramer [1902] 1995:60). In turn, when Samoan caretakers hold the baby, they face it outward, directing its attention toward the family or road where villagers pass (Ochs 1982; Odden 2009:171).

Devoted kin display a feeling Samoans call *alofa* (love, care), which children come to share and learn to extend to others beyond the family. The typical Samoan greeting is "*Tālofa*," literally "We love you": This sentiment is felt as collective. Samoans may say that they have alofa for another individual, just as in the United States one can say one loves a song or skiing, but in doing so Samoans redeploy an emotional experience that originates in childhood attachment to a group. This is not to say that Samoan families are free of animus, which may take the form of curses (parents cursing children, sisters cursing brothers, and so forth)—curses that many still believe can have dire consequences. Yet, family feeling supersedes interpersonal ambivalence and creates enduring identifications: Samoans proclaim that families are "one body and one blood" (Hjarno 1979/80:88–89; Schultz [1911] n.d.:26).

The Devoted kin family model also presumes communal rights. In pre-Christian times, the father's family had a right to a couple's first baby and the mother's family to the second baby. If they fancied an infant or toddler, any relative, particularly those considered siblings (all cousins no matter how distant) might ask for a baby. When Mead was in Samoa in the 1920s ([1928] 1961:42–43), children likewise had extended kin rights and might move households if elders became demanding—alleviating, she says "their sense of dependency." This independence persists into adulthood. The nineteenth-century missionary, George Turner, remarks, "A Samoan is very independent: he prefers liberty to money; any attempt to force him to do more than he feels inclined, would only cause him to turn on his heels and say, 'Good-by, I'm going' " ([1861] 1986:22). Colonists starting plantations in nineteenth-century Samoa had to import foreign labor because they could not persuade Samoans to do the work. Yet autonomy is not the declared aim of Samoan child rearing but its obverse. Today children who become independent are said to cut off their elders' hands and feet. The English word "independence" is absent from Pratt's early dictionary of Samoan ([1862/1911] 1977). In Milner mid-twentieth-century dictionary, the word is translated as *tū to'atasi*, literally "to stand as one person," meaning as an individual (1966:385).

Samoan Distancing Practices

I suggested earlier that Samoan caretakers use distancing practices to create ambivalence about interpersonal attachment. For the first six months, elders pick up a crying infant. After that, they ignore wails to prevent the child from becoming *matanana*, which in babyhood means inclined to tearful complaint and spoiled, but in adulthood means boastful and inclined to self-aggrandizing tales (Mageo 1998:49). This withdrawal of attention/attending becomes dramatic at weaning. Universally babies show most distress at their mother's absence between 9 and 18 months of age (Berger 1980:243). In Samoa, weaning is likely to occur during this period (Mead [1928] 1961:22; [1930] 1969:90; Schoeffel 1979:102, 126; Sutter 1980:31). For weaning, an infant may be sent to relatives in another household or village temporarily suspending all contact between the little one, its mother, and others who had attended on it (Freeman 1983:203).

If, as Klein (1988) argues, separation generates hostility to mother, weaning at this critical time would heighten this hostility, generating ambivalent attachment. One might think that a plethora of devoted kin would dissipate this effect, yet Samoan babies often display behaviors associated in US studies with ambivalent attachment during and for years after weaning. Freeman, for example, describes a 13-month-old infant taken to a grandmother in another village for weaning; after he returned to his natal family, "he would cry whenever his mother made to leave him" (1983:203). Gerber says such reactions are common: "One of the most frequent sights in a Samoan village is a child having a tantrum when his mother gets on the bus to go to town, even when his usual caretaker is standing right beside him" (1975:107). As soon as the child can walk, tantrums turn into pitched battles. Gardner (1965:154) tells us of a mother who must work for a chief elsewhere in the extended family compound; her toddler trails behind. When she sees him, she picks up a broom (children are often beaten with brooms). The boy cries and lingers until his mother calls her five-year-old daughter, who literally drags him back to their house where he sobs for half and hour until he falls asleep.

When little ones are around the age of two, older siblings, like this daughter, assume responsibility for their care and stop them from intruding upon adult activities (Mageo 1998:40–50; Mead [1929] 1961:24; Odden 2009:64). Siblings may not feed the baby adequately (Bindon and Zansky 1986), making this transfer acutely traumatic. After this time, elders communicate mainly through orders and avoid showing personal attachment to their children (Gardner 1965:145–146; Sutter 1980:37–38). Such displays are considered unseemly as they muddy the boundaries between age-grade groups. Yet, it is not that elders do not feel affection and occasionally they do display it. One of my best informants when I worked and resided in Samoa for 1980 to 1989 was my former husband, Sanele who is Samoan. When Sanele was a boy, Western ideas about weight had not yet affected Samoan eating habits; elders would sometimes feed a child until it lay down sick, saying, "Now you see how much *alofa* we have for you!" When a child is hurt, elders often become solicitous and attend upon the child as they do a baby, sleeping beside the convalescent and cooking for it. Yet, such practices are exceptions to the rule: normally, one pays no heed to the members of lower-status groups, leaving their management and care to their immediate superiors.

Children try to reestablish personal bonds through attention-getting behaviors, which elders respond to with name-calling. *Fiatagata*, literally "to want to be a person," for example, means a young person is pretending to distinction; *fiapoto*, that they "want to be smart"; or, since colonial times, *fiapālagi*, that they "want to be a Western-European." Most frequently, elders call youngsters *tautalaitiiti*, literally "to talk above one's age," but here talk is a trope for all forms of impertinence. Should the child actually talk back it is called *gutuoso*, "jumping mouth" (Mageo 1989). Jumping mouths are beaten until they dramatically relinquish demands for attention by sitting silently stock-still and lowering their gaze. Samoan infants range in temperament from more assertive to more compliant; the former incur the worst beatings (Odden 2009:170–175). Shaming and beatings are likely to increase youngsters' rage, which Klein's (1988) work suggests is likely to be projected back on elders, further undermining trust. The resulting insecurity creates an emotional gulf congruent with the status gulf between youngsters' age-grade group and that of their elders. To properly enact this hierarchical relationship, youngsters are expected to suppress their personal feelings, quietly carrying out elders' commands.

Childhood peer relationships echo these distancing practices. Children lambaste unfortunate features that distinguish a child from others (*faipona*), often by giving it a nickname like Splash Bowels, Sail Ears, or Black Lizard (a racial allusion). This shaming makes children so sensitive that even calling out the name of another's parent is to take this name in vain and may begin a fight. Girls in particular learn to gossip, telling stories about one another's disgraceful actions or humiliations. Schoeffel (1979:141–142) describes a girl gossiping about her rival in a village peer group by describing her as "black," as having "a fat bottom and skinny legs," and as talking too much. The first two comments, like *faipona*, point out personal features that Samoans consider unfortunate. The last comment evokes the most common childhood censure, *tautalaitiiti*, with its implications of presuming above one's proper status, an implication that was explicit in the gossiper's talk: her rival had been asked to be a bridesmaid, a distinction that the gossiper felt was her own status entitlement.

Under elders' direction, children also beat their same-sex contemporaries in other families or villages. The girls of another family once beat up one of Sanele's sisters. When she came home, her father divided her siblings into a female battalion and a male battalion, proceeded to the house of those girls' family, and demanded the family send its children out to fight. One time Sanele was visiting another village, and then waiting at a bus stop to return home, several boys attacked him at the behest of a village chief.

Shaming and beating by age-mates is likely to undermine interpersonal attachments to peers. Young Samoans whom I taught in a psychology of adjustment class in the 1980s routinely voiced doubts that their friends and lovers "really cared" (Mageo 2001:189–211). Distrust is likely to inhibit sharing personal thoughts, feelings, and desires, sharing that could otherwise strengthen personal bonds. So habitual is this avoidance in Samoa that people say one simply cannot know what is in another's inner world (Gerber 1985:133; Mageo 1998:10–11, 39–40). Strong attachments between individuals can breach group boundaries—just as Romeo and Juliet's attachment breached the boundaries between their respective families.

Samoan Defenses

From toddlerhood, Samoan elders encourage children to attend on others, *tautua*, which also means to obediently serve. I remember a scene in a waiting room at a Samoan hospital when a mother on one end of the room gave her toddler a note to take to a woman on the other end. This little one walked a bit unsteadily from one to the other, while both women smiled broadly at its performance. Attending on others, I soon argue, is a culturally constituted reaction formation through which children come to express/deny their rage and disappointment at elders' refusal to pay attention to them.[2] This transformation is not typically effected through individual praise, which is thought to spoil children, but by telling them what to do and shaming or punishing those who disobey—practices that, we saw earlier, tend to increase rage and the insecure interpersonal attachments that accompany it. *Tautua* comes to include: cooking, cleaning, massaging elders, maintaining the family compound and fields, caring for smaller children and grandparents, turning over a paycheck, or taking up a course of study in school that elders think will increase family status. One girl gave an illustration.

> All my life...I never did anything for myself...I was given to my grandparents, so I could run errands for them. My grandmother was put on a hemodialysis machine every four days within a week, and most of the time I was

> there with her...I learned how to put her on [the] hemo-dialysis machine...I gave her insulin shots in the morning, took her blood pressure rate after every meal, made her food to fit her diet the doctor told me to give her. I translated everything she felt to the doctor because she didn't speak English, but I did. I had to do all this and I was still going to Elementary School. I did this until my grandmother passed away...Then I took care of my grandfather till he passed away.

A reason why babies and children circulated so freely among kin in Mead's Samoa was because children were, and indeed are, the household work force, and much work is gendered. Since Christianization, girls' service is within the household; boys' is outside it (Mageo 1992, 1998:141–163; Shore 1981). Within the village, too, service is gendered. In the *'aumāga* (the untitled males' association), boys carry out the council of chiefs' decrees, and act as a public works crew, a police force, and formerly a militia. In women's groups, girls undertake a range of projects from singing and dancing at funerals, to sanitation, to raising funds.

Tautua is understood as enacting respect yet often betrays resentment toward elders. Thus, Gerber describes a scene (1975:67) in which girls sit talking, playing guitars, singing quietly, and combing each other's hair; their elders eat in the front room. A call comes for service. A "look of annoyance can be plainly read on all faces." Girls "arise clumsily with an exaggerated show of exhaustion," whispering, "Alas." Anger flashes briefly "as the servitors grimace and quietly mimic the words of the command." Spirit possession episodes often indicate similar resentment: A dead relative who outranks elders will possess a beleaguered girl and reproach her elders for their service demands (Macpherson and Macpherson 1990; Mageo 1998:174–190, 218–239). Boys' outside tasks make them harder to coerce but they too often resent demands for service (Mageo 2001:198–202). One of my informants, for example, said his family was "always chasing me and telling me to do this and do that...I remember my grandmother always telling me if I don't pick up the trash...she's going to send me to my mother. And she knows I don't like my mother's family."

What helps young people move past the rage displayed in separation tantrums and in jumping-mouth insolence, then partially disguised in resentful service, and move toward willing service is that, from childhood onward, *tautua* not only means subordination to elders but also command of subordinates. Thus, children may be saddled with sibling care but also have full authority to demand attention and compliance from younger ones and to beat them should they demure, which affords considerable opportunity to disguise and displace rage. As one girl put it: "If they [her younger siblings] don't listen to me, that's their problem. I told them what to do...I don't care how they feel...If they do something wrong, they have to be punished for it."

Humbly "standing at one's post," Samoans say, is the way one serves the group, yet every post is also a position of authority. The college where I taught in Samoa, for example, had a copy center. The Samoan who staffed it seemed to decide whether an individual instructor got copies or not based on what he judged to be their politeness and his personal preferences. After many complaints from white instructors, the college president spoke to him gently about the importance of copies to forwarding the purposes of the institution, which moved him to mend his way (a bit). In relation to copies, he was king, though he was in humble service to the president.

Sources from proverbs to daily discourse, moreover, tout *tautua* as the path to power and renown. Men awarded a title, the beginning of social ascent, are said to have done their *tautua* to family and village. Titled men's wives bear their own correlative titles. Samoans see titles as another form of service, but by investing the group's authority and honor in a man and his wife, titles exalt these individuals, reversing the name-calling and forced subordination of early childhood.

Delight in positions of honor and administrative authority, along with people's willingness to humbly serve, then, are two sides of the Samoan ethos. On the one side, the habit of humbly expressing respect is so endemic that Robert Louis Stevenson says that on the streets of nineteenth-century Apia, "Terms of ceremony fly as thick as oaths upon a ship...[C]ommoners 'my-lord' one another as they meet—and urchins as they play marbles" (1892:2). On the other side, the desire for titles in pre-Christian Samoa was so strong that wars were always about them (Gilson 1970). For this reason, in deference to the nineteenth-century missionary plea that wars should cease, the last paramount in the westerly islands decreed that his title should die with him (Gilson 1970:117).

Missionaries preached not only against war but also for nuclear family-style attachments: children, they told their congregants, should grow up with their biological parents (Turner [1861] 1986:86). In Christian rhetoric generally virtue was rooted in personal attachments to individual others: Christ, a parent, a spouse, or a neighbor one loved as oneself. For many decades, this rhetoric prevailed only in church contexts like Sunday services and mission schools but it provided a basis in thinking and feeling when US middle-class models of one-to-one bonding washed up on twentieth-century Samoan shores, carried on a wave of World War II American servicemen and then on successive waves of television, movies, and videos, which today tend to confuse youngsters' feelings about traditional elder-youngster relations (Mageo 1998:141–163, 2001). Christian attempts at psychological conversion continue: At one point, for example, I lived next to a Samoan Mormon family that on the advice of their church had weekly family meetings in which they shared personal feelings with one another!

Resilient Security in the Northwest

I draw the following portrait of the Northwestern attachment from my 2004–2006 work with 114 undergraduate students from Washington State University (WSU) along with many psychologists and anthropologists' research on development and bonding in the United States. WSU students are predominantly white and middle class, although decedents of Asian/American unions are common. Students' natal homes are Northwest-wide and hence both urban and rural. My project focused on dreams, which have long been an important source of data in psychological anthropology. Students kept dream journals, learned several projective techniques to help them associate to their dreams, and wrote dream papers in which they constructed their interpretations from these associations, which were typically to their personal relationships and family histories. Probably because of the period during which my students grew up and their socioeconomic class, many had stay-at-home moms and working dads. It was our common assumption that their dreams represented their individual psychology; I also asked them to consider how their dreams might reflect a cultural psychology. With 19 students, I conducted life-history interviews. At the end of each semester, in my absence, all students filled out a form indicating their willingness to have their papers and journals included in my study (IRB No. 5921). They contributed 995 dreams (400 from men and 595 from women), 217 of which were accompanied by their own dream analyses. This method of data collection has advantages and drawbacks that I lack space to discuss here (but see Mageo 2011:10–20).

I return to my first question: How do Northwestern middle-class attachment practices forge relationships of resilient security? For all but one of my 19 interviewees, their first and closest interpersonal bond was with mother. In Western cultures generally, the baby cradled in its mother's arms, each gazing into the other's eyes, is the icon and epitome of early attachment. This position promotes what Stern (1985) calls "intersubjective attunement" along with preverbal facial interchanges between mothers and infants. Cradling contact and reciprocal gaze further suggest individual-to-individual intimacy and anticipate mother's later role as an appreciative audience for the child's endeavors. I call these mainstream middle-class beliefs in the importance of intense mother-child engagement the Devoted Mom model. There are, of course, many models of child rearing in US society, from the Devoted Mom to more communalistic models in places like Appalachia and among working-class African American communities in Carolina (Rogoff 2003:23, 121). US mothers of lower socioeconomic status, moreover, usually lack time for one-to-one devotion (Kusserow 2004). The Devoted Mom model, however, is not only evident in my Northwestern students' dreams and self-reports but finds its way into attachment theory itself.

While attachment theory was originally meant to be a descriptive system, Casillas (2012) shows that its privileging of motherly devotion as a basis for emotional security is now widely accepted by the US pediatric community and in popular books that inform middle-class parenting (Leach 2007:113; Pantley 2002:51; Sears and Sears 2001:11). According to Giddens (1991:18–21), due to an explosion and fragmentation of knowledge, mainstream Americans tend to rely on experts; social science theory, therefore, has come to influence the organization and transformation of society. There appears to be a historical circularity between Ainsworth's documentation of middle-class US infants' responses to separation, the classificatory system she established to describe them, and attempts to reform practice to replicate that system's implied ideal. Indeed, the attachment practices predicated by the Devoted Mom model were not customary in the US middle class before the mid-twentieth century (Giddens 1992:98; Rogoff 2003:130), when attachment research and theory originated.

What then is father's role in US middle-class attachment? According to Benjamin (1988), fathers represent a larger world to the child along with the power, freedom, and danger of that world, and provide what Winnicott (1967) calls transitional space: a protected space in which the child can practice risk-taking in relative safety. Anthropologists question the universality of these "larger world" associations (Ackerman 2003; Leacock 1981). In old Samoa, for example, adult women like men were preoccupied with politics, while children were cared for by other children. In all 19 cases in which I conducted life history interviews, however, my Northwestern students still associated their father with freedom/risk-taking. One student with divorced parents, for example, said that while her mom always planned her time, her dad "shot from the hip, whatever he and his buddies were up to, the kids came along. It was always different." Her father represented "living life on the edge." Even a student who said that her working well-paid mom "wore the pants in the family" had a father who took her for thrilling rides when she was little, skidding his car in the snow for fun. I call this the Supportive Dad model. Risk-taking, I shall soon argue, counterbalances close mother-child attachment.

Northwestern Distancing Practices

Again, my thesis here is that middle-class Northwest distancing practices tend to amplify dependency feelings; these feelings undermine emotional separation and create insecure personal boundaries. I begin with practices common in the US mainstream middle class, practices characteristic of my Northwesterners as well.

Despite the fact that the middle-class attachment ideal is close personal mother-child engagement, after the first few months and sometimes earlier, a stranger without affective ties to the child periodically replaces mother. As a preteen and then a teen, I babysat for extra cash, as many US girls do. In my family, I had no experience caring for an infant. I remember times when a mother left me with a baby who cried unceasingly after her departure until it finally fell asleep. The only instruction she had given me was to take whatever I wanted from the refrigerator. I had no idea how to soothe the infant, whom I had never met and was afraid to touch.

Upper-middle-class families may have permanent help, usually one female with whom the baby is familiar or even bonded, which may soften the frustrated dependency likely to result from intermittent maternal absence. When middle-class families do not move for work or other reasons, babysitters too may become familiar figures, but are less likely to be so in early life. Through intermittent absence, US middle-class mothers also attempt to offset the burden of narrow dependency by creating a situation in which the baby, then the child, must rely on its own resources (McCollum 2002). Thus, even when mother is home, the infant and later toddler may be isolated in a room with the door shut for nighttime sleep or daytime naps to "develop her character," Mead remarks with irony in her film, *Four Families* (1959b, cf. McCollum 2002:127). I remember those naps because often I wasn't sleepy and sat up lonely and bored gazing at long afternoon shadows on the opposite wall.[3] Being intermittently absent is a distancing practice at least initially upsetting to children, as Ainsworth herself documents. Indeed, one could interpret the SS as her attempt, after observing nearly constant early contact in Uganda (1973), to reassure herself that this US practice, in most cases, was not emotionally harmful.

Today middle-class mothers are also likely to send preschool toddlers to day care. At home they favor disciplinary practices that recreate intermittent absence like sending children to their room or into a corner for a "time-out." Their reasons for doing so are complex, but intentional or not these practices underline bodily separateness, which is an experiential trope for individual separateness (the person as within the skin). Like intermittent absence, disciplinary practices that underline bodily separateness are likely to increase awareness of one's need for others and hence feelings of dependency.

Freud ([1930] 1964) argues that infants' first sense of self comes from introjecting pleasurable experiences, mother with them. It seems likely that mother introjection would be powerful in a culture where the early mother-child relationship is privileged (as in the middle-class Northwest) and where child-care practices accentuate dependency feelings: Internalization is a way to keep available an intermittently absent mother one badly needs to be present. Such internalization, however, is emotionally hazardous because the intense one-to-one regard predicated by the Devoted Mom model also has a surveillance function critical to the normativity that Foucault (1990) argues is central to the psychology of moderns.

For Foucault, the king and his phallic symbols, scepter and sword, symbolize social control via laws enforced by violence (whipping, hanging, and so forth), which he believes characterized premodern European society. In relation to child development, beating is the obvious analog here. In modernity, surveillance replaces laws and attendant violence. Northwest middle-class children, I propose, tend to internalize surveillance in maternal form: one's mother, as a voice in the mind, compares the self to normative ideals. This internalization makes secure personal boundaries unlikely. In consequence, young people can be touchy about mothers' attempts at influence.

Despite her athletic figure, for example, one student's mother once gave her a Slimfast shake for breakfast and another time told her sister to "watch sweets." The athlete, Scarlet, was "very upset"; her sister cried. These sisters were reacting to their mother's implied comparison of their bodies to an ideal—a comparison that was particularly painful because this ideal was not only external but also internal. Thus, Scarlet rose daily at 5:00 a.m. during high school to work out, however late she had stayed up the night before. Scarlet's workouts, however, not only evinced internalized surveillance; her pride in self-discipline indicated that workouts were also a way to assert independent control over her own body and to deny her frustrated needs for secure boundaries.

Scarlet is not alone. In the white middle-class US female dedication to dieting, the body is a site where girls and later women seek to replicate a normative ideal and at the same time to exert independent self-control. Eating crosses a boundary between external and internal; extreme eating routines often dramatize boundary insecurities. In girls' eating disorders, for example, internalized norms represented by top-model bodies compel young women, yet are also a way that anorexics and bulimics attempt to be self-determining and escape others' control (Brumberg 1988; Giddens 1991:103–108; Gremillion 2003).

Lest anyone wrongly assume that maternal surveillance and its effect on personal boundaries is universal, I turn back briefly to Samoa. One might think becoming part of a culture where people assert they are one in body with their family, as Samoans do, would also imperil individual boundaries. Yet, Samoan children are usually free from close personal surveillance because they tend to be regarded and treated as a group (Sutter 1980) and because they are mainly attended to by other children, who have neither the interest nor the ability to shape them in intimate ways. An exception is a lovely girl with long hair, a mark of particular attractiveness. Elders will closely watch such a girl to maintain her virginity and to ensure refined conduct in hopes of marrying her to a high-status male. Such girls sometimes cut off their hair to escape surveillance.

Returning to the Northwestern United States, the Supportive Dad model bolsters insecure boundaries. Inasmuch as one's father conforms to this model and is internalized, feelings of insecurity activate a "dad" voice in the mind that encourages autonomy by way of conquering fears and taking risks. The problem with this remedy is that American fathers are often emotionally, physically, or financially absent (Fields and Casper 2001:7; Kelly 2006; Mageo 2011:26–28). When fathers are absent, my Northwest data suggest, personal boundaries may remain porous.

Clark, for example, had divorced parents. In the divorce, his mom got a rural house and property that she had neither the physical nor financial resources to maintain without Clark's help. Clark had a dream about his mom's house in which he was on the sundeck and hit a skunk with a soccer ball. The skunk grew to "three times it original size, leaned down on its front legs with its butt in the air, and started spraying me in the face with his skunk juice. The spray was coming out so strong and fast, it was like water coming out of a fire hose." Clark runs inside and closes all the doors and windows, but the smell penetrates and "totally engulfed me." He cannot seal his boundaries: They are insecure.

Clark felt that the dream fear was "not being able to get the smell off." Clark also associated the skunk with anxious waking behaviors: "I have kind of a thing about being clean. I constantly wash my hands, use antibacterial gel, take up to three showers a day, and can only wear clean, just washed clothes." So for Clark skunk stink is a kind of pollution, associated with his mother (in his dream, the skunk sits on her deck), which reminds him of his compulsive purification practices. Such pollution fears evince boundary insecurity: As in Clark's case, a dirty external peril seeps inward.

Northwestern Defenses

Here again I begin with studies of middle-class mainstream US practices. From toddlerhood, mothers praise their child's early success with walking, talking, and a host of small self-care tasks (cf. Quinn 2005; Wiezbicka 2004). I suggest what this praise actually teaches children is that they can continue their dependency in the guise of soliciting mother's attention for independent activities. Thus, Whiting observes that when a US child draws a picture, she may go to mother and say, "See my picture." Mom responds: "That's a very good picture," nursing the child's self-regard (1978; cf. Weisner 2002). Inasmuch as children, through individual achievements, continue to express/deny dependency on mother and later others for attention, their achievement orientation represents a culturally constituted reaction formation, one that is likely to covertly carry forward the porous boundaries and vulnerability to surveillance this dependency posits.

As children's activities begin to range outside the household, maternal witnessing becomes remote through questions like, "What did you do in school today?" Remote witnessing means mother becomes an audience for children's narratives. US middle-class children, I suggest, internalize mother-as-audience by telling self-stories, first to her and then to others and to themselves. Children come to witness their personal struggles and successes and transform them into autobiography (Miller 1994; Nelson 1996). Middle-class fathers too, ideally, offer an appreciative audience, but more often for the child's risk-taking tales (Benjamin 1988).

There is evidence that US middle-class girls and boys defend against the porous personal boundaries produced by dependency feelings by enacting autonomy in gendered ways. Thus, Tannen (2001) records early childhood interactions in which two girls embrace, gaze into one another's eyes, and tell one another they are "alike." "Girlfriends" defend their personal boundaries by denying that the other is really outside the self because she is the same. They share secrets and personal feelings that nurture this identification while also demonstrating that the two are separate and different from others (Canaan 1990; Tannen 2001). In early conversations Tannen records among boys, conversely, they try to outdo one another—the goal being to rank as number one (Mageo 2005; Munroe et al. 1981). In one exchange, for example, a boy says his family is going to Disneyland next month; another boy says his family is moving to Disneyland. Thus boys, individually and in teams, learn to defend their boundaries by competing against others in this way garnering attention and asserting their differential rank on a common standard.[4]

For illustrations of how these gendered defenses operate in individual lives I turn to the dreams of a young woman mentioned earlier, Scarlet, and a young man, Van, but first I briefly review my own interpretative methods, explained at length elsewhere (2011:10–14, 23–26, 55–57, 62–64, 93–97). Like psychoanalysts, I take dreams to be metaphorical representations of dreamers' emotional life structured by symbolic transformations such as displacement and condensation. I also see dreams as metaphorical representations of the dreamers' personal experience of and feelings about the cultural psychologies in which they participate, psychologies formed in part by shared child-rearing practices. Cultural psychologies, along with their characteristic hazards and problems, are also metaphorically represented in narratives circulating in a society found in sources from grammar school history books to news reports to films and television to other popular media. Such narratives often enter dreams where dreamers combine and transfigure them in a multitude of startling ways (Mageo 2011:23–58).

Scarlet dreamed that she was driving behind a car carrying two Mexican boys and a white girl that crashed: "there's glass everywhere and blood from head to toe on one of them. I call 911. The ambulance comes and they act like it's nothing and I am just in a panic." Bleeding symbolizes a breach of boundaries—especially for women because it is part of the menstrual cycle and the beginning of sexuality. Scarlet believed the bleeding Mexican boy stood for her boyfriend: "Butler has a heart arrhythmia…Ever since I found out…I have…anxiety about not being in control." Ambulances are a normal part of life for Butler. If Scarlet marries him, moreover, she will be part of a Mexican family: his half-sister is Mexican; so are his nephew and niece.

In high school, Scarlet's family took three spring-break trips to Mexico: one to Cancun and two to rural Mexican villages. Later, Scarlet was a leader in a church group that she inspired to help poor people in Mexico. They traveled to a village and, in a week there, built a house for a woman with three children. The village had a "migrant house" where people learned how to sneak across the US border safely, and a long fence with crosses. Each cross was for a person who died trying to get across and one was for a boy just Scarlet's age when he died.

For Scarlet, then, the bleeding Mexican children are what Freud in his analysis of dreams ([1900] 1964) called a condensation: a dream image that is a pastiche of associations from life experience that have similar emotive significance. In the dream, Scarlet worries about the bleeding children as in life she worried about her boyfriend's heart problem and about the moral implications of a dead Mexican boy. All three images (the bleeding children, her boyfriend's unsteady heart, and the dead boy)—one present in the dream, the other two represented by it—demonstrate extreme insecurity and, I suggest, displace Scarlet's anxiety about her own insecure boundaries. Here some further explanation of psychoanalytic term "displacement" and its difference from "projection" is necessary.

Projection is a defense in which one attributes one's own feeling to another: for example, "I am not mad at mother, mother is mad at me." Displacement can be a defense in which one enacts one's feelings towards one object in relationship to another. A Samoan child, for instance, might be angry with her elders and so punish her younger siblings. Displacement, however, also refers to any dislocation of sentiment from its real source to another to disguise and alley anxiety (Freud [1900] 1964, [1925] 1926). It is not that Scarlet projects her own anxieties on others: In her descriptions of Butler in life and the Mexicans in her dream, they were all conspicuously relaxed about their boundaries, dismissing her concerns. Scarlet, rather than being aware of anxiety about her own boundaries, focuses on her fears about others' boundaries—fears that are more manageable because they refer to threats less close to home.

The dream also reflects one of Scarlet's defenses against boundary insecurity: She simply expands her boundaries empathetically to include all of humanity. While this expansion does not cure (indeed it may increase) her worries, presumably it lessens her feeling of being invaded by a world outside herself. Yet, Scarlet thought that her broad sense of responsibility was problematic: "I need to take care of everything," she remarked, "to fix things." Scarlet may be replicating the mother position in the white middle-class mother-child dyad, exercising surveillance-as-care and inadvertently trespassing others' boundaries. Scarlet thought the dream exemplified Americans' need to "fix others... we as a nation feel it's our right to intervene in other countries' problems."

For insight into how Northwestern masculinity expresses/denies the boundary insecurity that comes with early dependency, I turn to Van's dream, which opens with a fight that he described as like "a martial arts movie." The combatants attack innocent bystanders. Van does not "bother to help... because it is not my problem." Then the fighters "start to chase me. I do not run but instead I embrace them... The first person attacks me but I... flick him off like a bug." Then Van loses his "cool" and "it is on... I am hip throwing people and enforcing s-locks on them. I feel invincible, like no one can harm me. I feel like an indestructible machine."

Van's dream, like Scarlet's, begins with imperiled strangers and as in her case I suspect Van is displacing his own boundary insecurity. Indeed, he said he had variations of this dream recurrently since he began learning a martial art called Hapkido a year before: "The next day, I would go... and get the crap beat out of me." The dream, then, refers to a situation in which his bodily boundaries were at risk and to a defensive practice through which he responds to this insecurity. By virtue of these associations I suggest that, for Van, a fear of "getting the crap kicked out of me" (breached boundaries) in daily competition leads in dream life to an embrace of competitors in which others seem like bugs (a different order of being than himself) and thus inconsequential threats. Via this transformation, Van feels invincible: that no one can violate his boundaries.

Again like Scarlet, Van associated his dream with adolescence, that period when young people begin to master adult versions of gender identity: "I would get into a lot of trouble and fights. More importantly I had a lot of pride and I still do; I didn't put up with a lot of crap." So in Hapkido, he gets the crap beaten out of him, but as an adolescent he didn't put up with crap. The dream locale is Van's high school and thus condenses recent memories of Hapkido with memories of adolescent troubles.

Martial arts movies are a subgenre of "action films," an extremely popular US genre that enacts contemporary masculinities (Holt and Thompson 2004). The intertextuality of Van's dreams with action films suggests that his imperiled boundaries, along with the dream's defensive transformations, are common among US boys.[5] Van thought his dream exemplified Americans' need "to protect themselves and...to always be safe"—from weapons of mass destruction, for example?

Scarlet's and Van's dreams also betray problems with these gendered defenses. Scarlet's ambulance man says she's just panicking. He means she is overly emotional (a characterization of women that was once explicit in white middle-class culture); this denigrating judgment signals incongruence between a US "rationality" norm in which people are considered intrinsically separate from others and the intersubjective engagement nurtured by early mother-child attachment. In Van's dream, aggressors metamorphose from objects of an embrace into insects, while he himself becomes machine-like, transformations that metaphorically express and then deny his engagement with others and also represent defenses against insecure boundaries.

I admit that Scarlet's and Van's dreams represent exceptionally clear cases: Most girls do not build houses for poor Mexicans nor do most boys study martial arts. Nonetheless, Scarlet and Van evince boundary insecurities and gendered ways of denying these insecurities and defending against them that were widespread in my Northwest dream data (2011). These complementary ways—one enacted by trying to fix people(s), the other by overpowering them—may represent two sides of what one might call the US superpower ethos, an ethos that originates in cultural forms of attachment and separation.

For both sexes, of course, there are intracultural variations in these ways. US girls, for example, may form cliques where several "girlfriends" bond and marginalize or exclude others (Goodwin 2006). Cliques express autonomy from outsiders and defend against insecure boundaries in a manner similar to girlfriend relationships and represent a variation on them (Mageo 2011:54, 98, 117–132, 170). On school playgrounds, in hopscotch or jump rope, White, Latina, and African-American girls of middle and lower socioeconomic status are often aggressively competitive (Goodwin 2006), expressing autonomy and defending against boundary insecurity as US boys do. And boys like girls manifest temperamental variation, some being less competitive and more inclined to one-to-one bonding, as Clark is with his mother, and others more dedicated to winning (Holt and Thompson 2004).

Whatever the variations, mother-child attachments are obviously of unparalleled importance for mainstream middle-class US boys and girls today. Over the course of the twentieth century, American studies of early child development shifted from Freud's (1961) father-centric focus to the mother-centric focus evident in Klein's (1988), Bowlby's (1969), and Ainsworth's (1973) work, and in attachment theory more generally. The contemporary significance of the mother-child bond for US children and the tendency of surveillance concomitant with this bond to imperil personal boundaries may help to explain why.

Ranges and Recommendations

Cross-culturally different and historically changing attachment systems do not mean that we should abandon our quest for psychological universals but suggest necessary steps for finding them. First, researchers might document ideal care and its putative outcomes, not only in Western societies but also elsewhere. Samoans view secure group bonding and a willingness to serve elders as the ideal outcome of proper child rearing. In the middle-class Northwest, a capacity for secure one-to-one bonding and a willingness to explore the environment are developmental ideals. Such outcomes typically represent people's conscious hopes and intentions and, therefore, should be readily apparent in discourse and through skillful interviewing.

Second, researchers might attend to the underside of attachment systems—distancing practices, practices usually less conscious in that people do not intend their psychological effects. Samoans do not typically aim at intensifying children's rage, nor do Northwestern middle-class parents aim to create frustrated dependency and insecure boundaries in their offspring. Inasmuch as people notice these effects, they are likely to regard them as unfortunate if unavoidable. Yet, rage and dependency, acknowledged or not, are critical to reproducing each of these two cultural systems. Furthermore, distancing practices and their effects will be evident once researchers allow that cultural values, correlative ideal outcomes, and unfortunate aberrations from these norms, are not all there is to child rearing.

Third, researchers might consider the culturally constituted defenses revealed when one sees both the more and less conscious sides of child rearing. In particular, they might attend to how shared defenses inherent in people's understandings of gender establish major life orientations. Here techniques such as dream collection and analysis could help us to see how a defense operates and to thus detect the fingerprints of an attachment system on subjective experience.

In his discussion of a session at the 2011 meetings of the American Anthropological Association, Robert LeVine argued that, from its beginnings, attachment theorists had a moral and political agenda rather than aiming at a cross-cultural perspective on infancy and early childhood (LeVine, in press; cf. LeVine 2004). This chapter, I hope, offers a few starting points that may help researchers arrive at a developmental psychology that is empirical and descriptive rather than prescriptive.

Acknowledgments

I thank Naomi Quinn, Stanley Smith, Justine McCabe, and an anonymous reviewer for their useful comments on this chapter.

Notes

1. Attachment theorists later added a fourth category, "disorganized," for all behavior that did not fit their classifications. See Gaskins, chapter 1.
2. For other Pacific examples of children attending to elders, see Quinn, chapter 8, Ritchie and Ritchie 1979.
3. For a German parallel see LeVine and Norman 2001:93
4. The 1992 20th Century Fox film, *White Men Can't Jump*, suggests that other US ethnicities too display these gendered defenses.
5. Kristeva (1986) originates the idea of intertextuality in her analysis of literary texts.

References

Ackerman, Lillian. 2003. *A Necessary Balance: Gender and Power among Indians of the Columbia Plateau*. Norman, OK: University of Oklahoma.

Ainsworth, Mary D. Salter. 1973. "The Development of Infant-Mother Attachment." In *Review of Child Development Research*, vol. 3, Bettye M. Caldwell and Henry N. Ricciuti, eds., pp. 1–94. Chicago, IL: University of Chicago Press.

Benjamin, Jessica. 1988. *The Bonds of Love: Psychoanalysis, Feminism, and the Problem of Domination*. New York: Pantheon Books.

Berger, Kathleen S. 1980. *The Developing Person*. New York: Worth.

Bettelheim, Bruno. 1976. *The Uses of Enchantment*. New York: Alfred A. Knopf.

Bindon, J. R., and S. Zansky. 1986. "Growth and Body Composition." In *The Changing Samoans: Behavior and Health in Transition*, Paul T. Baker, Joel M. Hanna, and Thelma S. Baker, eds., pp. 222–253. New York: Oxford University Press.

Bowlby, John. 1969. *Attachment and Loss*, vol. 1. New York: Basic Books.

Brumberg, Joan J. 1988. *Fasting Girls*. Cambridge, MA: Harvard University Press.

Canaan, Joyce E. 1990. "Passing Notes and Telling Jokes." In *Uncertain Terms: Negotiating Gender in American Culture*, Faye Ginsburg and Anna Lowenhaupt Tsing, eds., pp. 215–231. Boston, MA: Beacon.

Casillas, Emily. 2012. "Purposeful Parents." Masters Thesis, Washington State University.

Fields, Jason, and Lynne M. Casper. 2001. *American Families and Living Arrangements, 2000. Document P20–537.* Washington, DC: United States Census Bureau.

Foucault, Michel. 1990. *The History of Sexuality*, vol. 1, Robert Hurley, trans. New York: Random House.

Freeman, Derek. 1983. *Margaret Mead and Samoa: The Making and Unmaking of an Anthropological Myth*. Cambridge: Harvard University Press.

Freud, Sigmund. [1900] 1964. "Interpretation of Dreams." In *The Standard Edition of the Complete Psychological Works of Sigmund Freud*, vols. 4 and 5, James Strachey, trans. in collaboration with Anna Freud, assisted by Alix Strachey and Alan Tyson. London: Hogarth.

Freud, Sigmund. [1925] 1926. "Inhibitions, Symptoms, and Anxiety." In *The Standard Edition of the Complete Psychological Works of Sigmund Freud*, vol. 20, James Strachey, trans. in collaboration with Anna Freud, assisted by Alix Strachey and Alan Tyson, pp. 78–178. London: Hogarth.

Freud, Sigmund. [1930] 1964. "Civilization and Its Discontents." In *The Standard Edition of the Complete Psychological Works of Sigmund Freud*, vol. 21, James Strachey, trans. in collaboration with Anna Freud, assisted by Alix Strachey and Alan Tyson, pp. 57–146. London: Hogarth.

Gardner, Louise C. 1965. "Gautavai: A Study of Samoan Values." Masters Thesis, University of Hawai'i.

Gerber, Eleanor R. 1975. "The Cultural Patterning of Emotions in Samoa." Doctoral dissertation. University of California at San Diego.

Gerber, Eleanor R. 1985. "Rage and Obligation." In *Person, Self and Experience: Exploring Pacific Ethnopsychologies*, Geoffrey M. White and John Kirkpatrick, eds., pp. 121–167. Berkeley, CA: University of California.

Geertz, Clifford. 1984. " 'From the Native's Point of View': On the Nature of Anthropological Understanding." In *Culture Theory: Essays on Mind, Self, and Emotion*, Richard A. Shweder and Robert A. LeVine, eds., pp. 123–136. Cambridge, England: Cambridge University Press.

Giddens, Anthony. 1991. *Modernity and Self-Identity*. Stanford: Stanford University Press.

Giddens, Anthony. 1992. *The Transformation of Intimacy*. Cambridge UK: Polity.

Gilson, R. P. 1970. *Samoa 1830 to 1900*. Melbourne: Oxford University Press.

Goodwin, Marjorie Harkness. 2006. *The Hidden Life of Girls: Games of Stance, Status, and Exclusion*. Oxford, UK: Blackwell.

Gremillion, Helen. 2003. *Feeding Anorexia: Gender and Power at a Treatment Center*. Durham, NC: Duke University Press.

Greenfield, P. A. 2009. "Linking Social Change and Developmental Change." *Developmental Psychology* 45(2):401–418.

Hays, Sharon. 1996. *The Cultural Contradictions of Motherhood*. New haven, CT: Yale University Press.

Hjarno, Jan. 1979/1980. "Social Reproduction: Towards an Understanding of Aborginal Samoa." *Folk* 21–22:72–123.

Holt, D., and Thompson, C. J. 2004. "Man-of-Action Heroes: The Pursuit of Heroic Masculinity in Everyday Consumption." *The Journal of Consumer Research* 31(2):425–440.

Kelly, Joan B. 2006. "Children's Living Arrangements following Separation and Divorce." *Family Process* 46(1):35–52.

Klein, Melanie. 1988. *Love, Guilt and Reparation: And Other Works 1921–1945*. London: Virago Press.

Kramer, Augustin. [1902] 1995. *The Samoan Islands: The Outline of a Monograph Giving Special Consideration to German Samoa*, vol. 2, Theodore Verhaaren, trans. Honolulu, HI: University of Hawaii Press.

Kristeva, Julia. 1986. *The Kristeva Reader*, L. S. Roudiez, trans. Oxford, UK: Basil Blackwell.

Kusserow, Adrie. 2004. *American Individualisms: Child-rearing and Social Class in Three Neighborhoods*. New York: Palgrave Macmillan.

Lehmann, Arthur C., James E. Myers, and Pamela A. Moro. 2005. *Magic, Withchraft, and Religion*. Boston, MA: McGraw Hill.

Leach, Penelope. 2007. *Your Baby & Child*. New York: Knopf.

Leacock, Eleanor. 1981. *Myths of Male Dominance*. New York: Monthly Review Press.

LeVine, Robert. 2004. "Challenging Expert Knowledge." In *Childhood and Adolescence*, Uwe P. Gielen and Jaipaul L. Roopnarine, eds., pp. 149–65. Westport, CT: Praeger.

LeVine, Robert. In press. "Attachment Theory as Cultural Ideology." In *Different Faces of Attachment: Cultural Variations of a Universal Human Need*, Heidi Keller and Hiltrud Otto, eds. Cambridge: Cambridge University Press.

LeVine, Robert and Karin Norman. 2001. "The Infant's Acquisition of Culture." In *The Psychology of Cultural Experience*, Carmella C. Moore and Holly F. Mathews, eds., pp. 83–104. Cambridge, England: Cambridge University Press.

Macpherson, Cluny, and La'avasa Macpherson. 1990. *Samoan Medical Belief and Practice*. Auckland: Auckland University Press.

Mageo, Jeannette Marie. 1989. "Ferocious is the Centipede: A Study on the Significance of Eating and Speaking in Samoa." *Ethos* 17:387–427.

Mageo, Jeannette Marie. 1991. "Inhibitions and Compensations: A Study of the Effects of Negative Sanctions in Three Pacific Cultures." *Pacific Studies* 14(3):1–40.

Mageo, Jeannette Marie. 1992. "Male Transvestism and Culture Change in Samoa." *American Ethnologist* 19:443–459.

Mageo, Jeannette Marie. 1998. *Theorizing Self in Samoa: Emotions, Genders, and Sexualities*. Ann Arbor, MI: Michigan University Press.

Mageo, Jeannette Marie. 2001. "Dream Play and Discovering Cultural Psychology." *Ethos* 29:187–217.

Mageo, Jeannette Marie. 2005. "Male Gender Instability and War." *Peace Review* 17(1):73–80.

Mageo, Jeannette Marie. 2011. *Dreaming Culture: Meanings, Models and Power in U.S. American Dreams*. New York: Palgrave-MacMillian.

McCollum, Chris. 2002. "Relatedness and Self-Definition: Two Dominant Themes in Middle-Class Americans' Life Stories." *Ethos* 30:113–139.

Mead, Margaret. [1928] 1961. *Coming of Age in Samoa: A Psychological Study of Primitive Youth for Western Civilization*. New York: Morrow Quill.

Mead, Margaret. [1930] 1969. *The Social Organization of Manu'a*. Honolulu: Bishop Kaloseum Press.

Mead, Margaret. 1959a. "Cultural Contexts of Puberty and Adolescence." In *The Bulletin of the Philadelphia Association for Psychoanalysis* 9(3).

Mead, Margaret. 1959b. *Four Families*. New York: National Film Board of Canada.

Miller, Peggy. 1994. "Narrative Practices: Their Role in Socialization and Self-construction." In *The Remembering Self: Construction and Accuracy in Self-narrative*, Ulrich Neisser and Robin Fivush, eds., pp. 158–179. Cambridge: Cambridge University Press.

Milner, G. B. 1966. *Samoan Dictionary*. Pago Pago: American Samoa Government.

Munroe, Robert, Ruth Munroe, and John Whiting. 1981. "Male Sex-Role Resolutions." In *Handbook of Cross-cultural Human Development*, Ruth Munroe, Robert Munroe, and Beatrice Whiting, eds., pp. 611–632. New York: Garland STPM Press.

Nelson, Katherine. 1996. "The Emergence of the Storied Mind." In *Language and Cognitive Development: The Emergence of the Mediated Mind*, pp. 183–223. Cambridge: Cambridge University Press.

Ochs, Elinor. 1982. "Talking to Children in Western Samoa." *Language in Society* 11:77–104.

Odden, Harold L. 2009. "Interactions of Temperament and Culture: the Organization of Diversity in Samoan Infancy." *Ethos* 37:161–180.

Pantley, Elizabeth. 2002. *The No-Cry Sleep Solution*. New York:.McGraw Hill.

Quinn, Naomi. 2005. "Universals of Child Rearing." *Anthropological Theory* 5:475–514.

Pratt, George. [1862/1911] 1977. *Pratt's Grammar and Dictionary of the Samoan Language*. Apia: Malua.

Ritchie, James, and Jane Ritchie. 1979. *Growing up in Polynesia*. Sydney: George Allen and Unwin.

Rogoff, Barbara. 2003. *The Cultural Nature of Human Development*. Oxford UK: Oxford University Press.

Schoeffel, Penelope. 1979. "Daughters of Sina." Doctoral Dissertation. Australian National University.

Schultz, Dr. E. [1911] n.d. Samoan Laws Concerning the Family, Real Estate and Succession, Rev. E. Bellward, trans. Housed in the University of Hawaii Pacific Collection.

Sears, William, and Martha Sears. 2001. *The Attachment Parenting Book*. New York: Little, Brown, and Company.

Shore, Bradd. 1981. "Sexuality and Gender in Samoa." In *Sexual Meanings: The Cultural Construction of Gender and Sexuality*, Sherry B. Ortner and Harriet Whitehead, eds., pp. 192–215. New York: Cambridge University Press.

Spiro, Melford E. 1961. "An Overview and a Suggested Reorientation." In *Psychological Anthropology: Approaches to Culture and Personality*, Francis L. K. Hsu, ed., pp. 484–491. Homewood, IL: Dorsey.

Stevenson, Robert Louis. 1892. *A Footnote to History: Eight Years of Trouble in Samoa*. London: Cassell.

Sutter, F. K. 1980. "Communal versus Individual Socialization at Home and in School in Rural and Urban Samoa." PhD dissertation. University of Hawaii.

Stern, Daniel. 1985. *The Interpersonal World of the Infant*. New York: Basic Books.

Tannen, Deborah. 2001. *He Said, She Said. Video*. Los Angeles, CA: Into the Classroom Media.

Turner, George.[1861] 1986. *Selections from Nineteen Years in Polynesia: Missionary Life, Travel and Researches*. Apia: Western Samoa Historical and Cultural Trust. [reprint].

Turner, George. [1884] 1984. *Samoa: A Hundred Years Ago and Long Before*. London: Macmillian.

Weisner, Thomas S. 2002. "The American Dependency Conflict." *Ethos* 29(3):271–295.

Winnicott, D. W. 1967. *Playing and Reality*. Harmondsworth, UK: Penguin.
Wierzbicka, Anna. 2004. "The English Expressions *Good Boy* and *Good Girl* and Cultural Models of Child Rearing." *Culture and Psychology* 10:251–278.
Whiting, Beatrice. 1978. "The Dependency Hang-Up and Experiments in Alternative Life Styles." In *Major Social Issues: A Multidisciplinary View*, J. Milton Yinger and Stephen J. Cutler, eds., pp. 217–226. New York: Macmillan.

Chapter 8

Adult Attachment Cross-culturally: A Reanalysis of the Ifaluk Emotion *Fago*

Naomi Quinn

In the language of the Micronesians who inhabit the island of Ifaluk, *fago* is an emotion that the ethnographer Catherine Lutz, in her 1988 book, *Unnatural Emotions*, translates as love/compassion/sadness. Here I reanalyze the meaning of *fago*, an endeavor made possible by the depth and detail of Lutz's ethnography, based on fieldwork conducted in 1977 and 1978. As Lutz footnotes in her book (1988:238, fn. 20), "The meaning of the concept of *fago* shows important similarities with related emotion words in other Pacific languages." She names and cites published references for descriptions of Samoan *alofa*, Marquesan *ka'oha*, Maori *aroha*, and Tahitian *arofa*. I was first attracted to this set of related emotion terms common to the Pacific islands because of how different these cases seemed to the American material I had collected. My realization that there might be deeper commonalities between the Pacific Island and American cases came later. I have chosen to focus on Lutz's Ifaluk case simply because I deem it to be the most ethnographically rich, for my particular purposes, among the set. It is likely, however, that much of what Lutz describes about Ifaluk *fago* is distributed more widely across the Pacific Islands.

In my reinterpretation, I rely on the aforementioned book, supplemented by a 1985 article of Lutz's and an earlier volume that includes a description of Ifaluk childhood by Melford Spiro (Burrows and Spiro 1953). This latter source, the only other modern ethnography of Ifaluk, is based on the authors' six months of fieldwork there in 1947–1948. Any such amalgamation of older and newer work must be done carefully, out of appreciation for the substantial changes that may have occurred on Ifaluk, and that I know to have occurred in the conduct and writing of ethnography, in the 30 years intervening between the two research projects and the even longer time between their publication.[1] However, with its attention to Ifaluk childhood and its orientation, at once more psychological and more behavioral than that of Lutz, Spiro's ethnography fills in some gaps in her description. At other points, too, the two accounts confirm each other. In no important respect do they disagree.

While, as I have said, Lutz's ethnography in particular is exceptionally rich, my use of the body of ethnography on Ifaluk is subject to a couple of further caveats. First, we do not have the kind of extensive description of Ifaluk child rearing available, say, to someone working in the United States with regard to American middle-class child rearing, based as that latter literature is on decades of research and analysis. Lutz's work is focused on adult emotional life. While the ethnography by Spiro does address childhood, that description, collected by a single researcher over a short period of time, is relatively slight.

Second, and in tune with the disciplinary times in which she wrote, Lutz's analysis is quite driven by word meaning, and much concerned with the problem of word translation. Lutz defined *fago*, a concept absolutely central to Ifaluk everyday life and values, and a term heard frequently in Ifaluk discourse, to approximate the compound meanings of three English words. I believe that, instead of comparing the Ifaluk word directly to American English words, we ought to be framing both cases in terms of their common roots and their variation around this common origin. It follows that there are two sides to the argument I will make. First, I marshal evidence that *fago* has common roots with our own American emotion *love*. These commonalities suggest that the emotions labeled by these two terms have a universal basis. This universal, I posit, originates in early attachment.

At the same time, *fago* and *love* exhibit quite different cultural forms. This cultural variation merits a different explanation, which brings me to the second side of my argument. How attachment plays out in adulthood results from the cross-culturally variable patterns of child rearing and the other local circumstances surrounding attachment in infancy and childhood. To the degree that these circumstances are shared by members of a given group, adult patterns of attachment will also be shared. One important source of this cross-cultural variation in adult patterns of attachment, so evident in the comparison between American *love* and Ifaluk islander *fago*, is the defense shared by members of a group against early dependency yearnings that must be dealt with in some way in adulthood. I will detail this cultural defense for the Ifaluk case, and speculate about its origins in early experience; I will only have space to sketch the corresponding American defense.[2]

As it unfolds, my argument will raise a series of challenges to specific assumptions made by contemporary attachment theorists regarding adult attachment. These challenges will emerge from my delineation of the way universality and variation play themselves out in a comparison of the two cases. At the close of my analysis, I will identify a pattern in these various challenges that calls into question the overall adequacy of attachment theory as a general theory of adult close relationships.

A Reformulation of Adult Attachment

I follow both attachment theory, and the work on falling-in-love stories by Chris McCollum that I will discuss shortly, in assuming that romantic partnerships, including but not limited to marriage, are the prototypical "refindings" (to use Freud's term) of adult attachment in American society. Certainly these are the adult relationships in which expressions of dependency are most pronounced. Other American relationships, such as love for siblings (sometimes called "fraternal love"), friendship, or mentorship, may also carry vestiges of early dependency and should not be ruled out as sites of adult attachment. My own work, on which I draw next, has been on American marriage.

In earlier published research (Quinn 1997a), I described three adult desires that emerged from what my interviewees had to say about marital love. These were the desires to be with the loved person, to have your needs met by that person, and, finally, to be assured that you will not be left by that person. I posit that these three desires arise from infantile concerns that find their way into the enduring schemas or, in John Bowlby's term, the "working models" of intimate relationships formulated in infancy and early childhood and presumed to have been internalized. In attachment theoretic terms, the three desires can be understood as reflections of the human infant's concern to keep the caregiver in proximity; its need for that person to feed it, protect it, and otherwise care for it in its dependent state; and its anxiety about the possibility of being abandoned by that person. Initially, here, I have cast these three desires in American terms. In particular, when Americans express these adult desires, they couch them in the singular, in terms of the one other person, in their internal working model of the caregiver relationship, who will care for them.

I am following the lead of my American interviewees in proposing these three features of early experience as enduring into adulthood in individuals' internal working models. My three-feature model partially overlaps with but partially departs from attachment theories of adulthood. Most attachment theorists (see, e.g., Hazan et al. 2004:57–58) search for the updated adult versions of four attachment behaviors readily observable in early childhood. The corresponding expressions of adult need are thought to be continuous with that earlier experience, though necessarily modified to take account of the increased complexity and sophistication of adult cognition and other aspects of development across the life course (see, e.g., Pietromonaco and Feldman Barrett 2000:162). Two of these orientations, maintaining proximity with attachment figures and experiencing distress upon separation from them, are clear analogs of the desire for closeness and the fear of loss in my formulation.

For many attachment theorists, as well, the adult partner to whom one is attached is said to serve as a secure base in the sense of allowing one to explore the world with a greater sense of security, and a safe haven in the sense of assuring one support in times of stress (Collins et al. 2004:212; Zeifman and Hazan 2008).[3] These remaining two adult orientations, secure base and safe haven, are viewed as more developed versions of the attachment behaviors that have been, for theorists in this tradition beginning with Bowlby, such important diagnostics of early childhood attachment to the primary caregiver.[4] The behavioral indicator that the young child is using the attachment figure as a secure base is the child's exploration of its environment, meanwhile staying in proximity with the attachment figure and keeping an eye on that person, monitoring her availability. In case of felt danger or anxiety of any kind, the attachment figure becomes a safe haven, the behavioral indicator of which is that the child returns to that person for comfort and reassurance.

In my reformulation, adult attachment is distinguished not by adult versions of secure base and safe haven behaviors adapted from childhood, but by one of three enduring dependency concerns deeply internalized in childhood. The concern that one be well cared for in the sense of having one's critical needs fulfilled is more general than is captured in any specific behaviors that young children exhibit. Such need fulfillment may come to mean many things for adults, and did in fact mean many different things to my married American interviewees. These interviewees may, for example, talk about the fact that they can be themselves at home in a way they cannot at work, which might be interpreted in terms of secure base, or that their spouse will support them through difficulties and give them confidence in themselves, which might be interpreted in terms of safe haven. They also talk about the complementary child-care roles they and their spouse play, teaming up with their spouse to accomplish shared goals, sharing tastes and enjoying the same pastimes, being able to communicate fully with someone, finding the other person intellectually and sexually stimulating, being understood and accepted for who they are, and about the ways that their spouses help them grow emotionally, "mother" them, give them space when they need it, and so on and so on (see Quinn 1983). Of course, such adult needs will vary widely cross-culturally. It is difficult, however, to argue for a strict relation between these varied needs fulfilled in adult American marriages (and other adult close relationships), and the safety afforded against grave dangers that may have threatened infant survival in early human societies (and that are posited to explain the evolutionary origins of early attachment). It is worth noting, as well, that even the needs of infants and young children extend beyond those reflected in their secure base and safe haven behaviors, to the needs to be fed, kept warm and dry, and otherwise cared for. By focusing so exclusively on adult analogs of so-called secure base and safe haven behaviors, these attachment theorists overlook the more general meaning that being cared for has for both children and adults. My reservations about this direct translation of childhood behaviors into adult concerns is shared by at least some attachment theorists. Pietromonaco and Feldman Barrett (2000:168), for example, conclude that "the aspects that define an attachment system in children may not have a complete parallel in adulthood."

There may be at least two reasons why the majority of attachment theorists view the caring dimension of adult attachment in terms of these two discrete behaviors. First, they may have fastened on just those early behaviors easiest to observe and measure, and for which measures have been established.[5] Second, they may be overly zealous in applying the distinction they attribute to

Bowlby, between attachment and feeding. The empirical association of attachment and feeding and the cultural symbolic weight given to this association in many societies are documented throughout this volume, and arise again and again in the analysis of *fago* to follow (see LeVine and Miller 1990:75–76).

Attachment theorists who share my disinclination to interpret adult attachment in terms of secure base and safe haven may turn instead to the concept of "felt security" (Sroufe and Waters 1977), defined as feeling free from physical and emotional threat, and confident in a partner's love, commitment, and responsiveness to need (Collins et al. 2004:212; see Meehan and Hawks, chapter 3, for application of this concept to children). This alternative approach is certainly in line with my own assumption that what survives into adulthood is not a suite of behaviors that were appropriate to early childhood, but early emotive concerns that have been internalized. However, I would argue, while the "secure base" and "safe haven" behaviors are over-specific in the adult context, "felt security" is over-general in that context.[6] I am proposing, instead, that attachment in adulthood revolves around the specific concern to be cared for in the sense of having one's needs fulfilled, along with two additional concerns: desire to be close and fear of loss.[7] My proposal is empirically based in research on American middle-class adults and, although tentative, gains further empirical support, as we shall next see, from an examination of the case of Ifaluk islander adulthood.

The Common Roots and Radically Different Cultural Shape of *Fago* and *Love*

The same three concerns regarding closeness, care, and fear of loss reappear in association with Ifaluk *fago*, though in plural rather than singular person and in otherwise different guise than they take in the context of American married love.[8] As Lutz (1988:153) summarizes, the conceptual structure of *fago* puts "cultural emphasis on the links between loss, interpersonal connection, and others' needs." She never explains satisfactorily why these three meanings should be linked together. However, an analysis in terms of adult attachment, which treats these three concerns as deriving from the preoccupations of infancy and early childhood, does make sense of their linkage in a single word.

Let us flesh out these three meanings of *fago*, adding detail from Lutz's ethnographic account of it, and comparing it, as relevant, with American *love*. First of all, you feel *fago* for those in need. "The primary contexts in which *fago* occurs," Lutz (1988:121) tells us, "are those in which the person confronts another who is somehow *in need*" (italics in original). Lutz suggests that *fago* is felt toward any needful other, usually another to whom one is socially related in some way. The occasions on which such need arises are several:

> The *gafago* (needy, poor) are those individuals who are lacking one or more of the necessities for a good life. The needy are identified by the Ifaluk as those who are sick or dying; those who must leave the island and their families for

> some period; those who lack the ability to procure their own food, such as children, the aged, and the infirm; and those who lack the mental abilities or social status that would enable them to make decisions and move as autonomous agents in the world.

Fago has a strong component of pity for another who is vulnerable—hungry, sick, or otherwise needy. For this reason, children are likely objects of *fago*. As Lutz (1988:131) says,

> The parent-child relationship is, along with that between sisters and brothers, the one most frequently understood with the concept of *fago*. The child is the quintessential needy person—vulnerable to illness and death and unable to get his or her own food—the ultimate subordinate and the ultimate object of *fago*. In needing the parents' care, the child needs the parents' *fago*.

"When Ifaluk parents talk about their *fago* for their children," Lutz (1988:131) adds, "it is frequently when the child is sick."

Other relatives, too, are objects of *fago*, depending on "the kinds of duties and benefits attached" to a given kin relationship—"Ifaluk ideas about what people need, and about how relatives serve to fill those needs" (Lutz 1988:131). Thus, for example, sisters typically *fago* their brothers, giving them cooked breadfruit and taro; and brothers, feeling *fago* for their sisters, bring fish to them. Because they fago their brothers, sisters feed, otherwise care for, and may adopt their brothers' children.

It is important to appreciate the context for this feeling toward the needy, namely that social relationships on Ifaluk are highly circumscribed and, in this small social universe, very dense. This is a tiny Micronesian island, with a population of 340 when Lutz was there in the 1970s (Lutz 1985:41). As she (1985:41) observes, "A person on Ifaluk typically has been born and will die within the bounds of the atoll's one-half square mile. If female, she has probably never left the island." The close quarters in which people live, Lutz says, makes observable the suffering of those in need. Moreover, the sheer density of kin relations provides constant opportunity for such observations, inspiring *fago*. As Lutz goes on to explain, the cross-cutting nature of social ties on the island is fostered by a number of institutional factors: large extended households and widespread adoption—a situation which, "in fact acts to give most individuals a kinship relation with a significant proportion of the total population of the atoll"—as well as exchanges due to communal work and consumption patterns, communal ownership of canoes, cross-cutting ties of matrilineal descent and patrilateral rights, and, finally, clan siblingship across distinct matrlines (Lutz 1988:151–152).

The person in need of care is not the person who feels *fago*, but rather the other who is the target or recipient of *fago*. Both *love* and *fago* invoke the expectation of care, but *fago* involves care for others, according to their neediness and their relationship to oneself. And unlike *love*, *fago* is nonreciprocal.[9] (Of course, the person who feels *fago* for another may him- or herself become the recipient of someone else's *fago* in some other context.) Why *fago* should be directed at others and nonreciprocal will be critical to the final part of my argument. The American cultural understanding of adult *love*, in contrast, heavily stresses reciprocal fulfillment by each person of the other's needs in an exclusive, dyadic relationship.[10] This American pattern has led attachment theorists to assume that adult attachment is universally played out in such exclusive, dyadic adult relationships. Some of these theorists (Zeifman and Hazan 2008; see Hazan et al. 2004:59 for the origins of this idea in Bowlby's thinking) make the further assumption that adult attachment everywhere depends on heterosexual "pair bonds" having universal adaptive functions. These assumptions are contested by the cross-cultural case of *fago*, which is targeted at many kin, rather than at one other person.

Not only the people targeted by need fulfillment but also the content of these needs contrasts strikingly in these two cases. On Ifaluk, the needs to be met tend to be tied to the very real requirements of physical survival and well-being (Lutz 1988:146, 152): one may give food, for example, to a person for whom one feels *fago*, or care for them when they are ill, or donate cooperative labor to their projects (although certainly the objects of these physical needs, and as I have pointed out, food in particular, can acquire powerful symbolic meaning). In sharp contrast with these physical needs, those needs that Americans who love each other endeavor to meet for each other are predominantly emotional and interpersonal, having to do with each other's psychological well-being.[11] Even sex, for most Americans an obligatory component of marital fulfillment, is never posed simply as a physical need, but is suffused with feelings of closeness and intimacy. These psychological needs, one's spouse's and one's own—identifying them, meeting them, and sacrificing to do so—are the focus of a great deal of the "work" of marriage (Quinn 1997b:163). Presumably because they are thinking in these same middle-class American terms, attachment theorists tend to the theoretical generalization that adult attachment needs are predominantly psychological in flavor. Thus, for one example, Feeney and Collins (2004:305) characterize providing a *safe haven* for one's partner as including the expectations that the caregiving adult must "be aware of the other's point of view, feelings, and intentions" and "encourage expression of feelings." Similarly, for these authors (2004:307) providing a *secure base* includes "responding to exploratory successes and difficulties in a way that is helpful and encouraging," and "promoting open communication regarding personal goals and desires."

It is unsurprising that American adult conceptions of need fulfillment by a loved one are heavily psychologized. So, in the American middle-class style of child rearing, is gratification of infants' and young children's other needs bound up with emotional and interpersonal satisfaction. Chris McCollum (2002:127) observes that "American caregivers strive to create moments of psychological closeness or intense emotional sharing" with their infants—efforts that shift to greater pressure toward emotional self-regulation as the children mature. In a similar vein, Thomas Weisner (2001:272) writes that (at the same time they are taught the value of independence and self-reliance) "children are encouraged to engage in intense interaction with a parent or parents, and there is a great deal of seeking attention, adult-child interaction, and emotional warmth with powerful adults who respond in kind." He (2001:282) concludes that "from a cross-cultural perspective, there is an extraordinarily high amount of verbally mediated parent-child interaction" among the American families he sampled. There is an obvious fit between what adults seek from their spouses or partners, and this style of child rearing. As McCollum (2002:133) concludes, romantic partners "recreate this intense emotional experience of togetherness through the sharing of their innermost thoughts and feelings." As we learn from chapter 5 by Chapin and chapter 7 by Mageo, this style of intersubjective attunement and intense emotional interaction is hardly universal, though it is often treated by attachment theorists as a necessary ingredient of secure attachment.

If *fago* is about responding to others' neediness, it is, secondly, about being with people. Again, this understanding of *fago* is superficially very different from the need Americans have to be with the person they love, for it is not the person you *fago* that you want to be with.[12] It is people in general. If you *fago* someone you have lost, for example, it helps to be with other people. Those suffering from grief over a death or from homesickness are advised "to stay among people so that one will not 'think/feel' about the loss" (Lutz 1985:52). Sufferers feel worse when they are alone (Lutz 1988:237, fn. 8).

In the Ifaluk case, being with people means being with kinsfolk. *Fago* is felt, therefore, for those who have no kin: the barren woman, the only child, the man without sisters (Lutz 1988:131), and all those "whose kinship networks are small or are missing crucial members" (Lutz 1988:128). "When the Ifaluk say that they *fago* the person who is without kin, they say that people need, above all, to be embedded in a network of others who 'take care of' them," Lutz (1988:134) says. Special emphasis is placed on having kinspeople to eat with. As Lutz (1988:129) explains,

> The tragedy of being without relatives is... that one then eats alone, and for the solitary diner, "food does not taste as sweet." Each meal is a reminder that one is denied the opportunity of sharing food with the relatives who are either permanently or temporarily missing.

A related preference is for working in groups; Spiro (Burrows and Spiro 1953:319) says, "The Ifaluk abhor solitude and solitary labor." Indeed, Lutz argues, in this society in which the group orientation of life is paramount, *fago* plays a key part in this communal orientation, forming "a central part of the motivational system which supports cooperation" (Lutz 1988:152), notably the sharing of food and labor. In another context, Spiro (Burrows and Spiro 1953:307) reports, "People are afraid to die, say many people, because they no longer remain in Ifaluk, and are consequently separated from their families." "Death," Lutz (1988:128) summarizes, "is seen not so much as the end of an individual life but as the end of a set of relationships."

This is undoubtedly why, as Lutz (1988:122) relates, "one of the most important goals of every adult on Ifaluk is to be at the side of close relatives at the moment of death," conceived of as the final leave-taking.

This difference between the American middle class and Ifaluk cases makes sense, again, in terms of very different infantile experiences. On the one hand the middle-class American child has been cared for primarily by one other person, typically mother, in a relatively isolated nuclear household. At the other extreme, the Ifaluk child has grown up in a large extended family and a wider network of cross-cutting kin relations, all important in the child's life, many in a caregiving role. This caregiving pattern is more than just an isolated practice: In Pacific cultures more generally there is a collective approach to children. The kin group has control over children, rather than, as in the American case, the parents having inalienable rights over them, and a child is seen as "ours" rather than "mine." Elise Berman (personal communication) has made this point to me for the Marshall Islands, as has Jeannette Mageo (personal communication) for Samoa.

As both Spiro and Lutz further emphasize, the common practice of adoption heightens the attachment to multiple caregivers. Spiro (Burrows and Spiro 1953:268) concludes that the main psychological effect of adoption on Ifaluk children is that it "diffuses their feelings by directing them towards a number of people," with the important social consequence of broadening the already diffuse pattern of mutual aid." As Lutz (1988:153) puts it, adoption on Ifaluk "encourages both child and adult to identify with a larger group of others, to see a larger number of individuals as vitally interested in one's well-being, and to view their interests as overlapping one's own." Taken together, the childhood experience of these practices and attitudes no doubt readies people to live communally.

The extended network of kin involved in a child's caregiving should not be taken to mean that there is no initial attachment to a primary caregiver, only that there are many additional caregivers. Indeed, a set of regularly told traditional stories collected from the nearby Micronesian islands of Chuuk have been interpreted as being all about a youthful transition away from the initial attachment to a loving parent and into the community, with the threats attendant on involvement in these new relationships—which may be with less caring kin or even those in rival matrilineages (Lowe and Johnson 2007:165–166). In spite of a child's early experience with multiple caregivers, it seems, the subsequent transition to the larger group is still emotionally fraught. This Ifaluk picture corresponds to that provided by other ethnographic cases in this volume, and typical of more communal societies everywhere, in which children and young people are weaned away from their primary attachment or attachments to one or more particular others, to a more diffuse attachment to the group.

Third, you *fago* someone upon their death, imminent death, or separation. This meaning of *fago* corresponds to the fear, in the American middle-class case, of losing a loved one. However, *fago* in this sense applies, once again, not just to the one special person you love as in the American case, but to all those many kinspeople with whom you are close. Moreover, the prototypical kind of loss, on Ifaluk, is far more drastic than the threat of divorce, the possibility of loss that middle-class Americans are typically most anxious about. For Ifaluk islanders, in contrast, loss means death or the threat of death. "The Ifaluk mourn each death massively, with wailing and sung laments" (Lutz 1985:63; see also Burrows and Spiro 1953:307–308). "The dying person is the prototypical object of *fago*" (Lutz 1988:125), we learn. Illness occasions *fago* for the sick person, not only because that person is in need of intensive care, but also out of "concern that the sick person will die or, in other words, one's sense that ultimate separation and loss are imminent" (Lutz 1988:122). The inadequate health-care system on the island (Lutz 1988:122) does nothing to relieve this expectation that illness will lead to death.

And, Lutz (1988:150–151, 196–198) notes, death is frequent on Ifaluk, due to both a high mortality rate for infants and young children, and the special dangers of atoll life.[13] As Lutz (1988:150) says, "when typhoons threaten, people begin to talk to each other about the eventuality that 'we all will die together.' " These annual typhoons not only threaten life directly, but wipe out the staple crop, taro, causing famine. There are, in addition, "sudden and devastating epidemics" (Lutz 1988:122). Not to mention less collective dangers: Men drown while fishing and fall from coconut trees.

Not only is the incidence of mortal injury and terminal illness much greater on Ifaluk than in middle-class America, and its possibility a much more present reality, but it is much more observable. And such observations and understanding come early. Lutz (1988:125) notes, "From a young age, children…recognize death as an overwhelmingly central to the meaning of the concept of *fago*." And, because of its frequency on the island, Ifaluk children are well acquainted with death and mourning. Nor are they shielded from it. Describing the prolonged ritualized wailing that accompanies a death in the community, Spiro (Burrows and Spiro 1953:308) comments,

> Babies and infants are brought to these wailing ceremonies. Whether or not the wailing is stylized is immaterial so far as its effect on the children is concerned. The abrupt change from the ever-friendly, smiling and laughing adults, to the wailing, sad, ones must leave a deep impression on them.

Moreover, this emphasis on death, coupled with a high mortality rate, means that the threat of one's own parent's death is ever present in Ifaluk infancy and childhood.

This possibility of abandonment by a child's biological parent is made real not only by the high rate of parental death, but also by the exceptionally high rate of inter-household adoption, already alluded to. This rate was estimated by Spiro (Burrows and Spiro 1953:267) at "more than one-third" in 1947–1948 and at a similar 40 percent by Lutz (1988:161) in 1977–1978. According to Spiro (Burrows and Spiro 1953:267), adoption is arranged during pregnancy, but the actual transfer of households is delayed until the child begins to walk, although, between birth and adoption the adoptive mother may be in the child's life to a considerable degree.[14] While both Spiro and Lutz recognize the effect of this pattern of adoption on the diffusion of children's attachments, there is a darker side to the practice: It is first of all a loss of the primary attachment figure. As Lutz (1988:153) observes,

> Children and adults may also receive and generalize from the message which [Robert] Levy posits is sent in all Oceanic adoption, which is that "relationships between parents and children are fragile and conditional" (1973:485). The dual message—that nurturance is expected from and for many of one's consociates and that relationships that were primary may be "lost" to a secondary place—can be spoken about with the "sadly compassionate" notion of *fago*. Adoption is, then, both a training ground for the emotion of *fago* and a cultural site for its utilization.

Given how routinely, and at what a crucial juncture in their young lives, children's adoptions take place, this practice looms large as a "training ground" for *fago*.

If death and dying are prototypical occasions for *fago*, another kind of separation that elicits this emotion is departure from the island. As Lutz (1988:134) observes, there is "minimal cultural elaboration around the emotions of (at least temporary) separation in the United States." On Ifaluk, though, as elsewhere in Micronesia, such departures may be for an extended stay, months or even years, often of uncertain duration, on another island. This is especially so for young people (see Lowe and Johnson 2007:165 on extended teenage travel from the nearby islands of Chuuk). Those traveling away from Ifaluk feel *fago* for those "who will be left behind, in some neediness, without recourse to the traveler's help" (Lutz 1988:129). In complementary fashion, relatives left behind feel *fago* both "for themselves in their own loss" and for the traveler as well. They *fago* themselves "due to the thought that one might never see a relative again" (Lutz 1988:130). *Fago* for the traveler is based on the horribleness of homesickness—a concept, *pak*, that Lutz (1988:134) says is often paired with *fago*. Lutz also mentions that, at the moment of leave-taking on the interisland steamship, relatives may kiss a departing child or adult. She (1988:237, fn. 7) reveals in a footnote, tellingly for the assumption of a link between adult and early attachment, that the practice in question is "sniffing" rather than kissing, a sign of affection ordinarily "used in parting and with babies."

In sum, the same constellation of infantile concerns that I have identified in the meaning of adult love to middle-class Americans, also structures the meaning of the concept of *fago* for adult Ifaluk islanders. To review, Ifaluk adults want to care for the needy, whom they *fago*. They also *fago* those who are social isolates, and gravitate to the company of other people in a variety of circumstances, most urgently when they themselves are grieving dead relatives or missing those who have gone away. And these circumstances for loss, when those close to them die or leave the island, are chief occasions for *fago*. These three adult preoccupations having to do with care, closeness, and loss, discernible in both the American middle-class and the Ifaluk islander cases, appear to be universal consequences of the human infantile experience. This interpretation makes sense of the fact that, in the language spoken by Ifaluk islanders, love, compassion, and sadness should be packaged in a single term. As I have also argued, it challenges a tenet held by many attachment theorists that adult attachment is to be understood narrowly as an adult version of young children's "secure base" and "safe haven" behaviors. Instead, the more general concern that one be cared for is one of a triad of lifelong concerns derived from infant and early childhood experience.

At the same time, these three concerns about care, closeness, and loss are radically culturally shaped, so much so that it may be difficult to detect the commonalities for the differences. For one thing, Ifaluk islanders seem to emphasize loss more than do Americans, who might be said to put greater stress on closeness and, secondarily, on fulfillment of one's individual needs. Moreover, certain features of the middle-class American case, assumed by most attachment theorists to be universals, do not apply to the Ifaluk islander case. These include, we have seen, the assumptions that adult attachment is universally dyadic and reciprocal, even rooted in a biologically determined "pair bonding"; that the needs it fulfills are largely psychological; and that it is everywhere accompanied by intersubjective attunement.

Next we will examine another way in which *fago* and *love* differ radically.

Fago as a Cultural Defense

The Ifaluk island and American middle-class cases differ strikingly, not only in the respective emphases placed on different ones of the three attachment concerns encapsulated by *fago* and *love*, and in the targets of these emotions, but in another critical way as well. I follow Chris McCollum (2002) in assuming that, one way or another, "regressive" infantile feelings of dependency are so threatening to the newer demands of autonomy that these infantile feelings must everywhere be defended against in adulthood. Indeed, the conflict between dependency and autonomy is so general to the human condition that not just individual but culturally shared, community-wide mechanisms have evolved to defend against it. This is also a theme taken up by several other chapters in this volume. In contrast, and in line with their inclination to see attachment as unproblematically continuous across the life course, contemporary attachment theorists typically view feelings and expressions of adult dependency as a normal, nondefensive part of secure adult attachment (but see Bowlby 1980). Presumably, securely attached people do not need psychodynamic defenses because they are good at dealing with all kinds of conflict and adversity. Only some types of so-called insecure attachment may be considered to involve such defenses. In particular, individuals classified as dismissing-avoidant have been said to have "well-developed defense systems that enable them to regulate negative affect by deactivating their attachment systems and reducing the accessibility of attachment-related thoughts" (Collins et al. 2004:219; see also Pietromonaco and Feldman Barrett 2000:160–161; Fonagy et al. 2008:784–785). McCollum and I presume a more central and cultural role for psychodynamic defense in adult attachment.[15]

In the two cross-cultural cases I am considering, very different cultural defenses are mustered against this universal conflict. While I can only summarize the American case here, I do so to make ultra-clear that defense against early dependency is not a uniquely Ifaluk invention, and is in no way "pathological"; such defenses are everywhere necessary and normal.[16] McCollum (2002:125), whose analysis focuses on the falling-in-love stories told by middle-class Americans, details a set of interrelated psychodynamic defenses that, in this American case, "reconfigure conflicting desires into more manageable form, but are never able to completely reconcile them." These conflicting desires are what McCollum characterizes as the progressive demand for individuation and the regressive desire for dependency.[17] In most of middle-class American life, he (2002:131) argues, the tension between autonomy and dependency "is transformed into an uncompromising assertion of one side of the conflict," that is to say, resolved through reaction formation or overcompensation. Dependency needs, for the most part, are split off and allowed free reign only in the context of adult love relationships. In American life, marriage and other adult intimate relationships take their intensity from the singularity of that burden. Even in this narrow context, furthermore, romantic fulfillment is reworked by means of compromise formation to seem to be "the outcome of individuation strivings rather than dependency needs" (McCollum 2002:132). This compromise formation, McCollum explains, is accomplished through the more specific strategies of paradox and rationalization. The paradox is that one must first establish oneself as fully autonomous before falling in love; it is considered unwise, for example, to fall in love "on the rebound." The rationalization, that one has no control over when and with whom one falls in love, transfers agency from the self to the external world and thereby disguises the infantile nature of one's adult dependency feelings toward another.

What I propose is that Ifaluk adults defend against their dependency feelings. The psychodynamic process of defense, at its most general, is one in which something that originates within oneself is no longer recognized as one's own. The philosopher Herbert Fingarette (1969) calls this "disavowal," a useful way of thinking about defenses that I will adopt here. He says (Fingarette 1969:87) that something is disavowed when "to avow it would apparently lead to such intensely disruptive, distressing consequences as to be unmanageably destructive to the person." As Fingarette (1969:67) explains, having committed to the self-deception inherent in the disavowal, the self-deceiver is then forced into protective, defensive tactics to account for the inconsistencies in his or her engagement in the world. Thus (Fingarette 1969:62), a person fabricates stories in order to keep his or her explicit account of things and the way things really are in some kind of harmony that will make the account plausible. Presumably, even at the level of unconscious processing, the mind demands such a plausible alternative account—not foremost to tell others, Fingarette (1969:62) makes clear, but to tell oneself.[18]

The various named defenses may be thought of as different strategies for giving plausible accounts of what has happened to what has been disavowed. So, for example, in the defense that is commonly called *projection*, something disavowed is experienced as belonging to or emanating not from the self but from another.[19] In the defense of *reaction formation*, another such device, something disavowed is experienced as in some sense the reverse of itself. I am speculating that the defense represented by the Ifaluk emotion of *fago* is a combination of these two strategies. That is, one's own feelings of neediness are not one's own, but others' feelings, and one experiences oneself instead as being the one who cares for those needy others. In adult American love relationships, it is true, one is supposed to fulfill one's partner's needs, but, reciprocally; one also expects to get one's own needs fulfilled. A one-sided relationship in which one partner is not being fulfilled is deemed problematic. That *fago*, by contrast, is focused so singularly and one-sidedly on the needy other is central to its work as a cultural defense. In projecting neediness onto other people, and adopting a compassionate stance toward these needy others, Ifaluk islanders are able to disown or "disavow" their own feelings of neediness. Managed in this way, these infantile feelings no longer come into conflict with a more adult, caregiving, way of being. Still, some of an Ifaluk islander's own neediness does seep through, in the possibility that one may *fago* oneself. This can happen when one is grieving for a departed relative, as we have seen, or for one who has died, or if one is suffering from homesickness or, often and tellingly (Lutz 1988:137), when men become very drunk.[20]

Several of Lutz's more subtle ethnographic observations, beyond the bare fact that *fago* is nonreciprocal, fall in line with my interpretation. For one, Lutz (1988:146) offers the following telling comparison of American *love* and Ifaluk *fago*: "both emotions can motivate nurturance, although this desire is more fundamental to the meaning of *fago*." Indeed, nurturance is so fundamental to *fago* that the ability to experience *fago* in its sense of caring for others "is seen as one of the central characteristics of the mature person" (Lutz 1988:140).[21] Again, comparing Ifaluk *fago* to the not dissimilar sadness Americans feel upon a death, Lutz (1988:148) puts the contrast this way: "Both the sadness [in American English usage] and the *fago* that are spoken of in death can be *about* the loss rather than *for* the lost object. But the emphasis in sadness, unlike in *fago*, is much more often on the implications of the loss for the self" [italics in original]. The emphasis in *fago* is on the other.[22]

I am further encouraged in this way of thinking about *fago* by an example discussed by Bowlby (1980:156–157; 206–209) in the third of his volumes on *Attachment*, the one on *Loss*. What Bowlby describes as a variant pattern of adult mourning over loss, found in some individual clinical cases, is remarkably similar to *fago*. Bowlby calls it "compulsive caregiving for others." Although he does not label it a "defense" or seem to be concerned with assigning it the name of one, nevertheless in his account it does the work of one (Bowlby 1980:156-157):

> Because a compulsive caregiver seems to be attributing to the cared-for all the sadness and neediness that he is unable or unwilling to recognize in himself, the cared-for person can be regarded as standing vicariously for the one giving the care. Sometimes the term 'projective identification' is given to the psychological process that leads to this kind of relationship.[23]

This is exactly the way the cultural defense embodied in *fago* appears to work.

I would be remiss to leave this topic without mentioning that Spiro (1961:488–489) has published his own rendition of what he sees as a central Ifaluk cultural defense mechanism. Like me, he views dependency as a universal problem that must be defended against in adulthood. But he argues that the way Ifaluk islanders defend against feelings of dependency is to sublimate these feelings in obedience to their chiefs, simultaneously gratifying their dependency need by enjoying the affection chiefs show for them, and by accepting food, a symbol of nurturance, that is ritually dispensed to them by the chiefs. While this summary does not do full justice to Spiro's argument, it does bring into juxtaposition our two versions of how the Ifaluk defense against dependency might work. Tellingly, according to Lutz (see fns. 9 and 13), chiefs are said to *fago* commoners, so that half of Spiro's account fits well with mine—although *fago* is much more widespread than that which chiefs express toward their followers. It is also possible that those at the receiving end of *fago* are being provided with a context for expression of otherwise prohibited dependency—expressed in this case as obedience to their chiefs who, Spiro tells, are described in pidgin as "all same pappa this place." Although I would not necessarily term this obedience to chiefs "sublimation" or even call it a defense, Spiro's characterization of what recipients of *fago* gain does add another psychodynamic dimension to the story.

Speculations on the Origins of the *Fago* Defense in Early Experience

What might explain Ifaluk islanders' adoption of this particular cultural defensive pattern? In other words, what are its origins in early experience? One possibility would be Ifaluk children's socialization into a reversal of roles. By this argument, the pervasive Ifaluk emphasis on hierarchy, coupled with the obligation, assumed by older children toward younger ones, to look after those below them, readies the islanders for an Ifaluk version of Bowlby's "compulsive caregiving for others." Indeed, *fago* is inextricably intertwined with hierarchy. For example, Lutz reports that "as parents reach infirm old age, the emphasis shifts from their *fago* of the child to the child's *fago* for his or her mother and father" (Lutz 1988:132), and to the child's obligations toward the aging parents.

However, such later obligations do not appear to weigh heavily on young Ifaluk children. While neither Lutz nor Burrows and Spiro are very revealing about children's work, neither ethnography reports the assumption by children of the heavy workloads described for some of the Polynesian islands that have concepts cognate with *fago* (see, e.g., Levy 1973 on Tahiti and Gerber 1975 on Samoa).[24] Spiro (Burrows and Spiro 1953:265) does say that Ifaluk children are "permitted" to participate in adult activities at a young age, and he (Burrows and Spiro 1953:269) reports that girls, in particular, begin assisting their mothers at women's work very early. (Of course, the age at which children begin to participate in economic activities in any other society than our own might seem young to a middle-class American ethnographer.) Boys, in contrast, are portrayed as having more leisure time and "no definite economic responsibility" (Burrows and Spiro 1953:283), deciding for themselves what work to do and when to do it. Both ethnographers do agree more generally that laziness is not tolerated by Ifaluk islanders.

More especially, however, children care for younger siblings. Burrows (Burrows and Spiro 1953:156), leaving a full discussion of child care to his coauthor, says only that "older children keep an eye on younger ones to a greater extent than with us." Spiro reveals that Ifaluk girls in particular, from the age of seven or eight years, serve as mother surrogates, often feeding and washing as well as carrying a younger brother or sister, and in general supervising and watching over him or her (Burrows and Spiro 1953:272, 283). In addition, he says, one or two girls around the ages of nine or ten years are routinely left in charge of larger play groups of younger children (Burrows and Spiro 1953:262). One might speculate that this involvement in child care might ready older children and older girls, in particular, to reverse roles—that is, to renounce and eventually disavow being needy themselves and experience themselves, instead, as caregivers of the needy. Such a scenario might also explain the special relationship that exists between cross-sex siblings, in particular the inclination of sisters to *fago* their brothers.[25]

Describing a feature of Ifaluk childhood that struck him forcefully, Spiro (Burrows and Spiro 1953:274) supplies another possible explanation for the disavowal of one's own neediness and its reconfiguration as caring for others. His account of the abrupt transition from babyhood to being an older sibling, once a new sister or brother is born, is so revealing of early attachment on Ifaluk that it is worth quoting in full:

> We have repeatedly emphasized the fact that the baby is king in Ifaluk. Not only are babies desired and not only are all their desires satisfied, but they are the constant center of attention. They are always the focal point of the household. This orientation, moreover, remains constant. The eyes of the adults are always focused on the babies, so that once the baby grows older he is out of focus, so to speak, and a new baby is now in focus. In other words, the king is dethroned. His place of centrality is now usurped by a younger infant. From a

position of extreme overt love and attention he is relegated to a position where he is relatively ignored. Adults are still concerned about him, but they leave him to shift for himself. He is free to come and go when he wants and to eat where he wants, so long as he is not too far from sight. But what is even more important, the constant overt affection to which he had become accustomed is now withdrawn. I have seldom observed a child four or five years old to be held in an adult's arms, to be kissed or hugged, or to receive any overt, physical affection. From a state of infancy—a state of overabundant love—the child passed directly to a state of adulthood, with regard to the display of affection. The result of this differential treatment is a child starved for affection.

Spiro was himself a test case for his hypothesis. He (Burrows and Spiro 1953:274–275) eventually figured out that the fondness Ifaluk children showed for him was due, not to the candy he gave them, but to the fact that he was

> the only adult in their world that showed genuine interest in them, that played with them, that displayed overt affect for them. In other words, I was playing the role that their parents and other adults had played when they had been babies. I was filling a deep emotional need in their lives.

This epiphany came to Spiro after one boy snuggled against him and then lay contentedly for an entire afternoon with his head in his lap.

Spiro (Burrows and Spiro 1953:275) adds:

> The minutest frustration of the infant is attended to immediately, whereas much greater frustrations of the child are not only ignored, but often provoke amusement.

For example, children may wail long and loudly over some grievance, without anyone responding to their distress. Spiro gives no explanation for such disregard for children who are no longer babies. It may be deliberate on the part of caregivers, if the Ifaluk Islander cultural model of virtue is anything like the Samoan model that Mageo describes in chapter 7. Mageo explains that after a child is around six months old, Samoan caregivers will ignore its wails in order not to spoil it (or, in Samoan, make the child *matanana*), and ultimately not to produce a boastful, self-aggrandizing adult.[26] Moreover, she says, Samoans consider it unseemly for even parents to display personal attachment to their child, as people of higher rank are supposed to pay no heed to members of lower age grades, leaving their management and care to their immediate superiors—in this case, older children. In any event, the Ifaluk and Samoan cases contrast sharply with that of middle-class American children (e.g., Weisner 2001; Whiting 1978), who remain the focus of parental attention and praise throughout childhood—and, indeed, in many instances, long into adulthood.[27]

Spiro is interested in the sharp rivalry characteristic of Ifaluk siblings, expressed most vividly in competition for food, which this displacement of older child by infant engenders in children.[28] I suggest that something else is at issue as well. The child cut off in this abrupt way from the attention and affection to which he or she is accustomed might well learn to disavow his or her own need for affection. Perhaps the dual effect of such an abrupt transition from an indulged infancy and subsequent recruitment, at a young age oneself, into a role of responsibility for others younger than oneself, explains the way in which *fago* works to project one's disavowed dependency needs onto the others for whom one becomes the caregiver.[29]

Before closing this final part of my argument, I must add that I am not the first to single out the early experience of displacement by a new infant as key to Ifaluk adult attachment. As Charles Nuckolls (1996) earlier put it, "In Ifaluk, a dynamic conflict exists between the desire for nurturance that is developed in childhood and the necessity of withdrawal that is forced on children when they begin to grow up." To present and assess Nuckoll's entire complex argument would require another whole article.[30] The larger thrust of his argument, explicit in the subtitle of his article, is that approaches from cognition and depth psychology must be synthesized in order to achieve an adequate analysis of culture. That is a premise of this chapter as well. However, I must dissent from Nuckolls in one key particular that is absolutely vital to my argument, and that is our interpretations of the psychological basis of *fago*.

In Nuckolls's (1996:713) account, not dissimilarly to my own, *fago* is a "knowledge structure" through which an Ifaluk islander "recalls and recaptures the attachment of childhood." He (Nuckolls 1996:716) views this emotion, as do I, as "a culturally constituted defense mechanism" offering "a kind of resolution" to psychic conflict. The conflict being defended against, as he sees it, is that between taking for oneself and nurturing others. This, with its emphasis on adult cooperation in adulthood, might be said to be the Ifaluk islander version (just as emphasis on self-reliance in adulthood is the American middle-class version) of the more general threat that infantile feelings of dependency pose to adult autonomy. But Nuckolls and I have very different views of how *fago* does its defensive work. "Attachment," Nuckolls (1996:713) says, "is signified by neediness in one person and the fulfilling of that need by another, expressed most commonly in the giving and receiving of food." In this construction *fago* is two-sided. That is, psychic resolution is achieved either by giving or by receiving. Contrarily, and in line with Bowlby's clinical insight, I see the defensive work of *fago* as being decidedly one-sided. In feeling *fago* for another who is needy, one is enabled to disavow one's own neediness. To my mind, this account makes better sense of the unidirectionality and nonreciprocality that are such marked features of *fago*. But it may still be the case that Nuckolls—and Spiro, in his interpretation of the Ifaluk defense mechanism discussed at the end of the previous section—may be adding a dimension to my account of *fago* that I have left out. It may be true that the needy recipient of *fago* is experiencing, not a disavowal of neediness, but an opportunity for direct expression and acknowledgment of it—much as the American marital relationship allows an experience of dependency and neediness that adult Americans must in all other contexts disavow.

Reprise

Of course, two cases are hardly conclusive. Nevertheless, I hope at least to have opened some new possibilities for thinking about adult attachment. First, by pointing to a pattern of similarities between the two cases, I have raised the possibility of a universal basis for adult attachment in infantile experience. Second, I have shown how radical can be the remaining cross-cultural variation in adult attachment, including variation in both the targets and the content of adult attachment relationships. I have suggested that one of the most profound of these differences in patterns of adult attachment cross-culturally lies in the variable cultural defenses adopted against early dependency feelings. Throughout, I have speculated as to the possible childhood origins of these cross-cultural differences.

As well, both the posited universals and the wide variation I have described have raised profound challenges to key assumptions made by contemporary attachment theorists about adult attachment. Taken one by one, these challenges may seem to be reparable. Taken cumulatively, however, the challenged assumptions reveal a disturbing pattern. Together they tell the story of a theory that has become so boxed in by its own predetermined concepts that its practitioners do not ask critical questions about the validity of these concepts. As LeVine and Miller (1990:79) have observed,

> Attachment research operates with assumptions about the human species derived from a theoretical model rather than from empirical findings.[31] Studies of maternal behavior in diverse human societies show a wider range of infant care and communication patterns than any developmental theory has anticipated.

The observation holds for research on adult attachment. This is so whether attachment theorists are adapting the concepts of "secure base" and "safe haven" from Bowby's original writings about childhood to the adult context without interrogating their appropriateness to this context in either our own or other societies; or inferring supposed universals such as adult "pair bonding" or a certain style of "intersubjectivity" in adult relationships from patterns of middle-class American child rearing, without questioning the ethnocentrism of these inferences; or assuming pathology, as they do when they treat adult defenses as the products of insecure attachment, rather than recognizing the normativity of dependency conflicts and the defenses against these cross-culturally.[32] In none of these cases have attachment theorists been motivated to check their assumptions about adult attachment against the range of naturally occurring arrangements for such relationships. Yet the natural laboratory provided by the ethnographic record offers just such an opportunity to test these assumptions from attachment theory.

Acknowledgments

I am indebted to Bambi Chapin for her introduction to, and tutorial on, Fingarette's concept of disavowal, and for her insights on the defenses. I am grateful to Christine Bachrach for reigning in my critique, in an original draft of this chapter, of functionalism in current attachment theory. I thank Holly Mathews for reminding me of the work of Charles Nuckolls pertaining to the Ifaluk. More generally, I am immensely appreciative of the close readings of this chapter in one or another draft form, and the astute comments on it, provided by all three of these excellent colleagues, as well as by Elise Berman, Jim Chisholm, and Jeannette Mageo. It needs to be said that these commentators do not necessarily share my perspective.

Notes

1. Perhaps the most superficial change in the writing of ethnography being the elimination of a blanket use of the third-person masculine.
2. Melford Spiro (1961:482–490) was the first to posit such culturally shared defenses, which he called "culturally constituted defenses."
3. There is a debate about whether secure base and safe haven ought to be collapsed into a single category (Waters and Cummings 2000) or not (Feeney and Collins 2004).
4. The idea that the adult partner serves as a secure base in the sense of allowing one to explore work, hobbies, and friendships with a greater sense of security, as Zeifman and Hazan (2008:449) posit, is so mid-twentieth-century American, so Human Potential Movement, as to warrant deep skepticism about its status as a universal.
5. Attachment theorists Kobak and Madsen (2008:23) bring a similar critique to the use of behavioral indicators of early attachment when they note that "behavior needs to be interpreted according to the context and the underlying goals of the child, instead of being reduced to simple frequency counts of discrete behaviors."
6. Once again, there are attachment theorists who share this view. Kobak and Madsen (2008:32), for example, point out that there are many other sources of feeling secure than reliance on an attachment figure.
7. The level of abstraction I am suggesting is anticipated by Rothbaum et al. (2000:1102), who call for a more thorough search and testing for universals "in the crucible of human diversity," after which "[W]e expect that a few attachment universals will remain but that these will be limited to abstract principles (e.g. pursuit of proximity and protection, suffering resulting from loss)." Their hypothetical examples capture two of my three proposed concerns.
8. Noting that the use of the first-person plural is nearly as common as the use of the first-person singular in statements about mental events, Lutz (1985:44) observes, "In the case of the emotion word *fago* (compassion/love/sadness), the

use of the first person plural is more common than that of any other pronoun." Linguistic conventions like this one are hard to interpret, though. Elise Berman (personal communication) asks whether this use of the first-person plural is simply a technique for distancing oneself from an emotion such as *fago* and not taking full responsibility for feeling it. Along these lines, she notes that children in the Marshall Islands, where she conducted fieldwork, use this construction to mean something like, "Everybody who encounters a situation like this would feel this way," as against meaning that they are one of many who do feel that way.

9. An exception to this nonreciprocality would seem to be the *maluwelu* or calm person, who is the Ifaluk cultural ideal. Chiefs among others exhibit this quality. The person who is *maluwelu* behaves gently and does not frighten others. By inference such a person exhibits *fago*, since "in being gentle he or she protects others from the fright and discomfort that they would feel in the face of aggression or other social disruptiveness" (Lutz 1988:141). At the same time, and uncharacteristically for this normally nonreciprocal emotion, this person elicits the emotion of *fago* from these others as well. Wierzbicka (1992:143–144), too, recognizes that the application of *fago* to those who are exemplary in their calmness and social intelligence does not fit her script for the word, and concludes that there must be two polysemous meanings of *fago*. Wierzbicka's departs sharply from the present analysis, however, in treating the second, polysemous meaning of *fago* as encompassing compassion and sadness, with its application to chiefs and other *maluwelu* persons as being just one specific application of that second meaning. Here is not the place to critique Wierzbicka's analysis of *fago*, with which I am in sharp disagreement, in that my analysis accounts for Lutz's tripartite definition of *fago* as love/compassion/sadness in terms of a single complex meaning of the word. I would just insist that whether the particular extension of *fago* to *maluwelu* persons is polysemous or not awaits further ethnographic evidence concerning this usage. As Wierzbicka (1996:14) herself remarks, "It goes without saying that polysemy must never be postulated lightly."
10. And one such reciprocal need to be fulfilled in this exclusive, dyadic relationship is that of sex. *Fago*, unlike *love*, has nothing to do with sexuality, the emotions associated with which typically being described, on Ifaluk, in other terms (Lutz 1988:145).
11. Many historians have documented the gradual and complex shift in America from marriage based on traditional roles to marriage based on mutual fulfillment. Perhaps the most nuanced of these accounts is by Coontz (2005:247–280).
12. With one exception to be further addressed shortly: when the object of *fago* is dying.
13. Lutz (1988:150) views *fago* as an adaptation to this unforgiving environment. Central to this adaptation is the institution of chiefs, "individuals whose *fago* for commoners helps to insure the well-being of the island."
14. Lutz (1988:160–161) contributes the added tidbit that, at least some of the time, a child's adoption takes place after the age of three.
15. It is not that attachment theorists recognize no conflict resulting from early attachment relationships, but this conflict is contingent, arising only when the attachment figure does not meet the infant's needs and expectations (Fonagy et al. 2008:784). When that happens, it leads to insecure attachment (and, in the case of the avoidant version of this, defenses of an unspecified variety); otherwise, attachment is secure. In contrast, McCollum and I posit that the conflict between dependency and autonomy is universal (and hence cross-cultural).

16. At the other extreme, we must resist any romanticizing temptation to see Ifaluk *fago* and the communal existence in which it is implicated as inherently superior to our own cultural defenses or our own way of life.
17. Jeannette Mageo (personal communication) comments that in Polynesia (and possibly also on Ifaluk and in other Pacific societies beyond Polynesia and other societies beyond the Pacific) the demand for interdependence is viewed as "progressive," and the demand for individuality as "regressive." Be that as it may, Ifaluk islanders, we shall see, disavow their own neediness even as they experience that concern as individualistic and the concern for others' neediness as an expression of interdependence.
18. Fingarette's notion of defenses as involving the fabrication of stories to account for perceived inconsistencies gains support from an unexpected direction: the account of defense mechanisms given by neuroscientists Michael Gazzaniga (2011:97–98) and V. S. Ramachandran (Ramachandran and Blakeslee 1998:130–136; 152–157). In Gazzaniga's words, defenses arise "because the brain arrives at the most probable and globally consistent interpretation of evidence derived from multiple sources, and then ignores or suppresses conflicting information." Both neuroscientists locate this process in a left brain capacity that Gazzaniga calls the Interpreter, and both provide extensive experimental evidence of the Interpreter unleashed due to right brain lesions that compromise the capacity of that side of the brain to do its complementary job of hewing to the "literal" facts and detecting anomalies in them.
19. Fingarette (1969:67) provides two clear examples of projection: that of the hallucinatory, who, having disavowed voices in his head, assigns them to supernatural beings; and that of the paranoid, who, having disavowed the destructiveness with which he himself is filled, assigns it to others. *Denial, reaction formation, repression, displacement,* and *splitting* can all be regarded as other strategies for what to do with that which has been disavowed.
20. Ifaluk island women do not drink.
21. This view can be contrasted with that of Western psychoanalytic theorists, who regard the ability to take both needful and need fulfilling roles in a relationship as a hallmark of mature love and perhaps the very measure of adulthood in our society (see Quinn 1997a:201–203).
22. When missionaries first came to Samoa, Jeannette Mageo (personal communication) relates, funerals were very dramatic, accompanied by lots of self-injury, and people typically said things like "how can you leave me like this" to the dead. These occasions illustrate, Mageo speculates, that in extreme emotional circumstances the original thoughts and feelings (in this case, of dependency) can break through the defense against them. (See also Mageo 1998:54, 62.)
23. Bowlby goes on to explain that he himself does not use the term "projective identification" or others like it because they imply a theoretical paradigm other than his own.
24. Another anthropologist who conducted fieldwork in Samoa, Bonnie Nardi, once told me (personal communication) how shocking she always found it, after her return to the United States, to witness American mothers jumping up from the dinner table to get the salt or some other forgotten item that one of the children asked for. At Samoan meals, she said, children would jump up to get anything that adults needed.
25. Holly Mathews (personal communication) raises the possibility that whether siblings become rivalrous or close, in societies like Ifaluk in which older children

are heavily recruited as child caregivers, depends on sibling order. The most recently arrived sibling, she speculates, "probably remains a rival for life." On the other hand, the younger siblings that a girl is old enough to care for become objects of her lifelong affection—in the Ifaluk case, of her *fago*.

26. By extension, this concern not to spoil the child, says Mageo (personal communication), is also why Samoans avoid the kind of American-style attunement between children older than six months and their caregivers, a style of interaction that, as I have noted, figures in attachment theory as a requirement for secure attachment.
27. Whiting and Weisner both go on to argue that this American middle-class style, coupled with pressure to independence, fosters an adult demanding of attention and praise on the way to personal success, one relatively non-nurturant toward others.
28. Middle-class American parents typically take pains not to show "favoritism" toward one sibling over another, regardless of their relative ages. This practice undoubtedly blunts sibling rivalry in these families.
29. Bowlby (1980:222) identifies two types of experience commonly found in the childhood histories of adult compulsive caregivers. It is suggestive that one of these experiences is "intermittent and inadequate mothering during early childhood," while the other is pressure in childhood to care for a parent. These two types of experience would seem to correspond to the Ifaluk child's experience of first, suffering an abrupt transition from being the object of assiduous, continuous attention to being sidelined, followed by being recruited to care for other, younger children and, ultimately, for one's aging parents. Of course, I would reject any suggestion that Ifaluk mothering is, in Bowlby's term, "inadequate." As I have argued, every cultural pattern of child caregiving has its consequences for the way the desire to return to infantile dependency is defended against in adulthood.
30. His argument is republished in Nuckolls (1998) as the second half of Chapter Two. I will rely on the earlier of the two published renditions, which are nearly identical.
31. To be clear, LeVine and Miller's is not a claim that attachment theory does not produce empirical findings. It produces reams of empirical findings. These authors are simply pointing out that, very generally, empirical studies by attachment theorists do not question, much less jeopardize, its underlying theoretical constructs.
32. Or even more central to attachment theory, when they treat some widely distributed cross-cultural patterns of both early and adult attachment as "insecure," a readiness to pathologize that is addressed by several other chapters in this volume.

References

Bowlby, John. 1980. *Loss: Sadness and Depression. Vol. 3, Attachment and Loss.* New York: Basic Books.

Burrows, Edwin G., and Melford E. Spiro. 1953. *An Atoll Culture: Ethnography of Ifaluk in the Central Carolines.* New Haven, CT: Human Relations Area Files.

Cassidy, Jude. 2008. "The Nature of the Child's Ties." In *Handbook of Attachment: Theory, Research, and Clinical Implications*, Jude Cassidy and Phillip R. Shaver, eds., pp. 3–22. New York: Guilford Press.

Collins, Nancy L., AnaMarie C. Guichard, Maire B. Ford, and Brooke Feeney. 2004. "Working Models of Attachment: New Developments and Emerging Themes." In *Adult Attachment: Theory, Research, and Clinical Implications*, W. Steven Rholes and Jeffry A. Simpson, eds., pp. 196–239. New York: Guilford Press.

Coontz, Stephanie. 2005. *Marriage, a History: From Obedience to Intimacy or How Love Conquered Marriage*. New York: Viking Penguin.

Feeney, Brooke C., and Nancy L. Collins. 2004. "Interpersonal Safe Haven and Secure Base Caregiving Processes in Adulthood." In *Adult Attachment: Theory, Research, and Clinical Implications*, W. Steven Rholes and Jeffry A. Simpson, eds., pp. 300–338. New York: Guilford Press.

Fonagy, Peter, George Gergely, and Mary Target. 2008. "Psychoanalytic Constructs and Attachment Theory and Research." In *Handbook of Attachment: Theory, Research, and Clinical Implications*, Jude Cassidy and Phillip R. Shaver, eds., pp. 783–810. New York: Guildford Press.

Fingarette, Herbert. 1969. *Self-Deception*. London: Routledge & Kegan Paul.

Gazzaniga, Michael S. 2011. *Who's in Charge? Free Will and the Science of the Brain*. HarperCollins Publishers.

Gerber, Eleanor Ruth. 1975. "The Cultural Patterning of Emotions in Samoa." PhD dissertation, University of California, San Diego.

Hazan, Cindy, Nurit Gur-Yaish, and Mary Campa. 2004. "What Does It Mean to Be Attached?" In *Adult Attachment: Theory, Research, and Clinical Implications*, W. Steven Rholes and Jeffry A. Simpson, eds., pp. 55–85. New York: Guilford Press.

Kobak, Roger, and Stephanie Madsen. 2008. "Disruptions in Attachment Bonds: Implications for Theory, Research, and Clinical Interventions." In *Handbook of Attachment: Theory, Research, and Clinical Implications*, Jude Cassidy and Phillip R. Shaver, eds., pp. 23–47. New York: Guilford Press.

LeVine, Robert A., and Patrice M. Miller. 1990. "Commentary." In "Special Topic: Cross-Cultural Validity of Attachment Theory." *Human Development* 33(1):73–80.

Levy, Robert. 1973. *Tahitians: Mind and Experience in the Society Islands*. Chicago, IL: University of Chicago Press.

Lowe, Edward D., and Allen Johnson. 2007. "Tales of Danger: Parental Protection and Child Development in Stories from Chuuk." *Ethnology* 46(2):151–168.

Lutz, Catherine. 1985. "Ethnopsychology Compared to What? Explaining Behavior and Consciousness among the Ifaluk." In *Person, Self and Experience: Exploring Pacific Ethnopsychologies*, Geoffrey M. White and John Kirkpatrick, eds., pp. 35–79. Berkeley, CA: University of California Press.

Lutz, Catherine. 1988. *Unnatural Emotions: Everyday Sentiments on a Micronesian Atoll and Their Challenge to Western Theory*. Chicago, IL: University of Chicago Press.

Mageo, Jeannette Marie. 1998. *Theorizing Self in Samoa: Emotions, Genders, and Sexualities*. Ann Arbor, MI: University of Michigan Press.

McCollum, Chris. 2002. "Relatedness and Self-Definition: Two Dominant Themes in Middle-Class Americans' Life Stories." *Ethos* 30(1/2):113–139.

Nuckolls, Charles W. 1996. "Spiro and Lutz on Ifaluk: Toward a Synthesis of Cultural Cognition and Depth Psychology." *Ethos* 24(4):695–717.

Pietromonaco, Paula R., and Lisa Feldman Barrett. 2000. "The Internal Working Model Concept: What Do We Really Know about the Self in Relation to Others?" *Review of General Psychology* 4(2):155–173.

Quinn, Naomi. 1983. "American Marriage and the Folk Psychology of Need Fulfillment." Paper presented at the Institute of Advanced Study, Princeton.

Quinn, Naomi. 1997a. "Research on the Psychodynamics of Shared Understandings." In *A Cognitive Theory of Cultural Meaning*, Claudia Strauss and Naomi Quinn, eds., pp. 189–209. Cambridge: Cambridge University Press.

Quinn, Naomi. 1997b. "Research on Shared Task Solutions." In *A Cognitive Theory of Cultural Meaning*, Claudia Strauss and Naomi Quinn, eds., pp. 137–188. Cambridge: Cambridge University Press.

Ramachandran, V. S., and Sandra Blakeslee. 1998. *Phantoms in the Brain: Probing the Mysteries of the Human Mind*. New York: William Morrow.

Rothbaum, Fred, John Weisz, Martha Pott, Kazuo Miyake, and Gilda Morelli. 2000. "Attachment and Culture: Security in the United States and Japan." *American Psychologist* 55(10):1093–1104.

Spiro, Melford E. 1961. "An Overview and a Suggested Reorientation." In *Psychological Anthropology: Approaches to Culture and Personality*, Francis L. K. Hsu, ed., pp. 484–491. Homewood, IL: Dorsey.

Sroufe, L. Alan, and Everett Waters. 1977. "Attachment as an Organizational Construct." *Child Development* 48(4):1184–1199.

Waters, Everett, and E. Mark Cummings. 2000. "A Secure Base from which to Explore Close Relationships." *Child Development* 71(1):164–172.

Weisner, Thomas. 2001. "The American Dependency Conflict." *Ethos* 29(3):271–295.

Wierzbicka, Anna. 1996. *Semantics, Culture, and Cognition: Universal Human Concepts in Culture-Specific Configurations*. Oxford: Oxford University Press.

Whiting, Beatrice B. 1978. "The Dependency Hang-Up and Experiments in Alternative Life Styles." In *Major Social Issues: A Multidisciplinary View*, J. Milton Yinger and Stephen J. Cutler, eds., pp. 217–226. New York: Free Press.

Zeifman, Debra, and Cindy Hazan. 2008. "Pair Bonds as Attachments: Reevaluating the Evidence." In *Handbook of Attachment: Theory, Research, and Clinical Applications*, Jude Cassidy and Phillip R. Shaver, eds., pp. 436–455. New York: Guilford Press.

Afterword: Cross-cultural Challenges to Attachment Theory

Gilda A. Morelli and Paula Ivey Henry

When our colleagues and I (Morelli) wrote about the cultural nature of psychology's most influential theory of relatedness in 2000, we did so in the hope of a rapprochement with theorists wedded to a more universalistic view of attachment (Rothbaum et al. 2000). We questioned the key tenets of sensitive parenting, secure base, and child competency and brought to bear what we knew about other community practices to make clear the ideological underpinnings of this theory—as others had done before us (e.g., Fiske et al. 1998; Harwood et al. 1995; LeVine and Miller 1990; Takahashi 1990). We spoke of the value of including communities with different traditions to learn what mattered to them about relationships to refine our thinking about attachment theory—not to dismantle it. We ended our essay noting:

> Opening the door to human diversity could greatly enrich the understanding of the myriad ways in which human relationships take shape, go awry, and undergo repair in social contexts around the world. Expanding the research agenda in this way may, in fact, reveal what an intellectual treasure chest attachment theory truly is. (1102)

Reflections on Changes in Classical Attachment Theory and Research

Since that time, traditional attachment theory and research have widened in scope. The interdisciplinary framework, a hallmark of early attachment theory development, now advances with inclusion of evolutionary biology and neuroscience research, and with the increasingly global study of non-Western experiences. Still, attachment research progresses, like much of psychology, in ways that parallel medicine in viewing developmental stages and outcomes as normative and individual variation as trait-based (Mayr 1982; Nesse et al. 2010). The promotion of fixed concepts of good parenting and healthy development, and the methods and instruments to study them, continues largely unquestioned, bolstered by assumptions about attachment and supporting processes. Researchers play down observations ill-fitted to established (Western-based) psychological constructs, and deny competitive place for alternative methodologies, which obscures variation and constrains rather than facilitates theoretical development (Arnett 2008; Henrich et al. 2010).

Even so, traditional attachment scholars are not indifferent to the cultural and contextual aspects of people's lives, and acknowledge their role in close relationships. The thesis that attachment is species-wide allows for adaptation to local conditions, and neuroscientific evidence of plasticity support this (Belsky and de Haan 2011; van Ijzendoorn and Sagi-Schwartz 2008). Such developments temper views on attachment theory and research. For example, insecure patterns of attachment are considered adaptive under certain conditions such as when parents are unable or unwilling to invest in babies—often as a result of living in ecologically risky environments. In these instances, babies adapt by avoiding parents and secure resources elsewhere (avoidant classification) or by being demanding and overly vigilant (anxious/resistant classification) and secure resources from parents at the most opportune times (Chisholm 1996; Simpson and Belsky 2008). Ethnographic analyses are seen as useful to expand measures of sensitive parenting developed by Ainsworth and colleagues (Belsky and Fearon 2008); and, researchers are more careful to interpret attachment classifications of babies who experience more or less stress in the Strange Situation than that expected by protocol, as related to their everyday care experiences.

These changes, though representing a more nuanced view of attachment, do little to transform the key tenets of attachment theory. Concepts of security continue to privilege autonomous functioning, and security of attachment continues to depend on how well a child balances the need for protection and felt security with the need for exploration and mastery of the inanimate and social world, both considered innate drives. Securely attached babies best do this; they derive comfort from proximity to caregiver and use the caregiver as a base from which to explore the environment. Insecurely attached babies fall short of meeting these criteria. While insecure attachments are thought of by some scholars as "optimal" (adaptive) in particular circumstances (Simpson and Belsky 2008), insecurely attached babies are portrayed often as making the best of a bad lot; and adaptations to risky environments may come at a cost—inadequate growth, development, and less nimble learning. Finally, exploration that fosters (and underlies) autonomous functioning continues as a goal of attachment. With all of this, prescriptive ideas about sensitive parenting still emphasize care that is servant to baby's endeavors, with prompt responses to baby's explicit signals.

The preservation of key constructs and methodology in most studies may be one reason why attachment research in communities outside of the United States and Europe yields findings consistent with theory. Observers select predetermined psychological constructs that "best fit" their subjective evaluations rather than expand the kind of information needed to better understand variation observed. Puerto Rican mothers, for example, showed an overall preference for securely (compared to insecurely) attached babies. But mothers praised these babies for respectful attentive and positive engagement, qualities salient to them but not the basis for the classification (Miller 2004). In cases like these, traditional attachment scholars are disinclined to entertain competing interpretations for what they view as consistencies in attachment across cultures (e.g., normative distribution of attachment classification). Not surprising. Their position is safeguarded by decades of scholarship, with generations of scholars sharing a deeply Western philosophy on human development. It is reproduced in the teaching and research of the upcoming generation of students educated in academic institutions around the world and representing fields such as psychology, counseling, social work, and medicine. (See Gaskin, chapter 1, for a historical and critical overview of attachment theory.)

Advancing Attachment Theory and Research

In this year, 2013, with the known panoply of infant social interactions that exists across culture, we must work toward a more robust theory of the ontogeny of human close relationships. Progress rests largely on efforts that privilege human variation over human universals, and that record, hypothesize, and test variability in biology and behavior across communities in the context of the habitats they encounter. Attachment theorists partnering with scholars that offer complementary perspectives will result in significant gains in our understanding of human close relationships.

The contributors to this volume exemplify the type of scholars we have in mind. The authors immerse themselves in the very life of the community in regions of the world far different from those typically represented in attachment research. They rely on ethnographic and ecologically based accounts of people's everyday lives, and attend to the interplay of biological, ecological, and cultural processes to craft their theses on the closest relationships children develop when they are young and as they grow up. Most approach their research with an interest in describing and understanding these relationships primarily in local terms.

The freshness of alternative cultural views is a singularly compelling reason that attachment theorists should take this volume seriously. The ethnographic accounts broaden what we know about the circumstances that support infant capacity to develop close relationships and the nature of relationships that develop. The contributions point to the difficulties of ongoing use of psychological constructs and criteria in communities that did not participate in some way in their development, and with little knowledge of how community members experience and express close relationships. The authors extend classical conceptualizations of attachment in the face of new data, and intersect with significant advances in psychodynamic, evolutionary, ecological, and cultural understanding of human development and social behavior.

With these accounts come questions about the adequacy of traditional attachment theory for the communities studied. We point to four issues raised by these questions that direct us to the very assumptions on which the theory is based. They include the cooperative nature of infant care; correlates of attachment security; conceptions of self; and adult attachment relationships. The details provided by the authors and their insightful interpretations cast these dimensions of attachment in a more refined light. Contributions such as these will lead to changes in attachment theory critical to accommodate the many people in communities around the world whose ways of relating are invisible to current theory.

Cooperative Care, Multiple Attachments, and Multiple Secure Bases

Bowlby's initial views on the singularity of the attachment relationship caused some stir in the psychological community. But he was quick to note that infants are able to form more than one attachment relationship (and probably do), but attachment to mother—the presumed main caregiver—was primary and attachment to others secondary. Interest in infants' fathers, siblings, and grandparents developed, and continues, at the edges of theoretical attention. But day-care providers, as the most consistent mother-substitute in Western cultures, remain a strong subject of consideration. The near exclusive focus on mothers elevated in importance her role in the infant's internal working model of relationships, set apart from the other relationships the infant develops. Under this paradigm, mothers, not others, define the quality of infant security.

Although the primacy of the mother in the life of her baby is undeniable, all of the contributors to this volume make clear that mothers are not singular providers of care. The sharing of care is likely a part of our human legacy and allows mothers, with the help of others, to keep themselves and all of their nutritionally dependent children healthy—as mothers alone are not able to meet the energetic demands of doing both at the same time (Crittenden and Marlowe; Meehan and Hawks, this volume). This volume shows that the experience and expression of care by infants and caregivers alike, the characteristics and contribution of providers, and changes in care over time are culturally and ecologically situated. It also suggests that babies develop close, trusting relationships with many, though probably not all, of the people who care for them; and these relationships likely develop more or less at the same time. In the context of such care, babies may develop multiple representations of relationships derived not only from relationships with their mothers; and multiple bases of security—similar though not identical—may coexist in time and place from which babies can navigate. Research in this volume, perhaps especially that by Meehan and Hawks, strongly supports this view.

Intriguingly, this evidence suggests that it makes little sense to consider close relationships in isolation of one another from either the infant or caregiver's perspective. Rather, they should be seen as constituting a network of relationships that engender feelings of security in babies. The care of babies by mother and others observed in these societies is likely the prevalent pattern of care. Present-day patterns derived from it developed historically as households split into smaller units characterized by nuclear families. This formation reduced attachment relationships to a few and isolated the psychological significance of the mother—with one or two others—as the baby's primary care provider and attachment figure. The availability of secure bases narrowed substantially and revolved mostly around mother.

Correlates of Attachment Security

Much of the research examining correlates of attachment security concentrates on parental sensitivity, and in particular maternal sensitivity—and factors influencing sensitivity such as household income, parental stress, and so on are of interest. The gold standard of sensitive care, which serves as a prototype for other measures, was developed by Ainsworth and colleagues (Ainsworth 1976; Sroufe and Waters 1997) and reflects the valuing of children's autonomy and related constructs. Examples are care that supports baby's endeavors and prompt response to baby's explicit signals, even when at odds with caregiver interests.

Many contributing to this volume acknowledge the sensitive care of children in the first months and years of life—but not by all caregivers and not all of the time. This care oftentimes is differently sensitive from the sensitive care described by traditional attachment theorists. Among the Sinhala of Sri Lanka (Chapin, chapter 5), mothers and seniors are keenly attuned to babies' subtle signals, and rely on them to respond to babies' needs before babies verbalize them (which is discouraged in young children). Over time, babies learn to trust that others know what they need without consulting them and without explicitly expressing what they want. Babies learn to wait patiently, not to complain, and to accept what is given.

Sensitive care—however defined—is only one aspect of caring for babies important to the close relationships they develop, but its study occupies much of attachment research. This volume takes up other aspects of care that must be considered going forward if scholars are committed to crafting a more inclusive theory of attachment. Food, feeding, and food sharing are central elements of care and "cross culturally it may be more common than not for attachment and food to be intertwined and mutually influential" (Barltow, chapter 6). Among the Murik (Barltow, chapter 5), acts involving food (originating with mothers) are expressions of relatedness, caring, and belonging; among the Alorese (Seymour, chapter 4), ceremonial foods and feeding ease tensions that are part of attachment.

Qualities of relating that engender troubling and worrisome feelings in others may be part of culturally mediated processes fostering attachment relationships to another or others. In Samoa, Mageo (chapter 7) argues that practices such as teasing, name calling, and beating a child cause feelings of rage that are directed toward specific others. This rage emotionally distances the child from these specific others and facilitates the child's emotional connections to the group as a whole. In Bhubaneswar, mothers push young children away so that they seek out others for emotional satisfaction (Seymour, chapter 4).

These contributions show that views on sensitive care vary across cultures; processes mediating attachment relationships extend beyond current notions of quality care; and near exclusive focus on dyadic relationships eclipses processes that emotionally connect children (and mothers) more broadly to others.

Conceptions of Self

Traditional attachment theory also is concerned with a child's developing sense of self, other people, and relationships; and theory and research build on long-standing philosophical and theoretical traditions that prioritize the individual and autonomous functioning. From this view, autonomy and related constructs are central goals for development of children in all communities. Care that fosters autonomy (e.g., nonintrusive, noncontrolling, taking the baby's lead), and attachment relationships that reflect autonomy (e.g., babies use their caregivers as a base from which to explore the environment, typically in isolation from peers, and at some distance from caregivers but critically aided by their support), are considered healthy and valued. But, are these values by which only some people—not all people—live (e.g., many US middle-class communities)? As observed in many East Asian societies, children and parents live in accord with the ethics of their various communities (e.g., interdependent self), which tend to focus on the importance of continuous union—social, physical, and psychological. The union of oneself to others, and to a broader community, encourages and facilitates the taking and sharing of perspectives. Qualities that promote social harmony by accommodating to others and to context, such as fitting in, self-restraint, and promoting other's goals, are valued.

This volume shows that people live by values other than autonomy and that they care for children differently from the care idealized and recommended by traditional attachment theorists. Because of this, the standard constructs and standardized methods used to study attachment relationships may be inappropriately applied to them. Moreover, many contributors question the utility of dichotomizing conceptions of self as independent (autonomous) or interdependent (heteronomous). And several of them struggle to reconcile current portrayals of self as (mostly) autonomous or interdependent with what they observed in their fieldwork where qualities marked by autonomy seem just as important to the developing psychosocial well-being of a person as qualities marked by interdependence. The Murik are described as willing explorers who take initiative and are confident in their abilities. They are also described as highly social with a keen responsibility to others; loyal to kin and community; and reliant on group membership for help and protection. Moreover, author commentaries call attention to the probability that the experience and expression of constructs such as autonomy are not the same across cultures. Chapin (chapter 5) notes that Sinhala youth:

> Evidence their maturity, capacity to make good choices, and independent good judgment not by differing from their parents…but by complying with them. It

> requires *a kind of autonomy* [our emphasis] to recognize the wishes of group, to judge them as worth following, and to defer to them. This exercise of self control...displays a young person's capability for independent evaluation, choice, action and self government.

What we take away from this volume is that notions of self do not adequately deal with the different ways an individual's sense of self in a world of others are conceptualized across cultures. A more complete understanding rests on ethnographic studies of the nature of relating in communities around the world using new frames of reference capable of fully exploring (perhaps the many) alternative conceptualizations. With this information, we are better positioned to develop a globally relevant theory of self and, as a result, theory of attachment.

Adult Attachment Relationships

Most traditional attachment theorists assume continuity of attachment needs from infancy to adulthood, met for adults in close relationship with adult partners. Secure base, safe haven, proximity, and distress on separation, appropriately translated for adults, are understood as critical to the adult attachment relationship. Quinn (chapter 8) evaluates these assumptions in her analysis of the Ifaluk emotion *fago*, with American middle-class conceptions of love as a point of comparison. She identifies three features of relationships that align with attachment theory—desire for closeness, fear of loss, and expectation of care—common to her populations that may be universally important; and makes apparent the cultural nature of these constructs, a theme common to this volume. What Quinn adds to the critique of attachment theory (as does Mageo in a different way) is the thesis that *fago*—the experience and expression of closeness, loss, and care—allow the Ifaluk to healthily manage feelings of neediness, which are part of early attachment relationships but in conflict with adult close relationships. Dependency feelings, Quinn maintains, are normative but ways of dealing with them (i.e., defenses) cultural.

Closing Remarks

The current volume provides many of the empirical and theoretical elements for understanding exactly how the conceptual framework of attachment must change to better examine and understand attachment relationships across the range of cultural environments in which infants grow. We credit this achievement to the authors' reliance on ethnographic methodologies to describe and analyze the ontogeny of social relationships, moving from proximate interactions in babies' lives to the concerns and pressures on their caregivers to the ubiquitous environment that structures the lives of both.

By dealing with the challenges this volume identifies, an ambitious attachment theory would result with significant advances:

a. Conceptual units of study and experimentation would be more appropriately designed to address regularities and differences in developmental processes within, and across, study populations. This would broaden the scope of attachment questions pursued, and, it is hoped, stimulate needed participation of scholars from other cultural traditions;
b. Research would embrace individual and ecological variation as core units of investigation and be better poised to connect and enhance rapid progress in development and behavior studies at the interface of the biological and social sciences; and
c. A more ecologically and culturally sophisticated attachment research agenda would provide more sensitive and appropriate prescriptive and intervention strategies for use in clinical and community settings. Attachment interventions would be better poised to meet child needs by integration and service to, rather than diminution of, social and environmental conditions and caregiver and family needs.

All of this is a critical requirement for a theory of *human* close relationships. To succeed in advancing theory we need attachment scholars to join in the effort. We need scholars who are willing to shed language that constrains thinking, step beyond the comfort of philosophical anchors, and develop a broad cross-cultural and empirical base by observing, talking, and listening to people as they live their lives, and in the contexts where human development actually occurs.

References

Ainsworth, Mary D. S. 1976. *Systems for Rating Maternal Care Behavior.* Princeton, NJ: ETS Test Collection.

Arnett, Jeffrey J. 2008. "The Neglected 95%: Why American Psychology Needs to Become Less American." *American Psychologist* 63(7):602–614.

Belsky, Jay, and Michelle de Haan. 2011. "Annual Research Review: Parenting and Children's Brain Development: The End of the Beginning." *Journal of Child Psychology and Psychiatry* 52(4):409–428.

Belsky, Jay, and R. M. Pasco Fearon. 2008. "Precursors of Attachment Security." In *Handbook of Attachment*, J. Cassidy and P. R. Shaver, eds., pp. 295–316. New York: Guilford Press.

Chisholm, James S. 1996. "The Evolutionary Ecology of Attachment Organization." *Human Nature* 7(1):1–38.

Fiske, Alan et al. 1998. "The Cultural Matrix of Social Psychology." In *The Handbook of Social Psychology*, D. Gilbert, S. Fiske, and G. Lindzey, eds., pp. 915–981, vol. 2. Boston, MA: McGraw-Hill.

Harwood, Robin L., Joan. G. Miller, and Nydia. L. Irizarry. 1995. *Culture and Attachment: Perceptions of the Child in Context.* New York: Guilford Press.

Henrich, Joseph, Steven J. Heine, and Ara Norenzayan. 2010. "The Weirdest People in the World?" *Behavioral and Brain Sciences* 33(2–3):61–83.
LeVine, Robert A., and Patrice M. Miller. 1990. "Commentary." *Human Development* 33:73–80.
Mayr, Ernst. 1982. *The Growth of Biological Thought: Diversity, Evolution, and Inheritance.* Cambridge, MA: Harvard University Press.
Miller, Joan G. 2004. "The Cultural Deep Structure of Psychological Theories of Social Development." In *Culture and Competence: Contexts of Life Success*, R. Sternberg and E. Grigorenko, eds., pp. 111–138. Washington, DC: American Psychological Association.
Nesse, Randolph M. et al. 2010. "Making Evolutionary Biology a Basic Science for Medicine." *Proceedings of the National Academy of Sciences* 107(suppl 1):1800–1807.
Rothbaum, Fred et al. 2000. "Attachment and Culture: Security in Japan and the U.S." *American Psychologist* 55:1093–1104.
Simpson, Jeffry A., and Jay Belsky. 2008. "Attachment Theory within a Modern Evolutionary Framework." In *Handbook of Attachment: Theory, Research, and Clinical Applications*, J. Cassidy and P. R. Shaver, eds., pp. 131–157. New York: Guilford Press.
Sroufe, L. Alan, and Everete Waters. 1997. "On the Universality of the Link between Responsive Care and Secure Base Behavior." *Newsletter; International Society for the Study of Behavior and Development* 31(1):3–5.
Takahashi, Keiko. 1990. "Are the Key Assumptions of the 'Strange Situation' Procedure Universal? A View from Japanese Research." *Human Development* 33:23–30.
van Ijzendoorn, Marinus, and Abraham Sagi-Schwartz. 2008. "Cross-cultural Patterns of Attachment: Universal and Contextual Dimensions." In *Handbook of Attachment: Theory, Research, and Clinical Applications*, J. Cassidy and P. R. Shaver, eds., pp. 880–905. New York: Guilford Press.

Contributors

Kathleen Barlow is a professor and the current chair of the Department of Anthropology and Museum Studies at Central Washington University. She is a psychological anthropologist whose research among the Murik of Papua New Guinea has focused on the lives of women and children, culture and learning, and the role of mothering in culture. She is a contributing author and coeditor, with Bambi Chapin, of the 2010 theme issue of *Ethos* (38:4) on "Mothering as Everyday Practice."

Bambi L. Chapin is an associate professor at the University of Maryland, Baltimore County. She is a psychological anthropologist who has conducted research on everyday life and interpersonal relationships in Sri Lanka since 1999. She is the author of the forthcoming ethnography, *Childhood in a Sri Lankan Village: Shaping Hierarchy and Desire.* She is also a contributing author and coeditor with Kathleen Barlow of the theme issue of *Ethos* (2010:38:4), "Mothering as Everyday Practice," as well as the author of "Transforming Possession: Josephine and the Work of Culture" (*Ethos*, 2008:36:2).

Alyssa N. Crittenden is Lincy Foundation Assistant Professor of Anthropology at the University of Nevada, Las Vegas. She is a behavioral ecologist and nutritional anthropologist who works among the Hadza hunter-gatherers of Tanzania. Her research explores the behavioral and nutritional correlates of life history, cooperative breeding, attachment, allomaternal care, children's foraging and food sharing, the evolution of childhood, and the evolution of the human diet. Her publications pertaining to childhood, juvenile foraging, and cooperative breeding, include "Allomaternal care among the Hadza of Tanzania" (*Human Nature*, 19:249–263, 2008) and "Juvenile foraging among the Hadza: Implications for human life history" (*Evolution and Human Behavior*, 34:299–230, 2013).

Suzanne Gaskins is Professor Emerita in the Department of Psychology at Northeastern Illinois University. She has done fieldwork in a traditional Yucatec Mayan village in Mexico since 1977, integrating psychological and ethnographic approaches to the study of children's everyday lives and their development. Her research is focused on cultural influences on development and learning in childhood, across a wide range of topics, including childhood learning in context, infant interactions with people and objects, the role of play and work in development across cultures, the developmental evidence for linguistic relativity beginning in middle childhood, and the influence of cultural change on socialization practices. She has coauthored two edited volumes (*Play and Development*, 2007 and *The Anthropology of Learning in Childhood*, 2010) and written numerous articles and chapters on culture and development.

Sean Hawks is a Ph.D. student in cultural anthropology at Washington State University. He considers attachment theory from a human behavioral ecology perspective. He is interested in hunter-gatherers, their worldviews and their relationships with neighboring groups. He uses both evolutionary and cultural theory to describe and explain the nature of these relationships.

Paula Ivey Henry is a research associate at Harvard School of Public Health. She is a biocultural anthropologist with primary interests in the evolutionary ecology of development and health. Her work focuses on the cooperative reproduction and development of mothers and infants among Efe pygmies, and the interaction of behavior and growth in a multigenerational cohort in the United States. Her leadership experience centers on improving the integration of ecological and developmental science into health innovations.

Jeannette Marie Mageo is a professor in the Anthropology Department at Washington State University. She is the author of *Theorizing Self in Samoa: Emotions, Genders and Sexualities* (1998) and *Dreaming Culture: Meanings, Models, and Power in U.S. American Dreams* (2011). She has published many articles and edited numerous volumes in psychological anthropology and Pacific ethnography. She consulted for and appeared in a documentary made for Channel 4 in Britain, *Paradise Bent: Boys will be Girls in Samoa*, framed by her historical interpretation of Samoan transvestism. From 2003 to 2007, she was the editor of The Association for Social Anthropology's monograph series with University of Pennsylvania Press.

Frank W. Marlowe is a lecturer at the University of Cambridge. He is a specialist in human behavioral ecology. He has conducted fieldwork with the Hadza hunter-gatherers since 1995. His research interests include: hunter-gatherers and human evolution, the sexual division of foraging labor, evolution of cooperation, mating and sexual selection, and life history theory. He is the author of *The Hadza: Hunter-Gatherers of Tanzania*.

Courtney L. Meehan is an assistant professor of anthropology at Washington State University. She is a human behavioral ecologist whose research investigates cooperative breeding and its role in the evolution of human childhood, maternal reproductive strategies, and family health. Her research is particularly focused on the effects of early childhood environment on child physical, social, and emotional development. She conducts research in the Central African Republic among a forager and several farming populations. She is the author or lead coauthor of several articles on Aka and Ngandu parental and non-parental investment in *Human Nature* (2005, 2008) and

Social Science and Medicine (2013). She has also published on maternal life history time and energy allocation trade-offs in *Human Nature* (2009) and the *American Journal of Human Biology* (2013).

Gilda A. Morelli is an associate professor in the Counseling, Developmental, and Educatonal Psychology Department at Boston College. She is a developmental psychologist with interests in the cultural aspects of human development and the role of resource scarcity in caregiver decision making and children's experiences. She has lived with the Efe pygmies of the Democratic Republic of Congo for over a 30-year span years to conduct ethnographic and psychological research on infants' and young children's close relationships, social engagements and opportunities for learning.

Naomi Quinn is Professor Emerita in the Department of Cultural Anthropology at Duke University. Her enduring interest is in the nature of culture. She asks how cultural meanings become internalized, shared, motivating, enduring historically and within individuals, and thematic across cultural domains. She has conducted research among Mfantse people of Ghana, and also in the United States, on Americans' cultural model of marriage. Among her published works, she has coedited *Cultural Models in Language and Thought* (1987), coauthored *A Cognitive Theory of Cultural Meaning* (1997), and edited *Finding Culture in Talk: A Collection of Methods* (2005). She is a past president of the Society for Psychological Anthropology, and she was awarded that society's 2009 Lifetime Achievement Award.

Susan C. Seymour is the Jean M. Pitzer Professor Emerita of Anthropology at Pitzer College. She has done long-term research in India studying children and changing family and gender systems. Her books include, *Women, Family and Child Care in India: A World in Transition* (1999), *The Transformation of a Sacred Town: Bhubaneswar, India* (1980), and (coedited with Carol C. Mukhopadhyay) *Women, Education, and Family Structure in India* (1994). She has recently completed a biography of anthropologist Cora Du Bois that will be published by the University of Nebraska Press.

Index

accessibility, 5, 20, 146, 226
Ackerman, Lillian, 202
Adolf, Karen, 44
adult attachment, 23–4, 215–34
  fago and, 219–33
  reformulation of, 216–19
Ahnert, Lieslotte, 85, 87, 99
Aiello, Leslie, 72, 76
Ainsworth, Mary, 4–5, 10, 24, 34–8, 41, 43, 45, 51–2, 56–7, 67, 86–7, 89, 101–3, 115–16, 143, 146, 159, 165, 171, 177, 179, 185n1, 191–2, 202–3, 209, 242, 245
Aka, 19–20, 25, 85–109
  allomaternal effects on children's emotional states, 105–6
  caregiver responsiveness, 98–101
  context of mother-child separations, 101–3
  maternal/allomaternal caregiving in infancy and early childhood, 93–6
  maternal/allomaternal responsiveness and sensitivity, 98
  maternal effects on children's emotional states, 103–5
  multiple attachments, 96–7
allocare
  allomothering, 7–9, 19–20, 71–2, 74–6, 86–91, 93–107
  alloparenting, 8, 77n1, 86–7, 101, 116
  See also distributed caregiving
Alor of Indonesia
  attachment, 122–5
  infancy and, 118–20
  later childhood and, 121–2
  overview, 115–18
  toddlerhood and, 120–1
Althusser, Louis, 24
Altmann, Jeanne, 90
Alvarez, Helen, 70
amae, 16–17
Arnett, Jeffrey, 242
attachment theory
  advancement of, 243–7
  challenges to current models of, 67–8
  changes in classical attachment theory and research, 241–3
  contact and proximity seeking, 53
  crying and consolation, 52
  cultural critiques of, 37–8
  differentiation between familiar people and strangers, 44–5
  exploration, 56–7
  fear of strangers, 55–6
  human evolution and, 68–9
  interactions with infants, 48–58
  Klein's psychoanalysis and, 191–200
  locomotion and, 33
  maturation process and, 43–8
  maturational and cultural contributions to, 42–58
  memory and, 45–6
  overview, 33–7
  separation anxiety, 54–5
  single vs. multiple attachment figures, 49–50
  understanding/sharing intentions and attention, 46–7
attunement, 21, 146, 150, 158, 201, 222, 226, 245
autonomy, 15, 18, 21–2, 40–1, 131, 143–60, 165–6, 169–71, 191, 194, 196, 204–5, 208, 226–7

Baker, Victoria, 161n5
Barlow, Kathleen, 8–9, 21–4, 67, 69, 120, 124, 130, 165–85, 251
Beals, Alan, 129
Bell, Silvia, 34–5, 41, 51–2, 89, 103
Belsky, Jay, 50, 68–9, 90, 242
Benjamin, Jessica, 202, 205
Bensel, Joachim, 107
Bereczkei, Tamas, 71
Berlin, Lisa, 35

Bindon, J.R., 197
Bird-David, Nurit, 88
Blurton Jones, Nicholas, 70, 86
Bobe, Rene, 71
Bogin, Barry, 69–71, 86
Bove, Riley, 71
Bowlby, John
  adult attachment, 217, 219, 221, 226, 228–9, 232, 236n23, 237n29
  attachment and infants and, 33–6, 43, 49–50, 53
  attachment theory and, 3–4, 19, 22, 24, 26, 29n9, 244
  autonomy through kinship, and food 165–6, 170–1, 174, 177–9, 185n1
  caregivers and, 143, 151, 160, 161n8
  cooperative breeding and attachment and, 87–8
  cultural psychodynamics of attachment, 191, 193, 209
  human evolution and, 67–9
  multiple child care and, 115–16, 118, 122, 125, 134–5
Brazelton, T. Berry, 44, 46, 51
Bretherton, Inge, 4, 10, 13, 27, 50, 87
Briggs, Jean, 9, 125
Bril, Brandine, 39, 48
Brown, Penelope, 47
Brumberg, Joan, 204
Bunn, Henry, 73
Burrows, Edwin, 215, 222–4, 230–1

Callaghan, Tara, 47
Campos, Joseph J., 37, 44
Canaan, Joyce, 205
caregiver sensitivity, 6, 12, 15, 18, 20–1, 26, 34, 49, 51–2, 57, 59, 93, 98–101, 105–8, 146–47, 150–2, 154, 158–9, 170–1, 184, 197, 241–2, 245
Carlson, Elizabeth, 35
Carlson, Vicki, 39
Carpenter, Malinda, 46–7
Casillas, Emily, 201
Cassidy, Jude, 27, 35, 165, 171
Chapin, Bambi, 21, 23, 25, 131, 143–60, 222, 234, 245–6, 251
Charnov, Eric, 69–70
Chavajay, Pablo, 53
Chiao, Joan, 29n4
Chisholm, James, 8, 36, 40, 68–9, 73, 87, 242
Clutton-Brock, Tim H., 72
Cohler, Bertram, 158
Collins, Nancy, 217, 219, 221
consistency in caregiving, 52
consolation, 52
contact, seeking out, 53
cooperative breeding and attachment
  Aka foragers and, 89–108
  allomaternal effects on children's emotional states, 105–6
  caregiver responsiveness to attachment displays, 99–101
  caregiver responsiveness to crying and fussing, 98–9
  maternal and allomaternal caregiving, 93–6
  maternal and allomaternal responsiveness and sensitivity, 98
  maternal effects on children's emotional states, 103–5
  mother-child separations, 101–3
  multiple attachment and internal working models, 87–9
  multiple attachments, 96–7
  overview, 85–7
  research methods of, 90–1
  results of study, 92–3
  sample size of study, 91–2
  SSP and, 89
Crittenden, Alyssa N., 8–9, 20, 67–76, 87, 118, 170, 244, 251
Crognier, Emile, 71
crying, 52
cultural bias
  of assessment measures, 37–8
  attachment categories, 38–40
  insufficient categories to capture all attachment systems, 40–1

D'Andrade, Roy, 151
Darwin, Charles, 68
defenses
  disavowal, 227–8, 230, 232–4, 236n19
  fago and, 226–9
  Northwest U.S., 203–9
  projection, 192, 201, 207, 228–9, 236n19

reaction formation, 25, 180, 194, 198, 205, 227–8
Samoa, 198–200
secure attachment and, 222, 226, 233
splitting, 180, 236n19
DeLeon, Lourdes, 47, 51
Demenocal, Peter, 71
dependency, 7, 16, 23, 25, 29n2, 129, 143, 158, 162n18, 176, 185n2, 192–4, 196, 202–3, 205, 207, 209, 216–18, 226–9, 232–3, 247
diffuse attachment, 130, 172–3, 178, 180, 183, 223
Ding, Yan-hua, 39
distributed caregiving, 8, 20, 53, 88, 108, 127, 134, 168, 171, 176, 180
Doi, Takeo, 16–17
Donner, Henrike, 132–3
Du Bois, Cora, 117–25, 133
dyadic caregiving, 19–20

Eibl-Eibesfeldt, Irenaus, 68
Ellison, Peter, 75
Emlen, Stephen, 72
Environment of Evolutionary Adaptedness (EEA), 8
Erikson, Erik, 52
ethnography, 9, 22–3, 25–6, 161n5, 215–16, 23, 234n1
Ewing, Katherine, 157–8
exploration, 56–7

fago
as cultural defense, 226–9
love vs., 219–26
overview, 215–16
reformulation of adult attachment, 216–19
reprise, 233–4
speculations on origins of, 229–33
familiar faces, recognizing, 44–5
fathers, 19, 50, 70, 77n1, 91, 108, 118, 120–2, 124, 126–7, 145, 152–3, 156, 169, 172, 176, 180, 195, 198–9, 202, 205, 244
fear of strangers, 55–6
feeding, 14, 18, 22–3, 52, 90, 118, 122–4, 129, 133–4, 147, 166–7, 173, 177–9, 184, 219, 230, 245
Feeney, Brooke, 217, 221, 234n3
Feeney, Judith, 179
Field, Tiffany, 101
Fields, Jason, 204
Fingarette, Herbert, 227–8, 234, 236n18
Fiske, Alan, 241
Flinn, Mark, 71, 87
folk theory, 5
Fonagy, Peter, 24, 227, 235n15
Fosbrooke, Henry, 73
Foucault, Michel, 203
Fouts, Hillary, 74, 90
Freeman, Derek, 196
Freud, Sigmund, 24, 49, 191, 194, 203, 206–7, 217

Gamburd, Michele Ruth, 161n9
Gardner, Louise, 195–7
Gaskins, Suzanne, 7, 9, 13, 16–17, 25, 33–60, 159, 166, 169, 251–2
Gazzaniga, Michael, 236n18
Geertz, Clifford, 193
George, Carol, 4, 173
Gerber, Eleanor, 196, 198–9, 230
Gettler, Lee, 74
Giddens, Anthony, 201–2, 204
Gilson, R.P., 207
Goodwin, Marjorie Harkness, 208
Gottlieb, Anna, 67, 87–8
Greenfield, P.A., 21
Gremillion, Helen, 204
Grossman, Karin and Klaus, 11, 39
Gubernick, David, 29n9
Gustafson, Gwen, 46

Hadza
attachment theory and, 69
child-care patterns, 74–6
human evolution and, 72–4
Hamilton's Rule, 72
Harlow, Harry, 22, 49
Harwood, Robin, 41, 68, 116, 144, 165–6, 170, 172, 178, 241
Hawkes, Robin, 9, 25, 68, 70–1, 73–4, 87, 93, 167, 170
Hawks, Sean, 5, 17, 20, 68–9, 85–109, 130, 219, 244, 252
Hayes, Sharon, 194
Hazan, Cindy, 68, 179, 217, 221
Heinicke, Christoph, 67
Henrich, Joseph, 242

Hewlett, Barry, 73, 86–8, 90, 98, 100–1, 107, 170
Hill, Kim, 71
Hindu Indians
 attachment, 130–1
 child-care practices, 126–7
 developmental outcomes, 131–3
 infancy and, 127–9
 overview, 125–6
 toddlerhood and, 129–30
Hjarno, Jan, 195
Holt, D., 208
Howes, Carollee, 50, 67–8, 85, 88, 108, 116
Hrdy, Sarah Blaffer, 8, 19, 49, 68, 71, 76, 86–7, 116, 134, 165, 170
human evolution
 attachment theory and, 68–9
 in comparative perspective, 69–70
 cooperative child care and, 76
 Hadza hunter-gatherers and, 72–5
 mothers' unique reproductive challenge, 70–1
 origins of multiple attachment, 71–2
Hurtado, A. Magdelena, 86

Ifaluk, 215–34. *See also fago*
independence, 21–22
infants
 contact and proximity seeking, 53
 crying and consolation, 52
 cultural differences in beliefs about interactions with, 48–58
 exploration, 56–7
 fear of strangers, 55–6
 sensitivity, 51–2
 separation anxiety, 54–5
 single vs. multiple attachment figures, 49–50
insecure attachment, 3, 12, 14, 17, 24–8, 108, 125, 130, 185n4, 193, 226, 233, 235n15, 242
 avoidant attachment, 4, 10–12, 14–15, 38–9, 108, 192–3
 disorganized attachment, 39–41
 resistant attachment, 38–9
Ivey Henry, Paula, 241–8, 252

Jacobson, Sandra, 85
Janson, Charles, 70
Japan, 5–6, 11, 14–17, 37–40, 101, 107, 150, 170

Kaare, Bwire, 73
Kahn, Miriam, 185n7
Kaplan, Hilliard, 35, 70–1, 86
Karen, Robert, 35
Keller, Heidi, 36, 53, 68, 75, 116, 121, 144, 159, 165–6, 170, 172
Kelly, Joan, 204
Kennedy, Gail, 70–1
Kermoian, Rosanne, 88
Klein, Melanie, 191–3, 196–7, 209
Kline, Paul, 99
Kobak, Roger, 146, 234n5
Konner, Melvin, 43, 73, 87, 103, 116, 118, 165, 170
Kramer, Augustin, 195
Kramer, Karen, 71, 93
Kristeva, Julia, 210n5
Kurland, Jeffrey, 71
Kurtz, Stanley, 68, 137n19
Kusserow, Adrie, 201

Lamb, Michael, 19, 68, 86–8, 90, 101, 116, 131
Lancy, David, 48, 87
Leach, Penelope, 201
Leacock, Eleanor, 202
Ledoux, Louis Pierre, 182
Lee, Phyllis, 70
Lehmann, Arthur, 192
Leigh, Steven, 70
Leininger, April, 161n11
Leonard, William, 72, 76
LeVine, Robert, 4–6, 10–13, 15, 26–7, 36–7, 40, 47, 67–8, 71, 88–9, 144, 150, 165–9, 173, 185n1, 209, 219, 233, 237n31, 241
Levy, Robert, 225, 230
Lewis, Charlie, 88
Lewis, Michael, 68–9
Lipset, David, 182
Liszkowski, Ulf, 47
locomotion, 44, 53
Lowe, Edward, 223, 225
Lutz, Catherine, 23, 170, 215–16, 219–25, 228–30

Mabulla, Audax, 73, 76
Macpherson, Cluny, 199
Maduro, Renaldo, 129
Mageo, Jeannette Marie, 3–28, 68, 76, 109, 119–20, 124, 134–5, 144,

166, 170, 174, 185, 191–210, 222–3, 231, 234, 245, 247, 252
Main, Mary, 35, 39, 56
Marcuse, Herbert, 24
Marlowe, Frank W., 8–9, 20, 67–76, 86–7, 118, 170, 252
marriage, 21, 123, 125–6, 131–2, 135, 145, 153–6, 158, 168, 179, 182, 217–18, 221, 227
Martini, Joyce, 70
Martini, Mary, 36
Marvin, R.S., 88
McCollum, Chris, 170, 194, 203, 216, 221–2, 226–7
McDowell, William, 73
Mead, Margaret, 48, 59, 68, 115, 135, 162n17, 195–7, 199, 203
Meehan, Courtney, 5–6, 9, 17, 20, 25, 68–9, 71, 73, 76, 85–109, 130, 167, 170, 219, 244, 252–3
memory, 45–6
Miller, Joan G., 29n11, 41, 243
Miller, Patrice, 4–6, 10, 36–7, 89, 165, 219, 233, 237n31, 241
Miller, Peggy, 205
Miyake, Kazuo, 14–15, 37, 170
Morelli, Gilda, 36, 54, 68, 116, 144, 167, 170, 241–8, 253
mothering
  allomothering, 19–20
  culture and, 7, 12, 115, 117, 149
  evolution and, 8–9
  exclusive, 115, 122, 132, 171–2
  feeding and, 177–8
  multiple, 6, 19–20, 127–8, 132
  secure attachment and, 18–19, 165
  sensitive, 20–1
  socialization for independence and, 171–3
multiple child care
  attachment and, 122–5, 130–1
  infancy, 118–20, 127–9
  later childhood, 121–2
  North India and
    attachment, 130–1
    child-care practices, 126–7
    infancy, 127–9
    toddlerhood, 129–30
  overview, 115–17
  toddlerhood, 120–1, 129–30
Munroe, Robert and Ruth, 51, 75, 117, 122, 205
Murik of Papua New Guinea
  attachment and gender, 179–83
  caregiving and childhood, 167–9
  cross-sex relationships and adult attachment, 181–3
  discipline and caregiving, 174–7
  food and attachment, 177–9
  gender roles, 179–81
  independent and interdependent attachment orientations, 169–74
  interdependence/autonomy in foraging adaptations, 170–1
  overview, 165–7
  primary attachment to a single mothering figure, 171–2
  relationship of primary and diffuse attachment, 172–4
  seniority, siblingship, food, and gender, 183–4
  socialization for independence/diffuse attachment, 172

Nelson, Katherine, 205
Nesse, Randolph, 241
Nuckolls, Charles, 232, 234, 237n30
nursing, 22, 49, 52, 54–5, 57, 74, 99–101, 106, 118–19, 122, 127–31, 134, 15–46, 149, 171, 173, 175, 177–8, 181–2, 192, 205

Ochs, Elinor, 195
O'Connor, Mary, 39
Odden, Harold, 195, 197
Olds, David, 87
Otto, Hiltrud, 68, 75, 116, 121, 179

Pagel, Mark, 70
Panter-Brick, Catherine, 71
Pantley, Elizabeth, 201
Piaget, Jean, 46
Pietromonaco, Paula, 217–18, 227
Potts, Richard, 71
Pratt, George, 197
proximity-seeking, 3–4, 14, 16, 28, 34, 42, 44, 49, 52–9, 87, 91–6, 98, 102–4, 118, 134, 143, 146, 165, 173, 177–9, 183, 193, 217–18, 247
psychodynamics, 18, 22–5, 116, 174, 179, 191–209, 226–33

Purves, Dale, 19
Purvis, Andy, 70

Quinlan, Robert and Marsha, 109, 185
Quinn, Naomi, 3–28, 76, 109, 124, 132, 134–5, 151, 160, 166, 170, 174, 180, 185, 205, 215–34, 247, 253

Ramachandran, V.S., 236n18
reaction formations, 25, 80, 194, 198, 205, 227–8, 236n19
Reed, Kaye, 71
responsiveness, 51–2
Rheingold, Harriet, 34
Robson, Shannen, 69–70, 72
Rodning, Carol, 39
Rogoff, Barbara, 53, 201–2
Rohner, Ronald, 122, 131
Roisman, Glenn, 179
Roland, Alan, 133
Roscoe, Paul, 170
Rothbaum, Fred, 10, 15–16, 26–8, 39, 68, 88, 116, 144, 150, 165, 167, 170, 234n7, 241

Sagi-Schwartz, Abraham, 13, 16–17, 39–40, 50, 85, 88, 242
Samoa
  compared to Northwestern U.S., 209–10
  defenses, 198–200
  distancing practices, 196–8
  resilient security in, 195–6
  tautua, 194, 198–200
Sanders, Laura, 136n15
Schmidt, Joseph, 182
Schoeffel, Penelope, 196–7
Sear, Rebecca, 68, 71, 87
Sear, William and Martha, 201
secure attachment
  accessibility and, 146
  amae and, 29n7
  classification and, 38–40
  communication and, 144
  cultural bias of label, 38–40, 125, 130, 165–6, 169, 174
  defense and, 222, 226, 233
  exploration and, 56
  fago and, 222, 226
  gender and, 179, 222
  independence and, 169, 171, 191
  insecure attachment, 25–6, 28, 108, 242
  interdependence and, 170
  Klein and, 192–3
  questioning, 23, 67
  responsiveness and, 51
  strangers and, 56
  study of, 35
Sellen, Dan, 71
sensitive mothering, 20–1
separation anxiety, 23, 34, 49, 54–5, 57, 59, 122, 191
Seymour, Susan C., 8–9, 18, 20, 23, 68, 88, 115–35, 158, 165, 170, 245, 253
Shore, Bradd, 199
Shostak, Marjorie, 170
siblingship
  aggression and, 181, 183–4, 199, 207
  attachment and, 123–4, 174–5
  caregiving and, 74, 119, 121, 126, 128–30, 134–5, 172–4, 180, 230
  cross-sex relationships, 167, 181–3
  development and, 168
  feeding and, 129, 147, 231–2
  gender divisions, 181, 197–8
  hierarchy, 171, 181
  love and, 217, 220
  rivalry, 166, 231–2
  security and, 195
  socialization, 171–2
Simpson, Jeffry, 68–9, 242
single vs. multiple attachment figures, 49–50
Smith, B. Holly, 69–70
Solomon, Judith, 4, 39, 173
Spence, Janet, 26
Spieker, Susan, 68, 85, 88, 108, 116
Spiro, Melford, 24, 194, 215–16, 222–5, 229–32
Sri Lanka, childcare in
  adolescence, 152
  attachment theory on sensitive care and self-expression, 150
  autonomy, self-expression, and attachment theory, 157–8
  caregiver sensitivity, 146–7
  communication, choice, and self-expression, 147–50

consent and choice, 155–7
increasing dependence and deference, 152–4
overview, 143–5
Viligama and, 145–6
working models of relationships, 150–3
Sroufe, L. Alan, 35, 179, 219, 245
Stearns, Stephen, 70
Stevenson, Robert Louis, 200
Strange Situation (SS), 3–4
Strange Situation Procedure (SSP), 4–6, 10–11, 16–17, 25, 27–8, 86, 107–8, 191–2, 203
cross-cultural applicability of, 89
cross-cultural critique, 4–6
development of, 4–5
Strauss, Claudia, 135, 151
Super, Charles, 35
supernatural, 124

Takahashi, Keiko, 5, 14–15, 37, 39–40, 88, 101, 107, 170, 241
Talbot, Margaret, 13, 27, 125, 135
Tannen, Barbara, 205
tautua, 194, 198–200
Thompson, C.J., 208
Thompson, Ross, 85, 96
Tomasello, Michael, 46–7, 76
Tronick, Edward, 16–17, 36, 68, 85, 88
True, Mary, 88
trust/distrust, 13, 24–5, 34, 50, 52, 87–8, 96, 98, 107, 123–5, 128, 130, 134–5, 151–3, 170, 191–2, 197–8, 244–5
Turke, Paul, 71
Turner, George, 196, 200

understanding and sharing intentions and attention, 46–7
United States
attachment theory and, 5, 8, 11, 17–18, 144–5, 157–8, 216, 242
attunement in, 146
autonomy and, 157–9, 236n24
compared to Samoa, 209–10
defenses, 203–9
development and bonding in, 193–5, 201
distancing practices, 202–5
family in, 132
infants in, 14, 35, 50, 54, 91
mother-child interactions in, 146–7
multiple-child care in, 116
resilient security in, 200–2
secure attachment in, 13, 23, 125, 143–4, 192–5
separation and, 225
SSP and, 4

van IJzendoorn, Marinus, 13, 39, 67, 85, 88, 242
Vincent, Anne, 73
virtue, cultural models of
Alorese, 125
attachment and, 17–18
Ifaluk, 231
Japanese, 14–15
Murik, 21, 167–8, 177
North German, 11–13
Sinhala, 21–2

Wall-Scheffler, Cara M., 74–5
Waters, Everett, 35, 219, 245
Weinfeld, Nancy, 4
Weisner, Thomas, 10–11, 13, 36, 54, 67–8, 88, 125, 136n3, 144, 165, 167–9, 173, 205, 221, 231
Whiting, Beatrice, 205, 231
Whiting, John, 68, 161n7
Wierzbicka, Anna, 235n9
Winn, Steve, 104
Winnicott, Donald, 49, 55, 202
Winslow, Deborah, 161n10
Wood, Bernard, 69–70, 72
Woodburn, James, 73
Wrangham, Richard, 72, 76

Yucatec Maya, 5, 9, 17, 45–57, 157

Zeifman, Debra, 68, 179, 217, 221, 234n4

Printed in the United States of America